WESTWARD
☆ TILT ☆

The American West Today

Neil Morgan

Foreword by James A. Michener

RANDOM HOUSE
New York

WESTWARD
TILT

The American West Today

MONTANA

Missouri River

Fort Peck
Reservoir

Yellowstone River

Big Horn R.

BIG HORN MTS.

YELLOWSTONE
NATIONAL
PARK

NGE

AHO

Great
Salt
Lake

WYOMING

FRONT RANGE

O

UINTA MTS.

Utah Lake

UTAH

Green River

T

A

I

N

S

COLORADO

John W.
Powell
Res.

San Juan R.

SANGRE DE CRISTO MTS.

CANYON
DE CHELLY

PAINTED DESERT

Little Colorado R.

ONA

NEW MEXICO

Rio Grande

Salt River

N

FOR
Reverend S. L. Morgan,
one of the best reporters.

Foreword

In my early professional life I left my home in Pennsylvania to take a job in Colorado, and for the first time caught the fire and fury that characterizes life in the West. As a teacher of sociology, I began to take mental notes on the differences between my old home and my new; and almost all that I saw I liked. It seemed to me then, as it does now, that a new type of man was being reared in the West. He was taller, ate more salads, had fewer intellectual interests of a speculative nature, had a rough and ready acceptance of new ideas, and was blessed with a vitality that stood out conspicuously to a stranger from the East.

Years later when I was working in the Pacific Ocean areas, trying to interpret them to America, I was freshly drawn into speculation about that part of our land which fringed the Pacific, and my earlier experiences were recalled. I began jotting down random notes concerning this vivid part of our nation. The more I studied, the more I became convinced that on our Western slope we were building what amounted to a subnation whose future was brilliant, chaotic and well beyond the imagination of any single individual. In fact, I became so impressed with the prospects of this new culture that I made tentative plans for writing an account of it.

At this point I returned to Pennsylvania, where comparisons between East and West were constantly forced upon me, for Pennsylvania stood in powerful contrast to a state like California. Pennsylvania was losing three seats in Congress; California was gaining eight. California had over three hundred thousand students enrolled in junior colleges; Pennsylvania had only fifteen thousand three hundred. In Pennsylvania backward-looking business leaders still clung to traditional industries that were on the decline: coal, steel, railroads; whereas California had shifted to electronics, the so-called brain factories, and aviation, whose horizons seemed unlimited.

As a result of these factors, our federal government was awarding to Pennsylvania only 3.6 percent of all federal defense contracts, while California, because of her superior educational system, was garnering more than twenty-four percent of all such contracts. If this trend was projected into the future, the rich West would get richer and the poor East would get poorer.

On the other hand, Pennsylvania preserved a rich, solid historical tradition; California always seemed to me deficient in this regard. Pennsylvania citizens had stable, if conservative, views on national problems; whereas Californians could not be depended upon for any consistent point of view. And the general stability of Pennsylvanians seemed more reliable than that of Californians.

I was considering doing a book on this subject when I had the good luck to visit the former American ambassador to Mexico, Robert C. Hill, as he was about to make a flying visit to the Western districts of Mexico, and I observed that in Mexico the same relative problem existed. But in Durango I discovered much more, for we were joined by a red-haired, taciturn newspaperman with a good reputation for accuracy. He was Neil Morgan, of the San Diego *Evening Tribune*, and he had made himself an expert on Mexico.

Late one night, after a poker game in the almost inaccessible port of Las Cruces in the arid state of California Baja Sur, Morgan and I began comparing notes, and I discovered that in his own way he had been studying the West as I had been doing, but with two improvements: he had been gathering his impressions from the inside; and his scope of speculation far exceeded mine.

I also discovered that he had already assembled most of the information that I was going to have to ferret out. And his generalizations were so perceptive and precise that I suggested he write the book and not I. He rose to the bait and outlined an approach that went well beyond what I had suggested. Then he asked, "Where could I find a publisher?"

I replied, "Bennett Cerf might take a chance," and within a few days the publisher had telephoned Neil Morgan and *Westward Tilt* was underway.

It has been completed with substance and insight. What Morgan has to say about the new leadership of the West and its portent—good and bad—ought to be heard. As our industrial giants begin to center in the West, as our more enterprising intelligence begins to operate there, and as our more inventive young men and women either are born there or migrate to the area, the capacity of the West will be multiplied.

Immediately after the census of 1970, when we witness the transfer of political power from East to West, we will all be forced to contemplate the things Morgan writes about now. And if, as I suspect, the American borderlands of the Pacific Ocean develop economically as the Atlantic borderlands have been developing for the last two thousand years, the world power of this area will also be enhanced, as well as the purely American power.

I have watched this growth from two opposing vantage points, one in the Pacific and one in Pennsylvania, and I must admit that I am perplexed as to which direction our new subnation will take. Many of my Eastern friends take pleasure in deploring the garish architecture, the John Birch Societies, the overemphasis on youth and the development of a culture which has only a parochial significance. I, on the other hand, view with envy the West's freedom, its wild joy in living, its vital experimentation in the arts, and its willingness to cultivate new industries and new ways of doing old jobs.

But until I talked with Neil Morgan and read his book, I was not aware that the region had already produced a journalist who understood what was happening in his own backyard. In the years ahead we must all come to grips with the philosophical, moral and political significance of Morgan's new lands. I am so glad we met and talked after that poker game in Las Cruces, for he has helped me to do some hard thinking.

JAMES A. MICHENER

Contents

Maps

DRAWN BY EDWARD HALSBERG

Prologue

THE FOOTLOOSE

MIGRATION

In that dimly recalled era when it was *de rigueur* to deplore California, even Frank Lloyd Wright was a conformist. He propounded a puckish theory that America was tilted, and everything loose was sliding into Southern California.

Today an awesome hunk of America has come loose. The move to Western America is the largest migration in the history of the world. Since the birth of the nation, its geographical center of population has been moving inexorably westward across West Virginia, Ohio, Indiana and into Illinois. Now it is within fifty miles of crossing the Mississippi River. California is supplanting New York as the most populous state. Americans are moving to California in greater numbers than today's entire immigration to the United States. The five boroughs of New York City would have to be emptied of every man, woman and child to match the population increase of the past decade in the eleven states between the Rocky Mountains and the Pacific Ocean.

The West is that one-third of the nation between the Rockies and the Pacific. It includes all of California, Oregon, Washington, Arizona, Nevada, Utah, Idaho, and much of Montana, Wyoming, Colorado, and New Mexico. Historically, this region has been a citadel of natural resources which has been raided and plundered by the East. There is poetic justice to the Westerner in this westward tilt induced by migration. Now the West is raiding the Midwest, the East, and South; stealing scientists, teachers, industrialists, and technicians— bright young men who have a restless probing spirit that drives them in search of some better life. The West is plundering the rest of the nation's most dynamic resource: human energies.

Yet the move West is one of the least-understood wonders of our modern world. Less is written of it than is written about Disneyland. Most reportage is understandably haphazard, shallow, or distorted. Most journalists who try to interpret the contemporary West parrot that malignant stereotype of the West created by Eastern editors whose rare forays to the region are for a whiff of Hollywood saffron or a sojourn in San Francisco—which they assume to be an oasis of urban- ity in an uncivilized desert. The Western past has been recorded with more charm and less bias than its present. Its stagecoaches are better understood than its freeways, its United States marshals than its city managers, its Gold Rush than the westward tilt of today.

Those lacking firsthand knowledge of the West cannot be blamed for their woeful misconceptions. Their source materials range from the Lewis and Clark *Journals* to television serials eulogizing Wyatt Earp or Matt Dillon; from *The Grapes of Wrath* to rosy, superficial magazine stories, designed to please food advertisers, about the California migrant worker of today; from tabloid reconstructions of the cultist scandals of the Southern California Thirties to breathless gossip by Hopper and Parsons of fresher intrigue; from Helen Hunt Jackson's pamphleteering against the United States Indian policy, to grave punditry in left-wing journals about conservatism afoot in the West.

In 1957, Walter Prescott Webb, a historian of the West, found that ten standard school histories of the United States devoted an aver- age of only six or seven pages out of each one hundred pages to the western three-fifths of America. He concluded that this disparity was due to the brief span of Western history, and to the relative scarcity in the West of the historic problems of labor, industry, urbanization, and the Negro. But if Webb's theory is true, American history is being written today in the West with a heavy hand and on many pages. The West has become one of the most urban regions of America. Its boom- ing cities and the influx of science and industry are the overwhelming facts of the contemporary West. Moreover, the Negro is moving into Western cities today in avalanches.

The truth is that this is a vastly misunderstood region, even by those who live in it, because it is exploding too fast in every direction. Interpreting its cities, in the words of one brilliant Westerner, Wallace Stegner, is "like trying to hold a stethoscope to the chest of an angry cat." Its subtleties and intricacies discourage those who prefer a tidy problem with only one answer. There is a startling absence of studies of Western mores and attitudes. The Westerner is easy prey for the quick-impression writer who knows he can buy his audience cheap through time-proven broadsides at seashore culture or freeway madness.

Americans have sought to interpret the twentieth-century move westward in historic terms, but this is a move without precedent. It does not fit traditional migratory patterns. This continental tilt has been born of a modern American phenomenon: a nation so prosperous and so mobile that its people are free to go in search of a more luxurious way of life. The Westerners of today are the first people in world history to attain that freedom in the mass.

They seek a wide spectrum of amenities: sunshine and warmth in California, Nevada, Arizona, and New Mexico, fishing in Oregon, boating in Washington, hunting in Wyoming, skiing in Colorado—and almost everywhere, the scenic extravagances of the rawboned West, escape from conventional urban crowding, the leisurely pace and more amiable human relationships which derive from that pace and which lead many toward concentration on the less tangible pursuits of the arts and the intellect.

Because of this quest, growth in the West has been at the rate of about forty percent each decade, twice the national average. Many cities of California and Arizona have grown at four to fifteen times the national average. There is an air of inevitability about Western growth, but its causes and its nature are widely misinterpreted.

Migration to Florida, heavily weighted by the retired, comes close to being a purely climatic migration, but the move West is a younger one. The median age of the West is falling below the national average. The millions moving there seek far more than warmth and sunshine; they are moving West to build their future, and they have dreams of the super-life.

As the new Westerner has been set free from other regions to seek these amenities, industrial evolution has provided a new world of industry so footloose that it can move with him, oblivious to the traditional industrial requirements of location. The industries of the space age are less dependent on pivotal market areas and power resources than on an environment which will lure the scientist and skilled technician. Western factories are short on smokestacks and spur lines. Their products may be electronic components so small that they are flown away, or the actual aircraft itself. One of the most significant products of Western factories is ideas; the "think factory" and the laboratory are the epitome of the industrial move West.

Thus, sustained by footloose industry, the newcomer to the West develops a sense of having discovered the life of tomorrow. The selectivity that dominates this migration provides a unity among its diverse people. They are integrated by common bonds of supreme self-confidence and hope in the future. And it is this common spirit of the new breed dominating the westward tilt which has unified for the first time the vast area between the Rocky Mountains and the Pacific Ocean. Its vitality is obvious from the pulp mills of Montana to the electronics plants of Phoenix, from the missile producers of Denver to the aircraft and space industry of Seattle. It is obvious in the rapid urbanization of the cities of every Western state.

This eleven-state West was unified until the past decade only tenuously, and largely by the overwhelming factor of aridity. As recently as 1957, another widely accepted Walter Prescott Webb theory labeled the West an oasis civilization, a land of deficiencies whose most dependable asset might be tourism. Webb called Westerners "a normal people trying to create and maintain a normal civilization in an abnormal land . . . seeking to conquer the Great American Desert." He noted that the West of that day had contributed less than its share of listings to *Who's Who*.

Then the explosions began in science, industry, and education—even in cultural affairs. Nobel laureates and scholars began the trek to Western campuses. Research men and industrialists found an eager market for their abilities everywhere—in the eternal sunshine of the Arizona desert, near the coves and straits of Puget Sound, beside the ski slopes of the Rocky Mountains, and in the air that had the smell of freedom all along the pounding Pacific Coast. During the first two years of the graduate fellowship program of the National Defense Education Act, from 1959 to 1961, Californians received far more fellowships than any other state. The University of California has bred or lured eleven Nobel laureates; no other American campus comes close. After them followed skilled technicians and workers. Museums, concert halls, theaters, and art galleries began to spring up at an accelerated rate. The Western newcomer was obviously moving with giant strides to plug the gaps of Western life, to speed the West through its muscle-bound adolescence, to create the super-America which the West has suggested in men's minds for more than a century.

Slowly until recent years but not with a rush, the West is shouldering its appropriate burden of leadership in the federal government. In 1940, Westerners in major Washington roles included one under-secretary, three assistant secretaries, four chairmen, fourteen members or commissioners, and four administrators or directors. In 1960, there was one cabinet member, the treasurer, two under-secretaries, six assistant secretaries, seven chairmen, fourteen members or commissioners, and five administrators or directors. The appointments of President John F. Kennedy reflect the rising tide of Western power.

The West has grown in waves.

Gone are the years when California nurtured Technocracy, the EPIC (End Poverty in California) movement, Old-Age Revolving Pensions, "Ham and Eggs," and the Townsend Plan. The Depression gave birth to more spurious mutations in California, itself an unsteady but besieged infant, than in any other state. Waves of utopia seekers, most of them elderly, washed up on the California shores in the years just before the Great Depression. Then, over much of the West, came the tides of migrant workers whose tragedy was immortalized by John Steinbeck. But the sons and daughters of many of their number now are prosperous ranchers in the fertile Great Central Valley of California, and more than a few of their grandsons and granddaughters drive sports cars between their classrooms and their fraternity and sorority houses on the campuses of California.

The aircraft boom of World War II brought new towns and cities, new industries, and new millions over the Rockies to the Pacific, from Seattle to San Diego. This wave was almost tidal; with it came the military, for millions of acres of land lay cheap and ready to bear its burden, and the war had turned toward the Pacific. But the cities were not ready; and the blight of the precipitous growth of those years still disfigures some of them.

The West anticipated the next wave, for there was the precedent of the westward migration that followed World War I. Millions like myself sensed something hopeful and exciting in their first breath of Western air. As fast as we could shed our uniforms after World War II, we became Westerners. It was not disturbing that the jobs we found at first did not always match our dreams; we knew that in such a fresh land, so serene and self-confident, we would have the chance to show what we had.

Something less impulsive and more orderly has been happening since the 1950's. This is the wave that is bringing new strength to industry, science, and education. It brings new millions of trained, responsible citizens who are acutely conscious of what the West offers and of the shortcomings of its adolescence. Already they are its leaders. They have every intention of helping to do what only mankind can do to augment nature's grandiose handiwork. They are the catalysts of the dramatic maturing process which is now so evident.

Climate has been vastly exaggerated as a cause of the westward migration. In fifteen years I have interviewed nearly five thousand persons who have moved West. Climate is one motivation, but it is a superficial one. In the golden sunshine of a dazzling February day in San Francisco, it is quixotic to inquire of a new native why he left Boston. He feels himself suspended between turquoise bay and azure sky, and he can only regard his questioner as an insensitive fool for asking. The world around him brims with reason enough. But that is only part of what brought him West, and he will admit it in moments when God and nature have not paralyzed his reasoning. To cross the mountains is an act of emancipation. Descending the western slope of the Rockies, the pilgrim imagines himself in the land of tomorrow. He is likely to try anything, because this land has little history of failure and less of restriction; since he assumes he will succeed, he has a better chance to do it. The West seethes with the spirit of *Why not?* It is young and eager, cocky and eternally hopeful.

Despite the regional unity of the new West, its surface pattern is a marvel of diversity. Party politics are unpredictable. Nine of the eleven Western states gave Richard Nixon pluralities over President Kennedy in the 1960 election. But after the 1962 elections, only eight of twenty-two Western United States senators were Republicans. Republican governors outnumbered Democrats by seven to four. Whatever his party, the Westerner is a political paradox. He has an almost emotional commitment to individualism, and a generally stronger abhorrence for federal intervention than the people of other regions. He is aggressively liberal in economic affairs, but distrustful of big debt. He is slow to move toward sociologic reform, lacking the cultural flexibility of older regions, and yet he bears the scars of some of the most extreme reform movements in American history. More recently, a voluble small group of extremists has unfairly stamped parts of the West as reactionary.

One characteristic shared by the states of the new West is the relative lack of social need. In this prospering land, the burning cause is the bizarre oddity. At Christmas, service clubs cast about frantically for targets for their charitable instincts. The migrant worker has the lowest net income in America, but often he is driving a late-model car; welfare systems, usually generous, give him a last-line bulwark against crisis. The slums of Western cities cannot be compared in misery with those of cities in older regions; no settlement house exists in the West. Racial conflicts are milder than in other regions; the few serious racial crises of the West have been related to the tensions of wartime. No strong voice of social consciousness has been heard in the

West since World War II; social crisis has not reached a level to provoke reform.

The mobility of the Westerner is another regional trait which ac-
cents his differences from other Americans. It is not surprising, since
he is the kind who has pulled up roots and migrated, that even in the
West he keeps moving. In 1960 barely one-third of the Californians
over five years old were living in the same house as five years previously. One in seven had moved to California within those five years.
In Northern California, utility-company records show that one in three
householders changes residence each year; in urban Southern California the figure soars as high as one in two. (Random comparison
shows that about one in ten householders move each year in Wauke-
gan, Illinois, and even fewer in Brooklyn.) The Westerner, usually
having experienced a major move already in coming West, is quick to
exploit opportunities for other moves which will bring him closer to
his job or to a better one, or provide him more amenities, or better suit
his changing family status. He is freer because generations have not
tied him to the land or to the home; nor is he usually as involved with
neighbors as are people in other regions. The Westerner who thinks
he can improve his status with a move picks up his telephone and
calls for a moving van.

Such mobility blurs the Westerner's sense of community responsibility and creates a fluid community pattern which often frustrates
accomplishment. Westerners have a lower rate of church affiliation
than those of other regions. Many problems of city planning in the
West are attributable to mobility.

But this mobility has its virtue. Because he travels more than the
people of other regions, the Westerner is less provincial. He has
fifty-two percent more passports than the national average. From 1951
to 1961, the total number of passports issued in the United States
tripled; in the Pacific Coast states, it increased nearly eight times. On
transcontinental flights, there are more Westerners than Easterners.
Statistics for the entire air transport industry are not available, but an
American Airlines survey of its 1961 passenger traffic on non-stop
flights between Los Angeles and New York showed that forty-five
percent of the passengers resided in metropolitan Los Angeles and only
thirty-three percent in metropolitan New York, an area with half
again as many people. Metropolitan Los Angeles only recently has
passed metropolitan Chicago in population, but another American Airlines survey showed that between those two cities more than twice as
many passengers reside in Los Angeles than in Chicago. The
growth rate of all airline passenger traffic in Western cities has been

far above the national average. The sheer fact of distance has made a traveler of the Westerner. A defense industry executive living in La Jolla made fifty-nine round trips between California and the East Coast during the year 1959. He flew at night to save time, and in that year he slept one night out of every three in the air.

It is distinctly west of the Rocky Mountains that the Western essence of non-provincialism is evident. To the east, where the Rockies drop off to the Great Plains—down from Montana through eastern Wyoming, Colorado, and New Mexico—the land goes to wheat and pasture, and the people begin to face toward Midwest cities and toward Texas. They do not think in terms of the new West. Their politics become more predictable. They are more traditional. Theirs is an agrarian economy. The plains states boomed before the turn of the century, and since then have lagged behind the national average of population growth. Of all the states of the nation, New Mexico has the most ingenuous tolerance of racial differences; but even on that state's eastern plains, oriented toward Texas and the South, ugly prejudice suddenly appears.

It is California which dominates the new West. Of every one hundred Westerners in the eleven states, fifty-eight are in California and twenty-five in metropolitan Los Angeles. Washington, the second most populous Western state, ranks twenty-third among the fifty states. There are four million more Californians than the combined population of the ten other Western states. In population, others rank as follows: Washington, Oregon, Colorado, Arizona, New Mexico, Utah, Idaho, Montana, Wyoming, and Nevada.

The casual student of maps (which only suggest the vast dimensions of the West) may need reminding of the contrasts in population density. There are so many more people in California than in the rest of the West that an almost colonial quality sometimes is detected in the relations between California and the other Western states. In 1961 I attended a conference of Western governors in Salt Lake City at which California's Governor Pat Brown arrived two days late. It was obvious that nothing much would be settled until Brown appeared. In those two days, resentments of other states toward California occasionally flared—most of them involved California's aggressive search for Western water and power, some were connected with California's tremendous market for raw products of the Western states which are less economically sophisticated. When Governor Brown finally arrived at this conference, there was a subtle closing of ranks among some other governors.

Although California leads the way, and certain tensions inevitably result from one state being so rich and so large, there is wide-spread economic strength among the Western states. With one-third of the land area of the fifty states, these eleven have fifteen percent of the national population, earn seventeen percent of personal income, produce nineteen percent of agricultural commodities, furnish fifty-four percent of its lumber, extract twenty-three percent of its minerals, and erect twenty-seven percent of its buildings.

Some of the notable misconceptions about the West are economic. The West is not agrarian. Agricultural employment represents a lower percentage of the labor force than the national average. More Westerners live in the cities than the national average. Industry dominates the job market—and so does the federal government. In New Mexico, Utah, and Wyoming, government employment by federal, state, and local agencies is the primary source of work. Only in Nevada, where tourism dominates, do services loom near the top as the source of jobs. Manufacturing is the leading source of employment in California, Oregon, and Washington, the three Pacific Coast states. In agriculture, crops are more important than livestock in the coastal states and in Idaho and Arizona; livestock dominates in the other six Western states.

The overriding factor in Western unity is growth. Between 1950 and 1960, the population increase of these eleven Western states was more than seven and two-thirds million. This accounted for more than one-fourth of the nation's growth. California's growth made up two-thirds of the growth of the West. The California increase of nearly five million persons was far more than the combined growth of Florida and Texas, the next ranking states in growth. California alone accounted for almost one-fifth of the nation's growth during that decade. Yet no Western state lost population rank in relation to other states between 1950 and 1960. Arizona and New Mexico each moved past three other states. Four states moved up one position: Colorado, Idaho, Montana, and Utah. The remaining five held their rank; among them, California is expected to pass New York by mid-1963 to become the most populous state.

California has been the hardest hit of the Western states by the four big problems of growth: urban sprawl, traffic congestion, air pollution, and water shortage. But it moves, often aggressively, to solve its problems; it must, or be buried under the avalanche. Again, Walter Prescott Webb's old theory of aridity as the unifying factor in the West is subordinated, though it still has some validity; the voters of California approved the largest bond issue ever submitted to American voters—one and three quarter billion dollars—to channel water as far as six hundred miles from the lush green north to the arid ocher south. In the opinion of the Stanford Research Institute, this water shortage will prove the simplest to solve of the four major physical crises of California.

Lewis Mumford wrote in *The Culture of Cities* that, "the natural conditions of a region, so far from being nullified by the increase of culture and technical skill, are actually magnified." Californians will argue that point; more than any other Americans, more than the people of any other country or any other age, they are controlling their environment with their technical skills, their massive self-confidence, their boundless energies, and their unprecedented prosperity.

It is yet to be seen whether Californians and other Westerners, having conquered their environment, will in turn be subdued by that environment into taking their hard-won ease and lolling in the sunshine. But there is increasing introspection among Westerners, and encouraging signs that the transition is being made from the raw, youthful phase of hacking out the clearing for a cabin to a period in which affairs of culture are of primary concern.

With California in the van, the West has struck out ahead of the rest of America like a scouting party of the future. The West has become a center of innovation. The newest ideas of industry and science go into quick, full use in its new cities. It is an unorthodox land to which people are driven not by poverty but by high energy, neuroses, and daring. Its social problems are not the conventional ones of prejudice, poverty, and oppression; rather they are the new social problems of finding worth-while goals, of aim and direction, of integrity.

The West is the most dynamic region of America today. It is the most intense in its feelings, the most open to commitment to causes, good or bad, right or left. But newness and bigness are not adequate in themselves. Rapid growth and vigor are not goals but symptoms. In dedication and direction, the West flounders like America, only more so.

The westward tilt is wiping out most of the American frontier finally and forever. The driving urge of the American to move on and conquer new lands soon will have nowhere to spend itself but in space —and space will remain an arena for the few. The westward rush in America has a somber element of the climacteric. Soon there will be nowhere else to seek new resources, new values, new meaning, except within ourselves.

If the new West is indeed scouting ahead in the directions which the nation will take, its responsibilities are awesome, and its actions deeply involve the future of America.

Part I

THE
REALMS
OF
CHANGE

THE GOOD LIFE

Trademark, Not Obsession

The regional culture which once was thought to make the West quaint is crumbling in the avalanche of the westward tilt. Highways slash through Mormon country now, and Mormons are leaving the farms for missile factories. Jetliners have put the homeland of Navajo and Hopi within commuting range of the Eastern anthropologist. Industry has begun to push logging aside in Oregon, and paeans to Northwestern forests have taken on an air of literary mustiness. San Francisco is threatened by freeway, slum and subdivision; Indians of the Laguna Pueblo have grown prosperous by mining uranium; in Nevada, the prospector has given way to the pit boss; Los Angeles grapples with the ravages of megalopolis. And yet the old jokes about barbecue culture have begun to boomerang.

The new Western culture is not a finished thing, but a few points are certain. There is very little of a regional nature about it. It belongs to the people of all the states of the nation; they form the composite of the Westerner today. Its common bonds are energetic creativity and supreme self-confidence. It does not pause to defend itself against charges of cultural immaturity; it is too busy, and it is not self-conscious.

After vast research, Earl Pomeroy, the University of Oregon historian, found the West Coast to be more prosperous and more urban than the nation as a whole, more literate and more criminal. In a privately distributed monograph, he wrote: "It reads more, drinks more, goes to church less, and has more automobiles and smaller families. It is more in favor of birth control and also of foreign cars. Its people move more, travel more, camp out more. . . . It has more space, more wilderness, and also more suburbs and more new suburbanites and newcomers generally. . . . It produces more doctors than its share in the natural sciences and in education, slightly less than its share in the humanities, social sciences and arts, but has fewer resident chemists, economists and historians. . . . It receives academic honors much more than the rest of the nation—nearly fifty percent more Guggenheim fellowships than its population justifies." To a somewhat less dramatic degree, these assertions are valid for the entire West.

Only within the past five years have Westerners sensed their common ties enough to consider that there is such a thing as a Western culture. In 1958 a two-day conference was held at Carmel, California, under the sponsorship of the American Council of Learned Societies. Significantly, the impetus for the conference came from an Eastern savant, Dr. Howard Mumford Jones of Harvard, who was spending a sabbatical at the Center for Advanced Study in the Behavioral Sciences at Stanford. It was Dr. Jones' impression that something of import was occurring in the West and he wondered if anybody knew what it was.

The participants concluded that there is nothing regional about Western culture in the old sense of the regionalism of the South or the Midwest, but that Western culture is showing accelerated symptoms of national trends; it is regional only in that Westerners, particularly along the Pacific Coast, are pioneering busily in advance of the national culture.

Such a premise is not easily accepted east of the Rockies, and certainly not in the cities of the East, whose cultural aristocracies are accustomed to the notion that they guard the national culture in family vaults. The assumption outside the West is that the Westerner still is a sybarite, excited only by the clear and present challenge of how to expend his unparalleled prosperity. This has been, until recently, a defensible generalization; it no longer is valid.

The changing cultural patterns of the West merit continuous study. On the surface, they are easy to dismiss as insignificant. A closer look reveals a hungry, energetic drive to compensate for lost time. It is epitomized by the transplanted family of the scientist, technician, or educator, which has hardly unpacked before it plunges into the civic symphony, little theater or art classes; the new arrival sets out to establish whatever accustomed amenity is absent on the local Western scene.

A casual, easy manner of living continues to be an inherent part of the Western culture, but people from other areas find it difficult to understand that this is not evidence of a shallow culture. The good life is a Western trademark, not a Western obsession. The new Westerner can both live better and do more.

The best gauge of the more superficial cultural tides of the West is the magazine *Sunset*, which calls itself "the magazine of Western living." *Sunset* has been both symbol and symptom of the West. More than thirty years ago it divested itself of its involvement with the arts and the world of thought; it had tried, and it had failed. It began to thrive when it adopted an undeviating absorption with the sensuous life of the Westerner. *Sunset* is the how-to bible of the Westerner in four matters: gardening, food, travel, and home. In the West especially, these interests are strong. The people of the eight states primarily served by *Sunset* (an area with only minor economic differences from the West as a whole) earn about fourteen percent more than the national average. In 1961, on a per capita basis, these Westerners were buying twenty percent more automobiles than the national norm (and one hundred and twelve percent more imported cars), eighty-one percent more frozen foods, twenty-three percent more paper products, fifty-two percent more passports, fifty-five percent more gardening supplies, one hundred and sixteen percent more new homes, twenty-five percent more wine, and forty-six percent more dishwashers.

Each year, *Sunset* publishes a cross-index of subjects dealt with in the magazine. Topics for 1961 included okra fritters; minus tides for June; sightseeing in San Francisco from a helicopter; how to behave around bears; booby birds of the Gulf of California; a bridge across your pool; how to banish skunks; roof-top gardens grown in artificial soil; how to have "happy" tomatoes.

Sunset has sensed and capitalized on Western regionalism. Its interest has been in the superficial phases of Western life which are distinct from those of other regions. Gardening is its closest tie with its reader; Westerners have been noted until recently for their aversion to apartment living, and most newcomers inherit gardens—often for the first time in their lives.

The circulation of *Sunset*, above seven hundred thousand in

1962, is almost entirely in the West, with close to half a million of that number in California. Only about one in twenty-three copies goes east of the Rocky Mountains. With this distribution, its editors are free to concentrate on the Westerner. The best-selling book in the West, after the Bible and the dictionary, is the *Sunset Western Garden Book*, published by the Lane Book Company, a subsidiary of the magazine. More than a million copies have been sold since its first edition appeared in 1939. The reason is obvious; garden books published in the East do not work in the West, a different horticultural world. Similarly, the Southern Californian has learned that the garden magazine he read back East is of little help to him when his patio contains eucalyptus, orange trees, fuchsias, and orchids, ice plant, bougainvillaea and geraniums. Even his mealybug and white grub may not succumb to the same insecticides as their Eastern cousins. His planting schedule is so different as to befog the mind of an Eastern or Midwestern gardener. In areas of the Southwest where frost never intrudes, the gardener has perpetual blossoms (and perpetual labors), and may grow three or four crops of vegetables in a year. His new enemy will not be ice or snow but the parching brilliance of the desert sun; he will not be forcing plants in hothouses, but by generous irrigation that will send his water bill soaring. *Sunset* slips an arm around him and whispers instructions with its "climate-zoned how-to handbook and Western plant encyclopedia."

Sunset has not only a thick monthly issue which tells the Westerner what he could be growing, building, or cooking, or where in the West he could be traveling; there also are more than seventy *Sunset* books with the same disturbing inference that he is not living Western enough. There is even a book on growing African violets—which sold at such a wild rate that *Sunset* book editors no longer scoff at any suggestion. Notably, these Western books are bought all over the world. If Western living means the sybaritic life, the whole world wants it. In a volume entitled *Landscaping For Western Living*, ten pages were revised with the result that the same book had a lively sale in the East under the title *Landscaping For Modern Living*.

Sunset promotions are as self-assured and flamboyant as the West itself, but the best of them center around its seven-acre home-office estate in Menlo Park, a suburban town thirty miles south of San Francisco and near the Stanford campus. The architecture had to be good, and it had to be Western; *Sunset* has developed such a following with architectural how-to-do-its that the American Institute of Architects has teamed with the magazine to make annual awards for Western houses. In 1951, with adobe, redwood, and glass, the magazine built a

low, rambling structure designed by Cliff May. It is more related to
the Spanish ranch house than to Madison Avenue, but in this garden
setting is the headquarters of one of the big money-makers in the magazine world (gross revenue in excess of eight million dollars a year, and
advertising pages among monthly consumer magazines second only to
Fortune). Forty thousand sightseers troop through the estate each
year; they find pretty editorial assistants padding about on deep car-
pets in their stocking feet, or sitting at desks beside picture windows
shaded by big oaks and looking out to a vast rolling lawn on which
the staff holds noontime putting contests. Employees wince as they
overhear the inevitable remark: "You mean they pay people to work
here?"

My first visit to *Sunset* left me with a strong awareness of the
flexible, self-sufficient spirit that pervades life in the West. The magazine had arranged to serve lunch for a group of visitors coming from
San Diego, five hundred miles south of Menlo Park. A Los Angeles
representative of the magazine drove to San Diego that morning from
his home in Pasadena, one hundred and twenty miles north of San
Diego, and escorted the visitors aboard an Electra made by Lockheed,
a California firm, and flown by Pacific Southwest Airlines, a California
intrastate line. The flight from San Diego to San Francisco took
seventy-five minutes, and we went from the airport to *Sunset* in another half-hour by bus.

Minutes after our arrival, San Diego and San Francisco friends
sat sipping wines from the nearby Napa and Livermore valleys. A
warm sense of neighborliness enveloped the group. The beams and
ceiling of the rooms, exposed on one side to the open air, were unfinished, crosscut California redwood. The floor tiles were from the California desert community of La Quinta. The chicken, raised nearby and
broiled on outdoor spits, was crisp and brown; the crab was California
seafood at its best.

The return flight after lunch took sixty-six minutes. The Pacific
glittered blue and bright to our right, its surf breaking like lace
against the rocky cliffs and beaches. On our left was the panorama of
California forests, valleys, mountains, and desert. When we stepped
off the plane in San Diego at mid-afternoon, husbands parted from
wives and returned to their desks. The *Sunset* man said he'd like to
stay and visit, but he had to make a speech that night in Los Angeles,
and he wanted to get home first to see his family.

The euphoria pervading that day was no accident; it was a con-
trived *Sunset* euphoria, capitalizing on the facets of Western living
which make it gracious and casual. But it also fitted the pattern of the

West drawn by critics of Western living who deplore its ease and sensuality. We had not heard a word that day about problems of any kind, except for a plaintive query about curbing crab grass.

But in the process of the westward tilt, even *Sunset*, the arbiter of the good life of the West, is developing a social conscience. However unsophisticated the California culture of the 1930's, it is vastly complex today. The importance of this transition is not lost on the magazine staff, which so far has made only the mildest of forays beyond its unique Western world of garden, home, food, and travel into the deeper new Western culture which is ambitious for more education, better government, public buildings that are more handsome, cities that run smoother, sounder economic balance, more productive use of leisure time, and a new emphasis on the arts.

A Stanford professor who had participated in that 1958 Carmel conference told me: "*Sunset* could be a terrific force for good in the West today, if they got into ideas and Western problems. They could spearhead an emerging sense of Western responsibility." If the West is to achieve some buoyant, aggressive culture, its goals must be etched in greater depth than the Western living patterns of home, garden, food, and travel. Although *Sunset* is the leading regional voice of the West, it is unreasonable to expect that it will fill such a role. The one regional news magazine, *Fortnight*, collapsed after a brave but barren decade of publication. The only regional liberal magazine of any importance, *Frontier*, has a circulation of less than six thousand. "There is enough blood to keep the patient alive, but not to get up out of bed and walk," sighed Phil Kerby, *Frontier*'s editor. "Yet we are showing a modest improvement."

The spotty history of periodicals in the West is evidence of the lack of any unanimity of tradition. The magazine *Los Angeles* and one in Phoenix called *Point West* are slick local journals modeled after the most successful city magazine of the West, *San Diego*. San Francisco, a graveyard for periodicals, has fostered two non-regional literary magazines, *Contact* and the *San Francisco Review*. Among historical magazines, *Montana* is the liveliest in the West; the Montana Historical Society has the second largest membership of any historical society in the United States, and *Montana* has more subscribers in New York City than in the two most populous counties of Montana. The pattern of university quarterlies in the West has been erratic and generally undistinguished.

Arizona Highways is the handsomest of all state-subsidized magazines and has the largest circulation: a four-hundred-and-fifty-thousand monthly average, about four times the circulation of the next largest state magazine. It carries no advertising. Its subscription revenue in 1960 was 1.3 million dollars, which came within sixty thousand dollars of meeting costs, requiring one of the lowest subsidies of any state magazine. Its editor is Raymond Carlson, a mild, graying rosarian who was plucked out of an anonymous clerical job in the Arizona Motor Vehicle Department in 1937 and handed the responsibility for the magazine. Then it was a homely, black-and-white technical journal which on more than one occasion had devoted its cover to an itemized budget for the Arizona Highway Department. Today it is a showpiece of the graphic arts. Carlson, who has shrugged off bids to join the magazine world of Madison Avenue, has a salary set by the Arizona legislature of less than one thousand dollars a month. But he has wide editorial latitude, and on one occasion the legislature hastily repealed an Arizona law to support him in a budget dispute with the state auditor.

There is a growing demand for a more mature approach to local affairs in the West; it is suggested by the success of city magazines such as those in San Diego, Los Angeles, and Phoenix, three of the fastest-growing cities of the nation. A study of newspapers in these three cities is also revealing. To a far greater extent than the Western average, newspapers of Los Angeles and San Diego have increased their coverage of national and international affairs and have widened their range of features and columns of opinion. In Phoenix, a competitive daily was launched in 1962, in contrast to the national trend of newspaper mergers, a trend followed even in San Diego and Los Angeles. With too few exceptions, the Western newspaper is more provincial than are many of its readers; most Western newspapers have not widened their outlook much since World War II, but their readers have. Generally, Western newspapers stress local affairs, and at a somewhat low level of sophistication. The Westerner's interest in intellectual affairs is appeased, like the interest of most people in the nation, by publications originating in the New York area. The strength of New York publications in the West is eloquent. The New York *Times* has inaugurated a West Coast edition. More copies of the *Wall Street Journal* are sold in California now than in the state of New York. Circulation figures of *The New Yorker* show Californians second only to New Yorkers, and *Harper's* magazine's circulation is greater in California than in New York.

Robert R. Kirsch, book editor of the Los Angeles *Times*, exploded in print one summer day in 1961 when praising a new Los Angeles magazine: "The mistake many publications [in Los Angeles] made in the past was to assume that their existence depended on a kind of regional loyalty: Southern Californians ought to support a local magazine to show Easterners we are not barbarians and to prove to

San Franciscans that they have no monopoly on culture. As long as
this show-them-back-East-and-up-North attitude persisted, local periodicals have swung between barely disguised boosterism and a kind
of citrus-belt imitation of successful Eastern periodicals such as *The
New Yorker*. I bear my share of responsibility. I have gone back to
New York loaded with statistics and anecdotes designed to prove that
we are just as literate, just as cultured, just as human as those who
live within commuting distance of New York City. Man, I am through.
We don't have to prove a thing. We merely have to act instead of re-
acting. Let *Time* magazine discover Southern California; let the New
Yorkers finally figure out that people out here buy and read books,
think, listen to music, look at paintings, compose, create. As the old
psychiatrist gag goes, it's their problem."

Although book publishing in the West is still in an exploratory
phase, books—like almost everything else—are bought by Westerners
at a greater rate than by the nation as a whole. They also are written
at a prolific rate. In the Doubleday office in San Francisco, the largest
editorial office in the West representing a book publisher, close to five
hundred book manuscripts are read each year. Writers, like scientists
and educators, have been part of the new pilgrimage to the West: men
as diverse as Joseph Wood Krutch in Tucson, Mortimer Adler in San
Francisco, Ted Geisel in La Jolla—and, from an earlier pilgrimage,
Stewart Holbrook in Portland, Oliver La Farge in Santa Fe, Aldous
Huxley in Los Angeles. And here, too, the sense of individualism is
sustained. A bookseller was found guilty of violating obscenity laws
in Los Angeles for selling *Tropic of Cancer* after Leon Uris and Frank
Baxter testified for the prosecution. In Marin County, across from San
Francisco, a bookseller was found innocent on the same charge after
Eugene Burdick and Mark Schorer testified for the defense.

In a three-storied Victorian house in San Francisco, Mortimer
Adler presides over the Institute for Philosophical Research, which is
supported by the Ford Foundation. He and his staff spent eight years
preparing *The Idea of Freedom*, the first volume in a series whose
purpose is to apply the inventory process to Western thought on great
ideas. Though more of the Great Books series chosen by Adler have
been sold in California than in any other state, he suspects this is because of a superior sales force in California.

But writers of the West are running behind their region. The
last big contemporary novel of the Western landscape was *The Grapes
of Wrath*, and it seems as obsolete in the West today as Booth
Tarkington. Most of the so-called beatnik writers have proved themselves untalented as well as unwashed, and have gone out to look for
work. Some of the more successful Western writers—Irving Stone,

Paul Wellman, David Lavender—find their Western themes in the past. Contemporary social fiction of the West only nibbles at corners of the scene; there are literary gold fields still unexplored.

Trade publishing of hard-cover books will not soon thrive in the West. One reason is sheer economics. Because of low volume, it costs about three cents in San Francisco to put a paper jacket around a book for which the same operation would cost one cent in New York. Some of the most active book publishers of the West are the University of California Press, Binford & Morts of Portland, and Caxton Printers of Caldwell, Idaho. There are also a few intriguing small book publishers—among them George Chambers' Arizona Silhouettes at Tucson, which reprints rare historical collectors' items; and Hesperian House, a modest firm with offices in a one-time Chinese overall factory in San Francisco's Jackson Square, which has a splendid two-volume anthology of California writing among its titles. Among university presses of the nation, California ranks third and Stanford seventh in volume of books published.

In music and in art, Los Angeles is the do-it-yourself center of the world; nowhere is there a greater saturation of weekend painters or of semiprofessional orchestras (fifty or more, playing for pleasure— their own, if for no one else's). California has led New York State since the 1957–58 season in the number of radio members who contribute funds to sustain broadcasts of the New York Philharmonic. On the 1960 tour of that orchestra, Leonard Bernstein recalled incredulously, "They stood and yelled for the Bartok Concerto for Orchestra in Las Vegas! Las Vegas was the wildest! We played for seven thousand people at ten dollars top. The only way I could send them away after three encores was to say, 'You want to get back to the gambling tables, and so does the orchestra!' "

Milton Katims conducts the Seattle Symphony in a new civic opera house before a loyal and musically literate audience (sixty-two percent of the symphony budget is provided through the box office, with almost five thousand regular subscribers—a startlingly high participation). A hypnotic twenty-six year old, Zubin Mehta, presides over the renaissance of the Los Angeles Philharmonic, soon to be performing in a new Music Center. The San Francisco Opera Company, which extends its season to the other major cities of the Pacific Coast, has had no more crises of impending collapse in recent years than has the Metropolitan Opera Company. From Salt Lake City and from Phoenix, the Mormon Tabernacle Choir and the Orpheus Male Chorus launch world tours. Summer opera abounds. None is more picturesque than those at Santa Fe, New Mexico (in an amphitheater which looks up to the Jémez Mountains), and at Central City, Colorado, high in the

Rockies. The programs of the Aspen music festival, founded in 1949, are consistently superior to any other in the nation; here in this same majestic setting are an annual jazz festival, a design conference, and the Institute for Humanistic Studies, a forum of cultural study for executives.

The Shakespeare festival of San Diego ranks with the finest of North America; and the one at Ashland, Oregon, is not far behind. Theater groups all over the West are giving vent to the Westerner's rage for experimentation and his passion for hyperactive use of leisure time. Hundreds were being turned away at almost every performance in the 1961–62 season of the Theater Group at the University of California at Los Angeles, which is led by John Houseman, the film producer. Theater-in-the-round burgeons in a dozen Western cities. Little theater is in every hamlet, and experimental theaters in every city and on every campus. Summer repertory is as rampant in Southern California as in New England. Touring companies of Broadway productions have been reaping rich harvests in the West. More than forty theaters are in active operation in Los Angeles. *Playbill*, which publishes all Broadway theater programs, launched a Los Angeles edition in 1962. In the summer of that year, *Time* magazine observed: "Los Angeles has been struggling for years against smog and a stigma of cultural inferiority. Only the smog remains."

Los Angeles vies now with New York as an art market and a center for collectors. Art critics deny the existence of a West Coast style, but they concede a vigor, an optimism, a freedom from academies. One can be certain only that new galleries, new wings, new acquisitions are being amassed all over the West. In Los Angeles, the success of gaunt young James Strombotne as an artist is measured in part by the names of Hollywood collectors who own his work. Sculptor Donal Hord dominates the San Diego art scene. San Francisco painters including Diebenkorn, Bischoff, and Oliveira pass in and out of the glare of discovery, from a school sometimes called New Figurative. New Northwest artists do not descend from Callahan, Tobey or Graves, or Southern Californians from Rico Lebrun, and San Francisco has three or four schools of painting, not merely one. The artists of Sante Fe and Taos cling to their unique position, and a half-dozen artists of the Southwest are roaring financial successes at one-man shows in New York and Los Angeles and at regional galleries.

In architecture, the ranch house, the sliding glass wall, the outward trend—all born or first accepted in the West—have moved on to every other region. The West is no longer infested with motley "homesick" architecture derived from many regions. The Western tradition in architecture—the most undeniably regional innovation of the West —has passed from Henry and Charles Greene, Bernard Maybeck, and Ellsworth Storey in Pasadena, Berkeley, and Seattle, to the interpretations of more current men: Belluschi, Wurster, Spencer, Campbell, Wong, Jones, Emmons, Ladd, Becket, Pereira, May, Graham, Thiry, Neutra, Mosher, and a hundred more. Thomas Church, the Western landscape architect, has suggested new directions for landscape architecture everywhere. In the field of medium-cost tract housing, the thousands of California homes built by Joseph Eichler are notable.

As Wallace Stegner wrote in a summary of that 1958 Carmel conference for the *Saturday Review*, there is "from Seattle to San Diego a tremendous stir, a great swell of energy and optimism and creativity, and this may be the truest, though not necessarily the most traditional expression of a really regional spirit. For the ferment is not simply economic, not just a building boom and the skyrocketing of the electronics and aircraft and missile industries. This society—urban, opulent, anxious, energetic, highly unionized, with a per capita income exceeded by that of only four or five states, growing at a furious rate, located in a region whose climate is on the whole more beatific and whose natural setting is more spectacular than those of any other section—this society is not sitting on its hands or relapsing into Spanish-California somnolence. In spite of the sports cars and the Rolls-Royces (thirteen of the forty U. S. Rolls-Royce agencies are in California), and in spite of the swimming pools and the homes that cost two, three, four hundred thousand dollars, this society strains for something more. . . . Contribute regionally to the national culture? We *are* the national culture, at its most energetic end . . . not a region but the mainstream, America only more so."

There is a thread that has run through the more sober writings of the West's past and present. Lord Bryce wrote: "The West may be called the most distinctly American part of America because the points in which it differs from the East are the points in which America as a whole differs from Europe." Again: "What America is to Europe, what Western America is to Eastern, that California is to the other Western States. . . ."

The Westerner thinks of himself less as a Westerner than as a Portlander, a San Franciscan, a Montanan, or a Pasadenan. There are sharp differences of outlook. But inexorable forces are bringing the Western states closer to each other and demonstrating the necessity for more regional consciousness in economic affairs and in matters involving natural resources. The unity is more easily achieved because of the yeasty emergence of a self-confident Western outlook concerned with both the casual life and the intense cultural drives of the new Western millions.

The excitement that is still inherent in the West pushes and prods its people. It is an asset, but it is not a guarantee. The highly urbanized West Coast may be America's newest city, embodying the risks and hopes of all American cities. The West of today is very likely a close kin of the America of tomorrow. It is a hopeful image, for from their high threshold of abundance and energy, Westerners are devoting time and patronage in support of cultural and scholarly activities at such a rate that they seem likely to accomplish within a century what it has taken most of the nation two or three hundred years to build.

2

SCIENCE, INDUSTRY, AND AMENITIES

High on a California mesa above the Pacific Ocean, on the northern outskirts of San Diego, lies the weathered and forgotten hulk of an amphibious landing craft, last used in training soldiers during World War II. A city block to the east, beyond a row of eucalyptus trees, scientists and secretaries move about the business campus of General Atomic, where nuclear reactors are old hat and physicists are coaxing the phenomenon known as nuclear pinch on toward the goal of controlled fusion.

This juxtaposition is symbolic of the maturing West. The onrush to the West has been in waves; the roiling eddies have not always subsided before the next wave roared in. The wave of immigration which brought General Atomic to California is distinct from the one that brought the landing craft. Yet in two decades no one seems to have had time to set fire to, or haul away, a useless relic of another era.

General Atomic provides an example of the new white-collar West. The demarcation between factory and laboratory exists less in the West than in any other region, and nowhere does industry place more emphasis on the laboratory than there. General Atomic produces commercial nuclear reactors while its research people in adjacent laboratories probe the outer limits of their scientific disciplines.

The wide open spaces of the West, its abundant power, and the geography of the Pacific war led to the establishment of aircraft and shipbuilding industries in the West during the Second World War. The postwar readjustment in Western industry was unexpectedly minor—industry underwent a rapid transition which is not yet understood by much of America. It still relies heavily on federal military spending, but it is long past the crisis in which it would wither to nothing were there a decline in armament. The unprecedented migration to the West has brought with it a solid industrial nucleus which now is inherent to the area. Not only people have moved West; small basic industry has moved there in a continuing wave. At the end of 1962, the atomic power divisions of three of the nation's leading corporations were competing to build a nuclear power plant for a group of New York electric utilities. All three of the divisions—General Electric, General Dynamics and North American Aviation—are based in California.

The scientist has spearheaded the move since the mid-fifties, when the West began to assume major stature in the exotic industries: space, missilery, and electronics. In 1961, one-third of the missile workers of the nation and one-fifth of those working in electronics were employed in California. But not all of Western industry is in the glamor category. It was only in 1946 that aircraft production supplanted food processing as California's major manufacturing activity, and today agriculture remains California's largest industry. The total farm income is the highest of any state; it exceeds three billion dollars a year, far ahead of Iowa and Texas. California supplies more than one-third of the nation's canned and frozen foods and vegetables, about one-quarter of the nation's commercial production of vegetables, more than one-third of its fruits, more than half of its nuts, and an encyclopedic list of two hundred other agricultural commodities from artichoke to zucchini. The state has seven million acres of irrigated farmland; even pastures are irrigated and sprinkled. The farms are large and mechanized; more than one-fourth of all the crawler tractors on United States farms are in California.

Urban sprawls are diminishing farmland in some areas. Continued expansion of California farm acreage is dependent on more water—primarily that promised by the one-billion-seven-hundred-and-fifty-million-dollar Feather River project which will pump water from northern California southward as far as six hundred miles.

Heavy construction is also an important economic factor in the West, and it draws on the steel output of two major Western steel mills—at Provo, Utah, and at Fontana, near Los Angeles—which were spawned by the Pacific shipbuilding industry during World War II. Japanese steel has become a major source of competition, but the Western steel industry predicts steady expansion in the decade ahead. In a move aimed at decreasing competition from steel mills east of the Rockies, the Kaiser Steel Corporation at Fontana cut its prices sharply in late 1962; the move was a big step in the direction of eliminating that historic phrase, "prices slightly higher west of the Rockies."

The steel baron of the West is Henry J. Kaiser, whose mill is at Fontana. Kaiser is the dominant Western industrialist, but his son Edgar, president of Kaiser Industries Corporation, is taking a larger role in the family empire. From the gently curving, twenty-eight story Kaiser Center beside Lake Merritt in Oakland, sixty affiliated Kaiser companies are directed. Offices in this showplace structure look down on a three-acre roof garden with lawn, trees and shrubs planted in a light-weight synthetic soil developed by the University of California. Into the building went Kaiser aluminum, Kaiser steel, Kaiser concrete, Kaiser aggregates, Kaiser dolomite, and Kaiser gypsum products.

The Howard Hughes empire, with assets estimated in the neighborhood of one billion dollars, sprawls through Southern California, Arizona, Texas and even into Scotland with operations that include electronic armament control systems, missiles, oil-well drilling, real estate, a brewery, and space vehicles.

San Francisco is the headquarters of such industrial giants as Standard Oil of California (ranked fourteenth among United States corporations as listed in the *Fortune Directory* of 1962), Crown Zellerbach, Foremost Dairies, and California Packing. Across the bay at Oakland are three Kaiser corporations ranking among the top two hundred United States corporations. Southward at San Jose is FMC Corporation.

In the Los Angeles area, the industrial kings are mostly in aviation and oil: Lockheed Aircraft, North American Aviation, Douglas Aircraft, Tidewater Oil, Union Oil of California, Carnation, Hunt Foods and Industries, Signal Oil and Gas, Richfield Oil, Northrop Aircraft, Rexall Drug & Chemical, and Litton Industries.

These first two cities of the West dominate the industrial pattern of the region. The only other corporations ranking within the top two hundred in the 1962 *Fortune* survey were Boeing at Seattle, Weyerhaeuser, the lumber, pulp and paper firm at Tacoma, and another lumber giant of the Northwest, Georgia-Pacific of Portland.

But the size and growth of Western business are understood better in terms of the individual than in corporate massiveness. In the summer of 1961, Gordon O. Baskin, a native of Albany, New York, then thirty-seven years old, founded and was installed as president of a new Los Angeles bank. Fourteen years before, he had been a cab driver. The father of five children, he had supported his family by selling hot dogs at football games in the Los Angeles Coliseum while he took a course in economics and business administration. Baskin's vice-president and secretary at the new bank was the former manager of the loan department of a Beverly Hills bank—the man who had agreed to give Baskin an unsecured loan of two thousand dollars with which he had launched his quick business spiral.

In the savings and loan field, Bart Lytton arrived in Los Angeles in 1940 with little but an extra pair of socks. By 1962, he personally controlled assets of about half a billion dollars, and showed a net worth approaching thirty million dollars.

Similar stories of business success are more common throughout the West than in the tightly regimented patterns of older regions and bear a kinship to the Eastern pattern of half a century ago.

One of the empire builders of the West was A. P. Giannini, a classic example of the aggressive, free-wheeling entrepreneur who became a Western phenomenon. His philosophy of the bank as a money store for those less than wealthy was typically Western in its conception, and it has profoundly affected American banking. Giannini was an innovator with flair and daring who took his bank into every crossroads of California and pioneered in making small personal loans. Now the Bank of America, from its brain center on the eleventh floor of the headquarters building on San Francisco's Montgomery Street, casts a shadow across the land from West to East. The largest non-government banking institution in the world, it has more than eight hundred branches in California, close to eight million deposit accounts, and total resources in excess of twelve billion dollars.

The reputation of Montgomery Street as the financial hub of the West is attributable in a large part to the Bank of America. A major skirmish in the nation-wide warfare over savings' interest rates in early 1962—involving banks and savings and loan companies— was set off when the Bank of America raised its interest rate on deposits, a heady gamble which cost the bank an estimated thirty-seven million dollars a year.

Near the Bank of America's headquarters is the office of James B. Black, board chairman of Pacific Gas and Electric Company, the behemoth of Western power. As much as any man in the West, he bridges the gaps in understanding and outlook between America's East Coast and West. Born in Illinois, the son of a flour miller, he graduated from the University of California and has lived since in the Bay Area except for eight years in New York. He still commutes to the East to attend board meetings of United States Steel, Shell Oil, and others; he has served as a trustee of the Ford Foundation. His distinctions are notably diverse: he is the only Western board member of United States Steel, and he also is Shirley Temple's father-in-law.

Black believes that New York bankers and industrialists have a firm understanding of Western growth. "You find some who don't think much beyond the Atlantic Coast, but they are in the minority. The people I know in New York are impressed by what is going on in the West and very interested in being a part of it. They are quite alert to what people in business in the West are doing."

Business, industry, and science have been more alert than most sociologists and editors in sensing the implications of the westward tilt. There are reasons; for one thing, the statistics of the tilt are less elusive than its motivations and goals. But the man of the white-collar West gives thought to why he is here, and he is capable of some crisp answers.

J. R. Dempsey, a blond, blue-eyed young man who was born in Alabama, is president of the General Dynamics–Astronautics plant at San Diego. How does he live? With his wife and three children in La Jolla on a hillside overlooking the golf course and the Pacific; in airplanes, much of the time; intensely, because he is obsessed with the seriousness of the world's predicament. He believes the larger assets of the West are freedom and freshness. As a missile manufacturer, he senses that Westerners are intent on one goal, and he believes it is the best that any people can have. "We've made a good start," Dempsey says, "toward eliminating the absurdities of life."

Young men like Dempsey are the new breed of the West in industry and science. In an era when they are sought after and wooed by industry, such men have come West, and factories and laboratories have followed them; they can do their work in whatever area offers them and their families the best life. In such a pattern, Motorola has come to Phoenix, Varian to Palo Alto, Beckman to Los Angeles— and hundreds of others. General Atomic at San Diego is a classic case.

In 1955 the late John Jay Hopkins, board chairman of General Dynamics, entrusted to Dr. Frederic de Hoffmann, an Austrian-born, Harvard-schooled theoretical physicist, the task of choosing the site for a nuclear research laboratory to be known as General Atomic. Many were startled that de Hoffmann chose San Diego. Before he toured the country to study possible sites, de Hoffmann had not visited San Diego. His impressions of the West Coast were relatively vague; he had been at Los Alamos from 1944 to 1955, but he was more accustomed to the streets of Washington, New York, Boston and Vienna than to those of Seattle, Portland, San Francisco, and Los Angeles.

I sat with de Hoffmann in his office, which faced the foothills east of San Diego, and asked why he had come West. He spoke with a passion that most scientists in the West display when they answer the question.

"A revolution is rapidly coming in the United States," he said. "Very modern, advanced industries need technical people to run them. You make better products if they are firmly rooted to their ultimate base in pure science.

"If you want to do this, you must choose an atmosphere where not just development and production can go forward, but where the thinking and the scientific part can flourish. This means an open atmosphere. This is possible in Chicago or New York, but it is no longer half so easy there as it is here. There is a surge of new life in the West much like the frontier spirit. There is a recognition that this area lives by its wits. If you are to make a good life in this part of the West, you realize it will be by having intellectually bright enterprises that will constantly stay up with the future. Everywhere I go in the West, this sort of world is much more in evidence than it is in the East. There is an excitement here, an alertness. The people of San Diego voted six to one to deed three hundred acres of city land to us for this laboratory. This has made an enormous difference in our effort in recruiting people. It told them that here was a community that understands; not just the city council, but eighty-five percent of the people."

General Atomic scientists and their wives are prominent in Parent-Teacher Associations' affairs, in musical and artistic circles, and in helping to interpret the scientific revolution to the citizens of the area. The warmth of their welcome has made their integration almost casual.

"The whole world is the realm of this laboratory," de Hoffmann went on. "We are building nuclear reactors on five continents, and people of many nations are moving constantly in and out. If you ask any of these people what they think distinguishes the Western United States, the first thing they mention is the politeness of Westerners. It sounds trite, but it is very true. The individual is much more honored, and is much more an *individual* here in the West. The man you meet casually on the street will almost always be friendly to you. In the East, he will be outgoing toward you only if you prove yourself to him first."

De Hoffmann has not overlooked the asset of Western scenery.

De Hoffmann said, "There is a chance in the West for us to get out into nature and see that we are not the only almighty thing but

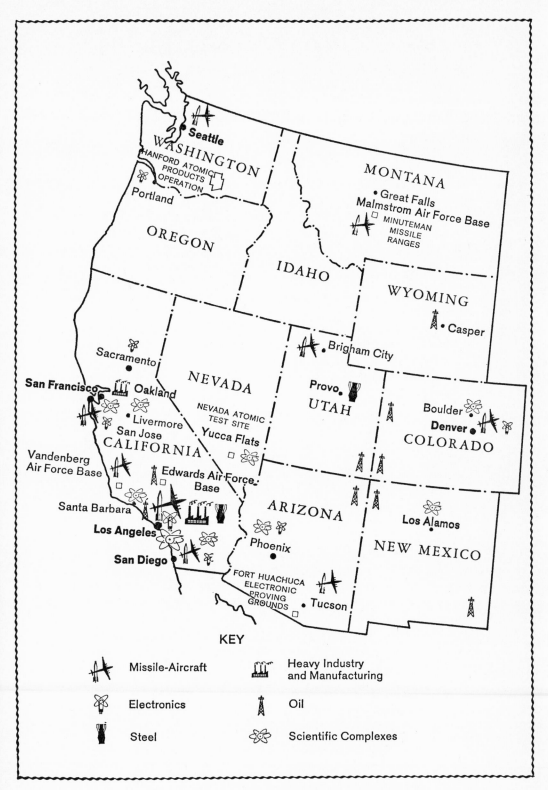

KEY

Missile-Aircraft   Heavy Industry and Manufacturing

Electronics   Oil

Steel   Scientific Complexes

Scientific, Industrial and Military Complexes

that there is something more almighty, and to get slightly humble. This is very hard to do when you live in a city of four or five million and never have the chance to contemplate anything other than your fellow man. There is a greater respect here not only for the individual but for nature. Somehow related to it is a stronger drive to think that almost anything that can be started, if only started with enough vigor, can be done successfully."

To a scientist of the new West like de Hoffmann, and to hundreds of thousands more, the cultural opportunities of the West have been a prime factor in their choice of the area. I wondered if de Hoffmann—a connoisseur of wines, an avid reader, a brilliant scholar, a collector of antique stamps—found the West a cultural desert.

"People from the East underestimate considerably what culture there is here now," he said. "They set up arbitrary standards of metropolitan culture. There is, in fact, a considerable appreciation of cultural matters in the West. We may have planned ahead enough, may have enough space, for instance, never to get into the question of really having slums, and at the same time be able to devote our attention more aggressively to cultural things."

De Hoffmann foresees a new dimension to cultural growth in the West. "East Coast culture is built on the traditional European pattern. There is culture for a few in the East. In the West, the benefits of education and nature are going to all. We can build cultural activities in the West in the same way, making them accessible to the larger part of the population. If we make this transition, we have a very large chance of keeping up with Eastern culture, and even surpassing it."

From the fervor with which he discussed it, I suspect that of all Western virtues, the one dearest to de Hoffmann is the freshness and diversity of its people. It is the virtue he most fears losing.

He left no doubt that he prefers the good life of the West Coast, where there is more leisure time. "More leisure may make kinder people," he said. "If there were more leisure time around the world, I suspect we would have fewer problems."

Several hundred yards away from de Hoffmann's General Atomic, on a steep Pacific cliffside, Dr. Jonas Salk's Institute for Biological Studies is being built. The design by Louis I. Kahn, the Philadelphia architect, is for a twelve-million-dollar complex including laboratories, a series of residences for seventy scientists which Kahn describes as looking "like a Pompeiian village," and a castle-like meeting house. Here, Salk says, "we will be looking into the most elementary processes of life." Some of the most eminent research men of the nation will converge to carry on their work in one of the most scenic settings in Southern California, which was donated to the Institute by the city of San Diego.

A few steps south along these Pacific cliffs is a new campus of the University of California, built in conjunction with the highly respected Scripps Institution of Oceanography. Dr. Herbert York, former Director of Defense Research and Engineering, with the Department of Defense, is chancellor, and men such as Dr. Harold Urey, a Nobel Prize winner, were entrenched on campus before the enrollment reached two hundred students. From the hub of this scientific community emanate underwater explorations of the Pacific and Indian oceans, and research projects in geophysics, planetary physics, atmosphere research, and molecular biology.

Such projects certainly are not without precedent, but a decade ago this San Diego scientific community—General Atomic, the Salk Institute, and the University of California—did not exist. The sites were owned largely by the city of San Diego under century-old Pueblo deeds. The city then had only the climate, the property, and the willingness to part with land in order to encourage the development of its future city. Other city land nearby went to provide the site of a million-dollar legitimate theater. City planners pored hard over designs for University City, a town with a projected population of about eighty-five thousand, rising on land adjacent to this new complex.

Part of this grand design has been the dream of Dr. Roger Revelle, director of the Scripps Institution of Oceanography and now the chief research dean of the University of California. Here again is the compelling voice of a California scientist: "I think we are developing less emphasis in the West on physical things and more on intellectual, esthetic, and moral matters. There are signs of greater interest in good art, literature, and drama—and, if you will, in a kind of religion which incorporates a set of values and sense of purpose. We need this in California perhaps more than most people, because here we tend to be uprooted. We will get it here because we need it, and because it naturally follows a life of intellectual and emotional fulfillment."

Certainly it is too soon to know if this remarkable San Diego scientific community will be as distinguished as anticipated. But rarely has a new little world been launched as auspiciously, in an environment of financial abundance, scenic delight, intellectual integrity and dedication. It comes close to meeting the terms of the vision which has lured men westward in search of the promised land and the better life, the quixotic goal held out for the West by Walt Whitman in *Song of the Redwood-Tree:*

I see in you, certain to come, the promise of thousands of years,
  till now deferr'd . . .
The new society at last, proportionate to Nature . . .
Clearing the ground for broad humanity, the true America,
  heir of the past so grand,
To build a grander future.

The Western man of science is not always so philosophical. A bar at La Jolla is a favorite cocktail stop for some of the bright young men of the San Diego scientific complex. Recognizing their creative drives, the proprietor lined the walls of the men's room with blackboards. Physicists and engineers chalk up imperfect equations to challenge each other, and Kilroy writes on the walls in Latin. At the nearby Navy Electronics Laboratory, an order was published that no more calendar girls were to adorn the walls. The men in the Human Factors Division, whose job is to predict the frailties of mankind, set an example of compliance. They moved their nudes to the ceilings.

Throughout the West, science and industry tend to travel in tandem.

The Martin Company chose Denver as the site for production of the Titan missile. Close by, the university town of Boulder gained sudden stature as a research center, primarily through the establishment there in 1960 of the National Center for Atmospheric Research.

Ever since the Los Alamos Scientific Laboratory was set up in 1943 and the Trinity Project came into being in southern New Mexico, industry involved with nuclear warfare has been an inherent part of the Albuquerque economy.

Even Arizona is feeling the birthpangs of a scientific community. "The world's largest hi-fi set" was built at Litchfield Park by the Arizona division of Goodyear Aircraft Corporation as part of an environmental testing facility. Old Fort Huachuca, founded in 1877 as an Army outpost to control the warring Apache Indians, is now the headquarters for a multimillion-dollar military electronics test range. The Hughes Aircraft Company has been making missiles in Tucson, not far from Kitt Peak, where a national observatory was dedicated in 1960. The industrial explosion of Phoenix—principally in electronics—has occurred because Arizona living has seemed attractive to thousands of scientific people and white-collar workers. Backed by the Rockefeller Foundation, the American Museum of Natural History has set up a biological research station in Cochise County.

Boeing long has dominated the industrial scene in the Pacific

Northwest, and its space research programs, centered at Seattle, are the prime intrusion of the laboratory into the more pastoral traditions of this region. There is an increasing emphasis on research at the campuses of the University of Washington and the University of Oregon.

But it is in California that the marriage of science and industry has reached full flower. Los Angeles presents the clearest example, but the pattern of white-collar factories for exotic products which has sprung up in the vicinity of the Stanford University campus, south of San Francisco, has much in common with the phenomenon of recent industrial growth near the Harvard campus on the opposite seaboard. While the output of many of these factories is concerned with the military establishment, the new scientific-industrial communities of the West can no more be dismissed as tenuous than can the Harvard–Massachusetts Institute of Technology complex. Today the layman, befuddled by the world of computer and transistor, tends to classify as "defense work" the production of items which already are an integral part of his everyday civilian life.

But the West cannot shrug off the hazards of its dependence on the federal dollar. California received twenty-four cents of each defense dollar in 1961. In research and development contracts, the state drew more than forty-one percent, as contrasted with twelve percent for New York. In the uneasy economy of the summer of 1962, this had become a national issue. Secretary of Defense Robert McNamara was defending his department on the grounds that contracts were going where the work could be performed most efficiently, by the people best qualified to do it; senators from the East and Midwest had begun to charge that California was pirating scientific brainpower. More than half of California's economic growth between 1947 and 1957 was attributable to defense industry. San Diego, which is even more dependent than Los Angeles, has had seventy-eight percent of its total manufacturing employment in the defense industry in 1959; the figure in Los Angeles recently has been estimated at less than fifty percent. Denver, Albuquerque, Tucson, Phoenix, San Jose, and Seattle also have an unhealthy reliance on the Pentagon. In most cases, dependence is declining as these cities struggle to diversify their economies with non-military industry. Cuts in defense spending, or elimination of specific production programs from Washington, react like tidal waves on the people of such cities; thus San Diego was depressed in 1963 through the staggering losses incurred by General Dynamics in its jetliner production, and by subsequent declining employment at San Diego plants when General Dynamics failed to bid successfully for new government contracts.

The dangers inherent in such federal cities have been described by Peter Madison in a study for the Falk Foundation Center for Political Research at the University of California at Los Angeles. The obvious danger is in the yoyo tendency that prevails because of the rise and fall of defense contracts. A more subtle danger is that the forces of a federal economy create a local federal elite "which is in the community, but no longer wholly of the community. The federal elite in the Los Angeles area—in science, industry, and the military— helps shape the great decisions of national security. Their counsel is and must be based on national needs. Yet the elite's decisions, also vital to this federal community, have been made with the community as a bystander. A federal city sees the ironic paradox of its own citizens helping shape its destiny without reference to community needs."

A former Los Angeles mayor, Norris Poulson, stated: "All they want or need from us is services and low taxes. . . . They give to local charities, they mean well; but they're just not seriously interested nowadays in local matters."

J. R. Dempsey of San Diego put it this way: "We spend a great deal of time at the plant. Most of our waking moments and energies are wrapped around building missiles and the other things we are building now. When we leave the plant, we tend to look for relaxation and not to participate in community affairs—probably to the detriment of upholding our real responsibilities in the community. In my work, I am traveling a good deal of the time, and an evening at home is something that I cherish. I don't like to go to civic dinners or lunches because it takes time. Time is our most critical commodity."

It was Thomas G. Lanphier, Jr., a former vice president of General Dynamics–Convair, who commuted from his home in La Jolla to the East Coast fifty-nine times in one year. His case is extreme, but not unusual. No community should hope for any degree of local involvement from a man who must live like this. The remarkable thing is the extent of community contribution that often is made by many men of this caliber, even in federal cities like Los Angeles and San Diego.

About one in every ten persons employed in Southern California is working in an industry which depends primarily on defense contracts; and while increased defense spending has heightened the potential hazards of the federal city in Southern California, another familiar hazard has proved to be exaggerated—that of Southern California's "weather-oriented" income. Only about one percent of the Los Angeles work force is in the movie business. Tourist spending accounts for only about two percent of California income. The elderly population coming to California for retirement is no longer a significant economic factor. California has a lower ratio of persons sixty-five years old or over than the national average: 8.8 percent in California, as against nine percent for the nation, and nine to ten percent in Ohio, New Jersey, and New York.

In vivid contrast with past eras, when the image of California was tinged by its aged, one of the most significant population resources today is the highly trained young technician and scientist. The number of California members in the National Academy of Sciences has climbed steadily in recent years until it is the largest of any state. In 1962, there were one hundred and thirty-five academicians from California, one hundred and four from New York, and ninety-three from Massachusetts. Yet the same problems of cleavage exist between the scientist and the community as between the industrialist of the federal city and his community.

It is not a Western phenomenon that the non-scientific community is woefully unaware of the work of the new scientific-industrial community; this is a national failing. But it may be most obvious in the West. A woman reporter in Los Angeles, assigned to interview a visiting Nobel Prize winner, asked him what he could tell her about his work.

"What do you know about physics?" he asked.

"Nothing, really," she said.

"Then I'm afraid I can't tell you anything," he said.

In San Diego, a poll in 1960 showed that only thirty-eight percent of the citizens knew the principal product of the city's largest factory, General Dynamics–Astronautics, manufacturer of the Atlas missile. The situation is probably not much different in other communities. Today's citizen is prone to assume that the product of the bizarre new factory which has no smokestacks, no railroad siding, and makes no odor is mysterious and complex. It is another thing when a man can smell the burning rubber at the tire factory, or see the steel desks being loaded into a box car. But the Atlas missile is taken from its birthplace under canvas, and a million dollars' worth of tiny electronics parts may roll out of the Motorola plant in Phoenix at night on a single truck and trailer. It is a pity that the layman does not make the effort to understand the missile or the transistor as he did the tire and the desk; the chasm widens between the scientist-industrialist and the rest of his community.

One of the most formidable fortresses of this kind of spurious mystery is the think factory, whose occupants usually prefer that their places of business be known by almost any other name. The most notable one in the West is a long low building on Main Street in Santa Monica. It is unadorned by neon or gaudy lettering, and it is protected by blue-uniformed guards. The RAND Corporation, once described by the Russians as "an American academy of death and destruction," has been more aptly termed an "arsenal for ideas." RAND was the first and has remained the largest of the pure think factories. It is a non-profit research corporation which was formed soon after the end of World War II, a time when Air Force generals grew disturbed by the fact that the scientists who had helped win the war were heading back to their campuses. RAND was conceived by General Hap Arnold.

It was unprecedented then to gather scientists together for studies vital to national security in a university-like setting rather than an industrial environment. Now there are others, such as Lincoln Laboratory at Massachusetts Institute of Technology, and the Institute of Air Weapons Research at the University of Chicago.

The RAND staff totals over one thousand, with a professional staff of about six hundred. Standard RAND gags give a hint of its functions. ("It has no IN basket, only an OUT basket"; and "RAND stands not for *research and development*, but for *research and no development*.")

RAND is in California primarily because Douglas Aircraft Company offered it a temporary home. An original RAND staff member recalls General Arnold's dictum: "Get as far away from Washington as you can and still be in the United States."

I spent an afternoon at RAND with Brownlee Haydon, an assistant to the president. He is a soft-spoken, patient and deliberate man who takes seriously his responsibility of bridging the gap between the lay mind and the research mind. "We have a sixteen-year record of not spilling the beans," Haydon said. "We are trusted with secrets both by industry and the Air Force." But without involving national security, some RAND accomplishments can be cited. For instance, the Air Force, the largest business in the world (it dwarfs General Motors), with its aircraft spread all over the globe a decade ago, was stockpiling replacement engines in hundreds of different locations. RAND told the Air Force to stockpile only minor, everyday replacement parts—and to airlift engines when necessary. This decision, reached by logistic research done by mathematicians at RAND, has saved the taxpayer millions of dollars.

In 1947, when the United States stood on the threshold of supersonic flight, even before the missile age, RAND turned to the study of exotic metals that were light, strong, and heat-resistant. RAND scientists examined the periodic tables and urged the United States to spend money in improving the ductility of beryllium; they called it a "dream metal." Today, beryllium is used in missile nose cones.

Although RAND is most closely related to the Air Force, the benefits of such studies go to all the services and are shared by the nation as a whole. RAND also does research for the AEC, ARPA, NASA, and other government agencies. In its work, the company wends its way meticulously along the thorny path of competitive enterprise, often playing a catalytic role. The Air Force once contracted with rival firms for two missiles. Both firms were working with RAND on design problems. One firm had failed to solve its propulsion problems. The other had guidance troubles. RAND advised the Air Force to take the front end of one company's missile and the rear end of the other, almost literally bolting them together for a test.

The Air Force listened, signed a joint contract with the two firms, and a well-known missile was the result.

A typical project at RAND involves many specialists. Chemist, propulsion engineer, material engineer, physicist, mathematician and aerodynamicist all may bring their training into focus on a single project.

An engineer at RAND may dream up a rocket which is then examined by his colleagues. A physicist would tell him how it can carry a weapon; an economist would tell him how expensive it would be; then a RAND social scientist might ask, "Do you really want that kind of weapon?"

RAND is a young man's company, but it has grown a little older since its start. The average age of personnel is about thirty-seven. More than half of those actually engaged in research have graduate degrees, and more than one-fourth of these are doctorates. A typical starting salary for a Ph.D. from Princeton or the University of Chicago at RAND is nine thousand five hundred dollars, but such men may have turned down pay of fourteen thousand elsewhere. "All my heroes are at RAND," said one young Ph.D.

To the science-oriented youth of the 1960's, the West indeed may seem as much a land of outsized heroes as to the schoolboy of another generation who found his heroes in the West of Zane Grey. Californians alone make up forty percent of the roster of men named in 1960 by *Fortune* as "great American scientists," and they number forty-seven percent of those named in the same year by *Time* (a variation of opinion between Henry Luce's science editors). The heroes of the new West are men not of the past, but of the future. That seems appropriate; the new West is dominated by the young, and best understood by them, just as the changing terms of science and industry are grasped most readily by the young. It is within the power of these fresh young waves of Westerners to give shape and meaning to the new world about which they display such intensity.

3

THE EDUCATION
RUSH

From the special public school classes for emotionally disturbed children at Las Vegas to the nuclear laboratories on the teeming California university campuses, the new West has embraced education as a
creature of its own discovery, a panacea for the ills of violent growth
and a talisman through which the West will fulfill its dream.

California has been building a new school a day. Sixty-two
cents of the tax dollar in California—more than a billion dollars
a year—goes to education of some sort. It is possible for a Californian
to ascend to the most obscure heights of graduate study at state expense.

At frigid Bozeman, Montana, a modern, circular field house
and a new chemistry building have risen on the campus of Montana
State College just across the street from a little white farmhouse and
a pasture which marks the start of the Montana rangeland. The six
campuses of the University of Montana have only eleven thousand
students, and the seven campuses of the University of California have
more than sixty thousand; but Montana is adapting the progressive
California master plan of education to its own needs.

Phoenix businessmen, restless at legislative budget delays, have tossed sure-fire real estate speculations into their Arizona State University Foundation; as much as half a million dollars has been available to begin a campus construction project before the Arizona legislature could clear its appropriation. Like all the West, Arizona is a state largely dependent on public educational facilities; the territory was settled after the state university had taken hold as a favorite American institution.

At Colorado Springs, in 1961, before the new Air Force Academy had reached its full four-year complement of cadets, three cadets were among the thirty-two Rhodes Scholars chosen in the United States. Only Harvard, with eight, and Yale, with four, exceeded that number. Three Western campuses ranked in 1962 among the top eleven in the nation in the cumulative number of Rhodes Scholars since 1904: Stanford, with twenty-six, and the University of Washington and little Reed College in Portland, each with twenty-one. (Selections from Southern California campuses have been notably sparse.)

Utah, thirty-seventh in the nation in personal income, leads the nation in percentage of college graduates. From the main Mormon campus, Brigham Young University at Provo, an educational empire has been launched by Dr. Ernest L. Wilkinson, a former Washington attorney who once won a thirty-five-million-dollar mineral-rights settlement from the United States government for the tiny Ute Indian tribe. Brigham Young, with more than twelve thousand students, is among the largest church-related institutions in the nation. Its student body was ninety-three percent Mormon in 1961. Smoking is forbidden on the campus; and the Mormon curriculum emphasizes courses in family living, sociology, social sciences and nursing. The church owns sites throughout the West where junior colleges are planned.

In the idyllic mountains of Santa Fe, New Mexico, a new campus is being built for the nation's third oldest college, St. John's College of Annapolis, Maryland. At Annapolis, St. John's confines itself to three hundred students and to a four-year liberal arts curriculum built around great books; it has abolished the departmental system and eliminated majors and minors at the undergraduate level. St. John's College in Santa Fe will be a Western echo of the Annapolis campus. Forty communities offered sites to St. John's; the selection narrowed to three sites in California and to Santa Fe. There, St. John's will be an institution unique in the Southwest.

The Berkeley campus of the University of California added its ninth Nobel laureate in 1961. With the two additional Nobel laureates on University of California campuses at Los Angeles and San Diego, the University is the runaway leader in the Nobel Prize sweepstakes;

it has enough of them to field a football team. (Stanford and Harvard have five, and the California Institute of Technology has three.) California has about nine percent of the nation's population and about eleven percent of its total personal income; but Californians are prone to boast that thirty-seven percent of the living United States winners of Nobel Prizes reside in California, and that twenty-eight percent of the living United States Nobel laureates earned degrees in California colleges and universities. Twenty-two percent of the members of the National Academy of Sciences live in California; in 1961, the University of California was tied with Harvard for leadership in number of academicians.

The stresses of growth among Western colleges are of such an awesome nature that higher education there has become more clearly a critical public challenge than elsewhere. Facing unparalleled quantity, Western educators and Western taxpayers have become acutely quality-conscious.

The college-age population of California will double between 1960 and 1970. In those years, the college-age group is expected to rise in New York by only forty-five percent, and in Illinois by fifty-eight percent. Only two states, both much smaller, will have sharper increases than California: Nevada's college-age group will rise from fourteen thousand to thirty-two thousand, and Arizona's from seventy thousand to one hundred and forty-five thousand.

The result of this challenge in California was an academic armistice which halted overlapping between state institutions and set an orderly pattern of growth. A master plan for higher education was enacted by the California Legislature in 1960. It laid down ground rules for the University of California, the sixteen state colleges and about seventy junior colleges. It committed the University to maintaining intellectual leadership by limiting its enrollment to the top thirteen percent of high school graduates, and by reserving for the university the right to bestow doctoral degrees. It restricted state college admissions to the upper one-third (junior colleges are open to all high school graduates). The bill also encouraged chancellors of the seven university campuses to develop autonomy and diversity, despite their joint budget and joint academic senate.

This pioneering California plan for education seems to be working. Sooner than the rest of the nation California faced the challenge of sheer quantity in higher education. Studying the successes and flaws of California techniques, other states have been girding for the new peaks of enrollment which lie ahead. There is something for everyone in this sharp division among university, state college and junior college; but it is designed to bring the better student to the better teacher and to avoid clogging the upper reaches of the university system with the casual student. Another revolutionary technique has been scheduled for inauguration in the summer of 1963: a year-round university operation created by the addition of a twelve-week summer semester. For the student, it will mean the opportunity to complete college in three years instead of four; for the University of California, it will mean accommodating more students in existing facilities, the equivalent of adding a new campus for seventeen thousand students at no further cost for buildings or equipment.

Thus the West is no longer an educational wilderness. At least three California campuses rank on any list among the dozen most distinguished of the nation: the University of California at Berkeley, Stanford University at Palo Alto, and the California Institute of Technology at Pasadena. Berkeley and Stanford have large enrollments: close to twenty-five thousand at Berkeley and nearly ten thousand at Stanford. Caltech is compared often to the Massachusetts Institute of Technology in everything except size; its student body is fewer than fifteen hundred, but its faculty is in excess of four hundred.

The significance of these campuses is not limited to science. The University of California began to achieve its preëminence in science at a time when Russian scientific advances had swung the United States' attention sharply in that direction. But the Berkeley scientific picture has been overemphasized; the humanities prosper also. The English department at Berkeley includes among its scholars Mark Schorer, Henry Nash Smith, Bertrand H. Bronson, George R. Stewart, and James D. Hart. The history department is outstanding; and philosophy, art, and music are strong.

The University of California's extent and influence is awesome. The unparalleled mechanization of California farms is due largely to the experimentation over the years at the Davis campus, which has made the transition from cow campus to a school of genuine agricultural science. The University reaches nine hundred miles away to operate the Los Alamos Scientific Laboratory, and it oversees seven oceangoing ships; it owns hospitals at Los Angeles and San Francisco. At its Livermore Radiation Laboratory, its physicists operate one of the world's notable nuclear research centers. It owns 25,877 acres, parks twenty thousand cars, employs three thousand professors, offers eight thousand courses, and spends more than a third of a billion dollars each year. Anxious that size not dominate, the University of California was busy early in 1963 with plans for a cluster of twenty small liberal arts colleges to be built on its Santa Cruz campus, a forested, two-thousand acre-expanse overlooking Monterey Bay.

The University Extension of the University of California is the largest in enrollment and scope, and its students amount to more than one-fourth of all extension students of public universities in the nation. The typical California Extension student is a married man, thirty-two years old, who has attended college. Three out of five Extension students have bachelor degrees, and one in ten has a graduate degree. In 1962, more than one hundred and fifty thousand Californians met under Extension auspices in two hundred and eleven communities for courses, discussion programs, and conferences on subjects ranging from Spoken Mandarin to Urban Development, from Mortuary Science to Thermal Management of Spacecraft. Two out of every three California lawyers sharpen their wits on current legal matters by attending Extension courses, and in the summer of 1962, a course for doctors involved a field trip to Japan for the study of the side effects of oral contraceptives.

There are more than one thousand Extension courses and seminars, which are mainly taught by academic men and women but often by high-powered specialists. Elizabeth Arden has been an Extension teacher, and so have Dr. Edward Teller, George Gamow, and Erskine Caldwell. Extension students have studied violin under Jascha Heifetz, physics under Harold Urey, and been taught creative writing by Aldous Huxley.

In the Los Angeles area it has become difficult to find enough buildings to accommodate University Extension students. Classes in philosophy conducted by Dr. Abraham Kaplan had to be televised by closed circuit. Classes in political science, announced during the Presidential campaign of 1960, were sold out so rapidly that more than five hundred refunds had to be made. A course in prehistoric and medieval arts conducted by Dr. Karl With was announced for a classroom which would hold thirty-seven students; attendance finally was frozen at five hundred and twenty-five after an elementary school auditorium had been acquired for the class sessions.

In a recent school term, fourteen Los Angeles men, each one a Doctor of Philosophy, went to Extension officials with a request for a night course in the Theory of Games. Extension knew just where to find its man; the mantle fell on a physicist from the RAND Corporation, a man not a bit awed by the caliber of his students.

Partly because of its hyperactive University Extension, California is the most-schooled state of the nation. It leads the states in expenditures for public schools, in number of high school graduates, and in enrollment and attendance at public schools and colleges. It ranks second only to Utah in median school years completed by persons twenty-five years of age and older. Los Angeles men and women in the 25-to-29 age bracket have an unprecedented median education level—beyond the thirteenth school year.

Though these facts seem hopeful, it is also true that California falls behind New York in conferring degrees (more Californians drop out of college) and in graduate study. It also lags in the number of public school teachers, indicating that larger classes still prevail than in some other states.

Only one in five California college students are on the campuses of private institutions. Stanford University is the most prestigious of the independent universities in the West. The University of Southern California (at Los Angeles) is the largest, with about fourteen thousand students. After Stanford, second in size, the independent universities drop away sharply in enrollment: among Denver University, Seattle University, the University of the Pacific (at Stockton) and the University of San Diego, there is no student body in excess of four thousand. Among independent colleges which do not rank as universities, California Institute of Technology leads the field in the sciences. Notable in many fields are the Claremont Colleges, a federation of five independent colleges east of Los Angeles, with a combined student body of fewer than five thousand.

Measured in quantity, the independent schools of California have a small role, but the quality of many is exceptional. They anticipate the ability to almost double their student capacity by 1975. Nevertheless, the staggering fact is that the college-age avalanche in California is so great that the independents' share of students by then will have dropped from one in five to one in ten.

Even at Stanford, which has a reputation in the West as a rich man's school, four out of five students are from public schools. This is an unusual proportion for a university like Stanford, but it is not unusual for the West. However, Western universities no longer are attended almost entirely by Westerners. Phillips Andover and Phillips Exeter lead in private schools contributing students to Stanford; both are Eastern schools, and the Stanford students coming from them are about half Eastern and half Western in origins. The California Institute of Technology has spread its net across the country; only about half the students are Californians. This has given Dr. Lee DuBridge, the president, a unique opportunity to explore regional differences in education. He has found that students attending *private* schools in the East often are better prepared for college than Western students, but he believes Western *public* schools prepare students better than do those of many Eastern states. Caltech is one of the schools which skim the cream of the high school market. With only one exception in its president's memory, every Caltech student who has been admitted has also been accepted at the other institutions to which he has applied.

The scholastic aristocracy of the Caltech student is exceeded only by that of the faculty. The average student IQ at Caltech is one hundred and forty-two; the average faculty IQ has not been made known. But that distinguished body includes astronomers, working under Ira S. Bowen, who man observatories at Palomar Mountain and Mount Wilson and huge twin radio telescopes at Owens Valley, all in Southern California. It also includes chemists like Linus Pauling, a Nobel laureate who has been outspoken on the issues of nuclear war, but who is not above probing the chemical qualities of a commercial chlorophyll deodorant (he once announced that a popular deodorant did not banish odor, but that it did paralyze the sense of smell). At Caltech young theoretical physicists like Richard P. Feynman and Murray Gell-Mann have pioneered in research on the decay of evanescent nuclear particles. It is not always easy to distinguish between the young faculty and undergraduates as they huddle in discussion in the sunshine of the sedate Caltech campus, or mingle in the Caltech laboratories, which outnumber classrooms by four-to-one.

The Caltech seismological laboratory has contributed as much as any on earth to the understanding of earthquakes, seismic waves, and the structure of the earth. A strain gauge devised at Caltech is sensitive enough to detect a shift of one-sixteenth of an inch between the West and East coasts. The jet-propulsion laboratory at Caltech is one of several departments which has fostered the space-age industrial development of Southern California in much the same way as Massachusetts Institute of Technology has fathered a scientific cluster near Boston. (In 1961, a wind tunnel at Caltech was junked because its maximum test speed, only 1.2 times the speed of sound, rendered it useless for testing aircraft and space vehicles then being engineered by the industrial companies which had pooled funds to build the tunnel with Caltech. It had been radically revised during the fifteen years since it had been built in order to double its speed, but by 1961 it was obsolete.)

This all-star faculty, with the highest percentage of members of any American college in the National Academy of Sciences, is the pride of President DuBridge, who has been referred to as the senior statesman of science. He was a post-doctoral fellow at Caltech in 1926, under his distinguished predecessor as president, Physicist Robert A. Millikan. Caltech in its present form was then only six years old. But by that year, Millikan had gathered a small group of able scientists on his olive-shaded campus and there was a spark of the devotion to pure science which later was to blaze. At Berkeley, the University of California was barely beginning to give warning of its future greatness. Across Los Angeles at Westwood, building was getting under way on the campus of the University of California at Los Angeles.

After recalling those early days at Caltech, Lee DuBridge said recently, "California scientists and educators were seldom seen in the East before World War II, and there was a kind of separate colony out here. Once you were in California, you might get back to see your friends in the East once a year, or once in five years. Very few Californians were on government boards or involved in the governing boards of professional and scientific societies."

Today, DuBridge's list of active affiliations in national societies and boards is enormous. "But I'm not even a good example," he protested, "because I've been reducing my affiliations. Many other Western educators have many more. It is common to see professors traveling back and forth to meetings in the East five, seven, ten or fifteen times a year. I see these same faces on the jets. Yet the Eastern educator who comes to California once a year thinks he has done a tremendous thing. We are trying to get our Eastern counterparts acclimated to the idea of three or four trips each year to the West to attend meetings and participate in affairs out here. Now it's the Easterner who needs to be educated. The Easterner has not learned that you can cross the country in four or five hours. He is the provincial one now!"

Caltech boasts of five alumni who are Nobel laureates: Pauling, Carl D. Anderson, who discovered the positive electron and the mu meson; Edwin McMillan, the physicist who went on to the University of California to work on the synchrotron; William Shockley, a physicist who did basic research with Bell Laboratories leading to the transistor; and Donald Glaser, who invented the hydrogen bubble chamber, now such an important tool in nuclear physics investigations. Two of these men, Anderson and Pauling, serve on the Caltech faculty. Three other Nobel Prize winners (Robert A. Millikan, Thomas Hunt Morgan, biologist, and George W. Beadle, biologist, now president of the University of Chicago), also served for long periods at the university. In 1961, a new and young member of the Caltech faculty, Rudolf Mossbauer, was awarded the Nobel Prize for his brilliant work on the emission of gamma rays from atomic nuclei. Other alumni who have made their names famous in technological industry are Marquardt, Beckman, Ramo, and Wooldridge.

Caltech students do not confine their high IQ to pure science. The word for their football team is sincere; it once lost twenty-five games in succession. The Caltech man excels in extra-curricular fields where the Caltech mind—and not the body—is challenged. Igniting a homecoming bonfire on a rival campus prematurely is not in itself an ingenious prank, but Caltech men once did it through the use of what seemed to be a log, but turned out to be a radio-controlled napalm fire bomb. The classic triumph of extra-curricular Caltech ingenuity occurred at the Rose Bowl game of 1961. One undergraduate posed as a reporter and interviewed the leader of the thousand-man University of Washington card stunt cheering section. During the next two days, in a frenzied burst of activity, and with the aid of a printer and a series of lock-picking invasions of hotel rooms occupied by Washington undergraduates, the Caltech men set their stage meticulously. At half-time during the Rose Bowl game, with all the nation watching over television, the University of Washington student body spelled out CALTECH instead of WASHINGTON, displayed a Caltech beaver instead of a Washington husky, and spelled HUSKIES—backwards. In the summer of 1962, a Caltech graduate student understandably called for help from Pasadena police when he faced the head of a seven-foot anaconda snake emerging from a bathroom fixture. Another Caltech student and two friends had been tugging on the other end of the anaconda from another apartment. The anaconda had been their own secret, and they faced its loss reluctantly. The opposing factions tugged for more than an hour before learning they were at odds over the snake; then the Humane Society took over.

With its raids on Eastern faculties, Stanford has gone far toward justifying its intention of becoming the "Harvard of the West." Stanford has been emphasizing the humanities and social sciences. Among the distinguished men who joined the faculty in 1961 were Gordon A. Craig, professor of German history, after twenty-five years at Princeton; Albert J. Guerard, literary critic, after twenty-three years at Harvard; Albert H. Hastorf, former chairman of the psychology department at Dartmouth; David M. Potter, American history professor, after nineteen years at Yale; and Emile Despres, former head of the economics department at Williams. Fifteen professors moved from Ivy League faculties alone to Stanford between 1957 and 1961.

Some of these men had their first introduction to Stanford—and to the West—during sabbatical years spent at the Center for Advanced Study in the Behavioral Sciences on a wooded knoll just one mile west of the Stanford campus. The center—referred to colloquially as "the Casbah," a vaguely phonetic attempt to meld the first letters of the Center's awkward name—was established by the Ford Foundation to provide one year's free work time to fifty post-doctoral fellows. The Center, which pays the salary of the fellow for the year, is a gem of Western architecture: redwood and glass, set informally in a grove of oak trees, with Stanford's Hoover Tower looming below in the flatland toward San Francisco Bay. It is reached by a narrow, winding road that rises from a terrain of rolling fields. Bicycles are parked beside the cattle gate which serves as the entrance to the Center, and an old water cistern stands nearby, enhancing the pastoral setting. A gardener and a cook are in attendance. Each fellow is provided his own office: an informal room with floor-to-ceiling glass facing outward toward the trees. Each office has a chaise longue and a desk with two file drawers and a dictating device. The Center requires nothing of its fellows; the result is that most of them work at a furious pace.

But even here, there is time for frivolity. When I visited the Center, a notice on the bulletin board had been posted by Dr. Abraham Kaplan, the philosopher from University of California at Los Angeles, that galley proofs of his book, *The New World of Philosophy*, were available in the Center library. "To those who are interested," Kaplan's memo concluded brashly, "my counsel is, lose no time in reading them!" Another bulletin-board notice concerned "an academic jazz combo" which would play at a forthcoming social for fellows and their wives. One of the American astronauts was in space on the morning that I visited the Center, but it was difficult in its insulated setting to find any relation between that world, and this.

The Center for Advanced Study in the Behavioral Sciences was established with a five-million dollar Ford Foundation grant in 1954. Directors had considered five possible locations in the areas of Boston, New York City, Philadelphia, Chicago and San Francisco. A poll had been made in 1953 of those chosen as the first fellows, and the vote clearly indicated a preference for a Western location.

"The reasons the Center was established at Stanford are simple," Preston Cutler, assistant director of the Center, told me. "There is a good year-round climate. There is a great deal of building in the area, and adequate housing available for the fellows and their families. There are leading educational and library resources in the area. Distance is of considerable importance. Most people who come to the Center are farther away from home here than in the other locations; geographical isolation is a positive factor for work like this. Then there is a rather strong component in the romantic idea of spending a year with one's family in California. For those fellows who later move to the West, and there have been many, it is partly the climate, partly that they see the West as a growing area with more academic opportunities, and partly just the simple fact of having made contact."

A sort of running mate to the Center, in the stratosphere of scholastic research, is the Center for the Study of Democratic Institutions. It was set up on a sunny hilltop estate in Santa Barbara by the Fund for the Republic under Dr. Robert M. Hutchins, who regards Santa Barbara as just as much in the American mainstream as his former haunt—the University of Chicago. The Center operates on a million-dollar-a-year budget. Its savants gather each morning at eleven in a conference room facing the Pacific; for two weeks each year, they are joined by many of the great scholars of the world. In the words of Dr. Hutchins: "We are the only institution in the world trying to carry on what used to be called a civil conversation . . . free from any ideology, without polemics, solely as a process of learning." Early in 1963, the Center was battling for funds to survive. The terminal grant from the Ford Foundation to the Fund for the Republic will expire early in 1964, and twenty million dollars is sought to underwrite the studies of the Center in the next decade. Political conservatives have labeled the Center as "little Moscow on the hill." But Justice William O. Douglas insists the Center is conducting the most important educational work in the United States today.

But what of the less esoteric institutions of the West? The University of California has been subject to sniping on the grounds that it uses its Nobel laureates as window dressing. Is the University emphasizing research to the detriment of the job of teaching its undergraduates? Is it not a mark of the academic *nouveaux riches* to cite its ascendancy in Nobel laureates, in Guggenheim fellows, in Rhodes scholars, in raids from Eastern faculties? At Berkeley, Allan Temko, an architectural critic and lecturer in journalism, told me: "Our students have little sense of custodianship, as at Harvard and Columbia, where they are taught—as students are in England—that they are the elite, that they are in training to run the country, to be the best."

The excitements—and the dangers—of higher education in the West were sensed acutely by Dr. Samuel B. Gould, who served for three years as chancellor of the Santa Barbara campus of the University of California before going to New York City in the summer of 1962 to direct an educational television network. Gould had come West in 1959 after five years as president of Antioch College in Ohio. His reputation in education is that of a fiery conservative. At Antioch he had made his name as an outspoken champion of intellectualism. His move to the West had shocked his scholastic fellows; his departure for the East reassured many of them that their biases against Western education were accurate.

"The picture that one has back East—I had it before I came here —of higher education in California is a kind of playboy picture: big athletic events, fraternities and sororities, and the wonderful outdoor life of year-round swimming parties," Gould said before he left the West. "In many ways it was true here at Santa Barbara. I have been changing that. We have the best freshman class scholastically in the history of the institution. This is just the beginning. We will be able here to create a climate for learning, the kind of climate that I think is going to make a tremendous difference on the West Coast.

"I came West to find out something. I was head of a very fine institution of excellent academic reputation. A lot of people thought I must be out of my mind to come here and take on a minor role in a tremendous university system that heretofore had never distinguished itself particularly. But I wanted to find the answer to one thing that's never been discovered, as far as I know: Is it possible in an institution of great size, as is going to be the case all over our country with many of our institutions, to build quality, and personal relationships between faculty and students? Can you get quality in mass education? Everybody says it is not possible—that you must adapt yourself to so many realities and make so many compromises that you might as well settle for a kind of mass mediocrity. I don't believe it. No one has ever kept foremost this matter of interpersonal relationships: the student as an individual and the things you can do for him as an individual, even though he is part of a tremendous number. This is what we are going to do here. The ratio here of student to professor is as low—or lower—as in some of the small colleges: one and thirteen.

"I think California is just coming into its cultural heritage," he said, "just beginning to mature, to take the place which it should have and will have in the whole American and world structures. Something different and exciting is happening here. To a certain kind of educator, this has tremendous appeal, even though he may have great security where he is. There also is a great feeling of adventuresomeness and pioneering in coming West. The center of the United States, and therefore the center of a good part of the world, is going to be concentrated here in the next twenty-five to thirty years. It is important, if you want to be in the mainstream of things, to be where these things are going to happen.

"We have a tremendous reservoir of all kinds of things here in the West and at Santa Barbara: human talent, energies, resources. Leaders in all walks of life are expressing their tremendous interest in helping us. Industry is seeking out combinations of physical and intellectual climate today, with a very important impact—adding a

new dimension to the whole conception of business. Today's enlightened industrialist is eager to have his people as close as possible
to the cultural influences that he knows will make a richer life for
them. We have it in Santa Barbara, with the coming of research
divisions of General Motors, Raytheon, General Electric's TEMPO,
and a host of smaller companies. This means that the whole feeling of
America has changed. This is happening out West, I think, more
than anywhere else. This is what I have great hope for, up and down
our coast.

"What lies at the heart of this Westward movement is something
that is a part of the American character. It's a good thing to have
it out in the open again. God knows we need it. Americans have
essential characteristics that many people have forgotten about. One
is that we are revolutionary. The second is that we are pioneers. The
two relate, of course. This is what took us out of New England and
Pennsylvania and sent us into Kentucky and later into Nebraska and
all the way to Oregon. There was a feeling that you've got to go and
do something somewhere else, for the sake of building something
else. Americans have a general unrest, an unwillingness to be shack-
led, to be put into a mold. These two characteristics of Americans
need to be cultivated continuingly, because we are in such danger of
falling into a stereotype. These are the spirits that are bringing people
to the West.

"Things can be done here. I think it's terribly important that
they be done, because this has become the center of a good part of the
American world."

And what of these aspirations for the West when in 1962 he
left the West for New York? Tacitly, he said he still believed it
possible to blend quality with quantity in the massive University of
California system. Although in his three years at Santa Barbara,
Gould had fought to bring in renowned teachers and new educational
ideas to bolster the undergraduate students, it was an era in which
the university was more interested in adding graduate research scientists to the faculties; prestige, rather than the personal and individual
development of the student, seemed a paramount consideration to
university regents. Gould's primary concern was with the undergraduate. He was silent on the subject, but many of his friends
speculated that his dreams had been stalled by the organizational
bureaucracy of the giant university system. Yet he said, earnestly:
"I would still love to come back to Santa Barbara. I still think the
West is the great potential for the United States of the future."

Western provincialism is more apparent among educators today
than in other spheres of Western life. There is an unwillingness to

understand that the West owes much to the East in education, as in other matters, and a lack of historical perspective can be injurious to the forward march of educational technique. Some Western educators are disbelieving when confronted with evidence that their pet theories or devices have been in use for years in the East. In educational fields one sometimes feels that the spirit of California is developing into a kind of nationalism. There is not always found in the West the same dedication of intellect that distinguishes some older campuses.

Yet the new symbol of the West is intellectual activity. It is a Western yearning to have an activity—even an avocation—that requires considerable knowledge and the exercise of brain power. The new Westerner is oriented to education and to the campus. With his prosperity and his leisure, he is able to insist—and he is beginning to do so—that new generations be schooled to a degree and in numbers heretofore unknown in world history.

Western education has outgrown some of the embarrassments of adolescence, like the loyalty-oath furor after World War II which for a time threatened to split the University of California. Its troubles are not over: witness the unhappy smear campaign, the product of a small band of extremist Californians, which helped to drive Dr. Buell G. Gallagher in 1962 back to the College of the City of New York, after a six-month tenure as first chancellor of the huge California state college system. But Western educators have developed an aptitude for innovation. They have learned new ways to encourage classical scholarship and research at the same time that they train engineers and practitioners. Necessity has fathered a flexibility in the West which will be influential in the American educational system.

In the West, prosperity has brought with it a compulsion to excel—to justify the region, and to justify the Westerner for having gone West. In the opinion of the Westerner, education is one way to do it. The motives for the education boom in the West may be held suspect by some, but the results have become impressive. With the continuing influx of distinguished scholars to Western campuses, its raw enthusiasm will be mellowed. If the West is to spur a golden renaissance of the nation, that stir of evangelistic zeal will be felt first on the Western campus.

4

OF ONE THING, LESS

Hate

Hillsborough is a suburban town south of San Francisco which has been a sanctum of inherited wealth. One Sunday afternoon in 1962, after visiting friends on the fringe of Hillsborough, I turned on to Skyline Drive for the run back along the hilly ridgepole of the San Francisco Peninsula to the city. Just outside Hillsborough, taken by the sight of a fog bank rolling in off the Pacific to fill the valleys while the sun shone with fine golden unconcern on the hills, I pulled off the highway and found myself at an attractive golf club called Crystal Springs.

In a moment, I had quite forgotten the spectacle of the fog. The bar and club rooms of Crystal Springs were almost filled with Negroes. A few whites were scattered through the club, but on the golf course, coming in from their games, were only Negroes. Notably, the bartenders were Chinese. One Negro woman, just in off the course, her hair in pin curlers, sat at the bar fanning herself with a ten-dollar bill. Whole families lounged in ease while their men golfed.

A small postscript, added to the Crystal Springs sign beside Skyline Drive, told the story: OPEN TO THE PUBLIC. Inside, on a bulletin board, was a placard announcing that another country club some miles distant was "now inviting public play."

Crystal Springs obviously was a weekend escape from the less glamorous living conditions of the crowded Negro ghettos of San Francisco. But in his suburban break for freedom, the San Francisco Negro was not ghettoized; Crystal Springs clearly was in rich man's country.

In the course of the next several days I discussed the status of minorities in San Francisco with some of the most knowledgeable leaders of the city. Not one of them had heard of any battle to desegregate Crystal Springs. There had not, in fact, been a battle. What I had stumbled on there was another scrap of evidence of the strong, silent evolution of minority rights in the new West. None of the San Francisco leaders to whom I talked seemed to be conscious of where Negroes were playing golf—or even if they were playing at all. This attitude was reminiscent of the story told by A. P. Tureaud, a long-time attorney for the National Association for the Advancement of Colored People, in New Orleans. He said he went to Thurgood Marshall, now a federal judge but at that time chief counsel for the NAACP, and asked him to take up the complaints of Negroes who were being barred from city-owned New Orleans golf courses.

Marshall was busy with dozens of suits involving school desegregation and lunch-counter sit-in demonstrations. He lashed out at Tureaud: "Golf! I'm not interested in Negroes playing *golf!*"

"But, Thurgood," Tureaud answered, "you've got to tend to the *whole* Negro, golfers and everybody else!"

It is a fact beyond challenge that in the West today, "the *whole* Negro" is exploiting his greatest opportunity for liberty in American history. That fact cannot be explained away by anything short of the gratifying truth: tolerance, in this new land of the West, is more prevalent and more a matter of custom than it is in any other region of America.

As Walter Prescott Webb has pointed out, the West clearly is the most cosmopolitan region of America. In the West live far more than half of the Chinese, the Japanese, and the Indians of the nation. Here, too, are Americans of Spanish or Mexican descent. And like the rest of the nation, the West has the heritage of the European civilizations.

Tolerance in the West has not evolved, as some have insisted, because the Negro is a minority so small that a sort of dignity of rareness imparts a reverse prestige to his status. There were only about five thousand Negroes in San Francisco on the eve of World War II, but by 1962, there were about eighty thousand.

Los Angeles is sometimes described as the second largest Mexican city, because Mexican-Americans traditionally have been the dominant minority there. They are no longer. In the past two decades, while Los Angeles County has grown in multiples exceeding that of any other American metropolis, its Negro population has grown at a far faster rate—from ninety-seven thousand to more than four hundred and sixty thousand. In the past decade, of the million and a half Negroes who have migrated from the South, about one in four have come to California. Negroes have entered Los Angeles County at the rate of two thousand each month; Los Angeles has become a focal point of the Negro migration. There was a ninety-one percent increase among California Negroes from 1950 to 1960: from 462,172 to 883,861. California, close behind New York, was the state with the second greatest Negro gain. The Negro migrated into other western states at a similar rate between 1950 and 1960. His number rose in Washington from 30,691 to 48,738; in Arizona, from 25,974 to 43,403; in Colorado, from 20,177 to 39,992; in New Mexico from 8,408 to 17,063; in Nevada, from 4,320 to 13,484.

"The Negro feels he has a better chance here," says John Buggs, executive secretary of the Los Angeles County Commission on Human Relations. The Commission, which is one big reason for that feeling among Negroes in Los Angeles, was founded by the Los Angeles County board of supervisors in the wake of "zoot-suit" or "pachuco" riots by Mexican-American youths in Los Angeles during World War II. Its educational program is directed through neighborhood councils. Another organization, the Los Angeles County Conference on Community Relations—with scores of affiliates—has been the largest local humanitarian group of its kind in the nation; its specialty is the quiet negotiation of potential racial frictions.

It would be easy for the Westerner to be chauvinistic on this subject. He could point with pardonable pride to a host of Western Negroes who have made good, who have fought for and been granted their liberties, who live well and under comparatively few of the pressures familiar to the Negro. Ralph Bunche came from the University of California campus at Los Angeles, and two Negroes have served as president of the student body, which now numbers about twenty thousand. One of the first Negroes to serve as stewardess with a major airline was Diane Garrott of Los Angeles. Her father, an attorney, was California's first Negro state policeman; her grandfather was the first Negro police captain in Los Angeles, her grand-uncle was the first Negro dentist in California. David Williams, a Negro, is a municipal court judge in Los Angeles, living in a hundred-and-fifty-thousand-dollar home in Bel-Air; his son was president of his junior class at Stanford University. Judge Williams' home was designed by Paul Williams, son of a Los Angeles fruit dealer and now a highly regarded Southern California architect. From his offices in Los Angeles, Norman Houston directs a seventeen-million-dollar life insurance business. In San Francisco, Negroes serve as municipal judge and deputy city attorney, and are ranking members of the California governor's staff. After twenty-six years as a state assemblyman, Augustus Hawkins of Los Angeles in the 1962 general election became California's first Negro congressman. In Arizona, a Negro has served a south Phoenix precinct in the State House of Representatives since 1951. Mexican-Americans and Negroes are not uncommon in the California legislature.

But the point is that except for occasional exhibitions of tolerance displayed for political and commercial exploitation, Westerners do not bother to play the tolerance game. Their consciences are not hurting. The test of Western tolerance is not that Westerners would be pleased to have dinner with Lena Horne or Ralph Bunche, but that relatively few are disturbed when a Negro family occupies the next table in their favorite restaurant. It is still a different matter when a Negro family buys the house next door; an empirical prejudice exists in such cases, involving the economics of real estate values, but such prejudice rarely is the blind hatred one finds in other sections of the country.

The Negro influx has been accepted more easily in most neighborhoods in San Francisco than in Los Angeles or San Diego. Apparently the greatest resentment among whites when a Negro moves into a previously all-white Western neighborhood comes from those who have lived previously in economically underprivileged areas of the nation, not necessarily the South. A greater proportion of inmigrant whites falls into this category in Los Angeles and San Diego than in San Francisco. Racial housing patterns are breaking freer in the West each day, but the issue still is sticky.

Negro leaders concede a high rate of tolerance in West Coast cities in regard to hotels and restaurants; discrimination rears its head more frequently in smaller towns and especially in resort areas. The NAACP has singled out the hotels and casinos of Las Vegas and Reno as making the Negro feel unwelcome. For once, perhaps, the Negro is fortunate; white Anglo-Saxons themselves are the objects of blatant discrimination in these casinos as soon as they begin to run out of money.

In San Francisco, the Fairmont Hotel on Nob Hill is owned by Ben Swig, a Jew who came West from Boston and regards San Francisco as freer from prejudice than any other city in the nation.

"I am supposed to have the fanciest hotel in the city," Swig told me, "but we take a Negro in here without any questions—into our dining room to eat, into our Venetian Room to see a show, or to rent a room. We had a Negro teachers' convention several years ago, and a few of our regular customers said they'd never come back to the hotel again. But every meeting of Negroes we've had has been well-behaved. There is less intoxication among Negroes than among our white people."

In San Diego, Negro fashion models have moved easily among the luncheon tables at Point Loma Inn, a resort hotel. The management employed a Negro model on its staff for the first time in 1962. There were only three complaints.

There is more social intermingling of Negro and white in San Francisco than anywhere else in the West, and more than I have found in any other city in the United States. It is centered in bohemian North Beach, where the Negro became a familiar part of the scene during the reign of the beatnik. The beatnik is gone, but the Negro has remained. A Negro man and a white woman drinking, dining or dancing, and seemingly unnoticed by predominantly white patrons, is a common sight in North Beach clubs and restaurants.

Defying such trends in the metropoli of the West are the pockets of prejudice.

Utah, regrettably, has not yet escaped its maelstrom of prejudice and counter-prejudice. Two-thirds of the citizens are members of the Church of Jesus Christ of Latter-day Saints, and all non-Mormons are referred to as gentiles. Many gentiles traditionally have been distrustful of Mormons in Utah, and there is an historic tension between Mormon and Mason. The beehive, adopted by the Mormon church as its symbol for industriousness, appears also in the older Masonic ritual, and Masons commonly believe that the Mormons "stole" their ritualism. Masons do not accept Mormons; inversely, it is rare that a Mason is converted to Mormonism.

Negroes have joined the Mormon church, but they are not known to have been granted temple rites or to have entered the priesthood. The Utah State Commission on Civil Rights, headed by Adam Duncan, a Salt Lake City attorney, in 1959 focused blame for prejudice against the Negro in Utah on the Mormon church. Mormon dogma proscribes that Negroes are the descendants of Cain, and that they are colored because Cain killed Abel. The Indian has his color, Mormon theology holds, because he is descended from Laman, son of the Prophet Lehi, who led the white tribe of Joseph from Jerusalem to the western hemisphere in 600 B.C. Laman sinned by rebelling against his father and his brother Nephi. It is notable that there were barely four thousand Negroes in Utah in 1960, less than one half of one percent of the population.

At a time when American industry has been self-consciously inserting non-discriminatory notices in help-wanted advertising, some Utah industrial brochures carry lines like these: "An overwhelmingly white population"; "A population composed almost entirely of those born in the U. S." By contrast, a smiling photograph of a pretty Negro girl employed as a mathematician by the Hughes Corporation in Los Angeles was appearing in 1962 in Eastern newspaper advertisements under the caption: CALIFORNIA AIRCRAFT CONCERN IS BELIEVER IN JOB EQUALITY.

A curious sidelight in Utah is that state statutes allow intermarriage between white and Negro but prohibit marriage between white and Oriental. This is in contrast to most of the West, where public feeling is not aroused by marriage between white and Oriental, but marriage between white and Negro is considered taboo.

The Navy has been a liberalizing influence for Orientals on the Pacific Coast in the years since World War II; Japanese war brides are numerous. The saga of the Japanese-Americans in the West since their deportation from the West Coast at the start of World War II has been one of the quietest but most exciting racial chapters of American history. Western whites do have a guilty conscience about this matter; the deportation was impetuous, brutal, and showed a hopeless misunderstanding of the Japanese-American. When the Japanese were allowed to return to their homes in West Coast cities, they had been dispossessed by the Negro—whose migration westward began with the demand for labor during World War II in West Coast war factories. With infinite patience and forbearance, the Japanese set out to rebuild their respect and status in the West. The job has been done, and in the process the noblest virtues of each race have been displayed.

The largest Oriental community in America is Chinatown of San Francisco. It is not an enforced ghetto but a voluntary enclave. Its people increased from fewer than 25,000 to 36,445 between the 1950 and 1960 censuses, as Immigration relaxed regulations applying to families of Chinese residing in the United States. (Los Angeles, with a population three times greater than San Francisco, has fewer than 20,000 Chinese.) At one time, close to 20,000 Chinese were jammed into a twenty-block area of San Francisco's Chinatown; they lived ten and twelve to a basement. The San Francisco Housing Authority helped to ease crowding with construction of large low-cost housing projects in and near Chinatown.

Also years ago, Chinatown was a scandal of tuberculosis, but the worst is over now, although the case rate among Chinese in San Francisco still is more than three times greater than among Caucasians.

Even the new housing projects of Chinatown maintain the insularity and tradition that have made the Chinese neighborhood of San Francisco so notable; multi-hued balconies and pagoda roofs brighten one of them. The herb shops, the daily Chinese language newspapers, the temples, and the tongs are in San Francisco still. This Chinatown has retained much more of an oriental atmosphere than New York's Chinatown. The abacus is still in use instead of the cash register at many places along Grant Avenue, and the clatter of dominos echoes from the windows of basement rooms. The visitor can enter Kong Chow temple, where Kuan Ti, the patron deity, rules. Beniamino Bufano's steel-and-granite statue of Sun Yat-sen stands at St. Mary's Square. The Chinese telephone exchange is housed in a pagoda on Washington Street. Chinatown is ruled from a building on Stockton Street which houses the "Six Companies," representatives of Chinese families who control community affairs—known formally as the Chinese Consolidated Benevolent Association.

But change is coming to Chinatown too. Family solidarity has begun to fade as newlywed couples establish their own homes, sometimes outside Chinatown where higher wages often are available to the Chinese. Perhaps one-fourth of the Chinese here now attend Christian churches. A six-story savings and loan building on Grant Avenue, in the heart of Chinatown, has been built in modern Oriental design—incorporating San Francisco's first outdoor elevator. Yet the community still has no rival in the matter of its traditional self-government. Family associations and religious and welfare agencies within Chinatown still are all-powerful.

San Francisco continues to regard its Chinatown with affectionate indulgence. A Chinatown leader recently appeared before the City Board of Permit Appeals in behalf of a poultry-market owner named Mar Yet, who wanted to move his market a block down Grant Avenue. Mar Yet had come up against a health code forbidding live poultry within twenty-five feet of a residence. Mar Yet had been operating within twenty-five feet of a residence at his old site, for there is hardly anywhere in Chinatown that is not within twenty-five feet of a residence. The lofty permit-board members nodded approval, and their usually grim-faced enforcement officers sat by smiling. Live poultry is to Chinatown what hot dogs and hamburgers are to the Caucasian.

Chinatown has a fourteen-million-dollar garment factory business which has been considered illegal under San Francisco zoning regulations. But more than two thousand Chinese are employed in its one hundred and twenty-five separate shops. City officials debated at length, and finally passed a compromise plan which allowed most of them to continue operation within a multi-block zoning sanctuary.

Many other parts of the West are almost totally free of prejudice.

There is an engaging tolerance in New Mexico between native (descendants of the original Spanish settlers and others of Spanish origin) and Anglo (everyone else). Anglos even refer to themselves as Anglos. It is a situation which has little precedent—one in which the Anglo-Saxon white has accepted a racial label, and proceeded to share it with Jew, Negro and Oriental.

Anglos in New Mexico enjoy telling how a native returned to the state and inquired one day in a barbershop how much was being paid for votes in a current election.

"Don't know," said the Negro shoeshine boy. "They haven't approached us Anglos yet."

Those who migrate to New Mexico are drawn, in part, by the racial and cultural diversities of the region. They tend to sharpen and illuminate these diversities because they place a high value on them. This may be chauvinism, but it allows for little prejudice. One of Santa Fe's most prominent Anglo families is Chinese. The patriarch of the family came to Santa Fe about the turn of the century, opened a laundry, and later became a restaurateur. Today they are completely accepted by Santa Fe's Anglo millionaires and artists. They are not the exception.

When a Negro family moved into the scientific community of Los Alamos not long ago, there was a faint undercurrent of grumbling. But when a physicist's wife took the new arrivals to church with her on the following Sunday morning and sat with them in a front pew, the incident was closed. Nothing more was heard.

Another white spot free of minority onus is the Basque community of the West. Basques from Spain first came to the West in Gold Rush times; most of them became sheepherders in the grazing lands of eastern Nevada, California, Utah, and particularly in Idaho and Oregon. In California and Nevada, French and Spanish Basques are about equal in number. In 1959 about six thousand Western Basques gathered at Sparks, Nevada, for a huge barbecue and music and dancing. In Boise, Idaho, during music festivals, the Basques, gay and vibrant, are the stars of the show. They are much sought after in inter-marriages. Though their temperament historically has been mercurial, they have become respected businessmen and community leaders.

For almost a century, Nevada had the sociological symptoms of

a feudal state. "We used to call Nevada 'a Mississippi with shoes on,' "
recalled Governor Grant Sawyer. "But now there is new thinking. For
ninety-six years, Nevada had been passing laws against minorities. In
1961 we put through a civil rights bill which would have been absolutely inconceivable two years before. Many of our statutes aimed
against Indians, against Mexicans, against inter-racial marriage, have
been found unconstitutional or have been repealed. We are sensing
our obligation to our sister states to take our place in national affairs."

The Mexican-American is a poignant example of the collision of
cultures. In the main, he has had no stomach for the hectic American
pace. He has stayed to himself in settlements of Los Angeles such as
Rose Hill, Happy Valley, Clover, Custer, and Bunker Hill. His family
table often provides the staples of his homeland: the flat, round *tortilla*
of ground corn, the *frijole*, or bean, the *sopas, enchiladas, tamales*.
His sons and daughters, like the Negro, drop out of schools at regrettable rates; often home does not offer adequate support of the new
customs which the sons and daughters are learning at school. Only
one out of ten California workers is a farm laborer, but two out of
five Mexican-Americans work on farms. Only a few of them go into
technical or professional work, although noticeable advances are being
made in training Mexican-Americans for such work and making such
jobs available to them.

There are about a million persons of Mexican ancestry in California, most of them in Southern California and in the agricultural
areas of the Great Central Valley. Some of them are direct descendants
of those early settlers who preceded the United States pioneer, and
these families are the aristocracy of their Mexican-American communities.

Thousands of the Mexicans in the West are *braceros*—migrant
farm workers brought in from Mexico under bilateral treaty, and
under the supervision of the United States Labor Department. These
people reach the United States under circumstances plaintively suggestive of the floods of Irish into the United States during the potato
famine. One of the five United States labor stations which process
braceros in the interior of Mexico is located near Guaymas. When I
visited there, four thousand Mexican men were standing behind a wire
fence in a vast, dusty field, waiting to be called forward by United
States authorities. Some had not left the compound for three days;
they had come by foot, by burro, and by bus from remote villages as
distant as two hundred miles, hoping that their papers would be found
in order, that they could pass the physical examination of the United
States doctors, and that the call from north of the border for workers

would be heavy enough to include them. If their luck held, they would be taken by train into the United States to work the harvests at rates of about seventy-five cents to one dollar an hour.

Late one night I stood in line at the Flower Street office of Western Union in downtown Los Angeles.

"I can't accept it," the clerk was saying. "This book doesn't show a telegraph office at Obregon."

The customer at the window, a Mexican man of about thirty-five, stared impassively. In his hand he held three ten-dollar bills. Behind him in a line were other Mexicans, all holding United States currency.

Another clerk, without looking up, said, "Look under Ciudad. That means city."

"Ah, there it is," said the clerk. "Ciudad Obregon. That's all right. I can take it."

The Mexican smiled and gave the clerk the money order and a message to go with it to be sent back home.

A few minutes later I was having coffee with the citizen from Obregon in a little café nearby. He told me that each week he sent home to his wife and five children, thirty dollars from his wages on a farm job near Los Angeles. Mexicans trust the telegraph; it does not occur to them to mail money. Western Union accepts United States dollars, and the Mexican national telegraph pays off in *pesos*.

"Besides," the man said, smiling gently. "My family needs the money soon. My sisters have many *muchachas*, too, all hungry. That is why I am here."

Even the lowest American wages, transmitted so faithfully to inland Mexico, can make princes of paupers in that poor land. When these *braceros* return to their villages, the sewing machine or the transistor radio that they bring home is the marvel of the season.

In Southern California, the Mexican-American is not the target of prejudice that he is in Texas. He is in a kind of limbo: neither accepted nor rejected. He is a vague part of that misty legend of early California, a residue of the *caballero* and the *vaquero*, and he is not in anybody's way. He is amiable and anxious to please, and he has inexhaustible energy and patience. Too few Californians have seen more of his country than the corrupt border towns; there is neither enough respect for the charm of Mexico, nor appreciation of the dignity of the Mexican. The Mexican is in California usually because poverty has driven him out of his own country. The Californian is moving too fast to notice, or to wonder why.

The incongruities of contemporary Western life for the Mexican-American, who is so little understood in his displaced status, are symbolized in the brisk message on a plaque erected by the Los

Angeles Board of Public Works on Olvera Street, at the heart of the original pueblo of Los Angeles. Olvera Street is a tourist attraction today, lined with stalls offering Mexican food, pottery, glassware, silver and fabrics. With a nervous eye on the insurance adjuster, the City of Los Angeles warns visitors:

IN KEEPING WITH THE ATMOSPHERE OF AN OLD MEXI-
CAN STREET, THIS STREET HAS BEEN COVERED WITH SPAN-
ISH TILE AND BRICK, THE SURFACE OF WHICH IS SOMEWHAT
UNEVEN. USERS DO SO AT THEIR OWN RISK.

The ghettos of Western cities are neither as cruel nor as desperate as those of older cities, but they exist.

In Los Angeles, the Negro community of Central Avenue was born with the coming of the railroads. Central Avenue begins at the railroad yards, and at first it was the home of Pullman porters and dining-car waiters. The avenue terminates twelve miles away in Compton, a defense plant city. As Wesley Marx has pointed out, Central Avenue is a "living display of Negro memories and aspirations." It teems with fish shops, second-hand stores and churches. Compton, a mass-produced suburb that hardly existed at the end of World War II, is itself a case study. In 1955 its population was about five percent Negro; today, Negroes are in the majority in Compton and there is very little racial tension. The more prosperous Negro families are breaking out into other areas of Los Angeles, especially along Adams and Western avenues. The Negro finds it most difficult to buy homes in new suburban areas; very few are open to minority groups.

In minority housing, San Francisco is unique. It is a city where people encroach on slums. The Fillmore district, where grotesque Victorian scroll-saw castles were unmercifully spared by the earthquake and fire of 1906, is reverberating to the blast of dynamite. The Fillmore is like a dusty attic jammed with mementos of the past. The fire raced up the hills from downtown San Francisco but was stopped short of the Fillmore by the width of Van Ness Avenue and by dynamite. Until San Francisco was rebuilt, the Fillmore was the commercial center of the city, but before World War II, it had deteriorated. It harbored "Little Osaka," the Japanese-American community. When the Japanese were interned, the Negroes moved in, and the Fillmore's curlicued castles were divided into apartments and furnished rooms. Antique shops gave way to television repair shops; vegetable stands became pool parlors or barber shops.

But now San Francisco is attempting to blast out the slums of the Fillmore. Whites are pushing back into the area. Houses formerly occupied by Negroes are up in price in anticipation of redevelopment.

New housing going up in the area is attractive to whites and too costly for most Negroes. The city has blundered as a result of a narcissistic determination to maintain its cityscape; it is driving the Negro out of the Fillmore by its slum clearance program.

When Fillmore homes were razed in the first San Francisco Redevelopment Agency project, the residential families forced out were paying a median monthly rental of thirty-nine dollars. With help from the city, these displaced families found living quarters elsewhere at a median rental of fifty-eight dollars a month. Apartment houses being built in these razed portions—and in the Golden Gateway and Diamond Heights projects—have a rental scale from one hundred and ten dollars a month for "efficiency apartments" without bedrooms to five hundred and ninety-five dollars for apartments with three and four bedrooms. Obviously, the Redevelopment Agency does not expect that many displaced Negro families will be able to go back once the slums are cleared.

A second project in the Fillmore was expected to evict about seven thousand persons. In the proposed redevelopment of white slum areas—the Tenderloin and Skid Row—another ten thousand are to be rendered homeless. San Francisco appears quixotic in its gestures toward making a place for these homeless. As Dr. Ellis D. Sox, public health director, asked bluntly in a meeting of civic leaders in 1961: "Where in hell are they going to go?"

One Negro minister in the Fillmore said, "Most of these people pulled up and left the South for the same basic reason that the Pilgrims came to America: freedom and opportunity. There are no signs in California which read: COLORED ONLY. But the Negro who walks into a lunch counter in many parts of the state still is not sure whether he faces an unpleasant scene. The law says we can live anywhere we want, but it's remarkable how often a home has just been rented or the last house in the tract has just been sold. Our people have more chance here, certainly. Some of them will say that they can get anything in San Francisco—except a job. That's an exaggeration, but unless he is better off financially than most, the Negro is living in a ghetto much like the one he left behind in the South. What disturbs me is that San Francisco hasn't faced the problem yet. And it is here. It is not going to go away."

Yet one Negro mother said, "I would rather take a little insecurity than no security at all, which we have been used to. At least my kids can go to good schools here. We see opportunity all around us here, whether we can grab hold of it or not. We smell freedom here, and maybe soon we can taste it."

Many Negro families who are being forced out of the Fillmore by slum clearance are spilling over into the Mission District in the east central area of the city, chosen in 1776 by Juan Bautista de Anza as site of the Mission Dolores. Today the Mission District sustains the highest incidence of juvenile delinquency in San Francisco. For years, it was the workshop of the city, a respectable working-class suburb, the center of the Irish population. But when the district started down, it went fast.

An Episcopal chaplain in the Mission District told me, "The Mission is tragically hard to escape. But San Francisco seems to insist on thinking of it in terms of the glories of its past."

Before our visit was ended late that night, the chaplain had employed all his wiles and those of his faith to ward off—as helplessly as Officer Krupke in *West Side Story*—a rumble quite as ominous as the celebrated stage rumble of the Jets and the Sharks. Within the shadows of one of his churches that night were the flash of knife blade and of needle, the seething teenage knots on street corners, the stalking watchfulness of private police. There were the feverish, frustrated, violent conversations of Negro, Puerto Rican, Mexican, Samoan, Oriental and white—boy and girl alike—and the urgent entreaties of their youthful contemporaries against violence.

The chaplain reported that Sunday school teachers from Methodist and Episcopal churches in the Mission District had met recently to ponder poor attendance. The Methodists even gave their Sunday school enrollment to the Episcopalians in an effort to hold together a semblance of organization for those who would attend either school.

In a Mission District high school, with a student body of hundreds, a graduating class of four was among the highest since World War II. In much of the Mission, women do not walk the streets after dark. A stabbing occurred on the steps of one of the churches in the Mission while I was in the city. In at least one Mission school, there had been bans on high pouf hairdos: they had served as concealment for scissors and knives.

All over the West, educators are beginning to seek special help in coping with the acute problems of the heavy Negro influx. They are the typical ones of the culturally and economically deprived: high truancy rate, drop-outs and disciplinary problems. In the Fillmore, under a Ford Foundation grant, about seventeen hundred school pupils have been receiving special classroom attention. About eighty-five percent of them are Negroes from low economic strata.

Across the bay from San Francisco, in Berkeley, a city about the size of Little Rock, more Negroes live than in Little Rock. Berkeley has only one huge high school, and it has been always totally inte-

grated. Yet residential areas are basically segregated, and thus elementary schools are generally Negro or white. This is, almost without
exception, the only kind of educational segregation that takes place in
the West. In Berkeley, its effect is that Negro and white students do
not meet until high school. There has been little discord, and evidence
of successful integration is abundant. In the spring of 1962, for the
first time, the Berkeley High School student body president was a
Negro.

Berkeley needs another high school, but its leaders have hesi-
tated, fearing it might be a step backward. Because of sheer geography, another school would provoke a districting situation resulting in
one mostly-Negro and one mostly-white school. This is an ironic facet
of the Negro situation in many Western cities. But there are leaders
of immense good will who guard the natural tolerance of their communities. If integration cannot be maintained at Berkeley, in the
shadow of the University of California, it cannot be maintained anywhere in the West. There is as little discrimination in the Bay Area as
anywhere in the country. Open testimony of this on the Berkeley campus of the university is that interracial dating has increased sharply in
recent years. A disproportionately large share of Freedom Riders
went into the South from the Berkeley campus. Reactionaries in
Berkeley consider such antics as evidence of the infiltration of Com-
munism into the University, but the tolerance of the Bay Area wraps
an insulating blanket around those who do not conform; it is in the
San Francisco tradition, and it is not necessarily Red.

South of Berkeley is Oakland, an industrial city with more than
fourteen hundred factories, where the Negro explosion has been immense. With less than half the population of San Francisco—367,548
compared with 740,316—Oakland had in 1960 a larger Negro
population: 83,618 against 74,383. At one time during World War
II, Oakland had a higher proportion of Negroes than any other city
outside the South. One high school, McClymond, is almost entirely
Negro; this, in the West, is rare, although elementary schools frequently have solid minority blocs. From McClymond have come two
noted athletes: Bill Russell to basketball and Frank Robinson to
baseball. At Technical High on Broadway in Oakland, the Negro
minority has become larger as the Negro residential districts have expanded. The Oakland Negro, once confined to one area, has broken out
of residential patterns through sheer force of numbers and lives in
widely scattered areas. A University of California study of the Bay
Area by Professor Davis McEntire showed that only 6.5 percent of the
residents of any area where Negroes had moved admitted to any

objection to their new neighbors. The Negro's job opportunities in the industrial East Bay are not so limited as those of the San Francisco Negro across the bridge.

The Negro nationalist—the Muslim—has not found a ready audience in the West. This movement, centered in New York's Harlem, has been involved in sporadic violence which has appeared relatively seldom in San Francisco and Los Angeles. (Its national membership was estimated in 1961 at about 3,000.) Richard Wright, the Negro novelist, has likened the Muslim movement to a Negro Ku Klux Klan. Its reputed goals are Negro domination of the white and a nationalist return of the Negro to Africa. The leader of the Muslims in San Francisco was convicted of draft evasion in the summer of 1961, but his case stirred small interest. A Muslim outbreak in Los Angeles in the spring of 1962 led to the usual sniping at police methods, but it was soon ended.

Negroes have become a potent political force in California. In Los Angeles, in 1962, there were Negro members on the fire commission and police commission; Negroes had been influential in the election of Los Angeles Mayor Sam Yorty, who upset the entrenched regime. A Negro judge, Thomas L. Griffith, Jr., was presiding over municipal courts. It is safe to assume that the California Negro was a crucial factor in Pat Brown's victory over Richard Nixon for the governorship.

Although the West is coping more effectively than other regions with prejudice, the heavy influx of Negroes in recent years has brought new problems.

In its first two years of operation, in 1959–61, the California Fair Employment Practice Commission heard about eleven hundred complaints of job discrimination, most of them involving Negroes. The FEPC found instances of discrimination in hiring in about one-third of the cases reported; all but four were resolved through conference and conciliation. Nevertheless, forty percent of the unemployed in Los Angeles are Negroes; a high proportion of the incoming Negro wave is still unskilled.

San Francisco was the first California city to establish a fair employment commission. Since 1957 it has served to open some doors of employment for the Negro—notably the municipal railway and the waterfront. But its budget has been cripplingly low and its scope meager; it has no authority to go into educational or conciliatory work in intergroup relations. Negroes are given employment opportunities in all city-related jobs; some of them operate cable cars, and the list of Negro police officers grows.

The head of a large San Francisco brokerage house told me that a Negro stock broker he had hired in 1961 was the first in the city. Another brokerage firm uses Chinese girl board markers exclusively. Many Orientals are hired in white-collar jobs and particularly in the garment industry, but Negroes still are on a last-hired, first-fired basis in most fields.

The crime rate of the incoming Negro, generally ghettoized, impoverished and under-educated, is predictably high. With just over ten percent of San Francisco's population, Negroes commit thirty to forty percent of its crime. Municipal Judge Albert A. Axelrod, in whose court vice cases composed a major component, estimated in 1961 that eighty percent of the defendants coming before him were Negro.

Poverty, as always, is at the core of the minority crime rate; cramped housing is the strongest indication of it. On the Pacific Coast, urban renewal projects have been augmenting rather than alleviating the concentration of Negro families in constricted areas. Negroes displaced by urban renewal projects have been finding alternative housing in pre-existing Negro sections. But in many communities, citizens' groups were springing up to encourage listing of housing for sale or rental on a non-discrimination basis. Many white real estate agents were co-operating, and some were joining citizens' groups. Even more important, the activities of such groups were not arousing heated controversy.

Universities throughout California have shown the lead in breaking housing barriers. Many state colleges and universities require non-discrimination pledges from prospective lessors who seek tenants through campus housing offices. Some teeth have been put into minority housing efforts by a California statute passed in 1959 which created a "right of action" for damages by any person denied housing of a "publicly assisted" status because of race; this applies to property which carries any loan guaranteed by federal or state governments.

Mexican-Americans and Oriental-Americans have a far greater degree of housing mobility in California than do Negroes; obstacles to their free choice of housing are disappearing at a faster rate than are the obstacles facing Negroes. As the Negro bursts out of his Western ghetto, he seldom moves singly into a previously white neighborhood; he moves with the group. The Mexican or Oriental is not so restricted and will strike out more often on a family-by-family basis, according to his economic level, to seek appropriate housing.

One silver lining appears, and it has a Western label. Here again is a suggestion that the easy, brash culture of the West may more readily make its way through the maze of contemporary American problems. A University of Michigan survey showed in 1960 that more and more whites had been moving from the San Francisco-Oakland metropolitan area to suburban areas, and that non-whites were taking their places in the cities. This is not unique—but an increasing number of non-whites also had been moving into suburban communities of the Bay area. It was the only area in the study where such a suburban trend was established.

Restrictive housing practices work to keep non-whites out of suburban areas in most parts of the nation. But in San Francisco, there are such desirable interracial suburban areas as Merced Heights and Ingleside Terrace; both have attractive sweeping views of coastline and city. Negro families are scattered through most of San Francisco's neighborhoods at all steps of the economic scale; the first volatile test cases in each neighborhood are history, and those following are easier. In most parts of San Francisco, those who can pay the price can make the grade. This is not true throughout the West yet; but as San Francisco has established trends in other fields, it is likely that this trend in racial patterns will influence other cities and finally other towns of the West. The path will not be rosy all the way; but it will be faster and more direct than the paths of older, more traditional areas toward the ends set forth by the verdict of the United States Supreme Court.

Prejudice is not as entrenched in the West as in older areas. Its patterns gradually are dissolving, and it cannot be thought of in the same sharp terms as elsewhere. Change comes easier in a newer environment; neither ethnic shadings nor prejudices are as strong in California as in much of the country. The Californian is new, he is absorbed in his unfamiliar surroundings, and he is so busy becoming a Californian that often he forgets to hate. He will find around him an unusual proportion who have not learned to hate, or who have lost the urge. He is not reminded of prejudice by the ever-present symbols of segregation that exist still in the South. If he is from Chicago, he has left behind the South Side and the memories of its race riots; if he is from New York, the ghettos of Harlem, the West Side and the Bronx seem a distant dream, and he is happy to find that there are very few streets or neighborhoods in the West where his wife may not walk in safety.

The new Californian may take his family to dinner at a restaurant which has been recommended to him, and find himself led to a table next to a group of urbane Negroes or Mexicans or Orientals. It may be the first time he has dined under such circumstances, but he is in territory new to him and he is less sure of its mores. It occurs to him that he may incur the hostility of his Western peers quite as readily by refusing to be seated as by being seated. He sits down and dines, and he notes, grudgingly perhaps, that no one has sustained any embarrassment. He is better prepared for his next encounter with racial equality. The tolerance factor of the new West is at work.

Rafer Johnson, the Negro decathlon champion who bore the United States flag in the Olympic Games at Rome in 1960, came from Kingsbury, a small farming town outside Fresno in the Central Valley of California. The son of a machinist who brought his family to California in 1945 from Dallas, Johnson became president of the student body at the vast University of California at Los Angeles. After his victory at Rome, a reporter asked him if it was the greatest day of his life. "No," Johnson replied softly. "That was when my father moved from Texas to California."

5

THE INDIAN NATIONS

Better Times for Many

The Indian is changing as markedly as any element of the West. His setbacks and his progress are clouded by the emotionalism of some of his white sympathizers, and by the expediency of those who, for political or financial gain, still stand in his way. Some of his friends are more dangerous than his enemies. Americans have been conditioned by history to mistreatment and neglect of the Indian, but after their sympathies have aroused them to action in his behalf and then they find themselves duped, they are seldom prone to take further interest in him. This happens much too often. Professional Indian sobbers easily can turn a fifteen-thousand-dollar-a-year profit by raising money purportedly to relieve Indian poverty; it is being done all the time, and it is one more example of the well-advertised gullibility of Americans.

The American Indian is not dying out. He is increasing rapidly. In the Southwest, under the enlightened administration of Indian affairs and with benefit of sudden wealth from oil, gas and uranium rights, Indians are prospering for the first time since their subjugation in frontier days. Through education and economic independence, they are moving toward integration as citizens with equal rights.

Ancestors of two major tribes of Arizona, the Navajo and Apache, came from the north late in the thirteenth century, when a twenty-three year drought was desolating the region. These are the two tribes which fought back hardest when the white man's squeeze play began with the arrival of the Spaniards. The darkest days for the Navajo came when Colonel Kit Carson rounded them up and marched into their stronghold at Canyon de Chelly, Arizona, in 1864; he led them on their notorious "Long Walk" to the Bosque Redondo on the Pecos River—after destroying their sheep and orchards and taking their horses. The United States' experiment with displaced colonization did not work. In 1868, the Navajos, ailing and homesick, were returned to their reservation. War, disease, and starvation had decimated the tribe; only about nine thousand were left.

In 1879, the Mescalerō Apaches under Chief Victorio left their reservation and started a four-year reign of terror in southern New Mexico and Arizona. Geronimo led the San Carlos Apaches from their reservation to join the Mescalerōs in all-out war. But the United States cavalry dug in, and Geronimo surrendered in 1886 to General Nelson A. Miles.

Thereafter, the Indians stayed home on the reservations, except for those who disappeared, quite understandably, to go get drunk when they had the money. Of course, this did not put an end to the white man's horror. But the Indians could not be blamed when Pancho Villa made his raids across the border, or when there was a big explosion at Trinity, near Alamogordo, in 1945.

Relations have been improving slowly between Indian and white man. The basic evidence is that the Indian is surviving more readily than before. The Indian population of the United States has shown an increase in each decennial census since 1930. The most abrupt increase appeared in the last census: from about 343,000 in 1950 to 523,591 in 1960. Of these, about 350,000 live on reservations. Arizona ranks first among the states in Indian population, Oklahoma is second, and then come New Mexico and California. There is less Indian land now than in 1900, but it has increased slowly since 1940. Almost half of it is in Arizona; virtually the entire northeast quarter of the state consists of Navajo and Hopi reservations. Today more than twenty-one million acres of Arizona is Indian territory; New Mexico ranks second with six and a half million acres, and Montana is close behind.

The Navajo tribe has doubled in the past quarter century to about ninety thousand in number. This alone is indicative of the Navajo genius for survival, for tribal lands in northeast Arizona and northwest New Mexico are part of the most formidable desert on the continent.

Paul Jones, the distinguished tribal chairman of the Navajos, talked to me in his office at Window Rock, on the border of New Mexico and Arizona. "My people say to me, 'We have been placed where only a lizard could survive. But our gods sent wealth from below the ground. We are not forgotten.' "

The Navajos' change is the most significant of all tribes; their progress in dealing with their problems is serving as a pilot for federal officials and for many other tribes. It is natural that they should lead—not only because they are the largest in number, but because their reservation is the largest (about the size of West Virginia), and the gross sum of their mineral royalties exceeds that of any other tribe. But beyond that, the modern Navajo has strong capabilities as a citizen. He is independent and dignified, but capable of infinite gaiety and subtle humor. (An Indian Bureau official found an old Navajo still practicing polygamy, once common in the tribe, and explained that this was against federal law. He advised the old man to decide which wife he would keep and to tell the others they were no longer wives. The Navajo stared through the white man as though he were not present, then answered amiably as he strode away, "You tell 'em.")

Much has been accomplished among the Navajos in recent years, by the tribe itself or with federal assistance. Leading United States lumbermen have been appointed to an advisory board to counsel the Navajos on their lumber reserves and on the operation of a new seven-million-dollar sawmill. Other jobs are being provided for Navajos in a thirty-million-dollar pulp and paper mill at Snowflake, to the south of the reservation. On the reservation itself there is a model farm to teach agricultural techniques. Many new schools have been built. A soil conservation program is under way to try to keep the meager topsoil from blowing away. A utility authority is being set up to provide power, gas and water. A park commission is working on tourist facilities. Two Congressional appropriations of twenty million dollars each led to the construction of reservation roads, particularly two paved highways: Indian Route 3 across the reservation from Window Rock to Tuba City in Arizona; and Indian Route 1, which runs southwest across the reservation toward Phoenix, and is highly traveled because it cuts the distance between Denver and Los Angeles by one hundred and ninety miles. Routes 3 and 8 were the first paved roads into

Canyon de Chelly, one of the most stirring juxtapositions of remote grandeur and gentle beauty in America. Indian wagons with rubber tires are pulled by small Indian horses along the floor of the canyon, where corn and peaches grow beside ancient Pueblo dwellings set into the soaring canyon cliffs. From the rim of Canyon de Chelly, the wagons look like toys. Far to the north against the horizon loom the wild, twisted skyscrapers of Monument Valley, memorials to the power of wind and erosion in this grotesque, gripping land.

The new highways into Navajo land—the first paved roads to venture deep into the reservation—reward the traveler handsomely, but Navajo leaders are pleased by the roads because they will help to feed their people.

One who has been on the Navajo reservation before is surprised to find that a paved road leads now to the Hopi town of Oraibi, perched precariously for centuries atop a mesa and probably the oldest settlement on the continent. The traveler is also jolted by the incongruity of the supermarket in lonely little Tuba City; not many years ago, most Navajos' furthest venture into sophistication was to sit on the floor of a trading post and eat peaches from a can.

Traditionally the Navajo has been a semi-nomadic sheepherder and dry farmer. But a recent survey showed that only twelve percent of Navajo income came from farming or sheep raising. The largest share, sixty-six percent, is from salaries and wages earned both on and off the reservation. The mean family income is about twenty-five hundred dollars annually, a sharp increase over past years. But an equally significant increase has been in the federal budget. In 1944, the total United States Indian budget was about twenty-six million dollars; in 1959, expenditure for Arizona Indians alone was about thirty million dollars.

An outstanding difference between Arizona Indians and those of other states is that the Arizonans are mixing widely with non-Indians and moving toward assimilation. They seem to be in a hurry; in many Navajo communities, there are more Indians in pickup trucks than on horseback, more Sunday sermons than native rituals, more treatment by white doctors than by medicine men.

The leader of the Navajos, Paul Jones, is a phenomenon in American politics. There is no more eloquent or reasonable spokesman for the Indian than he. He was unanimously nominated, and reelected to a second four-year term by the Navajos in 1959 over an aspirant who pledged to dole out Navajo royalties—then close to nine hundred dollars for each Navajo man, woman and child—on a per capita basis. Jones has insisted that tribal royalties be used to build roads, tribal halls, tourist facilities and sawmills, and to attract simple industry that will provide jobs. Such is the faith of the Navajos in Jones that they voted for him rather than for a man who stood ready to put cash in their hands.

Now nearing seventy, Jones is a stocky man with a big stomach, short-trimmed, graying hair, and glasses. He sits behind a modern steel desk in a simple government office looking out on the red stone ceremonial arch that gives the Navajo capital of Window Rock its name. On the wall behind him, beside a fine gray and beige Navajo blanket, are an American flag and plaques from the Boy Scouts and service clubs. When we talked he wore a gray plaid sports jacket and a braided leather tie studded with turquoise. Not only his dress and manner but his attitudes reflect compromise between the historic positions of Indian and white.

For the first hour of the interview, he spoke guardedly, obviously giving answers he had given before. But when we traveled around the reservation, he visibly relaxed. His own story is a modest saga of Navajo perseverance. "I had very little education. Like most Navajo children of that day who had any, I was picked up from my hiding place by force and sent to school. I graduated from the eighth grade on the reservation. A fellow who wanted to be a missionary to China— where he died later on—was going back to New York to study medicine. I wanted to see the country; I'd never been outside New Mexico. I had a little money saved, and I went along with him sight-seeing. I was eighteen. I saw New York and Boston and Washington. Then my friend said, 'I think you ought to go back to school. You do janitor work for me around the church here, and you can go to school from my house.' That's the way I started school in New Jersey. The following year I went back to high school, in Grand Rapids. That's where I graduated. When World War I broke out I was picked up out of Grand Rapids, and three weeks later I was on my way to France. I spent twenty-two months overseas. I was gassed, and my heart was broken down when I came back. I wanted to study medicine and be a doctor, but it took me two years to get back my health, and I was on the reservation here for a while.

"Then I went back to Grand Rapids to college and studied bookkeeping and typing. I thought I'd get a job easy—I was one of the first of the Navajos to get a college diploma. But it took me a year to get a job in Chicago. I went to work for the National Tea Company at the bottom and worked up to assistant shipping clerk in the whole-sale department. I married a Navajo girl and I lived in Chicago nine years. But my wife's health broke down with tuberculosis. The doctor said she couldn't be cured, but it might be nice for her to be with her people back on the reservation. So we returned. I started working for the federal government here. My wife died in 1938. I remarried two years later, and buried my second wife too. My third wife and I have been married for twenty years now.

"Since I had been working as an interpreter, both the Navajos and the Bureau of Indian Affairs thought I would be a good man to be leader of the tribal government, so in 1955 I resigned from government service and was elected to this position. I don't feel my efforts in trying to help the Navajos have been in vain. A lot of them have been appreciative, and I am grateful for that. I composed the tribal council of seventy-two members to operate by the committee system. They are working together very nicely. We have committees working on Indian health and on the problems of alcohol.

"I tell my people: 'Adopt new methods. Acquire vocational training and trades. The Navajos should be assimilated. There should be no reservations; we should be full-fledged American citizens.' "

The Navajos are moving in that direction. They and Jones have been helped immeasurably by Wade Head, an exceptional area director for the Bureau of Indian Affairs. Long at Gallup, New Mexico, he was transferred late in 1962 to the Phoenix office. "We can't build schools fast enough now to take care of Navajo children whose parents are anxious to educate them," Head said. This is a complete reversal from the days before World War II, or even from a decade ago. You don't make progress in this kind of work by trying to push people. The Navajos are proud and individualistic; they are taking what they like of our culture and keeping the best of their own."

They certainly are being exposed. At Window Rock, in the recently built Navajo Civic Center, Guy Lombardo and his orchestra played one night when I was there. Harry Belafonte and Fred Waring were future attractions. The Navajos are also seeing much more of the tourist.

For Wade Head, the completion of the highways in 1961 and 1962 was the climax to eight years of effort. Uranium, gas and oil discoveries had made his Gallup headquarters a hot seat. The bureau serves more than 130,000 Indians, including those of the nineteen pueblos in New Mexico, the Jicarilla Apaches and Mescaleró Apaches, and the Ute tribes of Colorado. The Mountain Ute tribe of Utah and Colorado, primitive and usually poorly educated, has cash assets totaling about twenty million dollars from gas and oil, and a potential income of about the same figure over the course of the next twenty years. There are fewer than one thousand Mountain Utes, and each family has elaborate plans for development, for housing, and for schooling.

"Some people think they are throwing their money around," Head said. "But most of the Indians are very philosophical about their new wealth. They enjoy the irony of it."

Some, in fact, *are* throwing it around. The Navajos, who have had no per capita distribution of this new wealth, sometimes find jobs tilling the fields of Apaches and Utes who do have cash. These *nouveaux riches* are prone to spend their time gambling and drinking. Although the liquor problem of the Indian has decreased since the bootlegger was pushed aside, only within the past decade has it been legal to sell liquor to Indians. The problem still is acute at Gallup, a dusty, dirty little railroad town in western New Mexico which is the closest thing to an urban center around Navajo territory. But it is not so bad as it was in the months after New Mexico had legalized the sale of liquor to Indians, and Arizona had not. Indians swarmed across the line and converged on Gallup. The population of Gallup is about fifteen thousand; one Saturday afternoon, a road check revealed twenty-two thousand Indians coming into town. Gallup still must have more liquor stores and bars than any town its size, and Navajo and white police can be found collecting drunks at almost any hour of the day or night. But the percentage of Indians who are drinkers is not as high as that of non-Indians. Those who do drink are learning to hold their liquor better, and they are getting better liquor than they did in the bootleg era. University and church groups have been participating intelligently in Indian seminars on the alcohol problems.

Still, even the casual tourist, tuning in his car radio in the neighborhood of Gallup, will hear wine commercials in the Navajo language. And Paul Jones said, "We organize groups around the reservation for public works, to improve roads and dig wells. The first pay they get, a good portion of it goes into liquor. The doctor over at the hospital says we are responsible for so many broken bones and so many killings that when our people don't have money to buy liquor, the hospital doesn't get filled up. Just the other night I was over at a ceremonial near the railroad. It was about fifteen hundred yards from the nearest bar, and the bartender had contributed quite a bit of money to bring the crowd to his location. We had our policemen there, and we had the police cars filled all night."

Jones explained that tuberculosis had been controlled among the Navajos, and child mortality had declined sharply, but that today the number-one killer on the reservation is alcohol.

"In what form?" I asked.

"In the form of the automobile," he said with a wry smile. "Liquor still is forbidden on the reservation, but Navajos now own cars and pickup trucks. They go into town and haul liquor back. There's all

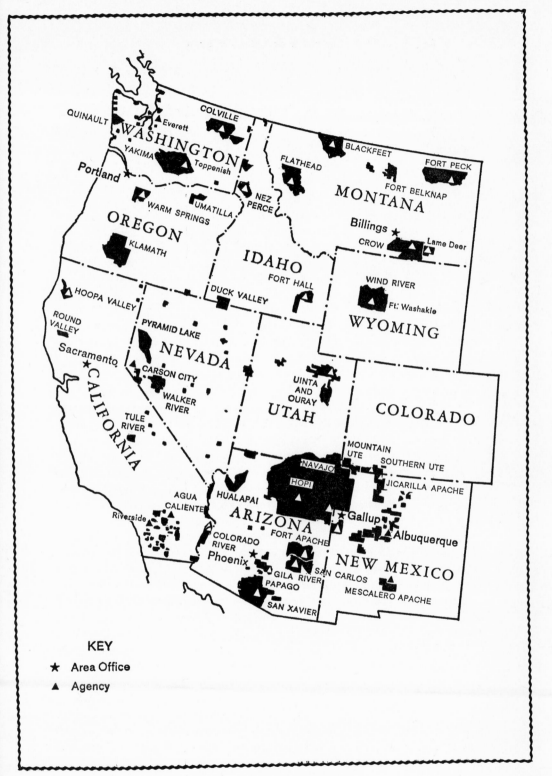

Indian Lands and Offices

kind of fighting and killing going on. They run over sheep, or they run over themselves."

Wade Head is optimistic. "The Indian is slowly learning about liquor, and Gallup is improving its attitudes toward the Indian."

Head's most dogged and persevering work on behalf of the Indian has been in the field of schooling. There are forty-nine boarding schools on the Navajo reservation. Close to five hundred Navajos are away at trade schools and colleges—many at the state universities of New Mexico and Arizona—and some of them will graduate. One was at Harvard in 1961; one has become a doctor. The tribe has set aside a ten-million-dollar fund whose income is used for educational loans. In 1954, half of the Navajo children were unschooled; by 1961, thirty thousand of them—more than double the number six years earlier— were in school. The federal government has built schools quickly, and Head has been one of the leaders in the fight to integrate Indian pupils into off-reservation public schools. About one-fourth of the Navajo children now in school are at Bureau schools away from the reservation. Off-reservation boarding schools were introduced during the Truman administration to accommodate unschooled Navajo youth in a five-year program designed to provide basic knowledge and trade skills. Now these large off-reservation schools are used primarily for regular schooling; in addition, twenty-four hundred Navajo children are enrolled in public schools in towns on the periphery of the reservation, and housed in dormitories operated by the Bureau of Indian Affairs. These are at Albuquerque, Gallup, Winslow, Aztec, Magdalena, and Ramah, New Mexico; at Flagstaff, Holbrook, and Snowflake, Arizona; and at Richfield, Utah. Navajo children living in these dormitories are as young as six years old, and attend both grammar and high schools. The Bureau of Indian Affairs pays in-lieu taxes to the host public school districts. There have been remarkably few problems of racial tension involved; Head is high in his praise of public school administrators in the three-state area who have participated in off-reservation schooling.

"The Navajos are on the move to get educated," Jones explained. "We've never had that before. Now parents use force to get the kids to go to school. In my time, they hid us from the white people. In World War II, many of our men saw the outside world for the first time and brought back the word that their sons and brothers should go to school. It has taken hold."

It is not that simple, of course. Navajo families living in hogans and huts seldom are able to pay for the several changes of clothing which their children must take with them when they leave the reservation for schooling. From tribal funds comes almost a million dollars each year to provide clothing for all children who go to school; this has proved a powerful persuader. But leaders like Jones and Head must also contend with Navajo prejudice. Just ahead of me when I visited Jones was a delegation of Navajos who had come to the tribal head-quarters to protest the assignment of a Negro teacher to their school. They insisted that she did not speak good English; she had a southern drawl, and these Navajos had not heard one before. Among the Navajos, as among some other Indian tribes, the Negro is not held in high esteem. Negro teachers, Jones said, have been assigned to the Navajo reservation only within recent years, and he himself felt that in general they were less sympathetic than white teachers toward the Navajo lack of education. For Jones, that incident posed a knotty problem. He was serving as a member of Senator Goldwater's advisory board on civil rights. "Now," he sighed, "I find my own people discriminating against colored people."

The impact of the great Navajo rush to the schools will be felt within a decade, and there is ample cause to hope that effective and unemotional redress for long years of Indian mistreatment and neglect is in store. Politically the Navajo is making himself felt; in his path, other tribes are sure to follow. There are still Navajo precincts without voters, but several thousand Navajos vote in each election.

The Indian's political renaissance began with a visit by Dwight Eisenhower to a Navajo tribal ceremonial at Gallup during the presidential campaign of 1952. He promised the Navajos that the federal government would consult them on Bureau of Indian Affairs appointments. It may have been blithe campaign oratory, but its impact on the Navajos was incalculable. An estimated ninety-five percent of the small Navajo vote went to the Republican ticket. After the election Navajos rallied behind Glenn L. Emmons, a Gallup banker, as their candidate for commissioner of Indian Affairs. In a full-page newspaper advertisement, the tribe pleaded its case in a manner Madison Avenue would have approved:

"Navajo life is an intense drama. The striving of the will of our people is the moving force in this drama. The Navajos must be turned from anticipated death, from fatalism to action, from inferiority to healthful pride; but under the leadership of the past and present in Washington, that goal is not yet reached. We cry out for a leader who will truly give us physical and spiritual life. If this does not occur under Republican leadership, we must be ready to meet the long Indian Night—perhaps the last.

"Democracy today is locked with anti-democratic forces in a world-wide struggle. The Navajos, and in a large measure every other tribe, have waged a comparable struggle for many lifetimes. . . .

"During most of its one hundred and twenty-seven years of operation, the Bureau of Indian Affairs has pursued a shoddy course of costly mismanagement and political maneuvering under administrations of both parties. At times it seemed that the Bureau was going far out of its way to force many American Indians to the status of second-class citizens. . . . Budget dollars for Indian reservation development have come grudgingly and in stingy amounts. The Navajos of Arizona and New Mexico are long-suffering testimonials of the Bureau's bad faith. Americans are rightfully proud of their treaties made and kept with other nations. Yet not once in the eighty-four-year period since the signing has the Bureau, or the Congress, lived up to the full terms of the Treaty of 1868 between the United States and the Navajo Indians. . . ."

Emmons was appointed. He helped the Navajos, and he helped Gallup too. After the Santa Fe Railroad converted to Diesels, Gallup, which had survived as a low-grade coal mining town, was dying out. Emmons brought Indian Bureau area offices and a hospital to Gallup. Federal payrolls boosted Gallup's economy.

Emmons gave way under the Kennedy administration to Philleo Nash. Under the two commissioners, Western Indians have turned an important corner in their relationship with the federal government. They regard Stewart Udall, Secretary of the Interior, as a staunch friend. Senator Barry Goldwater is another highly respected ally of the Navajos. He has visited every Indian reservation in Arizona, a remarkable feat even for a politician. Goldwater's conservatism coincides with the liberal attitude in the matter of the Indian: Do not abolish the reservation yet. Don't try to change the Indian overnight, even in the name of equal rights and full citizenship. Don't kick him out into the world; go slow. Give Indians a chance through education, through good health, through job opportunity, to make their own way, in their own time.

Even Oliver La Farge, the Santa Fe author and long-time critic of Indian policy (his Navajo novel, *Laughing Boy*, won the Pulitzer Prize in 1929) concedes that Indian policy in the Gallup area is enlightened. "The story with the Navajos is to protect Indian rights and encourage Indian enterprise. You can't ask within the same area that other tribes be treated differently; so the Indians have very little to complain about here and a good deal to be grateful for. But outside this area, you begin to run into the same old problems: sale of Indian land, and policies which tend to force the Indians out of their community."

The conclusion is inevitable that there is a strong correlation between the new wealth of these Indian tribes in the Southwest and their recent progress. In Oregon, where checks as high as forty-three thousand dollars were handed in 1960 to members of the Klamath Indian tribe upon sale of reservation lands, Indians paid their back bills, bought cattle and real estate, and invested in government bonds. For the first time, a Klamath Indian was initiated into a Masonic lodge. Promoters of get-rich-quick schemes who had moved into the area in anticipation of this Indian windfall were disappointed. There was no debauchery, no splurging on expensive new cars, no outbreak of indolence.

But few tribes have been so fortunate as to receive such wealth, or to have the opportunity to prove their capability of coping with it. Elsewhere in the West, very little of significance is happening among Indians. At Great Falls, Montana, the predominantly Indian community known as Hill 57 is a squalid, sequestered slum, a favorite target of federal Indian policy critics everywhere. Among the most pathetic of Indian tribes is the Papago, whose bleak reservation lies in the fiery desert south of Tucson. Some have become farm workers, miners and railroad workers, but many are nomads still weaving baskets, building their shelters from clay, and finding their food and medicine in desert weeds.

The Pueblo Indians of New Mexico, whose towns are the most picturesque of all American Indian settlements, are slowly turning away from their old traditions. There are about 21,000 of them, and in their everyday tribal costumes and long hair there is not a trace of the white man's influence. The Pueblos, as one tourist put it, are "more Indian than other Indians." But even they are coming down out of the hills to the white man's towns, drawn by the higher standard of living that city wages provide.

The first known inhabitants of the Pueblo country are referred to by anthropologists as Sandia Man. Artifacts from a cave east of Albuquerque place his era at about 35,000 to 30,000 B.C. An arroyo near Folsom in the far northeast of New Mexico gave up traces of human habitation dated at about 23,000 B.C. These later people are called Bison Nomads; they roamed the plains from Mexico to Canada.

The pueblos of New Mexico were the first apartment houses of North America. They were also the first annuities. Ancestors of contemporary Pueblo Indians did the building, but the smart boys of the twentieth century are charging admission. If one climbs to the lofty pueblo of Acoma, atop a mesa west of Albuquerque, one is presented with a list of photographic charges: eight-exposure black-and-white cameras, $1.50; 35mm. color cameras, $3.50; 8 mm. motion-picture cameras, $8; 16mm. motion-picture cameras, $15.

Taos is the northernmost of the pueblos, a relatively prosperous one and famed because of the nearby artists' colony. There is no more beautiful setting; one stands on the Taos plateau with a sense of awe. The blue mountains that shield the plateau are remote. There is a feel of other-worldness, a startling luminosity of colors, a tang in the brisk lightness of the air, an intimation of the eternal past in the adobe villages of native and Anglo and in the adobe pueblo of the Taos Indian. The Indians of Taos are eager to be photographed—for fifty cents. They might do better if they imported blankets from the Navajos, for they drape themselves in green-and-white checked blankets suspiciously like those offered at the J. C. Penney store in downtown Taos.

In the Laguna pueblo west of Albuquerque, where a Laguna Indian made the famed Jackpile uranium strike, Indians handle mechanical equipment and are the core of the mining work force. In the Santo Domingo pueblo, Henry Kaiser executives who sought to run a railroad spur to a gypsum plant found that their proposed route cut through a red clay mound which has provided ceremonial clay for the Santo Domingos. In three or four centuries, the Santo Domingos had taken out perhaps only a cubic yard of clay. Kaiser wanted to level the mound, and Kaiser men from Oakland came to talk the problem out with the Santo Domingo chiefs. After a day of immense corporate frustration, the spur line was re-routed.

In California, there are Indians in every county in the state, but in only six or seven counties do they number more than one thousand. About three-fifths of the Indian population live on insignificant reservations in unproductive hill country. Others live on land allotments or homesteads, work on ranches or, increasingly, find their way to industrial jobs in the cities. The Indian population of Los Angeles County quadrupled between 1950 and 1960. The situation in San Diego County is more typical. With no oil or uranium on their lands, very little timber and nothing whatever to attract the tourist, the eight hundred Indians on the county's reservations are impoverished and disheartened. The total Indian population of the county, just over two thousand, is almost the same as in 1910. Many who have left the reservations have jobs in construction work or as maintenance men and are living at somewhat higher standards than those who stay behind on the barren land. Many reservation Indians still show hostility toward Indian agents.

The most prosperous California Indians are the Agua Caliente tribe of the Palm Springs area. History does not credit their tribe with bravery or intelligence, and only about one hundred members of the tribe survive. Several picturesque canyons, two cemeteries and a church remain as tribal property. Most of the thirty-one-thousand-acre reservation, checkerboarded by land once owned by the Southern Pacific Railway, has been distributed among the Indians on an individual basis. Because the white man feels as he does about Palm Springs, the Indians are rich; they are worth an estimated three hundred and thirty-five thousand dollars each in land valuation. The city of Palm Springs in 1960 paid almost three million dollars for two sections of the reservation on which the city airport is located. The tribal chairman has been Mrs. Eileen Miguel, who lives in an eighty-five-thousand-dollar home on a bluff overlooking the new fifty-million-dollar Palm Canyon Country Club development. The Indians' old water hole, revered for the curative quality of its mineral springs, is in the center of downtown Palm Springs; it took an act of Congress to lease the springs for the construction of a luxurious spa, heavily patronized by the film crowd from Los Angeles. One John Joseph Patencio of the Agua Caliente tribe has a hundred-thousand-dollar business in Palm Springs which he describes as "the first Laundromat owned by an American Indian."

The major hope of other tribes and of the federal men involved with Indians throughout most other states is that the momentum of the Navajo movement will give impetus to better times for them, too. There are very few reservations in the other states whose land will support their population.

The Indians' cause would be spurred by the emergence of more leaders like Paul Jones. He says, "Since our old way of life is not paying, why stick to it? You can't just sit around in a blanket and have people come look at you. You have to work to live."

Also you have to know how. And you must have the chance. One persistent Indian problem becomes more critical as the education levels of the Indians rise: those who could help most are likeliest to abandon the reservation for a better chance at life. It is a rare person, Indian or white, who will return to a searing land like this after he has discovered how others live.

One of these rare men like Paul Jones is Peter Homer, chairman of the Colorado River Indian tribal council. His mother chose to live in the old way, but his father became a railroad hand and saw that education unlocked doors. As a boy, Pete Homer was chased down by Indian police several times and returned to school; invariably his father was the one who called the law. Finally he was shipped to Phoenix Indian School. His whole family on the reservation died in the flu epidemic of 1918; away at Phoenix, he did not know of their death for many months. A fine athlete, Homer played professional baseball and pitched for two years each in Oakland, Milwaukee and Hollywood. In *Rose Marie*, the Nelson Eddy–Jeanette MacDonald movie, he was an Indian spear carrier. His baseball career over, he returned to the Colorado River in 1937 with a Shasta Indian wife, six children, and a job with the Reclamation Bureau. He did not plan to stay, but a sense of duty prevailed. "Reservations will not be improved by education," he said recently, "if the best educated Indians all go away to live." Today Homer is just as intent on staying on the reservation as he was when Indian police dragged him away to school.

6

THE FIGHT TO SAVE

THE WEST

Wherever the impacts of spiraling population are felt, Westerners today begin to talk fast about saving the West that they knew, even yesterday. Because they are so mobile a people, they are vitally interested in both urban planning and in conservation of rural or wilderness areas. In each case, the motivation is their quest to create a controlled environment.

On days off, and on weekends, Westerners rush to beaches and parks—often to nearby state and national parks. They tolerate urban crowding with the reassuring knowledge that they are only a few hours distant from trout stream or ski run. But as they grow accustomed to the wondrous openness of park or wilderness, they ponder the failure of city or state government to exercise more effective control over urban growth.

It is this realization that makes Westerners begin to read and study, to join planning or conservation groups, in unprecedented numbers. Soon they are aware that the philosophy of Western natural resources is undergoing a transition in the westward tilt. When the West was sparsely settled, those who exploited its natural resources—

its timber, oil and minerals, its grass, water and farmland—became a powerful, vested political force. That power is declining.

The rising power is with the millions who have more leisure and more money and are more eager to travel than ever before. They are interested in preserving areas where they can fish, hunt, hike, swim, ski, and camp without being trampled by their neighbors from the cities. So the concept of Western natural resources has changed; through powerful organizations and lobbies, the sportsman, the conservationist, and the tourist are beginning to exert more political pressure than mine owners, cattlemen and lumbermen. But their interests are diverse, and the hunter on a motor scooter is as much an enemy of the wilderness as is the logger.

The new leisure power is evident on every side. One of the classic examples is in Jackson Hole, Wyoming, a saucer of gentle land overlooked on the west by the twenty-two summits of the most dramatic mountains in America: the Grand Tetons. John D. Rockefeller, Jr., stayed with his three sons in the Jackson Hole country in the summer of 1926. The next year he began buying lands there, and he didn't stop for more than twenty years. Rockefeller tried hard to give the land to the nation as part of the Grand Teton National Park. But it was 1950 before the opposition of cattlemen and local citizens could be overcome and the gift accepted for the purpose Rockefeller proposed. Teton County income in taxes on the striking, seven-million-dollar Jackson Lake Lodge (built and operated on leased land in the park by a non-profit Rockefeller corporation) is greater than the former income through taxes on those thirty-five thousand undeveloped acres of Jackson Hole which some residents fought so hard to withhold from public domain. Because of a Rockefeller endowment and the ingenuity of Raymond Lillie, who manages tourist facilities, Grand Teton is the bellwether among national parks in innovation and development of tourist services and facilities.

Beneath the sheer escarpments of the Grand Tetons, I watched a Cadillac limousine pull in among the pines of the Colter Bay shore. Its four occupants moved into two of the tent cabins designed and built in 1961 as a compromise between the rough outdoor life which fathers seem to like to recall for their children, and the softer life more favored in the realistic present. The cabins are an ingenious combination of log, canvas and concrete. Into one tent cabin went husband and wife; into the other, a nine-year-old boy and the family nurse. The rates were five dollars a night for each tent cabin. Five miles away, in the more posh confines of Jackson Lake Lodge, rooms with picture windows and private baths were available, but here was a family going camping with limousine and nurse.

It is not necessary to arrive at the Grand Tetons with tents, camp stoves, air mattresses, mosquito netting or sleeping bags piled on car roofs. Many families camp only rarely, but enjoy an opportunity to sample camp life without investing in equipment. All the items needed for camping are available for rental by occupants of the tent cabins— down to coffee cup and spatula. Axes are for rent, and there is abundant fallen timber so that fathers can make a great show of cutting firewood with their sons. This display lasts usually only for a day or two; when the camper has made his point, he may buy a sack full of chopped wood for a few cents.

Such understanding of the vacationer has been combined in all the Jackson Lake facilities with equal appreciation of the environment. Laurance S. Rockefeller, board chairman of the Grand Teton Lodge Company, is elated that the tent-cabins—at five dollars a night —are more sought after than the best twenty-five dollar lodge rooms; the more rustic setting is closer to nature, and to his heart. A small sign is posted beside the cashier's window of the Jackson Lake Lodge reminding guests that no one is making any profit from their visit. In such an atmosphere, there seems to be a keener sense of good fun than at many national parks.

One school teacher declined an appointment as superintendent of schools in a nearby Idaho county because it would have interfered with his summer job as a tour bus driver in Grand Teton National Park. Another teacher, from California, was my guide during a trip on a rubber raft down a fast but placid stretch of the Snake River from where the Tetons seem to loom almost vertically. The raft trip is another of Lillie's shrewd diversions for the vacationer. It is a thirty-mile trip, usually requiring about six hours, including a stop for a picnic lunch on a grassy shore of the Snake. There is very little white water this near the headwaters of the savage Snake—which begins its flow just north of Jackson Lake near Yellowstone Park, flows southwest to cross Idaho and turns northward through Hell's Canyon, deepest of all American gorges, finally meeting the mighty Columbia River in southeastern Washington.

A highway follows the course of the Snake through Jackson Hole; but from the water it is not seen, nor are motors heard. There is little trace of man. The guide stands manning the sweep as the raft slips silently downstream; the only sound is the lapping of water against raft and bank. On the shores and the islands in the stream are a succession of wonders. From a beaver lodge a canal leads into a grove of quaking aspen; the beavers had exhausted the supply of deciduous trees along the bank and cut their own aquatic skid road into the forest. From their tiny caves bored into a river cliff, a corps of cliff swallows emerge and dance their rhumba step along the bank. Above them is a wild splash of color: lupin, wild rose and Indian paintbrush; beyond those, buckwheat and sagebrush rim the top of the cliff, and a buck-and-rail fence of native lodgepole pine cuts into view at the edge of a pasture. A raven perches in solemn dignity on an island in the stream, and a moose with an awesome spread of antlers canters out of the trees to stare with hauteur at our leisurely, effortless passage through his domain. Far above us, clouds gather and curtain off from view the highest of the Tetons.

In the evening, after my trip down the Snake, a Fulbright scholar from India served me a cocktail. My waitress at dinner was a Paris girl who had transferred from the Sorbonne to the University of Wyoming, and whose eyes twinkled wildly when she talked of the contrasts. Later that evening I met a San Francisco builder, a vintner from Sonoma Valley and a New York City designer. All showed a keen interest in these mountains and in the Rockefeller improvisations aimed at bringing the casual vacationer closer to nature. Despite the crowding and cacophony of many of the national parks and most vacationlands of America, nature-minded visitors are growing more numerous, and their voices are raised more often in conservation affairs.

The national park system is predominantly Western, although by far the heaviest tourism at any park is at the Great Smoky Mountains National Park in North Carolina and Tennessee, the closest of the major parks to areas of large population. About eleven million acres lies in national parkland west of the Mississippi River, and less than three and a half million acres to the east of the Mississippi. The three parks most heavily visited in 1960 were Eastern, and yet the total attendance at national parks west of the Mississippi in that year was almost double that of Eastern parks.

Habits of the park visitor are changing. The house trailer, that monstrous enemy of mountain road traffic, has become a fact of life in the parks. The first trailer accommodations provided in national parks were at Grand Teton; now they are commonplace, and demand for trailer space is so great that parks are lowering the maximum duration of stay allowed for trailers. Between 1955 and 1959, while visitors to Yellowstone increased only three percent, the number of house trailers increased one hundred and ten percent, and the number of boats by one hundred and eight percent. Most of the boats are power boats, and their increasing use on waters such as Yellowstone Lake has set off controversy. The Park Service has closed three arms of Yellowstone Lake to motorboat traffic in the spirit of the 1916 law setting up the national parks "to leave them unimpaired for the enjoy-

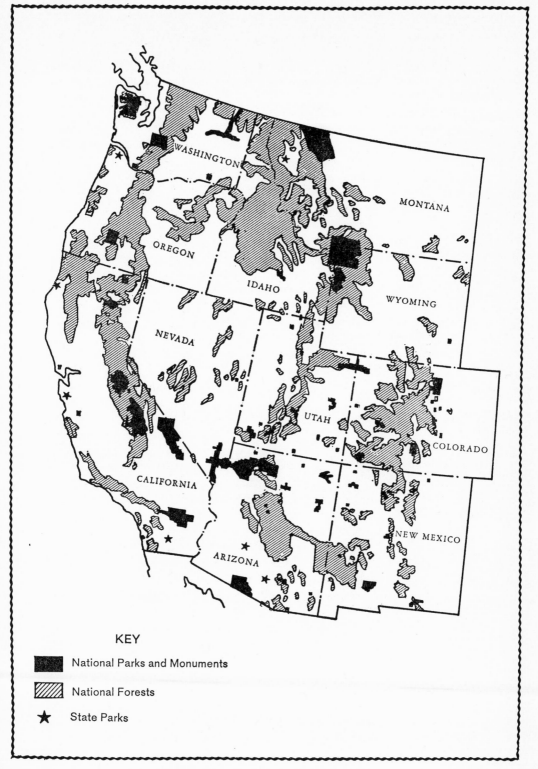

KEY

National Parks and Monuments

National Forests

★ State Parks

Government Parks and Forests

ment of future generations," and to guard, when compatible with other goals, the ancient virtues of peace and silence.

Another villain of park and wilderness lovers is the motorized trail scooter. Since 1958, more than fifty companies have gone into the manufacture of gasoline-driven, two-seater scooters; some of the scooters can negotiate a forty-five percent grade with a four-hundred pound load, and later fold down to fit into an automobile trunk. Their noise carries across remote mountainsides, sending naturalists into apoplexy; their wheels set off rock slides and dig ruts that lead to erosion.

The national parks wrestle with other problems which are unique to the characteristics of each park; crowding is a perpetual crisis at some parks, like Yosemite. The granite domes and towering waterfalls above Yosemite Valley make it, for me, the most compelling scenery in America. Nowhere else in the world have I repeatedly fallen so totally under the spell of nature. Obviously I am not alone in my attachment for Yosemite Valley. There are about eleven hundred square miles in Yosemite National Park, and fewer than ten square miles on the valley floor. Yet almost all of the more than a million visitors to Yosemite each year huddle on the valley floor, creating a condition of urban crowding during the summer which threatens to destroy the Yosemite spell. The Park Service combats crowding by encouraging visitors to explore the more rustic facilities of the magnificent Yosemite high country. But the crowding is rapidly making Yosemite the arena of a showdown in the battle between conservationists and others like the National Park Service, who contend that it is their prime duty to make room for the people. The narrow old Tioga Pass Road, which crossed the ridgepole of the Sierra Nevada in Yosemite National Park at almost ten thousand feet, has given way to a wide, high-speed and comparatively dull highway. The change was fought bitterly by many who believe that it is an irreverence to speed through scenic grandeur such as this.

Far to the north, Yellowstone tourism in the record-breaking summer of 1962 recovered completely from the earthquake of August 17, 1959, which took twenty-eight lives and caused an overnight exodus on the highways comparable only to Pasadena after a Rose Bowl game. One significant change in tourism at Yellowstone is that its southern gateway, through Jackson Hole and Grand Teton National Park, has displaced its northern portal as the most popular point of entry into the huge park. This is because more park visitors come now from California than from any other state.

Grand Canyon is unique in that visitors must leave the major highways, travel about sixty miles to the canyon, and then retrace their route to continue their journey. Park Service people at Grand Canyon like that; visitors are not there for a casual drive-through, but because they want to see the canyon. My most recent visit to Grand Canyon was in the chill, calm days of October. At sunrise I was almost alone outside old El Tovar Hotel, a few steps away from the rim of the earth's most violent aberration. Later I visited John S. McLaughlin, who had served as park superintendent at Grand Canyon for six years. He is a tall, quiet Scot with a mustache and an unswerving love for the outdoors. It is bizarre to associate anything as gargantuan and forbidding as Grand Canyon with a pet, but McLaughlin talking about Grand Canyon reminds one of a hunter's soliloquy about his favorite hound.

"One of the greatest thrills I get," he said, "is to go out to Mather Point in the afternoon and watch visitors stop their cars and take their first look at the Canyon. I like to watch their movements and hear what they say. Most of them are quite overwhelmed by it, and you can see it on their faces. This is true especially of people from the East and Midwest. Of course some Texans go up and take a look and turn around and walk away. They just don't want to admit it."

More people visit Grand Canyon than ever before, although the rate of increase has leveled out. In summer, visitors sleep in cars and jam hotels sixty miles away in Williams. By October, the North Rim is closed, and the Harvey hotels on the South Rim have empty rooms.

The same questions are asked today at Grand Canyon as were asked when the Park Service began almost fifty years ago: how did it happen, and when? To handle such questions, answered in every encyclopedia, the Park Service has opened a sleek modern visitors' center on the South Rim, and conducts nature lectures nearby. A new campground and trailer park have been added as part of the Park Service's Project 66 program—which sets 1966 as a target year for completing an ambitious series of improvements in national parks.

Even at Grand Canyon, there is change. "People don't stay as long as before," McLaughlin said. "A good percentage of them come to the rim and take a look, are here a couple of hours, and then get back to Highway 66. A few take the trail trips down into the Canyon, a smaller percentage than in past years. It takes at least a day—considerable time for today's tourist. The average American is not as interested in physical exercise as his father was. A great proportion of the people who actually hike to the Colorado River at the bottom of the Canyon are Europeans."

At Grand Canyon, as everywhere, the Park Service is anxious to maintain natural conditions as primitive as is compatible with accommodating the teeming visitors. At the Canyon, the Park Service has nature's wilderness on its side. Even El Tovar Hotel, built in 1905 and the overnight home of every United States president since that time, may disappear eventually from the rim; the Park Service is anxious to return the Canyon edge to nature. In the case of El Tovar, this is an awkward problem; the hotel was built by the Santa Fe Railroad eleven years before the Park Service was created. But the Harvey Hotels management concedes that the Park Service will win its point and the hotel will be rebuilt away from the rim. There is a certain fatalism in the air here, where millions of years can be measured in mere hundreds of feet of red rock.

One of the major national park fights of recent years was taking place as this book went to press: the effort led by Secretary of the Interior Stewart Udall to establish Canyonlands National Park, a remote three hundred and thirty thousand acre area in southeast Utah. Canyonlands would include the red rock gorges, buttes, and spires knifed by the torrents of the Green River and Colorado River in the area of their confluence near the uranium mining town of Moab. This is a wilderness reached now by only the very dedicated tourist, and it is one of the most rugged spectacles in America. The park, as originally proposed by Secretary Udall, would have included close to a million acres. But the boundaries were cut after Governor Dewey Clyde and Senator Wallace F. Bennett of Utah, both Republicans, had protested that the park would "lock up" mineral resources important to Utah's economy. Exploratory drilling has taken place in the area, but no oil or gas discoveries are known.

"This is the finest area in America outside the park system," Secretary Udall told me. "It has, in its way, greater variety and grandeur than the Grand Canyon. In some of the Western states, such as Utah, tourism is the future of the state. Even if oil were discovered here, it would be gone in fifty years; a park would preserve its scenic beauty, and have even greater value a thousand years from now."

Canyonlands is one of half a dozen proposed parks that Secretary Udall has been seeking in an effort to increase national park acreage; the rate of acquisition of Park acreage dropped sharply during the administrations of Truman and Eisenhower. This quest seems compatible with the report in 1962 of the Outdoor Recreation Resources Review Commission headed by Laurance S. Rockefeller. After a three-year study by its eight members of Congress and seven private citizens, the commission noted that "one of the main currents of modern life has been the movement away from the outdoors. It no longer lies at the back door or at the end of Main Street. More and more, most Americans must traverse miles of crowded highways to know the outdoors.

The prospect for the future is that this quest will be even more difficult." This is true, even in the new West.

Secretary Udall is among those who have sensed a desire for planning among the people of the West, at a time when they are receiving a great migration. "I think we have the opportunity now for the biggest push in conservation in this century," he told me. "Membership in conservation and wildlife groups is soaring. They are becoming more powerful, as they speak for the great mass of the people. What we save in the next few years may be all that we save. We must preserve the sense of spaciousness that America once implied. One source of our national strength has been that we have had a big land to test ourselves against."

About half of the land in Western states already is owned by the federal government, and some Westerners are appalled at the prospect that more land might go irrevocably into public domain under circumstances depriving the West and the nation of its natural resources. (Of the one hundred and fifty regions to be preserved under the wilderness bill considered by Congress in 1962, one hundred and thirty-nine were in the West.) Yet one of the firmest voices in support of the wilderness legislation has been that of the relatively small but influential Sierra Club, founded in San Francisco in 1892 with John Muir, the naturalist, as president. At the close of World War II, the Sierra Club had about six thousand members; the number tripled in the following fifteen years, and chapters of the club spread across the nation. Since 1900, the Club has conducted walking trips and pack trips into the Sierra Nevada. Many trips now are designed for full family groups, and are reserved months in advance. Board members of the Sierra Club include Supreme Court Justice William O. Douglas, one of the sturdiest and most literary of conservationists, and Ansel Adams, the nature photographer, whose magnificent book, *This is the American Earth*, was sponsored by the Sierra Club.

The Sierra Club sees as its role the job of awakening the American people from what it regards as nearly a mass oblivion of irrevocable changes in the national landscape, and loss of scenic resources. The Club fights for new parks and wilderness areas, and it urges that the public be given a broader voice in the management of national forest resources. In 1962, for instance, it led a fight for a protective dam which would prevent flooding of Rainbow Bridge in Utah by the waters of Glen Canyon Dam on the Colorado River. It works at lower government levels toward state parks, greenbelts, and urban open spaces.

The soaring membership of a club dedicated to such goals, and of other groups like the National Wildlife Federation, the National Parks Association, the Izaak Walton League of America, and the Wilderness Society, suggests a healthy rise of interest in nature and conservation. Many Sierra Club members have been active in the group since before 1920; they regard California as a state of rare beauty and wonder and want it to remain so. But the predominant part of the new membership is made up of younger Californians who have gone West for business reasons, or in search of amenities. They are acutely sensitive to the California movement and are usually aware of the hopeful contrast between the California environment and the one they left behind in older sections of the nation. They are looking for ways to prevent this bright new land from becoming as scarred and listless as the old.

"Not until 1961," wrote Edgar Wayburn, president of the Sierra Club in 1962, "could we talk in terms of a definitely rising tide in the conservation movement, both as a popular idea and once again as a political force, this time of the 'use-but-preserve' school. Of greatest import and interest to the Sierra Club is the increased and marked acceptance of the wilderness idea, the park idea, and the open space idea."

Among many Western people today such serious concern for the future environment is commonplace. At this moment, it would appear the Westerner has more hope of saving his wilderness than his cities. His political pressures are seldom organized enough to cope with his runaway world of urban growth. There is a rising tide of citizen interest in urban planning, but it is only now beginning to be translated into results at the government level.

There have been only a few planned cities in the West until very recent years; much more predominant are the cities that never meant to be.

Not long ago a University of Southern California sociologist suggested a plan for staggered weekends as a means of minimizing crowding of beaches and freeways. Implicit in his proposal, although not expressed, was the suggestion that the Sabbath be observed on varying days by varying segments of the population. Yet in the face of such drastic proposals, and with growth problems that dwarf those of every other state, Californians have been spending less per capita on statewide planning than the people of any other state except Indiana. The California State Office of Planning has existed on a smaller budget than that of many city and county planning agencies within the state. Its funds have been so limited that California has been unable to accept federal grants-in-aid for development of state plans—funds which have been exploited even by New Mexico, with a population only about one-sixteenth as large as that of California.

California will spend fifty-five billion dollars on public works within the next twenty years; yet because of the starvation budget of the State Office of Planning, the state has no comprehensive development plan to guide the location of its freeways and its aqueducts, no state land-use plan, no means of halting suburban sprawl, no plan for moving its urban growth pattern from valley smog to foothill airiness, no idea of when to stop the march of subdivisions over its best agricultural acreage, no statewide concept of air terminal locations, no program to aid the sparsely populated counties into which many of the coming millions of new Californians will have to settle. Instead, the California Legislature has voted down legislation to permit formation of metropolitan, area-wide policy agencies.

Each California county is required by law to maintain a planning commission and develop a master plan for land use. All major California cities do the same. But the plans become hopelessly ensnarled in metropolitan areas like Los Angeles County, which has seventy-three incorporated cities within its boundaries; or the San Francisco Bay area, with its nine counties and eighty-five municipalities.

Citizen interest in planning has moved ahead of the state government in California. A non-profit educational institution called California Tomorrow was formed in 1962 at Sacramento. "Our whole purpose," said Samuel E. Wood, a former official of the United States Agriculture and Interior departments, "is to achieve a greater public awareness of the growth problems that California faces."

In a booklet entitled *California Going, Going* . . . , Wood and Alfred E. Heller wrote: "The idea that there is no popular support for planning, and that planning has no political appeal, is outmoded. Every day thousands of citizens face the problems of growth as they give their time to cities and counties on planning commissions, zoning boards, and special citizens' study committees. Every year other hundreds of thousands attend hearings on general plans, central business district studies, zoning matters, school and park site acquisitions, and freeway locations. The subject of planning *is* people's homes and neighborhoods, their schools, their parks, their work places and how they get to them—it is where you live and how you live—it is the very bloodstream of California."

There is state planning in California, but it is unilateral.

The Department of Water Resources developed a water plan for California which was approved by the legislature in 1959. Voters sanctioned the largest bond issue in the history of any state in 1960:

$1,750,000,000. With that vote, the department was in the construc-
tion business; it was charged with building some of the water projects
outlined in its plan. But there is no overall state policy or state plan to
guide full development of concurrent recreational facilities at reser-
voirs, to prevent highways from crossing dam sites, or to guide the
location and growth of towns which will spring up along the route of
the new waterways.

The Division of Highways, with about sixteen thousand employees and an annual budget in excess of six hundred million dollars,
is sustained by a gas-tax fund set up in the state constitution. An
autocracy, it has been under fire incessantly because there is no state
policy directing the Division to work with other state agencies and
local interests in plans for freeway and highway routing, so that the
best use of the state's land for all purposes can result. The Division
has waived its authorization to buy parkland beside state highways,
and beach easements to provide public entry to state beaches. It has
evaded a stand on control of highway advertising.

A two-volume report by a special committee in 1960 produced a
California public outdoor recreation plan. But responsibility for recreation facilities in California is lost in a jumble of more than a score
of federal, state, and local agencies. There has been no dominant
single recreational agency. "As things happen now," wrote Wood and
Heller, "a tourist entering the state is not urged to take advantage of
[California] recreational resources—he is merely asked if he is accompanied by insect pests!"

The emergence of the California Tomorrow agency in 1962 was
a sign of California restlessness at state inactivity in the realm of
planning. It was evidence that Californians are growing uncomfortably aware that each passing day places new limits on the bright tomorrow of the golden state; each day brings fifteen hundred more people
into California and swallows more than three hundred acres of open
land. Backed by a distinguished advisory board recruited largely from
the San Francisco Bay area, California Tomorrow promised to be the
first effective rallying point for Californians against urban blight—or
the *slurb*, a word coined by the organization to describe the suburban
fringe destroyed by neon and subdivision.

Many other Western states, closely watching the effect of the
avalanche on California, have profited from its formidable example of
urban blight. Some of them are far ahead of California in terms of
state planning; they have made their moves in time to avoid some of
the worst of the state's catastrophes. Oregon virtually put its entire
coastline into a massive public beach system in 1913. Phoenix went on

a rampage of annexation in the 1950's which brought a huge suburban fringe under city planning controls. Seattle used the impetus of its World's Fair to create a handsome new civic center complex at the Fair site. But throughout the West, most towns and cities are growing in a string pattern which has evolved because land in the suburbs is relatively cheap and transportation is by automobile; the major arteries tail out through a melange of neon, jumbled signs and used car lots, into desert or fields.

There are, however, some bright spots.

One intriguing project is south of Los Angeles on the historic, ninety-three thousand acre Irvine Ranch in Orange County. The ranch had remained almost intact since the days of Spanish settlement until Joan Irvine Burt, twenty-eight-year-old beauty and an heiress of the ranch company, led a three-year battle with Irvine Company directors for a master development plan. The ranch, which her grandfather had founded, stood in 1961 as probably the largest undeveloped tract in an urban area in the nation.

Now it is being developed as a complete urban complex rolling from mountains to the Pacific—including a thousand-acre campus of the University of California, homes, hotels, golf course, beach facilities, business and industrial sites. The ranch includes eight miles of coves along the coast between the resort towns of Newport Beach and Laguna Beach.

The young heiress won a round in her battle with the directors after making public a letter to the company president in 1960 in which she cited the Irvine ranch as "an unparalleled and golden opportunity in the creation of new and lasting standards of community development." The president stepped aside, and Charles S. Thomas, former Secretary of the Navy, was called in to implement a master plan. It has been developed under the supervision of architect William Pereira; it is to be executed in three phases requiring ten years each. The result seems likely to be a brilliant example of community planning.

In some respects, Lake Tahoe is another hopeful example of planning. It is a mountain-ringed, oval emerald, high in the Sierra Nevada. The Cal-Neva Lodge straddles the state line; liquor cannot be sold after two in the morning on the California side, but a bartender on the Nevada half will cheerfully serve you a double martini at dawn. Despite such contrasts in the restrictive philosophies of the two states, they are joined in an unprecedented effort to develop bistate park and recreation sites on both Nevada and California shores of Lake Tahoe. Park commissions of the two states have been seeking an interstate compact to obtain property, and a two-state authority is con-templated to administer programs. It could be a breakthrough toward regional cooperation in planning among Western states.

There are powerful outdoor minorities.

California skiers showed their political strength when the state was persuaded to develop Squaw Valley as the site of the 1960 Winter Olympics at a cost to the taxpayers of sixteen million dollars.

Although naturalists shudder at his depredations, the hunter sometimes aids conservation. Contrary to the impressions of most non-hunters, he is often devoted to nature. The stiff licensing fees that he pays make possible strict policing and usually sound policies of fowl and game conservation.

In deer season, California overflows into that portion of southern Utah known as Dixie. In the 1961 season, by estimates of the Utah Department of Fish and Game, one hundred and sixty-five thousand hunters reduced the Utah deer population by one hundred and fifteen thousand in stiffly regulated hunting. Not quite all the hunters came from California. It is traditional in Dixie to shut down almost every-thing on the opening day of deer season. Local schools go on a three-day holiday, and even in Salt Lake City, two hundred and sixty miles to the northeast, a labor union contract with the Hercules Powder Company insures employees a holiday on the first Monday of deer sea-son. In the mountains between the Dixie towns of Cedar City and Panguitch there is every grade of hunter. Men road-hunt from motor scooters or skin their bucks outside two-bedroom house trailers.

There are far more fishing licenses bought in California than in any other state. The trout and salmon fishing of the Northwest is superb, but the catches of the California fisherman are enviable too. In coastal waters, marlin, albacore and yellowtail are prized sport catches. The California State Department of Fish and Game stocks fresh water streams and lakes with almost fifty million trout and salmon each year. At dawn on opening day of the trout season, it seems possible to walk across vast Crowley Lake, three hundred miles northeast of Los Angeles, atop the solid mass of fishermen's boats. More than thirteen thousand fishermen were present for the opening of the 1961 season there. California fishermen do not mention the good old days. A century ago, pioneers found better salmon, steelhead and rainbow trout fishing than today, but California offered fewer striped bass, shad, brown trout, eastern brook trout, or black bass—many of which have been introduced into California waters from other areas by the Fish and Game Department.

From 1947 to 1960, about thirteen million dollars in state revenue from horse-race parimutuel betting went into projects of the

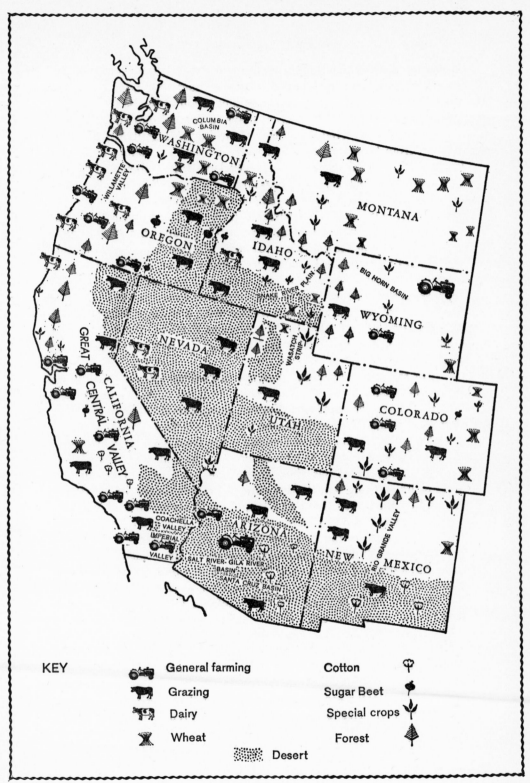

Land Use

Wildlife Conservation Board, which develops fish hatcheries, water-fowl management areas, and provides limited recreation facilities. California has a flair for maintaining separation of funds; some of the revenue received from fun always stays in fun. (From 1933 to 1961, California had received more than four hundred million dollars in revenue from horse racing. Funds were allotted for county fairs, col-leges and universities, and to the general fund; fifty thousand dollars of it was spent for gnat control research, and more than a million dol-lars went to a poultry improvement commission.)

Pleasure boating is big business every week of the year along the West Coast, and marinas along the Southern California coast cannot be built fast enough to provide moorage for the growing pleasure fleet. Marina del Rey, on the Los Angeles County coast, is a giant among marinas. It covers eight hundred acres and has six thousand boat slips, separated by four-lane thoroughfares on two-thousand foot long moles. Part of its cost was underwritten with a thirteen-million-dollar revenue bond issue floated by Los Angeles County. There are three hundred thousand small craft registered in California, one for every seventeen families.

For those who cannot find escape in boating from multi-million-dollar marinas, there is Georgie White. It is her specialty to conduct raft trips down the rapids of Western rivers for amateur naturalists, photographers, and any others who will risk a wetting for the wild joy of looking up into the Grand Canyon walls from a swirling, bobbing bit of rubber. Georgie White became enchanted with the Grand Canyon in 1944, and has since swum one hundred and twenty-five miles of its seething length. She runs the rapids on the Snake River, too, and on the Green River in Utah; she will see more of them now, because the new Glen Canyon Dam on the Colorado River above Grand Canyon has blocked her favorite river route.

Georgie White is a blue-eyed brunette of immense daring, but she is not a product of that older West in which physical courage was commonplace; she discovered the West after working as a comptom-eter operator in New York City's Rockefeller Center. She, too, is a part of the westward tilt.

The excitement of the land in the West is not yet destroyed by the migration of millions—and it need not be. There still is magic in Western land and sky and air and water. It is a prime asset of the region, and Westerners are well aware that it is worth fighting for. The excitement grips any sensitive observer, even at his first contact with it.

My father visited California for the first time when he was eighty-seven. His first glimpse of San Diego as his plane landed seemed to settle a question that had long puzzled him. As we walked away from his plane, his bright gaze roved toward the San Diego harbor and the long sweeping arm of Point Loma. It was sunset. He said he might forgive me for deserting North Carolina.

He sensed immediately that he was in a city unlike any to which he was accustomed. It is part of my father's nature that before he can accept a thing, he must understand it. In California as a visitor, he pursued truth as vigorously as he has from Southern Baptist pulpits all his life. Perhaps in the West, I reasoned, I could meet the test of his probing mind; after all, it had been my home for almost twenty years. But before our first evening had passed, he asked why it does not rain in the summertime in Southern California. I stared at him for a long time before confessing that I had no idea at all. (Weather men, I learned later, do not agree on reasons why storm paths from the north do not reach Southern California in summer. But the coastal temperature inversion is a prime factor.)

As we drove along the coast, he asked why, unlike most of the Atlantic coast, the Pacific coast has cliffs. (Later I got it straight. Half a million years ago, the Pacific lapped inland as far as ten miles from today's beaches. But then the earth of the always turbulent West rose hundreds of feet, forming what geologists call terraces.)

We settled down for a quiet afternoon at a beach. At eighty-seven, my father seemed to deserve a nap. But he was on his feet at the sight of kelp. Wasn't Pacific kelp quite different from Atlantic kelp? (Yes, I was told later at Scripps Institution of Oceanography. It is larger than Atlantic kelp and has floats which bring it to the surface, making it easier to cut for refinement into the emulsifying agents used in ice cream, paints, and surgical styptics.)

Something was missing, he mused later, in the California land of plenty. Why were there so few sea shells? (I had wondered for years, myself. Sea shells are calcium carbonate, a chemist told me patiently, and thus they dissolve more readily in cold water than in warm. The warm Gulf Stream of the Atlantic makes East Coast beaches a haven for shell-hunters. But even off Southern California, ocean temperatures rarely rise above seventy-two degrees.)

Most of my answers came too tardily to interest my father. Quite by accident, I learned that he had dropped in on an oceanographer and got the straight of it before I could. He had recognized the futility of embarrassing his son further.

Part II

CALIFORNIA
CENTER
OF
GRAVITY

7

SOUTHERN CALIFORNIA

The Restless Kind

In 1697 Loreto was the capital of all California. Now it is a dusty and awesomely remote Mexican town of fourteen hundred people on the wilderness peninsula of Baja (Lower) California. Since 1697 not much has happened, really, in Baja California, which has remained a part of Mexico. Settlement has been in what the Spanish and Mexicans called Alta (Upper) California, which Mexico surrendered to the United States in 1848; this is the state of California.

The contrast between the two Californias is indelibly vivid when sensed today from Loreto, which once was the forward outpost of California civilization; by current standards Loreto is an almost inaccessible dot in a vast wasteland. Not far from Loreto lives an Australian-born dentist, a little deaf, who chose to be a recluse in this land. Recently, for the first time in thirty-six years, he drove four hundred miles north—it takes a week over these rocky, rutted trails— to visit what we know as Southern California. He was impressed by the extent of electric lighting, the size and speed of freeways, and the bad coffee.

"Coffee in the States is awful, eh?" he told me. "But I found the people very polite. I was surprised, eh?"

The dentist thinks life must have been better among the primitive Indian tribes of Southern California, before the Spanish explorers, the missionaries, and ten million white men came. "All they did was hunt, fish, make love and sleep under the trees," he said. "They hadn't even discovered the fig leaf. The women spent their time picking fleas out of the men's hair, eh?"

Southern California has managed to forget its Indians, who were not among the brighter tribes, and to remember its Spanish soldiers and missionaries. It was the Jesuit order which established the first California settlement of the white man at Loreto in 1696. From there, in 1769, a crippled and aging Franciscan, Father Junipero Serra, led an expedition north to colonize Alta California. The major difference in the journey that the dentist took two centuries later was that he traveled by jeep. The scenery had changed very little.

Father Serra founded a mission among the Indians to the north at San Diego. That was the beginning of the California of today, for better or for worse. Juan Rodriguez Cabrillo had stepped ashore from his ship in San Diego harbor in 1542, but for two more centuries before the actual settlement of San Diego, California was thought by many to be an island or group of islands. So it is Father Serra who is the hero of Southern California history. Despite an ailing leg, he was a great walker. He was also a dedicated Christian and a man of sturdy principles—though some of the Spanish governors protested that the Franciscans punished the Indians excessively.

Father Serra's San Diego mission was first built on a bluff overlooking the bay; today General Dynamics–Convair sprawls beneath the bluff. Father Serra had trouble promptly with the Indians: soldiers fraternized with naked Indian girls, and Indian braves shot arrows at the soldiers. To minimize friction and to be nearer water, the mission was moved to a hillside in Mission Valley; nearby now is a hub of the Southern California tourist industry known as Hotel Circle. There, Father Serra's mission became the southern anchor of the chain of twenty-one Franciscan missions, each a day's journey by horseback, all the way to Sonoma, north of San Francisco. The missions can be seen today in varying stages of restoration.

Most of the Indians were brought in from desert and hills to live and work for the missions: there were more than twenty thousand of them by 1805. The settlements prospered, just as the South was prospering in those years before the Civil War, and for the same reason: slave labor. The Franciscans tried to convert the Indians, but also they used them to clear and till their fields, build their missions, dig irrigation ditches, herd cattle, and tan hides. Some were assigned as servants to indolent Spanish soldiers. Irked by heavy schedules of work and prayer and by cramped housing, many Indians ran away; if caught, they were flogged.

The San Gabriel Mission once owned seventeen ranches, three thousand Indians, more than twenty-five thousand cattle, two thousand horses, and fifteen thousand sheep. The fathers held the missions not as land grants from the Spanish Crown, but as trustees for the Indian neophytes. In the end, it didn't work out that way.

Mexico won her independence from Spain in 1821. Four years later, California became a territory of the Republic of Mexico. Castilian colonists had moved in on big land grants. Their names, and those of their heirs, are prominent still: Pio Pico, Juan Bandini, José Carillo. When the Mexican governor, Figueroa, began to secularize the missions in 1834, as planned, the Franciscans began to depart. Mexican and Spanish plunderers moved in, some with legal land grants and some without. The Indians fled. By 1845, all the missions had been sold or leased, and the era of the California rancho had begun. The Indians were paid now for their work, but in glass beads and bad booze.

The Mexican War didn't provoke much shooting in Southern California. The *Californio* generals on the Mexican side, Pio Pico in Los Angeles and José Castro in Monterey, fought between themselves, just as Southern Californians and Northern Californians always have done. The American forces, variously under Stockton, Kearny and Fremont, totaled only six hundred men, but it was a force about as large as the Mexican army, finally under a new Pico—General Andrés Pico—which surrendered to the United States. The terms were gentle: Pico was invited to give up his artillery and to promise to obey the laws of the United States. He agreed, and a boulevard in Los Angeles today bears the name of Pico.

Mexico gave up Alta California—that part of it from San Diego northward—in 1848, when the white population of California totaled about fifteen thousand. Mexicans have never quite forgotten their loss. A window in the national military academy at Mexico City shows a map of Mexico as she once was, her border snug against that of Oregon.

Soon came the first of many waves of migration into California, and, in 1850, statehood. That year, when San Diego became a city by law, whales rolled about the harbor in such numbers that a rowboat journey was hazardous. There were ten stores, eighty-eight houses, 2,273 Indians and 544 others of assorted breeding.

Philip Crosthwaite, the first San Diego treasurer, traveled by stage to Sacramento with two hundred dollars in tax money payable to the state. But he drew three hundred dollars in state funds for his travel expenses. State officials admonished him to stay in San Diego thereafter and embezzle the state funds.

In 1866 came Alonzo Horton, who bought one thousand acres encompassing modern downtown San Diego for $265. In 1884, La Jolla was advertised for sale; it was only a scattering of beach shacks.

The Indians found life little better under the rule of the United States than under the Franciscan *padre* or the Spanish *don*. They declined in number from more than eighty thousand in 1850 to fewer than twenty thousand in 1885. Their only revenge was in the heritage of names they gave to Southern California: names like Azusa, Cucamonga, Malibu, Ojai, and Pismo.

◇◇◇

In the high desert of Southern California, a pilot pushed forward the afterburner throttle in his TF106 jet interceptor and pulled up steeply from the long runway of Edwards Air Force Base. Ahead was nothing but blue sky. Behind us, it seemed, there was nothing but thrust. Four minutes later, at forty thousand feet, the pilot pointed toward a green speck on the Mojave Desert below. It was Barstow, a railroad and highway junction town. The trains looked like fallen bobbypins on a buff carpet.

Over the intercom came the pilot's voice: "We'll level out and make a speed run. We're on a west-southwest course that'll put us over the beach at Ventura. Watch the Mach needle. At Mach two, we'll be doing about fourteen hundred miles an hour."

Moving at twenty-three miles a minute, our plane was over the Pacific in less than six minutes. Southern California went from flat ocher desert to green timbered mountains, to rich fertile valleys and then to teeming coastal urban strip. The pilot eased back on the afterburner and we coasted up to fifty thousand feet. Now there was a hint of the curvature of the earth. Los Angeles sparkled and glimmered; from almost ten miles up, this sprawlingest city on earth seemed nestled cozily between the San Gabriel Mountains and the sea. Santa Catalina and the other offshore islands were brown warts on turquoise velvet. Our visibility was clear to the horizons. We saw almost all of Southern California: from Mexico, two hundred miles northward to the Tehachapi Mountains; from the Pacific to where the barren upland Mojave becomes Arizona.

Below us, in the ten counties of this largely inhospitable, arid desert beside an ocean, lived ten million people. Most of them old enough to vote had settled there on purpose. Just out of sight over the horizon to the east was the Colorado, the small, wild, desert river which is funneled off in pipes to sustain these millions.

These ten million have built their towns and cities in a narrow, benign strip between the coastal mountains and the ocean; ninety-four percent of them occupy less than fifteen percent of the land area of Southern California. They have made of that strip an American land that is neither Eastern nor Southern nor Midwestern. It is not even Western, in the conventional sense of easy pace, of dudes or cattle or openness—or any other sense. They have brought everything that is here now except the land and sun and sea and air. They have brought their own countless cultures, their own dreams, griefs, energies, indolences, prejudices and loves. They have shared all these with each other—how they have shared!—discarding and inventing, shouting down, raising up, experimenting endlessly, bustling about interminably, riotously busy both at work and at play. They move around more than any other people on earth; they are the restless kind. They are not the most sophisticated of Americans, but they are among the most vigorous. Their incomparable vitality is euphoric; it is born from an assumption of success which exists because so far their failures are quite dwarfed by their victories. In contrast with the mood of whatever place they left, they revel here in a conviction that anything is worth trying; they assume it will work, because everything else seems to be working. Everything, that is, except the things they haven't thought of trying, a category, unfortunately, which includes some very vital things.

The ten million are not burdened with a sense of regional history. They do not much care what happened here before they came, because so much has been happening since. Not many of them have stopped to look back over their shoulders to seek their bearings, and that, of course, can be their undoing. They are more involved with their environment than any other Americans. They sunbathe, swim, ski, water ski, sail, picnic, ride, hike, skate, fly, sky dive, throw, catch, race, hunt, shoot, fish, dig, plant, prune, pick, barbecue, paint and putter. Despite all this, they are not a part of their environment. They live *on* the land, but they are not *of* the land. This strange anomaly lodges fitfully in the subconscious of many visitors to Southern California. To them, it may imply impermanence, and it is a major reason that this is the most blithely libeled region of America. Hardly anyone seems to belong entirely to Southern California except the cowboy in the foothills and the commercial fisherman in his boat offshore. Even the Indian looks bizarre; he no longer appears at home on the land of which he once was a part.

There are good reasons for this inconsistency. Southern Californians have not been there long. No matter how ardently they deny it, a part of their nature leans toward the more familiar land of their birth; too often, their loyalties and resources can be more quickly drawn to a cause "back home" than to the multiple causes of their new home. They have not learned yet to sense the subtle welcome in dry brown hills as compared with the more obvious charms of cool green streams. Saddest of all, they may not respect the new land on which they live, since they are dominating it so handily. They build islands in their bays, make their harbors deeper and their beaches higher. They bring water from the desert through pipes which unroll like ribbon through chaparral, over wind-blown mountain crags, and down to the edge of the sea. They pare down mountainsides unmercifully for towns and freeways; they use dry lake beds for military aircraft runways and riverbeds for golf courses.

They are fiercely proud of their region, although this trait does not always show. When two San Franciscans pause on Union Square, they are likely to exchange a self-satisfied word or two about their city, but when two Los Angelenos greet each other on Pershing Square, they will rap the traffic or the smog. Southern Californians are most loyal to their land when they are away from it. They are more aware of it in absence than in its presence. When they long to get back to it, they realize—often with real surprise—that it has become home.

One of the most alluring things about Southern California is the image in the minds of its people of what this land can be. Those who do not feel the fire of the image may resort to ridicule; it is easy to deride the young, the eager, and the brash. Lately, Southern California has stopped hearing the ridicule. It is busy. It is not concerned about being accepted. It has been overwhelmingly accepted in a migration unprecedented in volume and velocity in the history of the world. In a sober mood, its leaders are fighting for the interest and support of the new millions by solving the problems of bigness which their coming has caused. Southern California is moving to offset its weaknesses and augment its amenities. It is coming on from behind with a rush like Silky Sullivan, the racehorse which was the darling of the area a few years ago. The question is the same one that the horse's nerve-wracked

Southern California

ARIZONA

NEVADA

SONORA

MEXICO

BAJA CALIFORNIA

Colorado River

95

66

466

91

UNION PACIFIC RWY.

A.T. AND S.F. RWY.

SAN BERNARDINO

MOJAVE DESERT

JOSHUA TREE NAT'L MON.

RIVERSIDE

60

IMPERIAL

Salton Sea

IMPERIAL VALLEY

El Centro

Mexicali

99

Palm Springs

DEATH VALLEY NAT'L MON.

Barstow

91

66

15

San Bernardino

Riverside

395

ANZA BORREGO DESERT STATE PARK

Borrego

SAN DIEGO

80

Tijuana

395

Edwards Air Force Base

6

LOS ANGELES

Pasadena

Fontana

Santa Ana

ORANGE

Long Beach

Newport Beach

Santa Catalina I.

La Jolla

San Diego

101

KERN

Bakersfield

466

TEHACHAPI MTS.

SOUTHERN PACIFIC RWY.

99

A.T. AND S.F. RWY.

VENTURA

Ventura

101

Los Angeles

Channel Islands

CHANNEL ISLANDS NAT'L MON.

SAN LUIS OBISPO

101

Vandenberg Air Force Base

Lompoc

SANTA BARBARA

SOUTHERN

Santa Barbara

Pasadena

Hollywood

LOS ANGELES

Civic Center

Long Beach

Santa Ana

SCALE: 45 MILES TO THE INCH

0   45   90

backers used to ask each other at the rail: has he made his move in time?

The overriding fact of Southern California life is its population growth. In 1950, California population was less than eleven million. Today Northern California alone includes about seven million people, living in forty-eight counties comprising the northern two-thirds of the state. Southern California lies south and east of the state's only east-west mountain barrier, the Tehachapi range. There are ten million people in Southern California, and almost six and a half million of them live in Los Angeles County. Another two million are in adjacent counties which are part of the Los Angeles Basin—an unfortunate name, but one which seems vividly accurate to the night traveler whose jetliner from the East begins to let down over Nevada or Arizona, and glides low across the rim of coastal mountains; with theatrical abruptness, the interminable carpet of lights from the Los Angeles Basin is below and around him.

The other Southern California metropolis is San Diego. This city in the southwest corner of the nation is the third most populous of the West (after Los Angeles and San Francisco), and, in 1960, eighteenth in size in the nation. Its metropolitan area, now far past one million in population, has doubled in size since 1950. It is the largest city in the nation to record that great a rate of growth. San Diego exhibits many of the characteristics of the Southern California region; in a way it is more typical of Southern California than is Los Angeles.

The San Diego population increase in the fifties was almost twice as great as during the previous decade, which encompassed the years of World War II. Thirty thousand dwelling units were built in San Diego in 1959, ranking it fourth among metropolitan areas of the nation that year in homebuilding, behind only New York, Los Angeles and Chicago. Factory employment rose in 1959 to a level three times that of 1949, just before the Korean War. But manufacturing growth has leveled out in San Diego, and now tourism is regarded as the richest potential for immediate economic growth.

San Diego is a classic example of the wave pattern of Southern California growth. There were three years of particularly intensive growth: 1942, when county population increased by about fifty-two thousand, and 1951 and 1959, when the increase was about sixty-six thousand each year. Outbreak of wars and subsequent war jobs explain the figures for 1942 and 1951; the 1959 figure relates to an increase of cold-war job opportunity in San Diego.

Unbelievably, in the wake of such explosive growth, San Diego has remained a pleasant and leisurely city. It glistens under a flood of

sunlight, and the toasted browns of its canyons and mesas form mount-
ings for pampered green lawns, burnt-red tile roofs, and pastel stuccos.
Its bays make abstract swirls of blue, merging with the deeper,
greener hues of the Pacific. The elements seem to have been pasteur-
ized in Southern California, and nature's blandness allows more time
for both play and work. Virtually anything that can be done in water is
done here. The climate and variety of surf and bay waters make
aquatic sports the dominant recreation of the young. There are sixty
miles of beaches in San Diego County alone. The fine natural San
Diego harbor is fourteen miles long. A second bay in mid-city, Mission Bay, is an aquatic playground with thirty-one miles of shoreline
and about two thousand acres of navigable water. Water fun is no false
front for the visitor; it is a way of life here in a land with twelve
months of sun and warmth.

San Diego is remembered by much of the nation either as the
drab and crowded town it was in World War II, when hundreds of
thousands of Americans in uniform saw it for the only time, or imagined in terms of sailing, fishing, swimming and sunning—the way
Southern California looks in the travel advertisements. It is neither.
Magazine photographers who are assigned to translate San Diego to
film soon find they are in for trouble. San Diego has happened so fast
and so spontaneously that no two citizens see their city alike. The
visitor receives wildly conflicting appraisals. For a frantic day or two,
photographers from out of the city are likely to race about from one to
another of the sub-cities of San Diego, along the glistening waterfront,
from great parks and old missions to Navy bases, from missile and aircraft plants to the squalor of the Mexican border. In frustration some
of them find that their best chance to contend with the vastness of the
city and its diverse personality is to shoot with their longest lenses in
every direction from any vantage point. The pictures will be fore-
shortened and they will not look like anything in San Diego—but they
may telescope the layers of San Diego into a perspective that suggests
something true about this strong, fresh, gangling city. Such photographs may show nuclear submarines and water skiiers in the fore-
ground and towering mountains behind the city, or lavish resort hotels
against a backdrop of missile gantries. But that is San Diego.

One gets the feel of the city best near sunset on a bright, warm
day, standing atop Point Loma. The boot-shaped main harbor, inky
velvet at twilight, becomes the main street of the city. It glows red,
white and blue in the lights of the sky line and those of descending
seaplanes or warships and yachts at anchor. The ocean and setting sun
are the backdrop to the west. To the east, sometimes capped with
snow, the Laguna Mountains of the coastal range stand sentinel.

Lights from highways and towns sparkle into infinity along the weaving Pacific Coast toward Los Angeles, more than a hundred miles to the north. Southward, the bold, barren wilderness of Mexico's Baja California fades off in a deceptively gentle azure haze past flat-topped Table Mountain. The San Diego city limits begin at the International Border, across from the dusty Mexican town of Tijuana. They extend thirty miles up the Pacific coast past La Jolla, a sparkling Riviera that has not always been prompt to identify itself as part of San Diego.

San Diego is at the end of the line. Not even that part of Mexico which lies south of San Diego can change that: Baja California is a savagely primitive peninsula almost as long again as California, virtually unpopulated south of the border towns, and separated from the mainland of Mexico by the storm-swept Gulf of California. Its largest towns are at the border—Mexicali and Tijuana. The staggering fact of the dirty, vice-ridden town of Tijuana is that more Americans visit Tijuana than all other foreign cities combined, including London, Paris and Rome: between eight and nine million persons annually. Americans visiting Tijuana are not always charmed by what they find there, but they have been to a foreign country the easy way. The city is a three-hour drive from Los Angeles, twenty minutes from downtown San Diego. At Pamplona, in the time of the bull festival, it is the bulls which stampede through the streets. In Tijuana, on summer Sunday afternoons, it is the *gringos*—pushing their way to bull fights, horse races, shops, bars, or gawking at film stars. It is possible at Tijuana to bet on horses, dogs, cocks (illegally), or people (jai alai is played here).

It is remarkable that more Americans do not find themselves in Tijuana jails. Tequila sells for less than a dollar a bottle. Standards of law and order are relative. The booking sheet at the Tijuana jail carries eight terms applicable to persons arrested while *ebrio*, or drunk. *Ebrio impertinente* is a fairly mild case. *Ebrio indignado* suggests that the prisoner talked back to the cop. *Ebrio escandaloso* carries the intimation of a full-scale spectacle. *Ebrio rinas* means he was fighting, and *ebrio lesiones* means he won. *Ebrio voltado* is a pass-out case—the tequila won. *Ebrio orinando en la calle* means the prisoner couldn't find his way to a men's room in time. Yet the most despicable of all, by Mexican standards, is *ebrio insultos al gobierno*—literally, drunk insulting the government.

The easy availability of marijuana and heroin in Tijuana is a grimmer menace. Narcotics are cheap and plentiful. The value in the United States of narcotics seized at the California-Mexico border each year is measured in hundreds of thousands of dollars. Customs agents concede that they are halting only a fraction of the flow at border gates.

(It is easy for smugglers to fly from small airstrips in Mexico and rendezvous in lonely areas of the Southern California desert.) Customs cannot halt all narcotics smuggling; it would require examination of more than eight million persons each year at the San Diego port of entry alone.

Southern California addicts find Tijuana wondrously accessible. The freeway winds southward to the border like ribbon candy. The greater tragedy is that many teenagers, taking courage from tequila in rowdy Tijuana saloons, have been introduced to narcotics in Mexico. There has been honest discord over a solution. A series of Pulitzer Prize winning articles in the *Los Angeles Times* in 1959, by Gene Sherman, urged closing the border unless joint action by the governments was taken. The State Department, studying the larger picture, has offered no such drastic solutions. There have been bilateral efforts to study and police the problem, including those of Governor Pat Brown of California, but they have been little more than a gesture. Open, cultivated fields of marijuana and opium poppies are not rare in parts of Mexico. In a country so poor, law enforcement is an imperfect instrument. In 1962, the United States Government allotted funds to the Mexican government in a highly practical attempt to get at the source of the narcotics flow.

At the United States Embassy in Mexico City, a student of Mexican affairs concluded my interview with him on border vice problems by quoting Sister Juana Inez de la Cruz, a gentle and eloquent Mexican poet of the sixteenth century: "Who is to blame? She who sins for pay, or he who pays for sin?" He did not believe closing the border between the two nations would deprive Americans of vice, or of narcotics. Instead, it would be regarded by Mexico as an affront, one which the United States cannot afford in Latin America today.

Amid all the furor over Mexican narcotics traffic, one powerful and effective procedure has proven itself: San Diego police authorities maintain a twenty-four hour police blockade at the border to prevent unescorted juveniles from going into Mexico. One member of a Congressional investigating committee charged angrily that the blockade was unconstitutional. Indeed it may be, but it has not been put to the test since it went into force in 1958. In its first four years, more than 25,000 juveniles were turned back, and more than a thousand grateful parents wrote their thanks to the San Diego police. In most cases, their teenage children had been stopped, their credentials checked, and the parents notified by letter that the youths had been turned back from the Mexican border. With appalling regularity, parents respond with shock to the news; their children, they often write, had told them they were spending the night at friends' homes nearby.

Prostitution flourishes openly in Tijuana, even in the saloons of Avenida Revolución, its main street. San Diegans are less grim about this vice. Because of it, San Diego—a city with a Navy population of fifty to one hundred thousand men—is free of organized prostitution. The Navy seems to accept the compromise gracefully. When the Navy operated a free prophylactic station at the border for personnel returning to the United States, a total of forty seven hundred men used its services in a single weekend. In the face of paternal consternation, the Navy abandoned this service, but there is no reason to suspect it is less needed than before.

With its scandals tucked neatly away in another country, however close, San Diego presents the image of a town of unpretentious Midwestern tastes, now sprawling outward and shooting skyward into the shape of a city. It is molded by an oncoming wave of sophistication, and it is becoming a center of research and exotic industry. The belligerent vigor of adolescence has taken hold in this no longer placid city of hills and bays, but it is tempered by an innate conservatism that prevails against every onrush of conformity and commercialism.

Yet San Diego ranks as the Western city most transformed by the newest wave of settlers. San Diego has changed even its mind. In suddenly becoming a metropolitan area of more than a million people, San Diego has accepted the missile, the atom, the laboratory, new campuses, and even a casual California sophistication—a commodity which World War II visitors thought foreign to its nature. Now, giving the lie to an old San Diego wheeze that you must pay dearly for the climate, has come a renaissance of attitude.

"For half a century," explains James S. Copley, a forty-five-year-old publisher who owns both daily newspapers, "there were opposing factions that came to be known in local jargon as 'Smokestacks versus Geraniums.' The issue faded with the arrival of jets, missiles, and nuclear reactors. Growth had come. There seemed to be no time to discuss whether it was wanted. Our duty clearly was to help make the growth solid and constructive."

In the pathology of Western civics, the patient has passed the crisis when majorities begin to pile up at the polls for vital bond issues. That has happened in San Diego. The role of the newspapers in guiding San Diego through its adolescence has been subtle but dramatic. Copley has been quietly in the wings as the San Diego stage has made room for new civic buildings, downtown redevelopment, major league football, new theaters, multimillion-dollar additions to its Fine Arts Gallery, development of freeways, sewers and water, and the new University of California campus on the Pacific cliffs overlooking La Jolla.

Copley's position is unique: as well as the San Diego newspapers, he owns eight dailies which surround metropolitan Los Angeles like a horseshoe. The Copley newspapers—there are five more in Illinois—are notably successful. Copley is a youthful, visionary publisher who sensed a Western trend and concentrated on it; his newspapers call themselves "home town newspapers." Local autonomy is stressed. His editorial policy strives to provide Southern Californians with what they direly need: the means to interpret, day by day, their astonishing environment. At the same time, Copley looks outward. He lends trouble-shooting executives to Latin American newspapers, produces newspaper-trade films available in Spanish, and has launched the most successful recent United States news syndicate, notable for thorough Latin American coverage. The future of the West and of the United States, he believes, is irrevocably involved with the emergence of Latin America.

Copley exemplifies the Western phenomenon: at first glance, a dedicated regionalist; on closer examination, a man who already has projected the West and himself into the position of leadership that the Westerner, by his nature, believes destiny demands.

Young men of stature are no rarity in San Diego. Bob Wilson, at forty-five, won his sixth term as congressman in 1962. New fortunes in electronics have been built by youngsters like Jonathan Edwards and Walter East, both forty, and Charles Salik, thirty-seven, who has three electronics investment firms of international stature. There are uncompromising but successful young architects and decorators in the same age bracket such as Robert Mosher, Henry Hester, and Gerald Jerome, whose work is of national significance. None of them is San Diego born.

The emphasis in San Diego is on youth; its overwhelming presence is obvious everywhere. The birth rate has exceeded the national average since 1940; the death rate is down to a startling 6.8 per one thousand, against a national average of 9.3. Even if the westward tilt were to cease, San Diego would grow sharply; the ratio of births to deaths is 3.6, against a national rate of 2.5. A recently built community, known as Cabrillo Heights, has a street named Haveteur Way. Its phonetic pronunciation is a bad pun, but it is related to census findings that the women of Cabrillo Heights led the city in fertility ratio—meaning, in this case, that each one thousand women between fifteen and forty-four had 1,325 children under five. The city is completing new schools at a rate of almost one each month. Long gone are

the days when San Diego was oriented to the retired; the median age
hovers below thirty.

Not long ago San Diego was young, and not certain she wanted
to grow up. When World War II brought its wave of migrants,
many of the established San Diegans drew their shutters and hoped
that people would go away. They didn't. New waves surged over the
widespread San Diego shores, across her raw brown hills, and into her
canyons. People came from all the states of the nation. Mostly they
were young and eager. They built a fresh, clean city around the
quaint town that once found its *raison d'etre* in Navy, tuna, tourism
and retirement.

Today San Diego is deeply involved in the scientific and industrial explosion of the West. She is yet too young as a city to have any
sharp-limned personality. Her old leaders are submerged by the onrush. Her new leaders materialize slowly and painfully, as her people
discover what goals they have in common. The transplanted cultural
roots of other cities and states are being nurtured as gently as those of
the hibiscus and bougainvillaea in patios.

Nature has blessed this city with the country's most benign year-
round climate, and it is largely smog free. But climate is merely the
most obvious answer to her growth. "People who are intelligent enjoy
living in a sunny, comfortable climate just as much as those who
aren't," said J. R. Dempsey, forty, president of General Dynamics–
Astronautics. This is San Diego's largest factory, a sleek and smokeless complex from which the Atlas missile emerged.

"Creative people come to us because of the excitement of our
project," he has said. "We need skills and brains, people who can think.
In San Diego particularly, you begin to see a concentration of this sort.
There is no raw material here. People who want to live here and
enjoy the climate must live by their wits. Hand in glove with the
California advance in technology is the development of our educational
system. The University of California at San Diego" (the new campus
on the Pacific bluffs overlooking La Jolla) "some day will be one of
the great universities. General Atomic, nearby, is one of the greatest
nuclear labs in the world today. I never mention climate when I try
to bring a man west. If there is one key regional factor, it is the sense
of freedom here."

Yet climate cannot be set aside. San Diego has even less temperature variation than Los Angeles, is generally free of smog, and is
equally sunny. Any city in which climate is dominant may lack the
driving vitality of cities where the living is not so easy. Those to whom
climate is all-important may be more prone to the wasteful search of
creature comforts than those who shovel snow from sidewalks. In San

Diego, there are some who fear that the God-given balminess of the city may condemn it to mediocrity. It is a sign of struggling maturity that such civic self-appraisal is prevalent in board rooms and at cocktail parties within the city from the beaches of La Jolla to the hillsides of Mount Helix, twenty miles distant.

The in-migration of thousands of the new breed like General Dynamics' Dempsey is a catalyst in San Diego and all over Southern California. The balance of social and economic power is passing into the hands of the young, the daring, the eager, and the informed. For them there are not the usual obstacles of entrenchment by older generations.

Civic indecision plagued San Diego in the years between World War II and 1960. There were new freeways, new shopping centers, new restaurants, new entertainment, but the community feeling was not present. There was nothing to make the woman in Alvarado Estates feel any kinship to the woman in Muirlands Village. A feeling of vagueness was in the air, a lack of direction. It lay heavy over Civic Center, where elected leaders seemed to be treading water.

The natives grew restive. More and more of the newcomers were from larger cities and from university campuses, and they sought the things to which many had been accustomed: better art and music, better buildings, better restaurants, better city planning. At the same time they welcomed amenities already present in San Diego to which many of them had been less accustomed: graft-free local government, benign climate, leisurely pace, a virtual absence of slums and blatant poverty. It was not difficult to conceive of a union of the new values to those already existing.

That dream is common today in San Diego, and to a notable extent throughout Southern California. It is not without basis, but whether it is realized depends on factors still imponderable:

How strong is the desire? Do enough of these new Southern Californians want that new world enough to demand the best schools and universities, the finest leaders, progressive urban planning by experts, and to pay the stiff taxes and approve the continued weighty bond issues that these will require? Will the amenities of this favored region be destroyed by the coming of those who seek them? The newcomers luxuriate in the sense of space which still exists in Southern California, but which decreases with each citrus-grove-turned-sub-division. They thrive on the unprecedented mobility which they enjoy, but can they control the traffic jams and smog which their mobility produces?

Some answers are being suggested daily. In the decades ahead the newspapers of Southern California will testify to the writhings of a generation which has barely sensed the deadly seriousness of its battle. There are many who believe that if California is to realize its stature, it will need a renaissance both in leadership and in the populace itself. The motivations of Californians must be more cohesive. More of them must sense some destiny. There are many who think it cannot happen; the good, easy life of California, they reason, is anathema to any mass sense of destiny. But the point is that California may be the *only* place in the nation where such a renaissance *can* happen.

There is much hope, and it is in the people. Sharp individuality and a lack of inhibition distinguish them. In San Diego a onetime member of the Al Capone gang has become a leader in Parent-Teacher Association work and a respected businessman. There is also a liquor dealer who some years ago was a priest in Chicago. There are farmers turned stock brokers, and bookkeepers turned ranchers. The mood of rebellion is contagious. It seeps from personal lives into community affairs and business. When it is channeled into constructive experimentation, it has usually been productive.

Southern California has, above all, a feeling of freedom and future. The feeling is shared by millions up and down this coastal urban strip which planners like to call a *megalopolis*, because it has one more syllable than *megapolis;* like Southern California, the word is bigger. The story of San Diego is one that is echoed in many of the other, smaller urban centers of Southern California.

Orange County is next in size after San Diego. In 1950 it was a placid citrus suburb of Los Angeles, not even tracted by the Census Bureau. Now eight hundred thousand people live here. The county is the fastest growing county of more than four hundred thousand in the nation; it is growing twice as fast even as Los Angeles County. Anaheim, once a gag word with Jack Benny—along with Azusa and Cucamonga—is the home now of more than a hundred thousand people. Some commute to Los Angeles, some work nearby in burgeoning industrial strips, and others choose to live here because it is sunny and warm and near the boating mecca of Balboa and Newport Bay. Some are here because they have jobs at Orange County's most famed enclave: Disneyland. A 1961 survey of Orange County showed that industry had risen five times above the 1950 level, buying power had quadrupled, and automobile ownership had almost tripled. Between those years, Orange County drew eighteen of every one hundred persons moving into Southern California: more than two hundred and fifty each day. Since 1952, it has exceeded both Los Angeles and San Diego in percentage of real estate sales. All that is declining in Orange County is oranges; they were still a twenty-eight-million-dollar crop in 1960, but more than half of the county's acreage in groves has been hacked out to make room for people.

On the northern side of the Los Angeles Basin, toward Santa Barbara, there is more open country, and room still for truck farming and lemon groves in the rich coastal valleys near Oxnard and Ventura.

Santa Barbara, near the northern outposts of Southern California, has done its best to avoid the explosive pattern of the two hundred miles of coast which lie between it and Mexico. It is the center of the romanticized, pseudo-Spanish tradition, preserved in architecture, in pace, and in its annual Old Spanish Days—an August fiesta of dancing, parades, and music, with a heavy accent on horsemanship. The Santa Barbara version of California's conquistador era is a close cousin of the Southerner's image of the ante-bellum South. Here the past is misted over in a montage of lace *mantillas*, flat-topped black hats, flaring red sashes, and stomping stallions.

Except for its lack of a seaport and its clear-cut antipathy for industry, Santa Barbara might have been invaded as decisively as San Diego. Its climate is superb; northwesterly breezes blow Los Angeles smog back toward its origin. The city is surrounded by great estates. For more than forty years, its destiny seemed to be in the hands of Pearl Chase, a woman of fanatic dedication to civic beauty and conservation. The Santa Barbara County Courthouse, an architectural masterpiece dedicated in 1929, more resembles an elaborate Spanish palace than a public building. The temper of the city, established in large part by Miss Chase and her disciples, has lured wealthy Midwesterners and Easterners into sumptuous retirement. For this reason Los Angelenos once were prone to refer irreverently to Santa Barbara as a cemetery-by-the-sea.

But of late Santa Barbara has found itself in what Bill Becker has described in the New York *Times* as the "mission-and-missile belt: the only section of the West where one can wind down unhurried roads past old-world missions to watch rockets of the new world take off for the unchartered Worlds of Tomorrow." Not far to the north are the major West Coast missile bases of both the Navy and the Air Force: Point Arguello and Vandenberg Air Force Base.

Lompoc, a tiny town of five thousand in 1950, lies in rolling fields of flowers from which seeds are extracted. Lompoc expected a placid future, until it found itself squarely between Point Arguello and Vandenberg. Its population has tripled since 1950 and it has called in professional planners to help solve its sudden civic crises. Its city council, which a decade ago conducted its business in an hour, often works until midnight.

Of deeper significance to Santa Barbara than its neighbors in missilery are the scientific and intellectual frontiers now being explored in the city. Research people have flocked to Santa Barbara largely because of the quality which Publisher Thomas M. Storke of the *Santa Barbara News-Press* emphasizes in calling his city "the ideal home of man." There are research divisions of General Motors, Raytheon, General Electric's TEMPO (Technical Military Planning Operation), and a host of smaller companies. On a sunny hilltop estate, Dr. Robert M. Hutchins leads the work of the Center for the Study of Democratic Institutions. At Goleta, on the northern fringe of Santa Barbara, a campus of the University of California has slowly been converted from a play school to a center of serious study.

Rising sharply to the east of Santa Barbara, and running irregularly southward, are the coastal mountains. These are the mountains to which Southern Californians go for big trees, high lakes, skiing—and to fight forest fires. These are the mountains that provide snow-capped backgrounds for tourists' pictures of orange groves and ocean swimmers. The Coast Range is a low mountain range compared to the Sierra Nevada, which runs parallel to it for much of the length of California. But the Sierra Nevada, on the eastern edge of California, turns and falters, then dies out in the furnace of the Southern California desert. The Southern Californian goes north from his one-third of the state when he wants trout fishing, hunting, or hiking in the Sierras. One big thing that the Southern Californian does not have is numerous big mountains. San Gorgonio, 11,485 feet, is its highest peak. Next is San Jacinto, 10,381 feet high; beneath its precipitous escarpment huddles Palm Springs.

Once one leaves the populous coastal strip of Southern California, he is in a different land. Thirty million acres of inland Southern California—ninety percent of the land area of its ten counties—have fewer than six hundred thousand of its ten million residents. It has become the vogue to refer to this vast desert area as the Inland Empire, a phrase long used for a somewhat similar region in the Northwest. It is arid but dotted with irrigated oases. The higher desert to the north is the Mojave. But the best known of the oases is Palm Springs, in the area of low desert to the south known as the Colorado Desert.

Palm Springs—and the strip of resorts which tail southeastward from it—is the most conspicuous flowering of all that is vulgar and futile in the Southern California philosophy. It is the Miami Beach of the West. To run away from it, but to retain their desert and their golf, other Southern Californians have concentrated their interest more recently on Palm Desert, an area fifteen miles south. Here is the golfing center which, for the moment, reigns as the crown prince of the fifteen golf clubs in the Palm Springs area: Eldorado, among whose residents is Dwight D. Eisenhower. Some of "the village's" other favorite visitors have been Harry Truman, Konrad Adenauer, Joseph Kennedy, David McDonald, Eleanor Roosevelt, and an infinite list of those made wealthy by almost any means, especially the entertainment business. (Mrs. Harpo Marx is a member of the school board.) Golf has become the Palm Springs bonanza, partly because it offers both built-in status symbols and the opportunity of real estate speculation with homesites along the fairways.

The weather, of course, has something to do with it. So long as the wind is calm, Palm Springs offers superb low desert warmth through the winter. On sizzling summer afternoons, the town drops early into the shadow of the San Jacinto range. It does not matter; everything is air conditioned, and there is a swimming pool for every two and three-quarters registered voters.

City Manager Daniel Wagner protested the results of the official United States census of Palm Springs in 1960 as low, although the figure (13,468) almost doubled that of 1950. "It's probably the best we can do if they insist on taking the census in April," he sighed. The community actually varies from a summer population as low as eighty-five hundred to a bustling fifty thousand on late winter or early spring weekends. "Within a few years we will have two hundred thousand people here," said Mayor Frank Bogert, puffing on a long cigar. He came to Palm Springs thirty-five years ago, when the town was a dusty village and the Agua Caliente Indians—who were granted checkerboard sections of Palm Springs in 1891—did not dream they would have per capita land assets by 1962 of about a third of a million dollars.

Southward from Palm Springs, desert resorts tend to become less flamboyant and often vastly more relaxing. La Quinta is favored by aristocratic regulars from the East. So is Borrego Valley, a placid resort community in an equally spectacular desert setting in San Diego's back country, around a spur of the San Jacintos from Palm Springs.

The resort business dominates this part of the Southern California desert, from it also comes ninety percent of the nation's date production. Date groves are common from Palm Springs south to Indio. On the Mexican border, through Imperial Valley, there are citrus groves, vineyards, truck gardens and cotton fields, many of them below sea level.

Here too is the Salton Sea, thirty-four miles long and about ten miles wide, an inland lake two hundred and thirty five feet below sea level and surrounded by barren flat desert. It is a prehistoric sink which was filled in 1905 by a whimsical, wandering floodtide of the Colorado River, setting off an epic two-year battle by the Southern Pacific Railroad to close the break and save the Imperial Valley from flooding. This freak of nature has been regarded by sportsmen and land speculators as a magnificent mistake. The level of the sea has remained fairly constant in a balance between evaporation and drainage from irrigated farmlands. The Salton Sea has been the site of a recent real estate boom, complete with yacht clubs in the searing desert. California authorities halted one runaway aspect of the boom. Midsummer temperatures of 120° and higher discouraged customers, and so they were being flown over the area on free charter flights from cities hundreds of miles distant to choose their lots by radio communication with a jeep and driver on the sites below.

In the higher desert to the north, the Mojave, only a few scattered, sun-parched towns break the sand-and-stone composure. From this desert come thirty-three minerals with an annual value of close to one hundred million dollars, including most of the nation's boron and much of its cement, both taken from open pits. Eight major military installations dot the Mojave, most of them involved with aviation and missilery. To the far northeast is Death Valley, the hottest and lowest point in the nation. But nothing except cheap distillation of ocean water can trigger a population explosion in this Inland Empire.

However, the coastal strip of Southern California shows few signs of slowing in growth. The Southern California of 1990, widely heralded as an urban area extending two hundred miles from the Mexican border to Santa Barbara, is visualized easily on any Sunday afternoon drive up Pacific Highway from San Diego. One must press the accelerator toward the floor to keep his place in traffic. The white lettering on a black metal sign at roadside reads *El Camino Real*. The sun to the left filters through the eucalyptus trees from over the Pacific, making their graceful trunks a blurring row of giant toothpicks.

Unlawful To Litter Highway.

In the coastal towns, blond, tanned boys and girls pick their way across El Camino Real—it is Pacific Highway now—through four lanes of traffic, carrying surfboards, rafts and towels homeward from a day in the sun beside the surf. Statistics prove they are taller and healthier than the youth of regions less favored by nature.

Citrus all Kinds $3.50.

In the station wagon that has been in the next lane for five miles, a mother calming her infant with a bottle turns and swats an older boy in the back seat. Juvenile crime in California has been rising steadily. The observer wonders if there is too much discipline in the back seat and not enough at home.

Tacos. Mexican and American Food and Surfboards.

Here at Leucadia, the California Highway Department cut down stately old eucalyptus trees from the center island because too many drivers were ramming into them. Now, drivers along El Camino Real have unlimited access to each other.

Visit Mission San Luis Rey Four Miles East.

Here are the world's largest poinsettia fields. The stalks are tall and green awaiting the flood of winter scarlet. The sun sinks behind a bank of coastal fog to the left, etching the murky gray with a silver fringe. The fog pushes up the rolling valleys to the right and the driver must close his car windows.

Follow the Swallows to El Adobe Capistrano.

The coastal cliff rises sharply at the right, north of San Clemente, leaving room only for four lanes of El Camino Real, the Santa Fe Railway, and one row of oceanfront homes. A new subdivision clings to a hillside; one wonders where California would be today without the intrepid, succulent ice plant. Its thick green watery fingers are plunged into place along the naked cliffs as fast as the earth moving machines depart, with the reassuring certainty that they will take root and hold back the earth from freeway and subdivision—usually.

Stay Right for Disneyland.

If the driver turns left he is in a sea of midget auto racers being trailered northward after a day of racing. Guiding each is a mightier chariot of the road with a young man at the wheel and a young lady close at his side.

Café Frankenstein Coffee House.

The homes sweep down the cliffs to the coves of Laguna Beach on the left. On the right, a mammoth ceramic gentleman with white ceramic beard beckons travelers to a pottery shack. The homes on the hills almost encircle the town, twinkling in the purple twilight haze, and the sharp tang of salt air drifts into the car.

Then it is dark and the driver speeds through the bright ocean of headlights and ruby sea of taillights, through odors of oil fields and dairy fields, and swings into the Santa Ana Freeway. Six lanes become eight. Cars roll like marbles into the slot of the freeway interchange at the center of Los Angeles and out onto the Hollywood Freeway.

The white letters loom out again: *El Camino Real*. Less than two centuries ago, it was a day's journey by horse between each mission, but the traveler has spanned four of them in three leisurely hours, driving through the heart of the new Western frontier.

8

LOS ANGELES

The Strong New Wave

"We find ourselves suddenly threatened by hordes of Yankee immigrants . . . whose progress we cannot arrest. . . . They are cultivating farms, establishing vineyards, erecting mills, sawing up lumber, building workshops, and doing a thousand other things which seem natural to them."

The plaintive voice is that of Governor Pio Pico, a reasonable man (but on the Mexican side), the year is 1847, and the place is Los Angeles.

Statehood came to California soon after Pico's words. The Census Bureau moved into California for the first time in 1850 and found Los Angeles to have only 1,610 inhabitants, mostly Mexican and Indian. And the climate was better then than now. But already Los Angeles was aiming high. Its county limits that year included everything between San Diego and Santa Barbara: thirty-four thousand square miles.

The Indian village called Yang-na had disappeared, and Los

Angeles, a town with a bad reputation, even in infancy, was rising on the site. Criminals banished from tough mining towns could find refuge in Los Angeles; wine from nearby vineyards was a major source of commerce; by 1870, there was a saloon in Los Angeles for every fifty persons.

Two seedless orange trees from Brazil were introduced in Southern California in 1873; they have had millions of descendants. The fame of Southern California citrus spread after it took first prize at the New Orleans International Exposition in 1884–85 and gave Easterners a suggestion of what the new California gold might be.

Even in the mid-1880's the city was trying to prove its sophistication to outsiders. The *Los Angeles Times* felt obliged to announce: "Los Angeles people do not carry arms, Indians are a curiosity, the G-string is not a common article of apparel here, and Los Angeles has three good hotels, twenty-seven churches, and three hundred and fifty telephone subscribers."

The Southern Pacific extended its line southward from San Francisco in 1876. The boom began when the Santa Fe Railway, cross-country into Los Angeles, was finished in 1886. The rate war which followed between the two carriers was a dinger: on March 6, 1887, the Santa Fe was selling tickets between the Missouri Valley and Southern California for one dollar.

The first migrants to come in the wave that followed were different from those Los Angeles had known. They were family people, usually well-to-do, such as Judge John Wesley North, a friend of Lincoln's who founded the town of Riverside, and Albert and Alfred Smiley, twins of some national distinction, who built a showplace at Redlands. But close behind the solid citizens came the sharpies and the boosters. In 1886, land speculation was as epidemic as the black plague. Subdivisions and cities that could have accommodated ten million people sprang up. Real estate transactions in Los Angeles County in 1887 totaled one hundred million dollars. In 1888 the bubble burst. Soon chaparral hid the speculators' stakes, and banks confined their loans to downtown property.

Then, with both the Southern Pacific and the Santa Fe underwriting California novels, magazines, and newspaper campaigns, the gospel of Southern California was beamed toward the Midwest. A special train ("California on Wheels") toured for two years with displays of mammoth fruits and vegetables, a brass band, and Los Angeles hucksters armed with booster pamphlets. This brought a wave of sober and God-fearing citizens to the area, but it also marked the start of a gaudy, half-century era of promotion.

Now came tycoons who would dominate Southern California for

decades: Chandler, Otis, Doheny, Spreckels, Huntington, Clark, Sherman, Garland. In 1892, Edward L. Doheny and Charles A. Canfield brought in the first Los Angeles oil well. That started another boom. In the next year, citrus growers formed their first coöperative, the forerunner of the powerful California Fruit Growers Exchange. In 1899, Los Angeles began to build breakwaters for its great unnatural harbor. By 1900, the population of the city, after boom and bust and boom, passed one hundred thousand, and Los Angeles was the most ballyhooed city in America.

But pious Midwesterners were in command. Gambling houses were closed, saloons were hemmed in, and churches thrived. By 1922, San Francisco was to vote against Prohibition, but Los Angeles to approve it overwhelmingly.

Eastern capital shied away briefly from San Francisco after its 1906 earthquake and fire, but Los Angeles thrived. Abbot Kinney, who had grown rich making Sweet Caporal cigarettes, put a fleet of gondolas on man-made canals in a beach subdivision he called Venice, and again a real estate boom flourished and burst.

Low wages and open shop conditions set the stage for the bloody union war in Los Angeles from 1907 to 1910. The *Los Angeles Times*, led by Harrison Gray Otis and supported by the Merchants and Manufacturers Association, was struck virtually from 1890 to 1910. Its battle for the open shop in Los Angeles became a national issue. On the night of October 1, 1910, the *Times* building was dynamited; twenty-one died.

Late in 1911, the trial began of three men: John J. McNamara, secretary of the International Association of Bridge and Structural Iron Workers; his brother, James B. McNamara; and Ortie McManigal, a professional pro-labor saboteur. Clarence Darrow led the defense, assisted by a corps of lawyers which included Job Harriman, who was on the verge of being elected mayor of Los Angeles on the Socialist ticket. With tension high all over the world, after seven weeks during which a jury had not even been impaneled, the McNamaras pleaded guilty to the dynamiting. Both the labor movement and Darrow were discredited, Harriman lost the election, and Los Angeles for three more decades kept its role as "the Gibraltar of the open shop." But McManigal, who had turned prosecution witness, later became a watchman in the Los Angeles County Hall of Records. When he retired after twelve years, county supervisors awarded him a scroll for faithful service.

In 1913 Los Angeles reached across the desert to Owens Valley with a two-hundred-and-thirty-three-mile aqueduct and brought water into the nearby San Fernando Valley. The farmers of the Owens

Valley, now almost waterless, believed they were defrauded of their water rights; but land speculators in San Fernando Valley, in league with the Owens Valley Aqueduct sponsors, grew rich. San Fernando was annexed to the city two years later.

For a few years Los Angeles had water to grow on, but by the mid-twenties, it needed more. With adjacent cities it formed the Metropolitan Water District and brought water from Parker Dam, on the Colorado River below Hoover Dam, through an aqueduct system five hundred and twenty miles long. The pipes pass through forty-four tunnels, including a thirteen-mile bore through the San Jacinto Mountains, and require a pump lift of 1,617 feet.

The Signal Hill oil boom began in 1921, Long Beach Harbor opened in 1925—and Warner Brothers made *Jazz Singer*, the first all-talkie movie, in 1928. Aimee Semple McPherson's Four Square Gospel enraptured the restless and unhappy transients of Los Angeles. Sister Aimee was a showman, but the newspapers upstaged her after she disappeared in 1926; she had not been kidnapped, as she insisted, but was off on an earthly tryst.

By 1930, Los Angeles had passed the million mark and ranked as the nation's fifth largest city. During the Great Boom of the Twenties, more than two million moved to California—over half of them into Los Angeles County. It was the first migration of the automobile age, but it was only the start for Los Angeles. There were booms in oil and movies, but J. B. Priestly wrote: "California will be a silent desert again. It is all as impermanent and brittle as a reel of film."

More than a hundred lost their lives in the Long Beach earthquake on March 10, 1933. At the nadir of the depression, 129,000 Los Angeles County families were on relief. But by 1937, Los Angeles had come back strong; it ranked fifth among industrial counties of the nation, and led in oil refining, aircraft manufacturing, and secondary auto assembly. In 1942, Henry Kaiser won a hundred-million-dollar loan from the Reconstruction Finance Corporation for a steel mill at Fontana, the first major steel mill of the West.

And after Pearl Harbor, as the nation turned its attention to the Pacific, Los Angeles began an era in which for the first time it would become more like other American cities than different from them. Henceforth its thronging people would be busy, as Governor Pio Pico had said in quiet desperation a century before, doing a thousand things which seemed natural to them.

New York and Chicago each have personalities. Los Angeles, the nation's third city, has had three or four—and none of them has taken. The outside world has remained an image or two behind in its concept of Los Angeles. The world should be forgiven, and so should Los Angeles; no other city has been so transformed by successive waves of migrants.

Not until about 1960 did the qualitative nature of the most recent wave of migrants become reassuringly clear and the earnest renaissance begin. It was high time; Los Angeles has become more interested in quality than in quantity.

Since its beginning, Los Angeles has been almost at the mercy of its migrants. From the turn of the century until after the end of World War II, through years of inexorable growth, Los Angeles came close to doubling in population during each of several decades. But each surge of new settlers came from progressively lower social and economic strata.

The great aircraft boom which began during World War II in Los Angeles set a pattern for the establishment in Southern California of footloose industries not bound to mineral deposits, abundant water or highly populated centers. The aircraft industry had brought laborers from the South and Midwest to work as welders and riveters. But the postwar trend toward electronics and space industries brought highly skilled, better-educated migrants to Los Angeles. California grew into a research center, with Los Angeles as its hub. As more of the intellectual elite settled in Los Angeles, pressures grew to supplement the amenities that nature has provided.

Some Los Angelenos who migrated west years ago have the air of zombies today. Their particular civilization lies two or three strata below the Los Angeles surface; they are out of circulation, and of them it can be said justly that they are vegetating in the sunshine. Others have grown with the city and the times, and are leavening this energetic renaissance with wisdom and a wealth of regional experience. But the primary impetus for the new Los Angeles stems from the newcomer, just as each stratum of the Los Angeles past has been formed by its wave of newcomers. These strata are clearly visible in the Los Angeles environment.

The farmhouse set in the cool green citrus forest of San Bernardino or Riverside is surrounded by subdivisions and shopping centers. Commuters look down into the grove from the overpass of a nearby freeway.

An igloo-shaped ice cream palace is toppled with one quick

shove of a bulldozer as steel girders are unloaded for a new apartment or office building.

Cavernous film studios which once held vast sets for movie spectaculars are partitioned into smaller stages for television film series; in the cafeteria on the studio lot lounge cowpokes, marshals and bad men, where once there paraded dancing girls and dapper dandies. Along the Sunset Strip, once the glamour showplace of Western America, the biggest names on marquees now are those of stars performing at Las Vegas hotels; the hotels lease spectacular signboard marquees along the Strip to advertise current shows more than two hundred miles away. At Schwab's, islands of toothpaste, hair sprays, and deodorants seem about to inundate the soda fountain where, film legend insists, stars are discovered.

In older, more central areas, there are interminable miles of dark, musty neo-Spanish stucco homes with tiny lawns, geraniums, and an orange tree or two. On the periphery of the city, these give way to more interminable miles of ranch houses, with their patio barbecues and picture windows. Dreary blocks of one-story shops are replaced with shopping centers and their acres of cars.

All over the city, the weird nightmarish shapes of the temples of bizarre cults are disappearing in a rash of first-rate church architecture. A colony of chic designers' studios has sprung up on Beverly Boulevard, and the show-place offices of architects give tang to the landscape.

Main Street, a sleazy skid row, is now giving way to a well-designed Civic Center. Pershing Square, the mecca of the dissolute and disenchanted, was lifted long enough for the installation of underground parking. Shabby depressed areas near the beach at Santa Monica and in the Bunker Hill area of the center city are on their way to becoming showpieces of urban renewal.

Not everything that is being done is outstanding, but it is better. There is always much more that needs to be done.

Everything important about Los Angeles today is in some way involved with bigness and newness. This is easily confirmed by spectacular statistics, of which Los Angeles always has had more than its share. But these figures have ceased to hold any meaning. Only a statistician senses the massiveness suggested by the word *trillion;* the terms in which the growth and spread of Los Angeles have been expressed have become trite to all but those most intimately involved.

To cope with Los Angeles in customary ways is out of the question, so the world reacts to the city by mocking its peculiarities. We laugh at its faddists. We slander its energies. We scoff at its bigness. We joke at its smog. We challenge its integrity. We babble away about its obvious and superficial externals—and pretend that these are the city. They are not. They are manifestations, but of what? Sociologists and anthropologists who have made careers of studying Los Angeles concede that they have only scratched its surface. The city will not hold still for their kind of study.

Los Angeles is the center of gravity in the westward tilt. It is highly urbanized, seething with change, surging with strength. It also is capable of being utterly ridiculous—but it is steadily becoming less so. Its leaders are a responsible and mature breed these days. Its current wave of newcomers is the most urbane and discriminating which has ever come to the city. Los Angeles is underrated. It has come alive with vitality. You may not care to love Los Angeles, but if you have the temerity to know the city, you will respect it.

In population, Los Angeles is larger than the next three largest Western cities combined, and larger than any Western state except California. The three counties of Los Angeles, Orange, and San Diego have added more population in each recent year than the total 1960 population of Nevada, yet Nevada has ranked first or second in percentage as the fastest-growing state in the nation. With increasing trepidation, Los Angeles County receives more than five hundred new residents each day.

Who are these people? Why have they come to Los Angeles? What are they doing? Seeking answers, I have interviewed hundreds of its citizens, pored over its newspapers, walked its streets, and studied a wildly diverse proliferation of writings about the city— which have less coherence than any writings I have read about any city of any era. The three primary challenges to its newspapers are indicative of reasons one cannot "understand" Los Angeles:

Size is a problem. The land area of the city of Los Angeles is the largest of any city in the world: about four hundred and sixty square miles. The coverage of its metropolitan newspapers encompasses an almost unbroken cluster of cities and towns—more than seventy of them in Los Angeles County itself. Such patterns foster the growth of more parochial interests and smaller community dailies—twenty-three of them in Los Angeles County.

Movement is a problem. Los Angelenos not only travel more, to work and to play, but they move their places of residence more often than the people of any other city. Their ties to a block or a town are not as great as those in more established regions. As their jobs change from one side of the Los Angeles Basin to another, as their economic status improves or as they have children (or children grow up and leave the home), they are likely to move.

Growth presents problems. When fifteen to twenty thousand

people move into a city each month, an honest editor must ask himself regularly if he knows anything about the newcomers. The old Los Angeles *Examiner* began a series of interviews with new families to find why they came to the city, but it was abandoned prematurely because the answers became repetitive: climate, job opportunity, year-round recreation, year-round gardening. (Some of those interviewed mentioned good schools, the built-ins of Southern California tract homes, and the absence of mosquitos.) A Sunday series offered ten dollars to readers for letters on the question: "Is there a Southern California way of life?" That died in a hurry, too; anyone who can answer that question deserves more than ten dollars. I asked one city editor how he covered his churning, sprawling area of ten million people. He pointed toward a map divided into zones and reeled off the number of staff reporters or stringers in each area who reported to him. (At that time this particular newspaper had only one man assigned to cover the San Fernando Valley, an area of close to a million people.)

The city editor spoke of pages made over to include regional news of various zones into which papers were distributed. "All we can hope is to keep up with running stories like water, weather, growth, and traffic, and watch standard news sources like the courts and police stations and public offices," he said, shaking his head. "Sometimes we wonder who they all are, and if nobody knows what they're thinking out there, or what they're doing when they're not killing each other and going to court. We know very little of what we'd like to know about Los Angeles."

His final sentence is an apt disclaimer for any comment on Los Angeles. But there are many canards about the city. More important, there are vital ingredients of the new Los Angeles personality which are not widely recognized.

Raymond Chandler called Los Angeles a "tired old whore." But Dr. Frank Baxter calls it the only city in which one is likely to see at one time, as he did, three Nobel Prize winners pushing their carts through a supermarket. In *The Natives Are Restless*, Cynthia Lindsay wrote that the garish Clifton's Cafeteria near Pershing Square was a refuge of togetherness for citizens who had come from somewhere else —which includes most Los Angelenos. Days after publication of her book, Clifton's closed for lack of enough togetherness to make the business pay. Near the site now rise large office buildings.

Los Angeles is known for Iowa State Picnics. Long Beach has been called "Iowa-By-The-Sea." But not even at the height of the Los Angeles effort to induce immigration from the Midwest in the early decades of the century was Iowa the leading source of new

Angelenos. The top states outside of the West, then as now, were New York and Illinois; Iowans just made more fuss about their picnics.

The spectrum of exotic cults has faded rapidly in Los Angeles. Once, ninety-six diverse stairways to heaven were available on the Los Angeles cultist market. The assortment now is sharply less varied, and the demand less. Waves of Utopia seekers, most of them elderly, washed up on the California shores in the 1930's. But today the median age, around thirty, conforms to the national average. Crackpot schemes have little chance on the ballot.

Los Angeles offers convincing statistics that now its smog is hardly thicker or more frequent than that of half a dozen other large American cities. The city was the first to try to control smog, in a campaign climaxed by the 1960 statewide bill requiring the gradual but compulsory installation (by 1965) of anti-smog devices for automobile exhausts. Los Angeles has spent twenty-five million dollars on smog control in the last fifteen years, reducing by about twenty-five percent the discharge of waste from production and consumption of petroleum products, which cause eighty percent of the air pollution.

Los Angeles is the only city of its size to take shape after the invention of the motor car. As a direct result, it has sprawled horizontally. The sprawl has had dire consequences, but some Los Angeles miseries are being minimized by a vertical building trend. Since 1958, more apartments have been built in Los Angeles than single dwellings. In 1952, apartment construction was only nineteen percent of the Los Angeles residential total; by 1961, it had soared to sixty-seven percent. Suburbia is losing its enchantment. Long noted for its preponderance of single dwelling homes, Los Angeles has almost as many apartment units now as homes.

The city's battle to keep pace with its cars, the greatest concentration in the world, is epic. There is one motor vehicle in Los Angeles for every two persons; in New York City, there is one for every six. Los Angeles County alone has more automobiles than any of forty-three states. More than six million gallons of gasoline are burned each day in the Los Angeles Basin. Since World War II began, one and one-quarter billion dollars has been spent on freeways in the three counties of Los Angeles, Orange, and Ventura. The present peak-hour jams, which slow traffic to a crawl, do not exist on the rosy drawing boards of the future.

California has no rapid transit; even its bus and streetcar systems receive declining patronage. The state's cars carry an average of only 1.7 passengers, but their role in transportation is increasing steadily. Both San Francisco and Los Angeles have been probing rapid-transit plans, but it will require increasingly staunch efforts to invoke them. In 1959 the California legislature approved a twenty-year free-way construction program which will add twelve thousand miles of freeway at a cost of more than ten billion dollars. The system will swallow up almost half a million acres of California land. By 1980, two percent of California land will be committed to the automobile.

Los Angeles is no longer a ballyhoo city. Harold Wright, its veteran Chamber of Commerce manager, told me that "there is no merit to any more people coming out here." The concern of Los Angeles leaders today is not to grow, but to cope with problems of traffic, air pollution, water and urban renewal—crises of a magnitude faced by no other metropolis. The startling thing is that Angelenos exude total confidence that they will solve their problems.

Men like Dr. Lee DuBridge, president of the California Institute of Technology at Pasadena, serve attentively as members of the board of directors of the Los Angeles Chamber of Commerce. "Our people in Los Angeles are of a steadily rising caliber," Dr. DuBridge said. "Here is the pathway of the future. Here are opportunities for im-proving, for building up a better community, a better world. You com-bine that with our particular type of beauty, and you find a special quality about the West Coast that is different from what you get in the East or Middle West. It is not yet built. There is still a chance for changing things. This country is young and flexible."

Los Angeles is led by men like Harold C. McClellan, whose paint business left him time to help lure the Dodgers away from Brooklyn, to serve as president of the National Association of Manu-facturers and as a trustee of Occidental College at Los Angeles. He is a former Chamber of Commerce president, but his is not the voice of a booster.

"I was born here and sold newspapers up and down Lamar Street right outside my office door. The thing that excites me most is that Los Angeles has begun to develop an enlightened look, not merely one of competence or efficiency. The first thing I would talk about is not our tremendous growth in business and industry, in employment and research, but in education. This is the forerunner of advance in any city or country. There is a spirit of enlightenment springing primarily from education and from improved liaison be-tween education and industry. I foresee Los Angeles as the center in an area of greater unity, from Arizona to the Northwest, a growing community of spirit born out of necessity and improved communica-tions, a rapidly growing population, expanding economy and closer trade."

Norman Chandler, president of the Los Angeles *Times*, talks of the city in terms of cultural maturity. The new Los Angeles Music Center and Art Center have been promoted aggressively by Chandler and his family and the *Times*.

"Los Angeles people think now in terms of cultural horizons that make a city great," Chandler told me. "Years ago they wanted no part of such things. But our new cultural assets draw better people from all over the world to make Southern California their permanent home. The population center of California moved long ago from San Francisco to Los Angeles. San Francisco still has the reputation of being the outstanding cultural community in the West. It does have more cultural assets, but that feeling is fast moving to the South as we mature. Los Angeles is not the most beautiful city in the world. Someday it will become more beautiful than it is today. But there is a sense of excitement here as great as any in the world."

Even the skyline of Los Angeles is assuming character. A building-height limit imposed after the Long Beach earthquake has been relaxed. The sixteen miles of Wilshire Boulevard from downtown to the Pacific at Santa Monica is in some ways as stirring a spectacle of construction as is Manhattan. New York goes up; Los Angeles, even with its new higher buildings, still goes out. At the fringe of Beverly Hills in West Los Angeles, on what once was the back lot at Twentieth Century–Fox studios, is rising a city within a city: Century City, an urban development which, its backers insist, will overshadow even Pittsburgh's Golden Triangle in scope and cost as the largest development ever undertaken by private capital. Century City is a skyscraper city with a twelve-year construction schedule. "There is nowhere left to go in Los Angeles but up," said one of its architects, Welton Becket, in a statement which until very recently would have brought only ridicule in this land of wide open spaces.

The Pacific Ocean has put a halt to the spillover of Los Angeles to the south and west. Its most notable direction of growth in the past decade has been to the north of the Santa Monica Mountains— part of the range is known as the Hollywood Hills—into the San Fernando Valley, still within the city limits. In the valley, about twenty-two miles long and ten miles wide, lie more than twenty communities, many with separate identities but hazy boundaries. It is primarily a suburban residential area, but there are footloose-industry plants dealing in rocket engine development, space research, electronics and atomic energy. More than half of the homes and plants in the valley have been built within the past ten years, and the population is about six times greater than twenty years ago. The homes are larger than the average for the city, and swimming pools are more numerous than elsewhere; so are the homes of movie stars, and so are horses. Most economic indices for the city of Los Angeles rank San Fernando Valley second or third, behind Beverly Hills—Westwood and Santa Monica. The valley has another distinction; it is the geographic center of population of California—a fact which suggests the dominance of Southern California in population. San Fernando now is the home of almost one million people; only eight cities in the nation have larger populations than that of this valley.

More than two and a half million people live within Los Angeles's four hundred and sixty square miles. But street signs often are the only warning to the stranger that he has moved from the city itself into one of the other seventy-two cities of Los Angeles County. Within the county are almost six and a half million people. The metropolitan sprawl of the Los Angeles Basin encompasses Long Beach, an aircraft, oil and shipping center with a population of more than a third of a million. The standard metropolitan area population of Los Angeles—Long Beach is greater than that of Chicago and second only to metropolitan New York. Also within Los Angeles County are Glendale, Pasadena, and Torrance, each with more than one hundred thousand residents.

The multiplicity of incorporated towns and cities within Los Angeles County complicates government services and area planning. Some are single-purpose cities. Dairy Valley was incorporated by dairymen in self-defense against encroaching subdivisions. So were two other towns in adjacent Orange County: Cypress and Dairyland. They are not cities at all but protective societies for cows. Such phenomena have led to drastic planning by men like Milton Breivogel, the Los Angeles County regional planning director. He is a soft-spoken, conciliatory man who came to Los Angeles in 1941 from Wisconsin and is working now on the assumption that Los Angeles County can assimilate another four million people (raising it past the ten million mark) without destroying the present environment.

One little corner of Breivogel's beat is the East San Gabriel Valley, an area of two hundred square miles, about as large as Chicago. "We have determined, on the basis of developing densities," Breivogel said calmly, "that this area ultimately will have a population of about one million two hundred and fifty thousand people. We are developing a land-use plan for the valley which sets aside enough land for industry so that people employed there can live in the valley. The same thing will be true of commercial centers of all types. With rare exceptions, the needs of the million two hundred and fifty thousand people will be satisfied in that area. Instead of traveling ten or twenty miles to work or to shop, they may travel two."

Will it work? Already thirteen cities in the East San Gabriel

Valley are planning together with Breivogel; highway and freeway systems are being integrated. There is support from the citizens. As might be expected by now, downtown Los Angeles businessmen do not protest such diversionary tactics.

Such foresight has worked before. To Breivogel, the most re-markable trait of Los Angeles citizens is their willingness to sacrifice personal plans when they interfere with the awesome community momentum. "They come to commission meetings all on fire," he has said, "and they usually leave pretty much satisfied that while what we are doing may inhibit their projects, we are doing something de-sirable for the community."

Breivogel's worst weeks were in 1953, when Antelope Valley, in the north desert area of Los Angeles County, began to experience a chaotic boom; the jet test centers of Palmdale and Edwards Air Force Base were burgeoning. County supervisors passed an emergency ordi-nance freezing valley zoning to agriculture only. Breivogel brought on an extra staff to develop a master plan for orderly growth.

"The first reaction was violent," he recalled. "But after several meetings, they went along. Within two years we had a plan for twenty-two hundred square miles of land. People agree now that it was the best thing that could have happened."

"Don't you ever view anything with alarm?" I asked.

"Oh, sure. These tremendous population increases. I wonder what it is going to be like and if we are doing the right thing. What we are doing today will determine the pattern of Los Angeles twenty years from now, whether it works or not."

But this public servant, one of the many whose hand is on the throttle of America's runaway metropolis, exudes that classic confi-dence of an honest man with four aces, a state of euphoria which applies today to most Angelenos.

If it were only a matter of prosperity under the sun, Los Angeles would rank as a roaring success. Since 1947, the city has hurdled Pittsburgh and Detroit to become the third-ranking United States manufacturing city. It will probably move Chicago out of second place by 1967. There are even warning signals that San Francisco is losing some of its corporate muscle to Los Angeles. Among the two hundred largest United States industrial corporations, as listed in the *Fortune Directory* for 1962, four are in San Francisco, three in Oakland and one in San Jose—a total of eight in the Bay Area. In the Los Angeles Basin there are twelve. Among the top five hundred, nineteen are in the Los Angeles Basin and fifteen in the Bay Area.

Metropolitan Los Angeles accounts for forty-three percent of all manufacturing in the eleven Western states. It is the nation's second largest retail trade center. Industrial expansion and capital investment in new plants average about eighteen million dollars a month. A well-designed seventy-million dollar air terminal has enhanced Los Angeles's position as a gateway to the Pacific. Import-export trade through the adjacent Los Angeles and Long Beach harbors exceeded $1.2 billion in 1961; their passenger traffic and cargo tonnage surpassed that of San Francisco, and ranked second to that of New York.

As a headquarters city, Los Angeles has an impressive roster. Metropolitan Los Angeles has periodically led the nation in new home construction and total volume of building construction. It ranks second to metropolitan New York in total employment, personal income, effective buying income, retail sales, and telephones in use. It follows New York and Chicago in manufacturing employment, wholesale trade and bank deposits. The heart of Los Angeles industry is in national defense, but the proportion has been declining steadily—even though as much as seventy percent of Air Force funds spent on military space programs have gone into Southern California industry.

The pattern of Los Angeles growth was emerging clearly in 1962. Business and industry are moving into suburban locations, but headquarters agencies are congregating in the central city. The new stadium at Chavez Ravine is near downtown. An axis of new construction lies between the Civic Center and a cultural-recreational area including the Sports Arena (site of the Democratic National Convention in 1960) and the adjacent museums, the Coliseum, and the campus of the University of Southern California.

Civic Center is a two-hundred-and-twenty-eight-acre complex in the central city with thirteen major buildings and four more under construction in 1962. It is the largest grouping of public buildings in any American city except Washington. In it is a twenty-three-million-dollar Music Center, due for completion in 1963, whose white marble columns and glass lobby will be a rejuvenating addition both to the architectural façade of the city and to its cultural ego. Civic Center has been dominated by the thirty-two story City Hall, built in 1928 and long a Los Angeles landmark. Until the 1960's it represented one of the few exceptions to the old one-hundred-and-fifty-foot height limit imposed because of past earthquakes.

Future buildings at Civic Center include a seventeen-story headquarters for the Los Angeles Department of Water and Power ($26 million), a Federal Building (with a $27 million Congressional appropriation), and a County Men's Detention Center ($13,630,000). Recent buildings in the downtown area house Union Oil and Signal Oil headquarters, and include the Tishman and Southern Counties

Gas Company buildings. A California Mart center is under construction, and there are scores of others.

Almost in the shadow of City Hall, private developers are investing the first of an estimated quarter of a billion dollars in rebuilding a 136-acre slum known as Bunker Hill. Tower apartments will rise in Bunker Hill for six to eight thousand residents in a walk-to-work location; many of them will be employed in office buildings and hotels which are planned for Bunker Hill.

A new freeway loop completed in 1962 around downtown Los Angeles has helped to rejuvenate the center city as a headquarters area. In 1953, thirty minutes driving in central Los Angeles took one about twelve miles; by 1962, a driver's range within half an hour had risen to about twenty miles—except during the peak hours of commuter traffic. The freeways work. Only because of them can Los Angeles residents continue to be the most mobile people on earth. Such movement is made necessary by Los Angeles's horizontal development as a city of one-family homes.

In a strange way, the freeways contribute to a sense of roots, an asset assumed to be in short supply in the city. Harold Wright, who has spent most of his life residing in South Pasadena, said: "My roots in Los Angeles now are spread over an area forty by seventy-five miles. People from the East don't understand it. Within that area are my family, my clubs and other organizations I belong to, and close personal friends who may live thirty miles away but whom I see regularly. South Pasadena is a self-contained, self-satisfied little community where a man feels he belongs to a body of people, helps raise money for charity, and cheers the high school football team. For those who both live and work there, such a feeling can remain. Recently I moved to an adjacent town, San Marino, where people eat and sleep and leave each morning on the freeway for God knows where. It is more impersonal than the same suburb would have been twenty-five years ago before the freeway era. But my roots are spread over the whole Los Angeles Basin, and I don't feel dispossessed. All over Los Angeles, people of like background think and act together. Even older, more cohesive cities have a hard time doing the things Los Angeles has done as a city, despite its sprawl and its diversities of background."

There is rising resentment throughout California of the philosophy of freeway development, which was facilitated by the Collier-Burns Act passed by the California Legislature in 1947. This act marked the birth of the massive freeway system of California and its powerful hierarchy in the state Division of Highways.

San Franciscans are notably anti-freeway. County supervisors there were blocking plans in 1962 for a seven-mile freeway which would have brought one hundred and seventy-three million dollars in state funds to the city. There is bitter resentment of the Embarcadero Freeway, which rims the downtown waterfront at an elevation which impinges on the view of the bay. Sacramento was protesting in 1962 because a freeway route would destroy historic buildings.

Angelenos, by contrast, realize they have scant alternative to freeway development. There has been organized opposition in Glendale and Malibu, but little has come of it. San Diego is fortunate: its excellent freeways are being built ahead of traffic congestion rather than afterwards; they seem better planned and less destructive of neighborhoods than those of other cities.

Several years ago a state highway engineer, Jacob Dekema, made one of the most explicit statements of freeway philosophy: "We find out where people are coming from and where they're going. Then we draw a straight line, and that's where we try to build a freeway. Of course, it's surprising how many people don't know where they're going." Something of volatile concern is likely to lie in the path of any straight line drawn in California, and that is where the furor usually starts. More recently, this same engineer, Dekema, made a more cautious summary of freeway philosophy: "We just try to sneak these freeways through town with as little disruption as possible." Wallace Stegner of Stanford refers to the California Highway Commission as "having nobody to control it, too much money, too much power, and an engineering mentality." Some citizens are concentrating on lobbying for more tasteful landscaping and screening of freeways.

More pungent criticism can be leveled toward the freeway autocracy in California and its seeming disregard for esthetics. But the simple truth is that the engineers have kept traffic moving in the state. Motorists—both Californians and visitors—have praise for most of the freeways being built, especially those between cities. Freeways reduce fatality rates by two-thirds and accidents by one-half, as contrasted to other rural state highways. They shorten distances and conserve time. They lower maintenance costs. By 1970, there will be twelve and a half million motor vehicles in California, and by 1980 about seventeen million. As James Mussatti, former general manager of the California Chamber of Commerce, put it: "This is not the time to throw 'monkey wrenches' into the program of freeway construction."

Instead, most Californians are learning to live with freeways. California Highway Patrol studies revealed a startling statistic: a car in a crowded left-hand freeway lane, moving fifteen miles per hour slower than the rest of traffic, usually will cause stop-and-go tie-ups ten minutes and five miles behind it. Warned the Los Angeles *Times:* "If a slow driver does choose the freeway, his civic duty is to step on the gas."

Freeway traffic in Los Angeles has led to a lore of its own. Some freeways there now handle more than two hundred thousand vehicles each day. Harrison Salisbury, the New York *Times* reporter, went West some years ago to write about Los Angeles freeways. He almost dismissed his entire series in one sentence: "I have seen the future, and it doesn't work." This is a first impression less frequently heard today than five years ago. Yet visiting drivers unaccustomed to moving on and off freeways have been known to hire taxicabs—not to ride in but to lead them through the freeway maze.

A highway patrolman pulled over to a freeway shoulder once to investigate a parked car with an Iowa license plate. In it sat a visitor, stark sober but unnerved and seeking to regain his composure. The patrolman nodded understandingly. "Would you mind," he asked, "if I sat down and joined you for a while?"

A woman driver turned too sharply at an intersection in Beverly Hills and ran over the left foot of a policeman who was directing traffic. A shrill plea from his whistle brought her to a stop. Helpfully, she flipped into reverse and backed toward the officer. An anguished cry rose up. "Now you got the other one," he roared.

One loyal citizen telephoned police headquarters to report a traffic jam. "Are you close enough to see what's causing the trouble?" the inspector asked. There was a moment of silence, and then the officer got his answer in a strange, tight voice. "Automobiles," the citizen said, and hung up.

One Los Angeles driver ran his car up on a freeway divider and could not drive away; his wheels were off the pavement. Ignored by thousands of passing cars, he greeted a motorcycle officer gratefully, but later testified that the officer roared off after telling him, "Get off the way you got on!" He finally was towed from the divider after mounting the top of his car and making a distress flag of his shirt.

The frequent and grim desperation of the motorist in Southern California sometimes goes out of control. Two New Jersey youths, driving south toward San Diego in 1961 on the Pacific Highway, felt that their car was being crowded by one driven by a Los Angeles man in an adjacent lane. At Oceanside, they stopped, pulled out a rifle, and shot and killed the California driver.

One issue in the balance during this present Los Angeles renaissance is its moral reputation. The city has been indicted over the years both as a reincarnation of the Bible Belt and as a world capital of moral obfuscation and moral imbecility. Los Angeles is capable of seeming to be blatantly anything, but it is certainly at neither of these moral extremes. It conforms to fewer established patterns of behavior than most cities, but there is no evidence that its median morality is higher or lower than that of the nation as a whole.

A University of California professor at Berkeley, a San Franciscan at heart, told me in vivid terms that Los Angeles is the most licentious city in the world, despite what he referred to as "its Bible-pounding fundamentalists." He regarded Paris, when contrasted to Los Angeles, as staid. The evidence he cited, when challenged, was a scene he had witnessed as he drove one afternoon at sixty miles an hour along a Los Angeles freeway. In a car in the next lane—a hot rod with a front seat he remembered as being covered in a leopard-skin fabric —a blond girl was enthusiastically involved in a sexual ritual with the driver which did not require his active participation, but which seemed more than likely to divert his attention from the hazards of the freeway. The scene does radiate a certain decadence, but to draw conclusions of the moral fiber of six and a half million people from it is unscientific. It reminded me of a night when I arrived at a Mexico City party, full of the story of how my taxicab had been delayed by a gun-battle between two natives in the streets of the city. A wise old professor from the University of Mexico listened to my story and shook his head sadly. "I have lived in this city for seventy-two years," he said softly, "and I have hoped from my youth to witness such a spectacle."

But in crime, as in so much else, California leads the nation. The 1960 crime index for metropolitan Los Angeles showed a higher rate in almost every major category than that for any other American city except Las Vegas. The crime rate in Los Angeles has increased at a disturbingly sharp rate: by some comparisons it doubled in the decade between 1950 and 1960. Experts tend to agree that this is because Los Angeles attracts criminals—for the same general reasons that it attracts new residents. Its high crime rate does not prove that it is an immoral city. Most Los Angeles people are as law-abiding as the average. California law enforcement standards are far above the national average, and the moral climate in which Los Angeles police operate is more strict than that even in San Francisco, a city with a sharply lower incidence of reported crime.

Part of the Los Angeles crime rate is blamed on the proximity of Las Vegas, where syndicate crime may not be in control but certainly is in evidence. Crimes involving narcotics are high, partly because Mexico is so close. Police Chief William Parker continually pleads for more law-enforcement officers, but already Los Angeles has a higher proportion of police in relation to its population than most cities. Their operations are made more difficult by the same three factors that complicate many phases of Los Angeles life: area, growth, and mobility.

One trouble spot in the Los Angeles battle against organized crime is Gardena, a Los Angeles suburb which has been the home of six poker clubs grossing more than five million dollars each year. Gardena is a city built of cards. It has stood firm for twenty-five years despite the huffing and puffing of thousands who deplore its major industry. To poker players, the funniest joke in California is that stud poker is gambling, but that draw poker is not. This notion has persisted since 1937, when a card shark discovered that draw poker was not specifically outlawed in California statutes. That fluke in the law, sustained that year by a state attorney general, permits the Gardena clubs to function on a local option basis. Three times the State Assembly has passed a bill to outlaw poker clubs, but the bills always have died in the upper house. They have survived three challenges at the polls in Gardena, although by decreasing pluralities, and in the latest test, in the November elections of 1962, county voters rejected a statute which would have wiped out card rooms throughout the county, including those of Gardena.

There are back-street poker clubs in several California towns; but in Gardena, half-million-dollar luxury clubs operate every day of the year, except Christmas, from 10 A.M. to 4 A.M. Each Gardena club has thirty-five to forty tables seating eight players. The stakes range upward from a dime. Most players wait their turns for seats at tables where the opening bet is one dollar or two dollars and the maximum bet is two dollars or four dollars. A girl collects the house percentage from each player every half hour. At the one-dollar-two-dollar table, it costs two cents a minute to play. There is not much idle banter, and a slow player soon may find himself alone at his table.

The lists of part-owners in these Gardena poker palaces include dozens of names from many parts of the West. Las Vegas and Reno names are prominent among them, and many Gardena citizens feel that their low tax rate (eighty cents per $100) and their handsome youth center are not adequate enough rewards to justify the clubs.

Police Chief Parker of Los Angeles once testified that ten ex-convicts and underworld figures are involved in Gardena gambling. In 1960, a bomb exploded outside the Rainbow Club. In 1950, an attorney named Samuel Rummel was ambushed and killed outside his Laurel Canyon home; police noted that he was a mouthpiece for Gardena gamblers. In 1942, a police officer was shot in a holdup at a Gardena card room, and fatally injured his attacker before dying.

In a club like the Normandie, the only suggestion of such sordid shenanigans is in the careful stares of oversized security officers. To the left of the entrance is a darkened television lounge, where players wait their turn to be paged—by initials only—when a place opens at a table. There is no bar. Signs warn that minors and liquor are equally unwelcome. But there are bars close by, and in the men's room I saw two players trading sips from a whisky bottle. There is a small restaurant with good food, reasonably priced. Waitresses bring coffee and snacks to the players at the tables.

I once took a turn at a two-dollar-limit table. A chip girl sold me ten dollars worth of chips—twenty-five-cent chips for antes, and one-dollar chips for bets. It was the least congenial card game I've ever played. At my right was a pale man in his forties who had been playing for seven hours and had lost eighty dollars. There were two men who appeared to be in their seventies. The other players were women in their forties or fifties, and at least half of the three hundred players seated in the big room were older women. They took their poker seriously. One of the women at my table, who was winning, asked me twice if I could possibly play faster. Once, when I drew one card to a flush and a winning hand, she called over a house man to protest that I had turned over my hand too soon. I had, indeed. But the house ruled that I still held the winning hand. She picked up her chips and stalked away.

"The old bag is a grouch," muttered one of the older men as he dealt. "But you ought to watch the game closer."

At the end of an hour I was even. I stood and picked up my chips gratefully. No one at the table looked up as I left. A house man signaled another player to my seat. The pale man at my right was still losing. He yawned and ordered coffee. It was 1 A.M.

The Gardena poker palaces wear an affluent look, but it is not cheering to look closely at their inhabitants. It is easy to associate with their tense faces the images many Gardena citizens associate with this principal civic industry: broken homes, lost jobs, and suicides.

Hollywood has its own westward tilt: television.

The movie studios, spread across Los Angeles from Culver City to Van Nuys, are busy with television. About eighty percent of the entertainment work in Hollywood today is for television. Far more network shows originate in Los Angeles than in New York; and television budgets in Los Angeles now exceed half a billion dollars each year. Almost all the major film studios are turning out television footage. Paramount is renting studio space to television producers. Universal-

International sold its studio in 1959 to Music Corporation of America and rents back a corner of the lot.

The new production aristocracy of Hollywood is led by the Music Corporation of America, which was formed forty years ago as a talent agency. Now it is a giant in television production, and has announced plans for three new fourteen-story office buildings on the old Universal-International lot, from where it proposes to "revitalize the film industry" with a foray into movie production. Despite antitrust action by the Justice Department, which resulted in divorcement of its talent agency operations, MCA prospers; in the 1962–63 network television season, programs produced by MCA accounted for one-sixth of all prime evening time on the three networks.

Box-office revenue from motion pictures shown in theaters is about $1.3 billion annually, compared with a peak of $1.5 billion in the final years of the old Hollywood—before television, and before major studios were divorced from ownership of theaters by government decree in 1948. There were as many as seven hundred movies made a year then; today the number is below three hundred—and almost half of these are made overseas. Runaway production, a fiscal device to avert payment of United States taxes and to utilize frozen overseas assets, has caused considerable unemployment among the one-time royalty of the industry. Rome, London and Tokyo are ahead of Hollywood in movie production.

But as the saying goes in Hollywood today, for a place that is supposedly dead, one can find a lot of life. It is an era when salaries are higher and movies more risqué than ever, but stars more folksy. At dinner in Chasen's, one night in 1962, Marlon Brando was being decidedly untemperamental; a calm and dispassionate colloquy on his difficulties with the press left him strangely placid at the end of two hours. Over on North Rexford Drive, Sam Marx was back from making a low-budget feature in Rome and involved again in the weekly card games with his neighbor Ira Gershwin, who has become one of the nation's leading art collectors. Nostalgia seems a trifle painful to them when they talk of old times and old friends such as the pretty twelve-year-old from around the corner, Elizabeth Taylor, who got her first part in *Lassie Come Home*. But on Academy Award nights, Hollywood still manages a flashback to the wide-eyed days of old— even though the ceremonies are no longer in Hollywood but at Santa Monica Civic Auditorium. Parsons and Hopper make it sound about the same as ever, and a new host of television columnists inhabit the Hollywood scene. Perhaps it is symbolic that one of the surest places to catch sight of a Hollywood celebrity is on one of the non-stop jets that wing between Los Angeles and New York in less than five hours.

It is only a rare film star who wins admittance to the Los Angeles Country Club, which is old-line Los Angeles still; and old-line Los Angeles, although it cannot look back very many generations, is capable of a casual kind of hauteur which is as assured today as the hauteur of Back Bay or Main Line. The Los Angeles aristocracy is dynamic, creative, prosperous, and confident. It relishes intercourse with the community of learned men who are bringing new stature to Los Angeles, and with scientists, architects and industrialists who have cast their lot with the West.

There is a surge of attention toward the arts; Los Angeles is moving forward rapidly with its symphony, its theater, and its art collections. The nation's greatest boom in the art market is occurring in Los Angeles; there is more serious money in art collecting in Los Angeles than in any other American city except New York. The city still is refreshingly unpretentious in its approach to the arts. In this it holds a clear advantage over the other cultural stronghold of the West, San Francisco. It is not too soon to hope that the two cultures of the two great Western cities—one in its ascendancy and the other in grave danger of decline—can find fresh and exciting alliances of effort which will give culture a full share in the robustness and vitality of the westward tilt.

Perhaps the canards which have most damaged the Los Angeles ego are those like Frank Lloyd Wright's jibe of the tilted continent, which bore more truth three decades ago than now. Another cliché of that era warned that those coming to Southern California should not bring with them anything which could not be taken back on the Santa Fe's *Chief*. But those days are gone. The new Los Angeles will not be beat.

"There is a feeling now in Los Angeles," says Harold Wright, "that you don't have to crash a fully-armed citadel of people, that everybody can come out here and find his place and, by God, then he can do it. Some of the newcomers could have done it elsewhere, but Los Angeles gives them the psychological push. It emancipates them."

To Henry Dreyfuss, the industrial designer, who commutes between offices in Manhattan and Pasadena, there is much to be said both for New York's "knowledgeable realm of *know-how*," and for California's "zestful climate of *why-not*."

A lovely image designed by the Los Angeles Chamber of Commerce, and labeled "Destination '70," expresses ten goals of Southern Californians: adequate jobs, rapid transit, clean air, adequate water, good government, improved traffic flow, better education, crime control, area-wide planning, and improved cultural and recreational life. It is significant that the Los Angeles Chamber of Commerce today is probably the most influential of any city in the nation, and that it has the support of its city to a greater extent than any other. It has an almost incredible record of having achieved its past goals.

Right or wrong, a great deal of the nation's thinking is being done today in Los Angeles, and inevitably a larger share of it will be done there. In science, education, business and industry, and in the art of living, patterns are being set in Los Angeles which are being followed elsewhere. It will be fortunate for all the nation if the new personality of Los Angeles now emerging proves to be a brilliant one.

9

SAN FRANCISCO

Narcissus of the West

The name of the town was changed from Yerba Buena to San Francisco in 1847, when eight hundred people lived beside the Golden Gate. Twenty years later, much of the nation had come to regard the town as a cultural rival of Boston, and a center of financial manipulation second only to New York. It was gold that did it.

In 1848 a thousand-ton sidewheeler, *California*, sailed from New York for the Pacific Coast. There were cabins for one hundred passengers, but none was aboard. Yet when the *California* anchored at Panama in January, 1849, hundreds fought frenziedly for passage to San Francisco. While the ship rounded Cape Horn, gold had been discovered at Sutter's Mill.

Between 1850 and 1854, one hundred and sixty fast clipper ships were built in the East for Pacific Coast commerce. Yet in those same years, San Francisco Bay became a graveyard of abandoned ships. Their crews had deserted to hunt gold.

Samuel Brannan, a renegade Mormon elder, had arrived in the

Bay area in 1846 and taken charge. He set up the first San Francisco newspaper, *California Star*, and led the first gold rush from the town to the American River in the spring of 1848. Only seven persons were left behind in San Francisco. But by the beginning of 1849, six thousand miners had appeared to join the hunt, and San Francisco was a tent town of about two thousand transients. Prices soared, gambling thrived, and violence erupted.

General W. T. Sherman, who later knew war to be hell, felt much the same way about San Francisco in 1853. He wrote: "Montgomery Street had been filled up with brush and clay and I always dreaded to ride on horseback along it. . . . The rider was likely to be thrown and drowned in the mud."

Fire leveled the shacks and tents of San Francisco six times in eighteen months. The fires were finally blamed on incendiaries. To halt them, Samuel Brannan became president of the first Vigilance Committee, which meted out a kind of justice of its own against lawless mobs known as Hounds (they hounded non-whites) and Sydney Ducks (ex-convicts from Australia). California had been a part of the United States since 1850, but Washington was busy with the slavery issue, and not even the slaying in San Francisco of United States Marshal William H. Richardson by a gambler brought much attention from the federal government. But when a city supervisor shot down a newspaper editor, a second Vigilance Committee was formed which eventually grew to nine thousand armed men with detachments of infantry, artillery and cavalry. It executed four men and banished thirty others from the state.

A new kind of panic swept the town in 1854 when the placer mines began to run out. Shipping dropped away, firms went bankrupt, and almost half the people of the town—now close to fifty thousand—were unemployed. Many left in 1858 to work the new Frazier River mines in British Columbia. But farming began to prosper. Sawmills thrived. Machine shops, set up to build mining equipment, were converted to construct flour mills, steamships and soon even railway locomotives. The treaty between the United States and the Hawaiian Islands permitted free entry of raw sugar, and a refinery was built in San Francisco. An immigrant German youth, Claus Spreckels, maneuvered his way from a small grocery business into a sugar fortune; his rise was helped when he won sugar plantations on the island of Maui in a poker game with Kalakaua, the island king. Soon, as the prime Pacific Coast port, San Francisco began to build conservative foundations in world commerce.

The role of the city as the financial capital of the West had begun with gold, but it was reinforced in 1859 when riches in silver from the Comstock Lode of Nevada began to flow through the city. Frenzied speculation in mining stocks centered in San Francisco. In 1862, forty men organized the San Francisco Stock and Exchange Board, and soon women brokers were peddling mining stocks on street curbs. William C. Ralston, who had grown rich on the Comstock Lode, loaned much of the money through his Bank of California for the building of the Central Pacific (later the Southern Pacific) Railroad. Two young miners, Mackay and Fair, teamed with two San Francisco saloon keepers, Flood and O'Brien, won control of the richest vein in all the Comstock, and then opened their own bank. Ralston, plunging to buy stock in a worthless mine, fell victim to a falling stock market. On an August day in 1875, his bank closed its doors. On the next day he went swimming off North Beach, as was his habit—but this time he drowned. From that day on, the financial capital of the West grew more orderly. Today, the descendants of those whose fortunes survived those heady days of silver speculation are among the most powerful Californians.

The first transcontinental railroad was built eastward by Union Pacific and westward by Central Pacific to meet in 1869 in Utah. Central Pacific was begun by four Sacramento merchants—Charles Crocker, Mark Hopkins, Leland Stanford, and Collis P. Huntington— who started with only fifty thousand dollars among them. To build their roadbed, they brought more than sixty thousand laborers from China. That was the start of San Francisco's Chinatown, and the start too of a long era of political domination of California by the Southern Pacific. Its rich holdings of California land grew to 1,349,000 acres, and its grip was not broken until the rise of Hiram Johnson in 1910. The success of the Central Pacific also led to Stanford University; Leland Stanford, who had come to California penniless in 1852, bequeathed eighty-three thousand acres of rich farmland and twenty-one million dollars for a private university.

San Francisco measures its modern era from April 18, 1906. At 5:13 A.M. the earthquake began; it ended forty-eight seconds later. The city was built almost completely of wood, more so than any other city of the nation. Yet it was not ruined by the quake; destruction seemed nominal at first. Then the fires spread, aided by explosion and by the collapse of the fire-alarm system. The fires raged for three days, until the mansions of Van Ness were sacrificed to dynamite and to back fires. The center of the city was destroyed; the loss in property was half a billion dollars, three hundred and fifteen bodies were recovered, three hundred and fifty-two persons were unaccounted for, and a quarter of a million homeless citizens camped in parks and empty lots.

As San Francisco was rebuilt, the natives distracted themselves with one of their liveliest graft probes. Abraham Ruef, most infamous of a long line of political bosses, was convicted—but not before his chief prosecutor, Francis J. Heney, was shot in the courtroom by a juryman. In his prison stripes at San Quentin, Ruef announced: "The zebra is one of the most beautiful and graceful of animals. Why, therefore, should I cavil at my attire?"

In the Atherton police graft probe of 1933, a defense lawyer gave what some San Franciscans still regard as a definitive statement of the *laissez-faire* attitude which has characterized the city. He told the jury that he was about to defend policemen who had been accused of taking bribes. He said he would show during the trial that not only the defendants, but the jurors themselves bore the same glory that he bore as a San Franciscan—they all were descended from the fun-loving Spanish.

The long labor strife of the city began to attract the attention of the world in 1916, soon after a longshoremen's strike, when a bomb killed ten persons during a Preparedness Day parade. Thomas Mooney and Warren Billings, arrested and convicted, became to American labor martyrs to injustice. In 1939, Mooney was pardoned and Billings released.

In 1934, longshoremen walked off the docks and shipping came to a halt. On July 5 of that year, a date still recalled by waterfront unions as "Bloody Thursday," two strikers were killed. On July 17th, in a general city strike, one hundred and twenty-seven thousand San Francisco workers left their jobs. The strike lasted three days, and from its settlement emerged the power of one of the city's three famous Bridges: Harry. (The other two were under construction. The San Francisco–Oakland Bay Bridge was opened to traffic in 1936, and the Golden Gate in 1937.)

◇◇◇

Among the cities of the Western United States, only San Francisco has the poise to laugh at itself. But self-ridicule comes seldom these days and is drowned by the sybaritic laughter from the city's Babylonian ghettos. Judged as the capital of the West, a role thrust on it a century ago by gold, contemporary San Francisco is an ingratiating failure.

There is small place in the image of San Francisco for the human miseries that increasingly haunt its majestic hills, for San Francisco is untroubled by conscience. It is narcissistic. It has had every right to be in love with itself, but because of complacency its beauty has been seeping away. In San Francisco and among its lovers all over the world, there is a wistful conspiracy to maintain the illusions of the San Francisco that has been fading: a virile, astute, cultured, fun-loving city, the city that knows how.

On its face, this is the most enchanting of all American cities. Its devotees ring the earth; its newcomers join the chorus in blithe paeans—or quietly move away, or stay and view the gathering storm with troubled eyes. If they leave, it is assumed that they couldn't make the grade. If they stay and fail to join the claque, they are "not San Francisco."

It is easy to be swept along in the conspiracy of self-devotion; the illusion has had talented creators. There are a host of them conveying the illusion in word and picture for an insatiable audience. There is a market almost anywhere for words about San Francisco, so long as they fulfill the image. It becomes unrewarding to remain objective about the city.

I asked a learned San Francisco cleric if he detected any disturbing note of narcissism in his city. He folded his hands and looked away for a long moment. When his eyes met mine again, they twinkled, as though his wit and honesty had been grappling with more theologic impulses, and had won. What he said came close to a revelation of pure San Franciscana:

"I make addresses and preach sermons in which I point out that San Francisco leads the cities of the nation in the end products of frustration and despair. From time to time we are ahead in alcoholism, in suicide, in drug addiction, in divorce, in homosexuality. I cite these statistics, and I listen to myself, and sometimes I have to say to myself: 'You sounded proud!' "

An advertising man remarked, "San Francisco is sort of a vertical Texas. San Franciscans assume you're going to think their city is the greatest place in the world, and they aren't interested in your compliments because they have all the oblivious confidence of a ten-year-old boy."

A former madame told me one night at a party on Telegraph Hill: "San Francisco is a town to ball in, baby!" And to paraphrase a comment which is currently popular among a handful of San Francisco *cognoscenti*, "San Francisco is the only city that can make love to itself."

San Francisco Bay, four hundred and fifty square miles of sheltered water, unites a metropolitan area as large as New Jersey.

The Bay extends forty-two miles north and south. The Bay area population is 3.5 million, but only one in five lives in San Francisco. Of these, only a handful are San Franciscans participating actively in the legend of their city. But thousands more are consciously, sometimes pridefully, enacting roles as supernumeraries.

In the custody of these hard-core San Franciscans, and their sycophants, is the urbanity of San Francisco. It is unique in the West. The compact center of San Francisco is as non-Western as midtown Manhattan. It is inhabited by those who are conscious of being a part of the scene, whether they are residents or tourists. "We all go to the same places at lunch," Stan Delaplane, the Pulitzer Prize winner and columnist, said. "The places are mostly within walking distance. I walk four or five blocks to the Palace or to the St. Francis—I hardly ever take a cab. We see each other all the time, which causes a certain unanimity of thought."

This urban center of San Francisco is set in an aquatic wilderness of contrasts.

From the Civic Center of San Francisco with its sumptuous, municipally-owned Opera House, the Bayshore Freeway unravels southward through a forest of signs and subdivisions, down the peninsula beside San Francisco Bay. In moments, the traveler is in South San Francisco, a glum industrial town, out of the seven-mile square enclave of San Francisco proper and the first of a long succession of sub-cities. Within an hour, he reaches San Jose, a vast new subdivision at the site of California's oldest incorporated town. The most intensive recent settlement of people and industry in the Bay area has been here. San Franciscans like to say that Southern California begins at San Jose. What they mean is that this new city of two hundred and twenty-five thousand has grown with the sudden explosive force associated with Los Angeles; what they are admitting is that proximity to San Francisco was not enough to endow the San Jose explosion of the 1950's with San Franciscan charm or grace.

Across the Bay to the east is another world, which includes industrial Oakland, seat of the world-wide Kaiser empire and the Western city most heavily settled by Negroes, and Berkeley, the home base of the wide-flung University of California. In population, East Bay rivals the peninsula across the Bay; some of its settlements are bedroom cities for San Francisco, and in the hills and flatlands east of the Bay lie other bedroom towns from which Oakland businessmen commute. Yet East Bay is detached inviolably from the San Francisco image. It is appropriate in San Francisco to dismiss the area loftily as "the mysterious East Bay."

To the north, past the restaurants and shops and galleries of Sausalito, lie the hilly residential and commuter towns of Marin

County, less thickly settled than those of East Bay; not until the
Golden Gate Bridge was finished in 1937 did this area fall within
commuter range. In Marin, the new breed of urban planner is trying
to blend rugged parkland with subdivision while there is time.

To the west is the Pacific.

In the center of all this lies a visually captivating city of only
forty-five square miles. Its hills and peaks, its ghettos and its skyscrapers bask in luminous color reflected on three sides by sky and
water. It has nowhere to go but up. The last of the sand dunes in the
far southwest corner of the city has been subdivided. This city of
seven hundred and forty-two thousand, and not the metropolitan Bay
area of 3.5 million, is the capital of the West. But it is no longer the
great city of the West; Los Angeles has overtaken it. Even the role of
San Francisco as the Western capital—implying influence, not size—
is under serious challenge. So many have fought so hard to keep San
Francisco the same that their effect has been felt. In many ways the
city is the exception that proves the rule in the theory of the westward
tilt.

San Francisco is blessed indisputably with *savoir vivre;* yet,
Samson-like, it seems ready to pull in its temple atop itself.

Its spires and towers rise indomitably from the edge of its great
bay and over its hills, haughty but enticing; yet half of downtown already is at the mercy of the automobile—a quarter of it in streets and
freeways, and another quarter in parking facilities. Its bay-windowed
streets beckon to the wanderer in search of a home; yet on closer look,
they are strangely ugly, and many are verging on slums.

While fifteen million dollars was spent on Candlestick Park for
the Giants, San Francisco's General Hospital was on probation for its
antiquated facilities and its two legitimate theaters tottered in seedy
obsolescence.

The city's reputation for tolerance is world-wide; yet as its
Negro population has risen from five thousand to eighty thousand in
twenty years, it has developed ghettos in the Fillmore and Mission
districts which are the worst breeding grounds of crime in the West.

Its two great bridges brought the city a dynamism and a visual
focus; but its freeways, its new office buildings and pending waterfront apartment developments threaten its historic vistas, even though
they are symbolic of progress.

Like its opera, the San Francisco Symphony Orchestra has been
a soothing source of smugness through the years, but in 1962, George
Szell canceled the second week of a series of concerts in which he
served as guest conductor. Baited by a San Francisco music critic
to explain, he finally exploded with a criticism of orchestra personnel

and policy. "I found the saddest state of musical affairs in any American or European city during the almost fifty years of my active conducting career," he said.

Because a 1948 civic bond issue failed, San Francisco has lagged in convention facilities. Its people always have assumed happily that conventioners would continue to gravitate toward their city, but they were jolted in 1962 by a warning that San Francisco now is forced to compete for conventions with Los Angeles, Denver, Portland, and Las Vegas.

The city grasps at the new to avoid self-strangulation—yet in the new it loses the charm of its past and begins to wonder who it is. It is a city with its finger in the dike, which must hold on and risk the ravages of drought, or let go and brave the flood.

Three factions are the heirs to San Francisco, and at the moment none of them seems likely to keep alive the flame. At dead center are the unimaginative descendants of the city's pioneers, largely bent on maintaining family fortunes. Slightly more attractive are the energetic newcomers who have learned to capitalize on the illusion of San Francisco. Most hollow of all is a voluble segment of intellectuals, who gloat in the sensual serenity of the city and enjoy it as a forum for their innocuous but highly glossed ideas. This group largely ignores or idly deplores the waste of the robust and peculiar strengths of the city.

But there are San Franciscans who are concerned. Wallace Stegner, the novelist, returned to his accustomed haunts on the Stanford campus after a sabbatical year in Florence and Rome and was stunned by the architectural dreariness that greeted him. "San Francisco has wealth, prestige, and the power to swing things," he told me. "Instead of a good city, it should be an absolutely spectacular city. It is a failure in zoning. The opera and symphony are fine, but why shouldn't they be among the best in the world? The theater in San Francisco as yet amounts to little. With the greatest opportunity of any city in the world, San Francisco has muffed it. Our cultural agencies are too self-contented."

A blindness among San Franciscans toward "what is really wrong here" is sensed by the Right Reverend James Albert Pike, Episcopal Bishop of California. He is a churchman of extraordinary intellectual brilliance, who embraced a clerical career after serving as an attorney for the United States Securities and Exchange Commission in Washington.

"Nobody bothers much about the San Francisco statistics of divorce or suicide or alcoholism," he told me in his chancery beside Grace Cathedral. "The beatnik philosophy is a counsel of despair, that *the moment* is all there is. I am not totally critical of it; it is a fact of our culture. It goes beyond the old beatnik haunts here in North Beach, permeating even the Pacific Union Club here on Nob Hill. San Francisco has the largest proportion of single persons of any major city. This leads to a great deal of loneliness. The friendliness of the San Franciscan is sometimes not so vividly and continuously expressed as in other areas. There is often a lack of involvement with one's neighbors. They don't care much who's around, which results in less participation in community affairs.

"There is less basic religious affiliation. There is a fresh new feeling that there are worlds to conquer, but the church was *back there*, and the need for it is felt less after the move to the West. San Francisco is the image of the last chance—the last place out—and it is a hub of anxieties and restlessness. It has the lowest degree of religious affiliation: twenty-eight percent as against thirty-two percent in Seattle and sixty-seven percent on the national average. With this low affiliation, it is not a coincidence that San Francisco is at the top of almost anything you name that shows unsolved personal anxiety.

"In growing areas of the West, our clergy are busy with financing and designing churches and in all kinds of activity involved with bringing in new people. The clergy in the San Francisco Bay area are so busy as promoters that sometimes they fail as ministers; they do not have enough time to read, or there may be no second priest in many parishes because of the expense of a high mortgage and the need to keep building.

"Yet the life, culture and gaiety of San Francisco are tremendous. The feel is different from the East. Back there, people say, 'We never did this before; why should we do it now?' In the West, at the suggestion of a new idea, laymen or officers of a parish usually say, 'Let's go!' The result is much creativity."

Scott Newhall, the dynamic executive editor of the *San Francisco Chronicle*, is one of the most outspoken and least complacent citizens. He is a fourth-generation San Franciscan, but he is certainly not typical of the city. He says, "The thing that frightens me is the world myth of San Francisco, and how our present generation and most of the people who have come here in the last generation are doing nothing to deserve it. They are sitting on a reputation. I don't want this to explode. This is a wonderful city. There is vitality here, but it must be put back to work. I think San Francisco is basically inactive. It is in the hands generally of cultural idiots. The civic approach to planning and architecture is completely distasteful. We keep demolishing things. There hasn't been a piece of statuary to be commissioned, of any size or scope, for a generation. City Hall is more or less populated by ignorance, conformity and mediocrity. It is the spirit of our city not to bother too much. What City Hall needs is a Lorenzo de Medici, and not just another cost accountant in an executive position. I have yet to see any Lorenzo on the horizon."

Instead, City Hall has been led by a Greek-American dairyman, Mayor George Christopher, who lacks the polish of the prototype San Franciscan but brims with the raw vigor of earlier eras. (In 1962, he was the losing Republican candidate for lieutenant governor of California.) He often seems to feel he is not a San Franciscan: he refers to its citizens in the third person. My first visit with him at City Hall was soon after a national magazine had devoted an issue to a hopelessly romanticized interpretation of San Francisco.

"Somehow," I told Christopher, "you and the San Francisco I read about don't add up."

He laughed, unconcerned. "Like many presentations of San Francisco," he said, "that one tended to glamorize the city in a way that reminded everybody of the glorious past. I suppose that's fine. I'm not going to quarrel with anybody who wants to glorify San Francisco. But the future of this city lies in energy and guts. It's good for these people to have sentiment. It gives them something to be proud of, and when people are proud and have sentiment, they usually try to better themselves."

City Hall towers higher than the Capitol in Washington, but like too much of San Francisco, what happens inside has failed to live up to the promise of the outside. The city planning department has been cited as one of the best in the nation; yet little of its long-range planning has been implemented. Its master plan includes subways, trees and small parks downtown, larger neighborhood parks, Civic Center additions, and the renewal of blighted areas in a traditional style which would blend with the rest of the city. The plan reposed, almost unnoticed, as civic officials overrode planning-department recommendations for the regulation of skyscraper heights to prevent blocking of views, and ignored the pleas of planners for the acquisition of federal land to make more parks.

Urban redevelopment bogged down for years in indecision and scandal—including the resignation of a mayor's aide who owned stock in a slum properties combine. The stalemate was broken in part after the *Chronicle* angrily labeled the civic redevelopment team "Dawdle, Dawdle, Bumbling & Pokery, specialists in deceleration." Soon, under a new director, the redevelopment agency began to stir itself.

Mayor Christopher was thrust abruptly into the planning vacuum soon after he took office. Since 1910, mayors who had tried to redevelop the blighted produce area adjacent to the Montgomery

Street financial district had been threatened with recall and even bodily harm. Every mayor backed down until Christopher. He gained courage with the support of the Blyth-Zellerbach Committee, whose businessman members volunteered five thousand dollars each for an engineering survey which led to the planning of the Golden Gateway Project. The latter became the nucleus for what Christopher has referred to as a "five-hundred-million-dollar redevelopment project all over the city," and what the Chamber of Commerce calls "The Big Build." But all of this is still nebulous. The Golden Gateway Project is far from completion.

Faced with massive, citywide obsolescence, San Francisco is moving toward rebuilding itself, but its feet are made heavy for the task by nostalgia and by the grim knowledge that it can never be the same again. It may be that nothing ever again will be quite like San Francisco.

The city was born in the ebullience of an incomparably exciting era of American development. Much of the zest and fervor which have impressed its admirers in years past were built into the city. As its façade begins to crumble and change, only calculated shrewdness can keep San Francisco from taking on the neuter trademarks of cities across the land.

In his recent book, *The Face of San Francisco*, Harold Gilliam, a former San Francisco art commission member, observed: "In the past, the city's uniqueness, its individuality, its incomparable variety and diversity developed spontaneously, with very little planning of any kind; in the future it is probable that these qualities can be maintained only by planning—on a scale far greater than any now officially under consideration. . . . Sometimes, San Francisco's incomparable natural advantages seem to be matched only by its determination to destroy them."

Sober warnings like Gilliam's have not made much impression on most San Franciscans. After all, they can pick up books and magazines by the score which reassure them that theirs is the finest of all possible cities. A Paul Revere in San Francisco today must cope not only with the complacency of the San Franciscan but with the flattery of the outsider.

Most of the dissension these days seems to be generated in the warring between San Francisco newspapers, and especially in the pages of the *Chronicle*, but even here it is sugar-coated with a trace of narcissistic bemusement. ("With something akin to admiration for the magnitude of the blundering that has marked the cable-car program of alterations and repairs," read a *Chronicle* editorial, "we have attempted to discover just how the trick was done.") The formula is working; the *Chronicle* has pulled ahead in its circulation war with the rival Hearst *Examiner*. In the process, San Francisco newspaper readers have embraced an extraordinary era of personal essayism and almost conscienceless sensationalism (VANDERBILT DIED DRUNK, screamed a page-one banner headline in the *Chronicle*.)

The newspaper war in San Francisco, like the breeze that whips through the city, keeps San Franciscans edgy. The opinion of Dr. Chilton Bush, a close student of the San Francisco newspaper war when he was head of the journalism department at Stanford University and dean of Western journalism professors, was that the primary interest of both San Francisco morning dailies was not in the news but in the extinction of the other.

Whether or not this is true, Editor Newhall of the *Chronicle* is the pivot man in the city's newspaper war; he is captain of the winning team. While many Western editors are thinking in terms of what they did in Omaha or Pittsburgh, or remembering that a lost kid story always is good for page one, Newhall is exploring restlessly what makes his San Francisco audience different. He improvises constantly. He decided, for instance, that there was a place in his newspaper for a male scold like Count Marco, a one-time hairdresser who proceeded to chide woman readers of the *Chronicle* for not taking baths with their husbands.

The *Chronicle* fought the Embarcadero Freeway, which is like a thimble on the shimmering fingertip of downtown San Francisco, rising high to shut out sea and sky. Losing the fight, Newhall called editorially for demolition of the freeway. It still is there, but Newhall made his point.

The success of the Newhall pattern of journalism is eloquently revealing about the contemporary San Franciscan, who is sophisticated, more confident of the past than the future, possessed of a wide-spectrum sense of humor and a somewhat narrower-spectrum tolerance, smug but facile in avoiding the embarrassment of being caught at it, hyperactive, glib in the patois of the intellectual but less dedicated to his truths than to his technique.

It is a favorite pastime in San Francisco to speculate on the nature of the new San Franciscan. He is often pictured as a crew-cut young man on Montgomery Street—an apprentice financier, perhaps, or an advertising man. He is certainly a martini man, and a ladies' man. He has come from Chicago or New York or some other city of more modest size and has read a few chapters of San Francisco history —or at least Sunday supplement features. He is pleasantly titillated about the contemporary city, and he finds it in vogue to be alarmed by the new freeways which obstruct some views of the bay and disgorge great traffic jams into downtown. He is knowledgeable about restaurants and a bit of a jazz buff. He is interested vaguely in urban renewal because such projects sound upbeat. He has heard something about the crime problems created by the heavy influx of Negroes and their crowded housing. Probably he participated in a vehement city-wide protest against junking the last of the cable cars. Before marriage, he shares an apartment in the city; after marriage, he buys a home in a new subdivision on the peninsula to the south—or, if better-heeled, across the bay in Marin County.

Can the city expect leadership from this kind of picaresque *bon vivant?* There is always the chance that he will mature, but the newer generations, both native and in-migrant, are deficient in two essentials: strength of character and indifference to public opinion. Instead, they are eager to conform to an image of San Francisco created by prior generations, and they lack the heart and the flair to live up to the myth. One wonders if they can create a new myth of their own.

It is a facet of the new San Franciscan that he has decided Los Angeles is not, after all, the very worst place on earth. Artists find a far readier market of collectors in Los Angeles than in San Francisco. Three or four restaurants in the southern city are comparable to the best of San Francisco. In the business world of the West, long dominated by San Francisco, Los Angeles is pulling ahead by the brute force of volume. The rapid population growth of the southern city is scoffed at by San Francisco—which *lost* population between 1950 and 1960. But some canny San Franciscans sense that, while growth itself is no virtue, a kind of virility is emerging in Los Angeles which is more aptly compared with their city of half a century ago than that of today.

"San Francisco has the greatest harbor in the world," says James D. Zellerbach, chairman of the board of the Crown Zellerbach Corporation in San Francisco. "But we have sat on our harbor and let Los Angeles and Long Beach and San Diego grow and develop what were not harbors into harbors. We have let Los Angeles become—I won't say a metropolis, because it isn't—the largest city in the West. That may be good or bad; for me, if I lived in Los Angeles, it would be bad."

James Zellerbach, a small, brisk man, was United States ambassador to Italy from 1957 to 1961. His grandfather came to California seeking gold. Zellerbach was born in San Francisco in 1892, graduated from the University of California, and rose to head the second largest company in the pulp and paper industry. He is a traditional San Franciscan who looks at his city in his senior years with conservative pride and considerable trepidation, but he has made the most effective salute to the present on the whole San Francisco skyline: the Crown Zellerbach Building, the first glass tower in San Francisco. He regards its construction as a step toward his vision of San Francisco as not larger, but more beautiful.

"San Francisco is now almost like New York in that it's hard to find a native San Franciscan," he said. "I don't like it. That's probably being conservative. Probably for the good of the whole community it is better that the West does grow. The old blood is running out."

I said that in traveling about the West, I had found a regional syndrome that approaches hysteria in some cities: an absorption in growth, sometimes at almost any cost.

"You don't find that in San Francisco," he snapped. "That is why San Francisco still has a spirit and feeling that is different from the average American city. This isn't a chamber-of-commerce city. We have lived here, and planted our branches in Los Angeles and in a lot of other cities where we wouldn't want to live. We took advantage of the growth of other areas, and also advantage of continuing to live in this kind of community. People in San Francisco aren't keen about growth of the city itself. They have mixed feelings about it."

Zellerbach has led the push for San Francisco redevelopment. He has been president of the San Francisco Symphony Association and a director of the Opera Association.

"I want San Francisco to continue to be the cultural and educational center of the West. If we are alert to our responsibilities, it will —if we don't let it go by default. There always is a risk of losing things that you don't put a high enough value on. This is what has disturbed me. I got stirred up in connection with designing this building and trying to find a site for it. I waited to see what was going to happen on redevelopment, and found that nothing was going to happen. Nobody was taking an active leadership in supporting the mayor or trying to get anything done in San Francisco. All the special pleaders were at work preventing things. That disturbed me—that, and seeing the apathy of people with their hands in their pockets when their support was needed for cultural things. But it has taken a turn in very recent years. People are getting stirred up in San Francisco again."

Indeed, there are hopeful bellwethers. Self-appraisal, too long absent from the temperament of the city, has set in, with several encouraging results: San Franciscans finally have decided that their slums must go, and the blast of dynamite echoes through the Fillmore —that preposterous reminder of what passed for opulence in 1875. This is progress, but still needed are housing developments which are priced at rents the dispossessed residents could pay. San Franciscans also are wrestling with the tremendous problem of devising a rapid-transit system; almost eight hundred million dollars was voted in November, 1962, for a transit district which is scheduled to set fast trains in operation by 1966. San Franciscans have been guided toward more awareness of what is good and bad in architecture by controversy over a smattering of new downtown buildings and a spate of freeways.

Herb Caen, the *Chronicle* columnist, has a stake in the San Francisco legend, and he is more thoughtful about it than most of his readers suspect. Not long ago, he interrupted his panegyrics to his city to inquire: "Can delayed maturity follow the premature senility that came on the heels of an extended adolescence?" Could this be Caen's Baghdad-by-the-Bay of which he wrote so coolly? It could, indeed. "This atmosphere of self-doubt rises from the hills," he continued, "like a mist."

Caen senses a change of mood in San Francisco. "There is more concern among older people over tradition, as though they were girding for the battle," he said. "The newer people are out to move ahead—meaning up—with tall buildings, and to hell with the view, like New York. We're on the way to sacrificing a heritage of broad visions. The old-timers are dying off, and the new ones don't have the same feeling for the city. All of the city that escaped the fire and earthquake is going to go. Glass and concrete things keep popping up. This will be the city of the future, I guess. The natural attributes will live on—the hills and the water and the bridges—but I don't know if we can sustain the myth of San Francisco much longer."

Such cries have been heard since Josiah Royce, in *The Californian*, at the turn of the century, deplored the exploitation by ugliness of what he called the most beautiful city site on earth. Sporadic self-criticism like that of Royce's is a form of flagellation, indulged in only by those obsessed with beauty, perhaps, but there is a challenge today, both from without and within, to the San Francisco of tradition.

Many factors work in favor of San Francisco's attempts at rejuvenation. It is a young city in a beautiful setting; unlike many, it was born to wealth. If urban renewal can succeed anywhere, it should succeed in an enviroment like this. San Francisco can meet the challenge, as it has met earthquake and fire, if it cares enough.

Wallace Stegner says, "You cannot live here a week without thinking, 'How much energy! How much talent! How much good will, and good intentions—and most of it undirected!' "

With awareness of its need and direction of its energies, San

Francisco must give up basking in its image and go in search of its Medici. There is not much time.

"Throughout the country," said J. D. Zellerbach, "we are washing our islands of individuality into sameness. I think we are losing something. Here in San Francisco, I suspect we will resist that trend for the next ten years. How much longer, I don't know."

If San Francisco cannot resist conformity, then the threat of sameness is grave throughout the West. The trends that move through the West often have originated in the urban core of San Francisco. If the city cannot manage to maintain itself as a city different, with all its brilliance and its wealth, one of the great hopes of the West is dying. If the West is America tomorrow, the warning shadow of a national resignation from individuality may be passing over San Francisco.

Indeed, recent newcomers to the Bay Area have not provided much flamboyancy. Before World War II, Henry Kaiser took on some of the old, accepted families; he broke up a Western combine by manufacturing his own product when he couldn't buy at a satisfactory price. He went on to build an empire, but he never has been accepted in San Francisco by San Franciscans; he has never conformed. But today it is difficult to point to men of Kaiser's individualistic stature in San Francisco.

One sanctum of non-conformity in San Francisco is a twenty-five-foot-wide building on Pacific Street—the old Barbary Coast—which served for years as Fire Station No. 1. When it went up for public auction in 1959, two advertising men in their forties bought it as the unlikely site for their agency and remodeled it. The ground floor serves now as an art gallery with a courtyard and fountain in the rear. Above, there is a series of stairways and ever-narrowing offices. Howard Gossage, one of the owners, has his office in a tiny room at the foot of a steep stairway leading into the old hose tower, which itself is almost totally occupied now by a large bed, where he occasionally sleeps. Gossage's mind does not travel in the usual paths; he has been involved in such abstract schemes as a move to repeal women's suffrage (somehow vitally connected with the advertising of a Western ale), and a five-year plan for a chain of service stations dispensing pink air for automobile tires. He once urged Americans to be the first in their block to win a kangaroo, as a gift from an Australian airline. He was quoted in San Francisco newspapers as proposing to solve traffic problems by building a forty-mile bridge lengthwise down San Francisco Bay from the Golden Gate to San Jose; he still treasures a letter from a University of California professor, proclaiming interest, offering encouragement, and requesting further information. Any affectionate writing in the public prints about Irish whisky within recent years probably was scrawled by Gossage at this desk below the hose tower—or on one of his jaunts to Ireland to absorb color, and Irish whisky.

Gossage was the author of the advertisements for a California champagne which read: "You know the feeling. The married breakfast is an uneasy time, no matter how much in love the participants . . . Face up with champagne." This brought an explosion from Evanston, Illinois, the site of the office of the president of the Woman's Christian Temperance Union, who countered with the words of Isaiah: "Woe unto them that rise up early in the morning, that they may follow strong drink . . ."

Unabashed, Gossage moved on into the fine arts. Sales of the Western ale he represents soared after the Gossage agency introduced sweat shirts emblazoned with portraits of Bach, Beethoven, and Brahms. As an afterthought, Gossage added Mozart, because his first name was Wolfgang—a splendid name, Gossage sensed, for the sweat-shirt set.

Irreverent but idealistic, intuitive and a facile writer, Gossage at work or at play is at home in the non-conformist environment of San Francisco's bohemian North Beach. Graying and handsome, he shares the presidency of the agency with Joseph Weiner, a bearded family man who commutes from Marin County. It was Weiner who won one of the firm's accounts after a Western brewery executive had decided to question advertising agencies on their corporate goals. A New Yorker answered frankly: "We want to become one of the ten largest agencies in the country." Weiner answered just as frankly: "Our ambition is to get out of the advertising business."

I attended a meeting with Weiner and Gossage and executives of this same company. One of the brewery men was protesting a forthcoming ad which puckishly warned women against drinking the company's ale. The Gossage ad copy was based on the premise that women have no business drinking ale—or doing anything else whatever that men do. The brewery man pleaded that the ad be somewhat less explicit.

Gossage threw up his hands. "Gentlemen, if you're going into a campaign as ridiculous as this one," he said, "go all the way or throw it over." The ad ran, and Western women dutifully took the bait.

Gossage describes the advertising industry as "a twelve-billion-dollar sledge hammer driving an economy-size thumb tack. We don't really disapprove of trivia, but we don't sell whisky like it's holy water, either. We sell it with the idea that you are going to get drunk if you drink enough of it." All their work is on fee, not commission. They have fought to keep their personnel down to nine people; it is a small agency in every sense of the word, but Gossage and Weiner and their heretical attitudes toward the business are notorious.

Gossage is in demand as a speaker, even before national advertising agency groups which are not known for their ability to jest at their profession. He has not been called on by the restaurant association for his irreverent comments on San Francisco food, however. "The chief thing in favor of San Francisco restaurants is that they are sort of homogenous. You lose the address and stumble into the wrong restaurant, but you get the same meal."

Another of the West's noted non-conformists lives and works not far from the Weiner and Gossage fire station. He is Melvin Belli, one of the most controversial attorney of recent years. San Francisco's North Beach is an appropriate setting for Belli—a man of soaring ebullience and satin-voiced restraint, worldly, dedicated to the dramatic, with total disregard for precedent and tradition.

After he had focused international attention on his innovations in trial procedures of personal injury cases—forcing monetary awards up to new highs in many states, and incurring the wrath of insurance and medical men—Belli chose a relic of San Francisco's past and transformed it into an architectural showplace. The two-story Belli Building on the edge of Telegraph Hill, converted from an ancient overalls factory operated by Chinese, suggests—like Belli—a paradoxical blend of the Old Bailey and a Gold Rush bordello.

Belli's certificate of membership in the American Bar Association hangs in a basement bathroom, hard by a steam room with symbols of Bellian contempt worked into the design of the floor tile. He thus displays his scorn for organized law, which has not always condoned his courtroom spectaculars. On one occasion, he introduced Mickey Cohen under an alias to his fellow lawyers, and they listened intently to the gangster as he lectured on provisions of federal income-tax law.

Between the law books in the vast shelves of Belli's main office —which more resembles a prosperous madame's parlor—are emptied whisky bottles and apothecary jars filled with embalming fluid.

At the crest of Telegraph Hill is a three-storied Victorian mansion which Belli owns and at the top of which he lives. The slanting rays of sunset on his roof garden seem to bring the Bay Bridge into fingertip reach. In patchy fog, the apartment becomes an island above the city. At sunrise, the kaleidoscoping spectrum of San Francisco light is introduced by a golden bomb which shatters slumber. In this setting, Belli rises at four A.M. to prepare cases, dictate his books, and keep in contact with offices and associates in almost every state and several countries. Trials and lecturing take Belli away from San Francisco on increasingly lengthy stays. A great part of his practice is now in Los Angeles; he has another home there and an adobe law-office building in Beverly Hills which is as appropriate to the environment of the South of California as his other is to the North.

But Belli is the kind of San Franciscan who will remain, even if his practice forces a move to another city. I asked him if he could explain what instills that spirit.

"San Francisco is a venal city," he said. "It has to be sophisticatedly so. If only one could psychoanalyze the San Franciscan to find out what makes him want to get back to the nostalgia of the street car, the earthquake, the lunch pail, the steamed beer, the ferries! Why do we have flocked wallpaper? Gaslight clubs? San Francisco still has the stamp of that era. They're trying now to scrub and perform surgery on San Francisco. Sometimes you see the skyline changing and think it's been scrubbed already and the surgeons are standing around ready to put in their scalpels, to take the cable cars away, put up something in that goddamned plastic, or strip off the virgin breast ornaments from fine old buildings. With so many new people coming in, they're trying to standardize us. They want us to do more business around the cocktail hour, for instance. They are trying to departmentalize us.

"We've had two mayors—Robinson and Christopher—who have been real squares, with no appreciation for the background of this city. To show you its vitality, we have resisted their regimes in every way but our conforming skyline of glass and steel, which I think is criminal. We maintain San Francisco individuality not by any civic plans or programs or committees—but through a sort of informal striving of every individual. You can't get anywhere with a unified civic drive; but things get done. Some of our civic efforts are atrocious. The Coit Tower is hideous; it looks like a thing ready to ejaculate. But look at the individual gardens, the individual old-time buildings!

"You can't organize the San Franciscan. No matter how thickly you disguise a group effort, he'll sniff it like bait in a bear trap and circle it and walk away. If it takes a card or a key, to hell with it. Key clubs don't last here, but at the cocktail hour San Francisco has a one-place feeling. Take a circle of eight blocks from Grant and Post Street, and you can drop into almost any place at five o'clock and think the city is just one big party: Paoli's, El Prado, St. Francis, the Palace. The maîtres d'hôtels treat you as though you're tired out and they want to put you in front of the fire and make you comfortable. They're not averse to taking a tip, but they don't stand in front of the door like the horse guards at Buckingham Palace. It's a big city with roots all around the world; yet the confines of the cocktail circuit are small. The San Franciscan is more a member of a group than any other society in the United States."

At lunch time, Belli strode into Doro's restaurant next to his offices and introduced a luncheon guest as the Chief Justice of New Hampshire. Belli's friends and associates seemed properly awed and the guest fell to talking law with them. The guest was, in fact, Fred Demara, the accomplished *poseur*, whom Belli was considering using as a legal investigator. (He decided against it, but not without regrets; he was sure it would have provoked fresh storms of protest from his colleagues.) Belli later introduced Demara to Mayor Christopher as Derf Aramed, Commissioner of Corruption from Abyssinia. Belli insists that the mayor shook hands and inquired, "What county was that?"

It is no coincidence that men like Gossage and Belli have chosen the same neighborhood of the West as their base of work. On the shoulders of such honest and inborn non-conformists lies the awkward burden of keeping San Francisco different. They are the inheritors of the tradition which built the city in the raucous Gold Rush era. There are a few such men around, men of vast energy and keen mind and good, though often bizarre taste, whose egos and whimsies are strong, who play as hard as they work and have time for everything except fretting over the censure of others. The more flamboyant of these Westerners are to be found in San Francisco, and some of them, like Gossage and Belli, in North Beach.

North Beach is a swirling eddy in the changing capital of the West. To the tourist, it is a lively center of night life. It is the Manhattan of the West for night club music and comedy, a fountainhead for Mort Sahls and Kingston Trios. To the old San Franciscan, it is the home of Vanessi's and New Joe's and a dozen other unpretentious Italian restaurants which remind him of how it used to be, when San Francisco was intimate. To the Italian, who once dominated North Beach, it is less and less home and more and more an area in which to profit from the visitor.

The most interesting aspect of North Beach is its appeal to the homeless youth, the runaway from his own world, the rebel who assumes that he must write or paint, but more likely finds his place as an extra in the North Beach scene. It is a place with vague ante-

cedents in the Paris of the 1920's, in the Greenwich Village inhabited by the lean and wistful on the eve of World War II, and in the
beatnik movement which had its genesis near North Beach on upper
Grant Avenue, flourished grotesquely for a time, and died a listless
death without a funeral.

Once the waters of Yerba Buena Cove lapped at its feet, but
there is no beach at North Beach these days. It lies in the narrow
valley between Telegraph and Russian Hills, a bustling area of
apartment houses two and three stories high, their bay windows
projecting over sidewalks in their search for light and air. Columbus
Avenue slashes across its streets at a diagonal, dividing North
Beach into a geometric irregularity which shapes its blocks and
buildings and even the lives of its residents and its visitors.

The irregularity of life has helped to make North Beach the bohemia of the West. It has been a lure for youth from all over the
West searching for tolerance, excitement and cosmopolitanism in
the age-old hope of finding themselves—or at least having a hell of
a good time trying. They live with one foot in surrealism, in a never-
never land far from reality, and nothing much seems to be coming
from this group. It seems dated for young people to try to shock
each other, but if they must, North Beach is as good a place as any
for them to try.

The decline of the beatnik movement in North Beach began
with explosive newspaper stories about violent deaths of several beatniks in 1958. Police moved in on the Co-Existence Bagel Shop and
the Coffee Gallery. The beatniks' Bread-and-Wine Mission now is
an automated laundry, and the Cassandra, which featured Zen soup
at twenty cents, is a record store. The Co-Existence Bagel Shop has
most recently been a jewelry store. Gone are the beatnik aristocracy:
Reverend Bob, Dr. Fric-Frac, Linda Lovely, Barbara Nookie, Mad
Marie, Lady Joan, Big Rose, Groover Wailin', Taylor Maid and The
Wig. Most of them went to New York; some moved south to Big
Sur or Monterey, or farther down the coast to Santa Monica or Venice
(near Los Angeles). Ralph Gleason, a jazz writer and observer of the
North Beach scene, explains it this way: "They attracted too much
publicity and too many amateurs, and the cops closed them down.
The weekend commuters to bohemia and the tourists increased in
strength until the police reacted." Toward the end, sophisticated college youths from as far away as San Diego, five hundred miles to the
south, mocked the beatniks on weekends by invading North Beach
wearing leotards and stage beards, and faking it for gawking
tourists.

Some of the basic factors which made the beatnik movement are still present in North Beach. Four-fifths of the beatniks were from outside San Francisco. Most were from middle-class backgrounds. Most were in their twenties. They had better than average educational backgrounds; many had dropped out of college for emotional or financial reasons. They were their own worst enemies, given to drunkenness, drug addiction and sexual deviations. They worked little. They were lonely, depressed and anxious. Their sex life was traumatic. They were idle, thriftless and often dirty.

Though the beatnik is a name of the past, the bohemian with related traits is still in North Beach today. I met a talented architect who had left his wife and job in Los Angeles to frequent the North Beach haunts. He sought a job which would not require office hours, and finally found drafting work he could do in his room. On my next visit to San Francisco, I learned he had thrown that over and gone westward to Hawaii on some illusory search.

A restless and beautiful young woman whom I met in North Beach had left a housekeeper with her husband and children in a distant Western city and come to North Beach to open her own night club. She had more experience with women's social committees and the Parent-Teacher Association than in night-club management. In her mink and diamonds, she was as much a rebel as the runaway architect, and she stubbornly made her place in North Beach. When she felt the urge, she would return home to visit her family. She had an air of forecoming doom, but for the moment she seemed almost happy.

Across San Francisco Bay at Sausalito, but in a setting similar to North Beach, lives Marsha Owen. Under the name of Sally Stanford, she earned her reputation as the last of San Francisco's fabled madames. She still is successful but now as a restaurateur. At her Valhalla, on the shore of the bay, she converses raucously with her parrot Loretta amid gaudy Victorian trappings calculatedly suggestive of an earlier era. She recalls that era warmly. "San Francisco isn't as much fun any more," she sighed. "We don't have the big spenders we used to. There are too many strangers." When I last saw her, she was seeking election as a city councilwoman in Sausalito, implying the endorsement of the California governor. "Pat Brown paid me a high compliment," she said. "He said I've accomplished by myself what it usually costs the state a lot of money to do—complete rehabilitation." But she ran third.

Also in North Beach is the City Lights Book Store, operated by resident author Lawrence Ferlinghetti. He is associated with the beatnik movement, but in City Lights he has provided himself with some capitalistic insurance against artistic blight. The three floors of City Lights offer the most obscure and peripheral of periodicals and paperbacks. Among them are:

The Ladder, a pathetic little monthly pamphlet published for lesbians by the Daughters of Bilitis, Inc., a San Francisco-based women's organization which cites as its purpose the "integration of the homosexual into society"; a male homosexual periodical called the *Mattachine Review*, published in San Francisco by the Mattachine Society, Inc., an organization chartered in Los Angeles in 1950 "in the public interest for the purpose of providing true and accurate information leading to solution of sex behavior problems, particularly those of the homosexual adult"; a slim volume, *The Gospel According to Thomas*, described as a collection of the "sayings of Jesus of particular interest to homosexuals."

Of slightly less specialized interest are some of the paperback booklets published by Ferlinghetti under his City Lights Books imprint, most of them the work of the beatnik school: Allen Ginsberg, Jack Kerouac, Gregory Corso and their followers.

Ferlinghetti is listed as one of the editors of an occasional journal which made its first appearance in the fall of 1961, *Journal For the Protection of All Beings; a Visionary & Revolutionary Review.* The first number was listed on the masthead as the "Love-Shot Issue." This note followed: "Due to the transitory nature of life on earth, this Journal is not sold on a subscription basis. . . . Issue No. 2 may appear in 1962." The editors' statement is a credo equally appropriate for North Beach itself: "We hope we have here an open place where normally apolitical men may speak uncensored upon any subject they feel most hotly and coolly about in a world which politics has made. We are not interested in protecting beings from themselves, we cannot help the deaths people give themselves, we are more concerned with the lives they do not allow themselves to live and the deaths other people would give us, both of the body and spirit."

Considerably more polished, and certainly in more conventional balance, are two San Francisco quarterlies: *San Francisco Review*, which is printed in England but edited and distributed from San Francisco; and *Contact*, a sleek review with a modicum of advertising and a smell of success. To Ferlinghetti, although he sells them, such quarterlies are "an advertising man's idea of what a quarterly should be."

Whatever other merit he may have, Ferlinghetti offers the highly functional professional courtesy of a bulletin board and mail service at City Lights. Transient writers and artists—and who in North Beach cannot pretend?—are invited to use City Lights as a mailing address. In the pigeonholes can be found a distressing array of manila envelopes which bear every earmark of rejected manuscripts.

North Beach is not all phony. Sitting over coffee late at night beside the sidewalk at Enrico's, one suspects that here remains an arena for the curious and the open-minded, a liberal expression of civic tolerance in a city with a liberal past. This spirit of freedom helped make the city great as well as raucous. Yet North Beach seems basically touristy today, not nearly so ingenuous in this period of relative financial success as when club proprietors were struggling to pay new talent five hundred dollars a week instead of five thousand.

Possibly no one can discuss North Beach adequately unless he has been a part of its past. If so, Walter Straley, more recently of Seattle, and president of Pacific Northwest Bell, is qualified. He is saddened: "I'm a little tired of the San Francisco cult. I'm an old San Franciscan, and I still go there once or twice a month as part of my job. Of all the interesting things I've observed in cities as I've moved around the country, the growth of the San Francisco phobia has been one of the most interesting.

"I now get the full treatment there. The only place I can go and feel as though I am back home again is Vanessi's in North Beach. I sit up at the counter. Every place else, I have the feeling I'm being taken quite willfully and not too damn skillfully. When I get taken in New York, it's worth the money. But they feel kind of sorry for me in most places in San Francisco now because they're sure I'm just one of the tourists. They haven't developed the generations of skill that the waiter cult and barber cult and all the rest of the pros in New York have in giving you a show for your money."

Outside the tourist haunts, and beyond the confines of North Beach, *joie de vivre* still reigns sometimes in San Francisco. After a superb sole marguery with friends upstairs at Jack's, it became my responsibility to see a vacationing physician into a cab for his hotel. We walked outside together, but his attention was diverted by a hook and ladder truck and its sweaty, begrimed crew preparing to leave the scene of a fire. He rushed over and with unerring aim settled his hand on the fire captain's shoulder.

"What's been going on here?" he asked, much in the tone he might use to demand a scalpel.

The captain looked him over calmly, welcoming the chance to catch his breath. "We had a little fire," he said finally.

"Set it again," my friend demanded. "I missed it."

I have seen men led away and booked for less. I tried to intercede. The captain waved me off.

"My boys are tired," he said. "If you could just as well wait until tomorrow night, we'll promise you a good time."

The suggestion seemed acceptable to my friend, and we got the hell out of there.

No dialogue quite like that ever reached my ears outside of San Francisco. It was the kind of moment that the city understands. San Francisco was born in a spirit of fun, and often a twinkle still can be detected. In such a moment, Enrico Banducci, the noted entrepreneur of the hungry i, was the victim of foul play. The assault was led by Joe Rosenthal, the San Francisco newspaper photographer and Pulitzer Prize winner, and three tourists happily collaborated. The four of us felt a need to meditate with Mort Sahl, and there simply was no room to squeeze more chairs into the club. Rosenthal withdrew into a dark depression, and Banducci asked if he were ill.

"No," said Rosenthal, "it's nothing."

Banducci pressed a glass of cognac on him, but Rosenthal pushed it away. With that, Banducci showed real alarm. Rosenthal consented to explain. "It was simply a promise I made. These three men," he said, waving his arm grandly toward us, "these men are the only survivors of the group I photographed, raising the flag on Iwo Jima."

It was an inspired plan of attack. I was emaciated from a siege of hepatitis, one of my companions was taped and hunched from back surgery, and the third had worn a hearing aid since childhood. We were not conscious of our pathetic appearance, but Rosenthal obviously had been, and after one look for himself Banducci had no doubts. A party was ejected from the club and a table was placed for us at Sahl's feet. Sahl paid us a stirring patriotic tribute, and there was no check.

In the face of such nostalgia, it would be patently unrealistic to disclaim a personal affection for San Francisco.

North Beach is only a tiny backwash of the city. San Francisco is afflicted with a dulling conformity and with the conservative quiescence of middle-age. But the shadow of its dashing, spirited past has not entirely faded. Even tainted as it is with narcissism, the conformity of San Francisco is more interesting than are the wilder sprees of most cities.

10

NORTHERN CALIFORNIA

A Vast and Virile World

When Sebastian Vizcaino sailed into Monterey Bay in 1602, he embellished its scenic beauty so much in his log that the next white man on the scene, Gaspar de Portola, marched by in 1769 without recognizing it.

Portola returned the next year and built a fort. Father Junipero Serra built another of his missions at Monterey, and completed the chain of twenty-one with one in Sonoma Valley. Padres still make good wine in this area. Everyone tries to coöperate; in 1961, the Internal Revenue Department made a compromise settlement on a multi-million dollar income tax case against a religious order involving profits from the Christian Brothers winery in nearby Napa Valley.

The Franciscans left their missions soon after Mexico won its independence from Spain in 1821 and California became a Mexican outpost. There followed an era in which the rich got particularly richer, and the poor—mostly Indians—grew unbelievably poorer. England and France had their eyes on California, but it was being settled primarily by American pioneers. The American settlers were welcomed by the gracious *Californios*, and so were the New England clipper ships which brought cloth and plows, pots and needles. Yankee trappers roamed the Sierra Nevada and found their way into the Great Central Valley.

President Andrew Jackson offered to buy Northern California from the Mexicans in 1835, but got nowhere. In 1842, Commodore T.A.C. Jones received a message that war had broken out between the United States and Mexico and that a British naval force was standing offshore to seize California. Hastily he raised the American flag above Monterey. Within hours he learned there was no war and no British fleet; promptly he lowered the flag, apologizing profusely to the polite Mexicans for the little misunderstanding. Everyone had a drink.

It may not have been a misunderstanding, four years later, when Captain J. C. Frémont, on a surveying expedition for the United States, precipitated a skirmish with Mexican forces and raised the flag over Sonoma. Within weeks, the Mexican War had indeed begun; the American flag was raised over Monterey again, and California was claimed for the United States. Finally, in 1848, Mexico ceded California to the United States in the treaty of Guadalupe Hidalgo.

The bragging about California got under way in earnest. In 1846 a New York newspaper called the state "a perfect paradise, a perpetual spring"; it was the same year that members of the Donner party, trying to cross the Sierra Nevada, escaped starvation only by eating others who had frozen to death.

In January, 1848, James Wilson Marshall, a wagon builder from New Jersey, picked up a nugget half the size of a pea from the tail race of a saw mill on the south fork of the American River. That nugget set off a movement which has become the greatest migration of people in the history of the world. There were fewer than ten thousand white persons in all of California before the Gold Rush—at a time when New York State numbered close to three million. It was the first chapter of the westward tilt; by 1860, there were 379,994 persons in California. But the Gold Rush has never ended.

Much of California's wealth has been agricultural. The pattern for its big farms was set by the Spanish-Mexican rancho. John Sutter, a Swiss-born farmer, was the first American to settle the Great Central Valley, and he prospered with crops and cattle until gold was discovered at his mill. "My best days," he later wrote, "were just before the discovery of gold." As miners began to disappear, farmers appeared. Cattlemen were almost destroyed by a drought in 1862, and then land speculators moved in and hit pay dirt with California land promotions that brought speculative money from the East. Wheat boomed for an interval in the 1880's. In 1875, forty-five men owned four million acres of California, and the Grange was organized to protect the interests of the small family farmer. The saga of the Great Central Valley really began toward the end of the nineteenth century with the development of irrigation projects.

In 1861, the new California legislature formed a commission to improve the new state's wine industry. Soon Colonel Agoston Haraszthy sailed for Europe, and returned with more than one hundred thousand cuttings of vines. They became the foundation of the California wine industry, which grew smartly until the almost fatal hiatus of Prohibition.

Labor unions found strength in Northern California while Southern California was still a stronghold of the union shop. But labor's strength was concentrated in San Francisco, and not in the towns or on the farms. In 1933 and 1934, there was a wave of agricultural strikes up and down the state, and vigilante methods were used to put them down. The American Federation of Labor and the Congress of Industrial Organizations united in 1938 to lead in the defeat of a statewide anti-picketing proposition.

But life was improving too slowly for the refugees from the Dust Bowl, who made up much of that first great wave of migrant workers in the Great Central Valley. In the classic, *Grapes of Wrath*, John Steinbeck wrote of their misery. To the grower in the Great Central Valley, the plight of the migrants never was as bad as Steinbeck portrayed it; to labor-union organizers, it is still just as bad today as Steinbeck portrayed it. When it comes to the migrant worker, for once California's troubles have not been because people were bragging about the state.

◇◇◇

Whatever comes within its tight confines, San Francisco will remain the economic hub of Northern California, a vast and virile world of redwood and rain forest, volcano and glacier, fog-cloaked seacliff and searing desert. Its irrigated farmlands stretch flat to the horizon; its vineyards roll gently over purple hills; its teeming subdivisions abut the wilderness. It is a wildly incongruous land, encompassing the noblest of nature and the most pitiful of human squalor. Almost anything that can be said of any part of the nation can be said of some part of Northern California. It is a region which has known everything but doubt.

Even Californians forget that one-third of their state lies north of San Francisco. It is an area that understands solitude, one foreign to any image of contemporary California that the stranger may hold, primarily because it is sparsely settled. It is the country of huge brown trout and mule deer, of sequoia and buckthorn, of dove and wild turkey.

To be precise, San Francisco is not in Northern California but in Central California. But Northern California, in its accepted sense, includes the forty-eight counties that lie between the Tehachapi Mountains in the south, and the Oregon border in the north. Northern California has grown vigorously in the postwar years of the westward tilt. The population of San Francisco declined by 32,502 between 1950 and 1960. In those years, the whole of Northern California, including the Bay Area, grew from 4,654,248 to 6,560,512, an increase of forty-one percent. During several years of the 1950's, the rate of population growth in Northern California exceeded that of Southern California.

The power lines of one of the largest utilities in the world form a seventy-five-thousand-mile web of wires serving seven million people in forty-eight Northern California counties. Pacific Gas & Electric Company, the behemoth of Western private power, is a scarred but unbowed warrior of the Western battle between public and private power. The regional divisions by which PG&E has shaped its operations provide a convenient route to glimpse the Northern California country and its people. There are thirteen divisions, and each can be seen by driving an elongated oval route beginning and ending at San Francisco. Such a tour easily could be a two-week affair, and its contrasts would be rapid. Across the Golden Gate Bridge from San Francisco are bayside commuter towns like Sausalito, Belvedere, and Tiburon. Northward lie the coastal redwoods of the Humboldt. Moving on to the far north of California, dominated by snow-capped Mount Shasta, the oval crosses the mountains eastward to the high desert and volcanic country of Lassen, on the edge of the Great Basin. Southward, the route swings into the heart of the Sierra Nevada, awesome in the high mountain grandeur of the Donner Pass, and nostalgic in the ghost towns of the Gold Rush era. Still

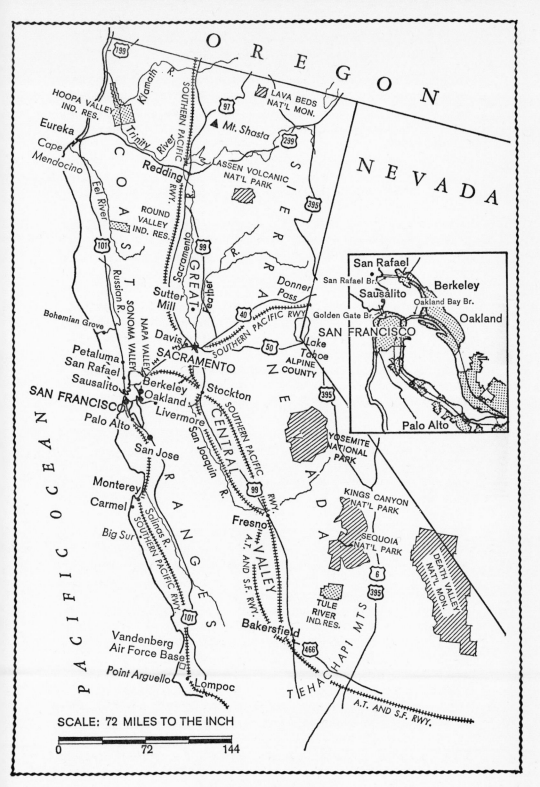

Northern California

southward is Sacramento, near the heart of the gold country and the center of the turbulent California political world. The Stockton division, still farther south, extends from the delta tidelands east of San Francisco to the snowy summits of the Sierra Nevada Mountains. At the south bend of the oval is San Joaquin, the agricultural heartland of California. Westward, at the Pacific Coast, are Santa Maria and the missile belt surrounding Vandenberg Air Force Base and the Pacific Missile Range headquarters at Point Mugu. The hills are smaller now, the oak trees sparser. Northward again are oil and cattle fields, sugar-beet farms, the precipitous wildness of the Big Sur, and then the Monterey peninsula. Finally there is San Jose, the fastest growing city of Northern California, at the foot of the San Francisco Bay peninsula. The oval is complete.

This is the shell of Northern California. What lies inside?

Where there is water and industry, rural areas and small towns have burgeoned as rapidly as any of the great Western cities. Where tourists come, mountain and coastal hideaways have become thriving resorts. But within this oval are regions almost as unspoiled as at the turn of the century; their residents scorn boom talk and make it plain they want to be left alone. Sometimes they are; with increasing frequency, they are not. Their isolation is pierced by encroaching subdivisions, new highways, and most frequently by science and industry, hand-in-hand on the prowl for settings which capitalize on climate, scenic beauty, water and power—and that commodity which is becoming dearest even in gargantuan California: space. Retracing the oval more slowly, it is possible to see a rural kaleidoscope of the westward tilt, a sort of frenetic pastorale.

The mountains of Marin County thrust down into the Pacific and into San Francisco Bay like jagged brown fingers. The skyline of the city lies behind, to the south; ahead, along the Pacific shoreline for more than six hundred miles, is country. Portland is the next city, almost a state-and-a-third distant.

In Marin the impact of the metropolis appears in commuter towns of such varying elegance as Mill Valley, Kentfield, and Ross. Cows and chickens are giving way to subdivisions. For the tourist, such towns are a base for exploration of the southernmost grove of two thousand-year-old coastal redwoods, Muir Woods. From San Rafael, a bridge second in length only to the Oakland–San Francisco Bridge spans an arm of the San Francisco Bay for more than five miles to industrial Richmond, making San Rafael a commuter town both for San Francisco and for the East Bay. Twenty miles north is a town with a name which is the standard reference for rurality among

North Beach comedians: Petaluma. It shamelessly calls itself "the egg basket of the world," and its poultrymen are fighting economic extinction with automation, so that seven million hens may keep on laying fifty million eggs a year.

Inland from the coast lie the fabled valleys of Sonoma and Napa, from which come some of the finest of all table wines. Autumn is the time to be there, during the crush of grapes, when the vineyards are bronzed and golden and the aroma of the grape lies heavy in the lazy sunshine. The massive redwood and white-oak aging tanks; the cool, deep caves where bottles of champagne are turned each day by hand to push the sediment into the bottle neck; the ivy-grown stone buildings in the European style; the bottling rooms and cellars—all these are little changed from fifty or seventy years ago, steeped in a New World tradition. In a new land like California, tradition is a luxury; it is a land where oldness is simulated often because it is novel and desired. But the wine valleys were born old. The California vintner is set apart from the big industrial farmer of the Central Valley by his leisurely, loving dedication to his work.

The finest New York City restaurants stock only second-rate California wines. The explanations of California vintners (not enough of the best wines) and of New York restaurateurs (California wines have no snob value) make equally little sense. The best varietal wines from California are on a par with all but the most exceptional European wines, but they are not abundant. The urban Westerner has grown conscious of California wines; and unlike California fruits, the best California wines are consumed near at hand and are readily available in the West.

(In Rutherford, a tiny Napa Valley town, El Real restaurant has a wine list of sixty-seven varieties, all from the nearby coastal valleys. That is almost as many people as live in Rutherford.) Only a few classic European wines exceed the Cabernet Sauvignon, a robust but satiny claret produced primarily in the Napa, Sonoma and Santa Clara valleys; or white wines like Johannisberg Riesling and Pinot Chardonnay, grown primarily in the Livermore Valley of Northern California.

The finest California wines come from these four valleys, all within a hundred-mile radius of San Francisco. Napa and Sonoma are separated only by a range of purplish, oak-studded hills. The Santa Clara Valley is south of San Francisco. To the east is Livermore, most famed for the white wines which evolve from its gravelly soil.

Livermore presents the most vivid contrasts. Until the nuclear age, it was a placid rural center for ranches and vineyards. The wineries are there still, but Livermore has become a hub of scientific sophistication. In Livermore now is the University of California's Lawrence Radiation Laboratory, its cyclotron, its Bevatron and its corps of nuclear scientists. The Sandia Corporation, the work horse of the Atomic Energy Commission, is here too.

The environment is more fitting at the Cresta Blanca winery five miles south of Livermore. A young vintner led me on a tour of this classic old winery. As we nibbled quail and sipped his premium dry sherry, he told me that he had graduated from an Ivy League university as a chemist, and had gone into the wine industry at a lesser salary than he would have commanded in many others. It was obvious that he loved his business. Not long before we talked, chemists had announced some success with an instant-mix coffee which is almost indistinguishable from brewed coffee in both taste and aroma. Fresh from an unsettling look at the nuclear laboratories of Livermore, I asked my guide if it were not likely that some day the same thing would be done with wine, and that the caves and kegs and cellars of Cresta Blanca would give way to stainless steel and tile laboratories.

He nodded thoughtfully. "I could do it myself," he said. "We could perfect a process which would enable us to sell a powdered wine concentrate and the alcohol separately. The customer could mix them with water in whatever proportion seemed to fit the occasion. But when that day comes, I'm getting out of the wine business."

There has been change in California winemaking, of course, since the California legislature formed a commission in 1861 to improve the new state's wine industry. Since vineyards were revived after Prohibition, they have set consistently higher marks for quality and quantity. Close to a hundred and thirty-five million gallons of California wine were shipped in 1961. California grows ninety percent of all grapes and produces eighty-five percent of all wines—and one hundred percent of all raisins—consumed in the United States. The states' vineyards and winery properties are valued at almost three-quarters of a billion dollars. There are two hundred and forty-nine bonded wineries and wine cellars. Annual returns to farmers from vineyards are nearly one hundred and fifty million dollars and the annual retail value of wine production is more than half a billion dollars. Though such figures are dwarfed by the statistics of California citrus or cotton or sugar beet, they bear witness to the revival of an amenity closely associated with Western life.

Some California winegrowers, like James D. Zellerbach, are gentleman farmers intrigued with the insidious charm of the vineyard. Frank Bartholomew, chairman of the board of United Press International, for years owned Buena Vista, one of California's oldest wineries, in the Sonoma Valley.

The wine industry is by now so accepted on the California scene that citizens may write the University of California Department of Viticulture on the Davis campus and receive state-researched instructions on how to make wine in gallon jugs at home. It is done, especially by European immigrants who need no instruction, but the procedure is not recommended by Fred Lang, a veteran vintner of German descent who showed me through the Charles Krug winery at St. Helena, the largest of the Napa Valley wineries.

"We do not have the barefoot any more," he said, pointing to the Garolla crusher which swallows the boxes of grapes as they come from the trucks, spits out the stems, and passes the juice, pulp, seeds and skins on to the fermenting tanks. In the weeks of the autumn crush, the increasing scientific concentration on winemaking is obvious. Karl Wente, a crew-cut young man who is a third-generation winegrower, said, "Europeans think of us as young people in a hurry. But to get good wines, you must sit with them. From the first crush, usually in September, until the first of November, I seldom get home. I crawl in the car and sleep for an hour; then I get up and change the cooling unit to another tank of wine."

The University of California recognizes the role of wine in the state with a full professorship for Dr. Maynard A. Amerine, chairman of its Department of Viticulture and Enology, and a member of its faculty on the Davis campus since 1921. Amerine is no ordinary cow-college man; he holds a Ph.D. from Berkeley, and one of his years of studying European winemaking was on a Guggenheim fellowship in 1954. His published writings number more than one hundred and twenty-five books and articles. His department offers nine scholarships each year to youths studying to be vintners, and the competition is keen.

North of the Napa Valley lies the apple country of Sebastopol and Guerneville, and the Russian River, a noted fishing stream. Nearby is Bohemian Grove, a 2,437-acre grove of redwoods owned by the Bohemian Club of San Francisco, the site since 1878 of the club's High Jinks, when only men gather for two-week summer encampments. Bark-covered logs are the seats in a large outdoor theater where many of the world's distinguished men have been both cast and critic. Founded by a cadre of artists and writers, the Bohemian Club draws a select membership from all over California. It was at Bohemian Grove that the Republican move to nominate Eisenhower for the Presidency took shape. Year after year, respectful attention has been given to Herbert Hoover's annual discussion of world affairs. The summer encampment, attended by about fifteen hundred men, is the most sought-after retreat in the West. It is a despotic operation. A captain is appointed by the club board; he is judge, jury and hangman. If any member or guest invites discipline, the captain has full power to throw the offender out of Bohemian Grove. It has happened, and it usually causes a flurry in the San Francisco columns.

Northward, the redwood groves thicken, the sun breaks through infrequently, the highways narrow and darken in the awesome stillness of the towering forests; and the northwest corner of California is at hand. The coastal cliffs face huge offshore rocks battered by waves, and through them roar the Trinity, the Klamath, the Mad, and the Eel Rivers, after their descent through deep wooded valleys from the coastal mountains. This is a California rarity: rain country. As much as one hundred and twenty inches may fall each winter in the isolated Mattole Valley on the coast. Rain forests of redwood and fir stretch into infinity. In this untroubled land of the lumberman, the dairyman and the fisherman, the air hangs heavy with wood smoke from burning waste at log mills.

The tourist sees his redwoods, is impressed, but presses on. The trees are aged, they are immense, they dwarf the soul and mind; the tourist finds himself restless, somehow disturbed, and he drives southward to San Francisco night life, or northward toward Portland, Seattle, and the Canadian border. Like rich food and rare wine, the big tree country is not for everyone; one must be ready to make peace with oneself before he can be at home with the redwoods.

Here in this corner of California is the Cape Mendocino Lighthouse, the westernmost point in the continental United States; the town of Petrolia, the site of the first oil discovery in California; Arcata, which calls itself the lumber center of the world; and the twin lumbering towns of Rio Dell and Scotia, which claim the world's largest redwood mill. It is a region isolated by distance, by mountainous terrain, and often by heavy winter rains. Some of the region is in economic limbo. Big lumber firms are buying out small loggers for their timber holdings. They are seldom in such a hurry to cut trees as the small logger.

Moving eastward across Northern California, the traveler cannot escape from Mount Shasta, which dominates the landscape for a hundred miles. It is solitary, symmetric, ghostly white in winter and summer, reigning over wooded, tumbled mountains and valleys. A former volcano rising 14,162 feet, it ranks only fifth highest among California peaks, but it is perhaps the loveliest. The Coastal and the

Cascade mountain ranges meet in its shadow, sealing the north end of the Great Central Valley of California. To the south is Shasta Dam, second highest and second largest dam in the United States, the chief unit of the federal Central Valley Irrigation Project, which cost more than one hundred and seventy million dollars. The dam is five hundred and sixty feet high and thirty-five hundred feet long; behind it, Shasta Lake backs up fifty miles from end to end. The towns of Shasta country are bleak: lumber towns with weather-beaten houses and battered fences, grimy business districts, great lumber mills with stacks of pine and fir boards. There are hamlets named Hayfork, Peanut, and Big Bar.

In tiny Weaverville, where James Hilton visited before writing *Lost Horizon*, there has been agitation by the local newspaper editor that the town be renamed Shangri-La. The Western individualist has his stronghold in country like this. Weaverville was enraged in 1961 when it was designated a depressed area clearly entitled to federal aid. The Weaverville *Journal* greeted this news with an irate editorial entitled, "Lie Down and Be Depressed, Damn You." Bank deposits were at an all-time high in Weaverville, a new supermarket was about to open, and the *Journal* insisted that Weaverville wanted no help. The background of this anomaly was significant: Pacific Gas & Electric had fought for, and lost, the construction of the nearby Trinity River Dam. It became a federal project and Weaverville enjoyed a modest boom. In anticipation of the completion of dam construction, and subsequent recession in Weaverville, the depressed-area classification was applied to the little town. Weaverville wanted none of it. "Big Brother is watching us, all right," concluded the editorial, "but he's myopic."

The Trinity River people are not lacking in ingenuity: one plant has been experimenting with using the oils of the graceful, red-barked manzanita trees to make rocket fuel; another company uses manzanita as a base for cattle and hog food. In these towns around Shasta Lake, the family cars sit at the curb, and nearly every garage holds a boat. PG&E workmen know this area well: they must dynamite in lava beds for pole holes, cross rivers in a bos'n's chair to read meters on snowy peaks, maintain flumes and canals. One PG&E employee is a cowboy whose sole job is to patrol company-owned grazing land. Linemen are flown by helicopter in winter to clear ice from the power lines of the Redding television transmitter atop a spur of Mount Shasta. Yet in the thirty-five hundred square miles of its Shasta division, the utility averages only one customer per square mile.

In the northeast corner of California are harsh lava beds, forested mountain wilderness with undisturbed game, and high desert country. Lumber and hydroelectric power are the major resources, although there are scattered ranches and orchards. Fishing, hunting and skiing bring seasonal tourism. But people are the scarcest commodity of all. Some of these counties have shown sharp population drops since World War II. Nothing much seems to be happening. This country is a long way from anything, and the young people head for the cities. Lassen County showed a twenty-six percent drop in population between 1950 and 1960. Almost as large as Connecticut, it is inhabited by fewer than fifteen thousand people; at that, it is a relatively populous county. Along the eastern border of California, Plumas County has fewer than twelve thousand; Sierra County has twenty-three hundred, and in the last census Alpine County had three hundred and sixty residents.

With seven hundred and seventy-six square miles of area, most of it up and down the crest of the Sierra Nevada, Alpine is a county of lakes and mountains, no railroad, only ninety-three miles of surfaced road, and no incorporated city. So subordinated to nature are affairs of state in Alpine that county court sessions are scheduled to coincide with the fishing season. Alpine is not alarmed. It would welcome a modest share of the population explosion, but it does not aim for the stars. Its board of supervisors advised its representative on the California-Nevada Compact Commission to reserve enough water for an ultimate population of ten thousand in Alpine County. That, the board agreed, would be quite enough. Members ridiculed a report that the California Department of Water Resources had projected a population figure upward of fifty thousand for Alpine. "If that ever happens, I tell you, I'll leave," said Frank Sasselli, the Alpine board chairman. Alpine intends to go on doing what it has been doing: preserving wide open spaces for fishing, hunting, and skiing. But the county has not buried its head. A subdivision of twenty-five lots was approved at the same session at which the water-planning matter exploded; furthermore, the board moved toward a uniform county building code.

Moving southward on the eastern side of Northern California, there appear some of the highest, most scenic and forbidding mountains of the West. At Donner Summit, Highway 40 and the Southern Pacific Railroad snake over the Sierra Nevada at 7,135 feet. In the lower hills west of Donner is the Mother Lode country: it is here, in the gravel bed of the American River at Sutter Mill, that gold was discovered in 1848. To power company men, winters here mean snowshoes and skis; maintenance men stake warning flags for skiers over high-tension transmission lines buried in snow which may drift to four hundred inches in depth.

The transition of the gold country is another dramatic example of the changing West. For almost a century the region thrived on gold, until inflation made the flagging ore more costly to mine than it was worth. Like others, the North Star mine, once the deepest and richest gold mine in the world, is idle today, its yards in Grass Valley filled with weeds and rusting machinery. (It yielded more than eighty million dollars in gold, with one producing shaft ninety-eight hundred feet below ground.)

The Mother Lode country is not scenically spectacular. There are stands of old oaks in the foothills; higher ranges lie dirty-green with pine and manzanita. Orchards of plums and pears are watered by ancient miners' ditches. Beside every road lie the black scars left by the miners, surrounded by weed-grown, barren acres of tailings. The small towns of the Mother Lode are dependent today on the tourist who makes nostalgic explorations of the ghost villages: Poker Flat, Slumgullion, Bedbug, Chinese Camp, Rough and Ready, Angels Camp, Rawhide, Port Wine, Grizzly Flats, Poverty Hill, Shingle Springs, Dutch Flat, Fiddletown, Copperopolis. In most of these are valid remnants of the Gold Rush—plank sidewalks and colonnaded balconies—and less valid plaques and inscriptions boasting about Mark Twain, Bret Harte, Wells Fargo, and any number of vast gold strikes. But little gold is being mined today, and most of the miners have moved on to other work, like Aerojet-General's rocket-fuel plant down the slopes of the Mother Lode at Sacramento.

Sacramento is the largest of the towns along the four-hundred-and-fifty-mile length of the Great Central Valley, the oblong trough of California which lies between the Sierra Nevada to the east and the Coastal Range to the west. The new world of California has hit this area broadside. Nowhere else in the West is the collision of old and new more vivid.

As the gold nearby petered out, Sacramento began to perceive its destiny as an administrative capital city and a traffic hub of rail, highway and river for the agricultural riches of the Great Central Valley. Promptly it felt the impact of the new Western industrial revolution. Its elm-shaded streets became snarled with traffic; and the impressive golden dome of its capitol rose above old iron-front and brick buildings which were no longer the nostalgic mementos of the Gold Rush but had become a festering scab of cheap hotels, saloons, rooming houses, and warehouses. Emblazoned on the pediment of the State Office Building was the poet's plea, "Bring me men to match my mountains." Instead, there was Artie Samish, soon to be exposed and imprisoned as a boastful and over-industrious lobbyist, entertaining and wheedling in the shadow of the capitol while downtown businessmen pondered the population drift to the suburbs which was leaving them stranded. While a nine-hundred-man staff muddled in the state architect's office, grinding out banal, cheerless public buildings up and down the booming state, Sacramento civic leaders called in Richard Neutra and Robert Alexander to chart a course for the redevelopment of their capital city. The voluble and courageous *Sacramento Bee* awoke to the threat of freeways and slums, and threw its considerable weight behind redevelopment.

Today the change is in full swing. Much of central Sacramento has been pulverized to make way for a capitol mall which will be a green-fringed approach to the capitol; for Capitol Towers, a garden-apartment center for government workers; and for new business buildings aimed at eventually replacing the blight of sixty-two blocks between the Sacramento River and the capitol. Adjacent to Capitol Park, an airy brick executive mansion, designed in an architectural competition, will replace the eighty-five-year-old Victorian home of past governors. Many citizens are fighting to preserve historic structures of Old Sacramento near the river front—such as the hardware store on K Street over which Collis P. Huntington, Charles Crocker, Leland Stanford and Mark Hopkins met to plan the first transcontinental railroad; and the B. F. Hastings Building, at which a horseback rider arrived in 1860 to finish the first cross-country trip by Pony Express.

Sacramento is placed second in the population-growth projections for 1960–70 by Stanford Research Institute; with its strategic location and natural resources, it has been discovered by industry. It also faces heavy increases in state-government employment to cope with the swelling population of the state. Sacramento receives its share of the soaring California state budget (close to three billion dollars), which has become the largest state budget in the nation.

The Great Central Valley is larger than Denmark; the Appalachian mountain range of the East would fit into it easily. The upper valley is called the Sacramento and the lower the San Joaquin after the rivers which traverse each area; topographically, the valleys merge indistinguishably into the Great Central Valley. It is the home of about two million people, who are notably open, relaxed and industrious. More than eight million acres are under cultivation. They are irrigated by wells, and also through twenty thousand miles of man-made canals that make up the Central Valley Water Project, which redistributes the waters of the Sacramento and San Joaquin over a three-hundred-mile distance. The Great Central Valley is an agricultural wonderland; with water and rich soil, the California sun is free to work its miracles. This is the heartland of California's three-billion-dollar agricultural industry, which provides one-third of the nation's canned and frozen fruits and vegetables. Virtually every can of fruit cocktail and every canned peach in America comes from California. The major crops in the valley are cotton, grapes (table, wine, and raisin), peaches, apricots, plums, olives and melons. The towns of the valley break the monotony of high-speed, north-south Highway 99, from Redding at the north, through Chico, Sacramento, Stockton, Modesto, Merced, Madera, Fresno, to Bakersfield at the south.

Somewhere between Fresno and Bakersfield, at the southerly end of the valley, San Francisco newspapers give way on newsstands to Los Angeles newspapers. Most of the valley is tied closer to the northern city than the southern, largely because the south of the valley is closed off by California's only east-west mountain range, the Tehachapis, which marks the northern boundary of Southern California. But valley residents seem content to see the vast valley in terms of their own fifty-mile radius, within which most of their needs are filled. The loyalty that counts in the Great Central Valley is loyalty to the soil. It is found among owners as well as foremen, although owners spend more time in urban offices, supervising vast holdings and relaying orders. In Kern County, airplanes and helicopters outnumber draft animals.

Today most crops are machine harvested, but until a few years ago, mechanized harvesting in the Great Central Valley was limited primarily to cotton and sugar beets. Recently machines have been used to harvest almonds, filberts, and walnuts. Booms shake the nuts from the trees and pickup devices gather them from the ground. A tomato harvester now cuts off the entire vine, separates the tomatoes, sorts them and conveys them into bins. Experimental equipment is being tested for the automatic harvesting of peaches at the speed of two minutes per tree, of prunes at one minute per tree, and of lettuce at three hundred and twenty cartons per hour.

Such harvesting procedures are the current chapter in the saga of labor in the Great Central Valley. In 1939, Carey McWilliams wrote angrily of labor exploitation in his book, *Factories in the Field*. This same valley is the locale of Steinbeck's *Grapes of Wrath* and of human misery not yet absent. In the summer of 1961 the American Federation of Labor and the Congress of Industrial Organizations abandoned another drive to unionize farm labor; it had failed in the Great Central Valley after a two-year organizational effort. At about the same time, farm-labor camp inspectors of the California Housing Division padlocked a Fresno County camp. Many other substandard labor camps were protected by retroactivity clauses in new county and state housing and sanitation codes. One of these, still operating in 1962, was the Three Rocks camp in the melon and cotton country forty miles west of Fresno. Three Rocks has fifty shacks of frame and tarpaper, with electricity and bottled gas, but without sewerage or running water. Water is carried by bucket from a service station several hundred yards away. The rent for these shacks rose in 1961 from $3 to $15 a month, after Fresno health authorities urged the camp operator to install water lines; with this additional income, he hoped to install lines before the 1962 harvest. Most of the tenants were Mexican-American. They seemed generally undisturbed at their surroundings; their men had work in nearby fields, and they saw no prospect of cheaper quarters. Eleven members of two families were occupying a one-room shack at Three Rocks in the summer of 1961, yet above many shacks in farm labor camps all over the valley, television antennas rise, and outside, late-model cars are parked.

Most of the camps have running water. Tightening provisions of the law in the late 1950's led many farmers to clean up labor camps on their property; some were closed. Many farmers have begun to understand that better housing attracts better migrant workers. Some workers, sensing prospects of steady employment, settle down and buy their shacks and begin to impove them. One happy example of improved conditions is the ten-thousand-acre farm of Frank Coit, a Fresno cantaloupe-and-grain grower. His farm has a hundred and fifty permanent employees and a million-dollar payroll. In melon harvest season, eight hundred and fifty temporary employees and their dependents congregate to occupy two dormitories and seventy-five family cabins on his ranch. There are showers and toilets; such facilities are not uncommon today in the Great Central Valley.

The migrant worker is becoming less of a social problem; with California industrialization, he is moving slowly toward becoming a city dweller. In Fresno County, about sixty-five thousand farm workers are permanent residents. Another twenty thousand migrant workers appear at the peak of the grape harvest in late August and early September; about three thousand of them are *braceros* from Mexico, most of them melon-pickers, present in the United States under a bilateral agreement which has been furiously contested by organized labor.

Despite their repeated failures during recent years, labor organizers claim credit for forcing valley employers to install sanitary facilities in the camps. Undoubtedly they have been a factor in raising wages. To the north in Monterey and Santa Cruz counties, seven hundred growers in May, 1961, headed off a Teamsters' Union attempt to organize laborers in lettuce and celery fields by granting a minimum $1 hourly wage, a demand which they had fought hard in Washington and Sacramento. But the migrant laborer can expect to earn these wages for little more than half the year. His annual income is likely to be around one thousand dollars, the lowest wage in the American economy. Increasing focus on bringing the migrant worker under social and labor legislation is having a profound effect on practices throughout the Great Central Valley. There was strong opposition to the extension by Congress in 1961 of the pact to import Mexican laborers, yet the *bracero* is favored by growers over many American migrants; he is often a harder worker. His presence under federal sanction has been a staggering blow at union drives to organize American farm laborers. Union organizers attributed their failure in the 1960–61 effort to a lack of education among farm workers. Noting that migratory workers show little interest in unions, employers are confident that they will avert unionization. Moreover, their continued trend to automation in the fields works on their side.

The migrant moves on from the Great Central Valley in midwinter to pick oranges in Arizona, and thence to Oregon and Washington. Throughout the winter, migrant children pick up bits of schooling here and there, but their challenge to educators is enormous. At Westside Elementary School in Fresno County, Principal Norman Jaco has learned that his pupils, most of them migrant children, cannot be taught until they are fed. If they are embarrassed by inadequate clothing, they first must be clothed. The cafeteria luncheon is the only adequate meal of the day for many of his pupils. But it is not always enough; the children, loyal to sisters, brothers and parents, slip food in their pockets to take home. At Westside, a parents' club maintains a clothes warehouse and dispenses surplus oatmeal or rice with honey and milk. Schooling is more basic than elsewhere. Children learn to repair shoes and clothing, to make mouse-proof chests from cardboard boxes and chairs from tree branches. They develop an interest in cleanliness by washing school buses.

The historic labor scandals of the Great Central Valley, in terms of numbers and overall importance, are past. The greed of the grower has been tempered by social and union pressures, by law, by prosperity, and by the enlightenment of newer generations. Those who seek causes can find them anywhere. But it is difficult to foresee any combination of circumstances in the Great Central Valley which could become the setting again for the sorry tragedy of the Depression era. Abuses exist in sufficient quantity to support the production of an occasional film documentary or the lament of a magazine article. But I have traveled the valley in and out of harvest season, on the byroads and back roads, and I have talked to scores of workers and been inside their shacks. The fact is that it is hard to find villains among the industrial agriculturists who dominate the valley today. The novel of the great-grandchildren of Steinbeck's Joads should be written. Not infrequently, they may be found today in their Thunderbirds and Triumphs on the campuses of Berkeley or even Stanford. But such a novel would be poor reading. It is not the same stuff of drama as the offering of a milk-laden young breast to a starving stranger in a barn.

It was not merely for a better job that a once-powerful regional voice like that of Carey McWilliams, the most effective modern spokesman of the California oppressed, moved on to an editorship in New York City. His years in California as a gadfly to the oppressor were not wasted. But in this golden land of plenty, the gadfly must search ever deeper to find his vulture.

The long narrow oval which takes in Northern California turns northward and back toward San Francisco through the coastal counties of Central California. The missile boom has struck Santa Maria: seventeen miles to its west begins the one-hundred-and-three-thousand-acre Vandenberg Air Force Base, and Point Mugu, headquarters of the Pacific Missile Range. The highest rate of population growth in any part of California between 1960 and 1970 is predicted for this area. Eight of the old Franciscan missions lie within these coastal counties. There is also the lush Salinas Valley, center of lettuce and artichoke production; Hearst's famed castle at San Simeon; plants for sugar-beet and magnesium production; the artists' colony of Carmel; the savage grandeur of Big Sur, the cliffside artists' retreat where the Santa Lucia Mountains fall off precipitously to the Pacific and bold redwood homes are poised like pygmies on the cliffs, hundreds of feet above the surf; and the majestic Monterey peninsula, one of the most compelling juxtapositions of sea and land in the world. South of Monterey is mostly rural territory and parkland, sparsely settled but traversed heavily by Los Angeles–San Francisco traffic on the fast freeways of Highway 101 and the tortuous, precipitous coastal road, Highway 1, which follows the dizzying heights of the coastline. North of Monterey are agricultural valleys, larger and more frequent towns, and finally San Jose, the epicenter of Northern California's population explosion.

The total population of San Jose in 1950 was only 95,280. By 1960 it had moved past the two-hundred-thousand mark and was soaring steadily. The population of Santa Clara County, of which San Jose is the seat, has quadrupled in twenty years and is expected to pass the two million mark before 1985, giving San Jose a population in excess of San Francisco. Already metropolitan San Jose contains more people than San Francisco.

PG&E has been adding customers at the equivalent rate of sixty-five thousand people each year in Santa Clara County. The whole county gives the impression of a giant construction camp. San Jose payrolls have been swelled by electronic plants. Lockheed employs fifteen to twenty thousand workers at Sunnyvale, producing the Polaris missile. Nearby are Ford, IBM (which Khrushchev visited), General Electric's atomic power equipment department, FMC Corporation (129th-ranked United States corporation in 1961), Ames Laboratories, and the National Aeronautics and Space Administration wind tunnel at Moffett Field. There is even a cement plant which uses oyster shells dredged from the San Francisco Bay.

Why did all this happen to San Jose? The cry is heard plaintively all through the Santa Clara Valley from those who remember it as a quaint agricultural community, a distribution point for prune and apricot, a dried-fruit packing center; or from those who knew that San Jose had been California's first Spanish pueblo and first incorporated town; or from those whose parents and grandparents remember that the willow trees along the Alameda, a main thoroughfare, were planted for protection against wild cattle. It was not long ago that its Municipal Rose Garden was the pride of San Jose, and a visit to it in May was an event to be talked of for days. The roses have escaped the bulldozers, but all the wild cattle in the West could not so thoroughly have uprooted the life that was dear to a lost generation of San Jose residents.

Building-permit statistics for 1959 help to place the San Jose story in focus. Among United States cities issuing permits that year in excess of fifty million dollars, Los Angeles, with two and a half million persons, ranked first by far over Manhattan and Chicago. San Jose, with two hundred thousand residents, ranked tenth—far ahead of Milwaukee, Atlanta, San Francisco, Washington, and Detroit.

More startling even are per capita building-permit values. San Jose led the nation with a staggering $639. Next were San Diego with $358, Manhattan with $266, and Los Angeles with $265.

Until 1955, when it became abundantly clear in San Jose what was happening, the citizenry had gotten along quite well with an antiquated city hall for which the cornerstone had been laid in 1878. With the authorization of a bond issue for a new city hall in that year, San Joseans turned their backs on the prune-and-roses culture of the past and underwent a profound change in attitude. They began approving bond issues for municipal improvements, and with minor exceptions, they haven't stopped yet. The city has voted close to one hundred million dollars in street and highway improvements, a sewage-treatment plant, parks and playgrounds, fire stations, libraries, public-works yards, central police facilities, health department facilities, a communications center and a municipal airport. The county has joined the fun with a new jail, hospital, juvenile hall, and a complete new complex of administrative office buildings.

San Jose has not exploded by chance. Every typical factor of the westward tilt is in play here. This combination of elements has brought what more conservative cities would regard as an overwhelming avalanche that could only result in chaos. Astonishingly, San Jose is not chaotic, though its last decade has been hectic. Its schools are not on double sessions, and space has been made for its graduates in nearby colleges and universities, including San Jose State College, Santa Clara University, and Stanford University. Some smog is developing, but Santa Clara County is a strong participant in the Bay Area Air Pollution Control District, which is making some progress; in the absence of smog, the climate is superb. San Jose has been a perpetual construction camp, yes, but not a barren one. Much of the orchard acreage has been preserved by green-belt zoning. Charming homes nestle in the foothills above the subdivisions of the valley floor. There are rather more bowling alleys than some would prefer, and certainly there is still a deficiency of good music and theater, but San Francisco lies at the other end of the Bayshore Freeway and the Monterey Jazz Festival and Carmel Bach Festival are over the hills to the south. The ocean is less than an hour to the west.

San Jose has not had time to develop great restaurants, but again, San Francisco is not far distant. Yosemite is due east, a four- or five-hour drive. And at home in San Jose, so close to such amenities, is a proliferation of sophisticated employment opportunity: glamour jobs in new smokeless factories and in offices which look out to the white clouds that dance over the green, oak-studded foothills. San Jose is no masterwork of a city. Perhaps it will never have as much either to lose or to gain as a city like San Francisco. But most San Joseans would far rather live in their city than in San Francisco. It is a compromise of many things: largeness and smallness, urbanity and rurality, big business and casual business practices, conservatism and informality, traditionalism and modernity. In these ways, San Jose may be the prototype of the new city, and its people the prototypes of the new city dwellers. This is not a city that will become great, but big business is being done here, its people seem a little more serene and compatible than most, and they are here because they wanted to come here. That is more than can be said of most cities. But it will take a longer test to find whether San Jose represents the good life, or merely a novena to mediocrity.

The potentiality of life in San Jose was not overlooked by the thousands of men in uniform who discovered the town during World War II. This was the first of the classic factors which has made San Jose a microcosm in the westward tilt. The war caught this prune town, with its proud heritage, flat-footed. San Jose State College, the oldest and largest school of its kind in the California system, had a handsome campus in the Spanish-California architectural tradition. Natives pointed out the home of Edwin Markham, the poet, as the birthplace of *Man With the Hoe.* But soon San Jose was a crossroads for servicemen from Fort Ord, Monterey, and Moffett Field. Its gracious people, never subjected to city pressures and untrained in the defenses of the more urbane, were hospitable and open-handed. San Jose developed a reputation as a good liberty town, and thousands of men of all services vowed to settle here after the war.

As though divining the future need for jobs, the San Jose Chamber of Commerce set up a realistic program in 1943 to attract industry. It was a fateful decision, made several years before industrial wooing became as chronic to the West as a hotelman's smile. This commitment, pursued diligently, was the second factor in reshaping San Jose.

Sometimes in cities of the New West, the confrontation of established residents and their traditions with the incoming thousands has been as turbulent as the meeting of the massive warm and cold currents of the Pacific—the Kuroshio and the Oyashio, described so vividly in Eugene Burdick's *The Blue of Capricorn.* At that point in the Pacific, Burdick wrote, the ocean "coldly smokes" with the condensation of the conflict. San Jose was fortunate; the smoke cleared rapidly from initial skirmishes between old and new. Most San Joseans did not show deep prejudice against infiltration, and the new breed turned out to be not bean pickers and welfare-hunters, but electronics technicians and nuclear physicists, young Harvard Business School graduates and wives who rushed out to join the Parent-Teacher Association or to organize a neighborhood chamber-music quartet.

A San Jose executive who has lived there since 1939, and has a considerable understanding of both old and new factions, described the coming of the new: "We realized they were city folk. They set right in to bring the amenities of city living to a suburb whose lawns and shade trees had helped to attract them here initially. Some of the old corporation hands from GE, IBM, and Lockheed came from Schenectady, Poughkeepsie, or Los Angeles. Maybe the professional scientists and engineers would stay out of community affairs, but their wives made up for their lack of participation. Corporation executives are active now in proportion to the stress their firms place on 'community relations.' In general, newcomers of all social and economic strata have turned out to be active in civic affairs. Very soon after their arrival they acquire the feeling that this is their community. It doesn't take long these days to become an old San Josean—anywhere from three to five years will do. You can find people who have been here that long complaining more loudly than any others about San Jose being 'overrun by strangers'! There really isn't any conflict between old-timers and newcomers that justifies so strong a word. Of course, higher tax rates rankle the retired old-timer particularly, and no wonder. Everybody else is making enough not to mind the bite."

In San Jose there was no moneyed, entrenched old guard inclined to oppose the inevitable urbanization of the valley. There was, instead, a cadre which wisely sensed that growth was inevitable, and that it should take a paternal hand in directing that growth intelligently. The guidance was not always motivated by sheer statesmanship; usually the orchard owners who have been forced out by subdivisions are leaving San Jose rich, or investing profits in rental property, the San Jose equivalent of coupon clipping. Thus San Jose was spared the trauma of one classic pattern in the westward tilt: it was not becalmed by indecision resulting from a stalemate of power between old and new. By 1955, enough of the new people had arrived to overcome the remaining inertia and opposition to change of the more rural-oriented population. They brought a new enthusiasm to San Jose—and they brought votes. When they were numerous enough simply to outvote old San Jose, the city began to change in earnest. In 1955, bond issues for civic improvements began to pass.

San Jose is a classic example of the quick-change from Old West to New. That is the third factor in its effective explosion, along with its initial exposure in wartime to thousands of young men at the start of adult life, and the realistic solicitation of jobs by community leaders.

Industry would not have come to San Jose if adequate water, power, and land had not been available. It would not have come except that San Jose offered extraordinary attractions to business and industrial people as a place to live: climate, schools, universities, recreational and cultural proximities, and the nebulous feeling of future. All of these forces combined in San Jose, and that is why it has been the fastest-growing city in California.

The job is far from done. San Jose has always drawn its main supply of water from wells, and now the water table, quite naturally, is dropping. Water importation, an established fact of life in Southern California and in San Francisco, is at hand; the mechanics of importation are a source of dissension. San Francisco, with surplus water in its Hetch Hetchy reservoir system from the Sierra Nevada, would like to sell water to San Jose and use the proceeds to refurbish its own crumbling domestic distribution system. Transit is another problem. San Jose is not allergic to freeways, like San Francisco; it cannot get them built fast enough. Traffic problems are immense, and rapid transit is needed. Proliferating local government units are becoming an overlapping maze, and advocates of metropolitan government are gaining support. But everywhere at hand is the same confidence that prevails in all the areas most massively involved in the westward tilt: San Jose has no doubt that she will get the job done, that the super-city and the super-life are within her reach.

Some of the intellectuals are less sanguine. At Stanford University, eighteen miles northwest, Dr. John Wendell Dodds sighed and told me, "People want to come to a place that is different. When they get there, they make it a place that is not different. The glow on the horizon becomes factitious." Down the hall, in Stanford's English department, Wallace Stegner said, "Periodically, I ask myself, 'Where is the least attractive place in the world?'—because I want to go there after another five years or so of this. I want to go where people have a little of the dignity of rareness. I live out in the horse pastures. They've been kind of slow to develop. But even they will be gone in five years." At work on a book of monumental length, living almost in seclusion at Stanford, Bruce Bliven said, "The problems we have here are the problems that confront all America, exaggerated in size because of our rapid growth. No matter what the quality of these in-migrants may be, their sheer numbers make an almost impossible problem. But probably we are moving toward a solution in that we are becoming conscious of the problem."

Back in San Francisco, at the start and the end of the northern California oval, James B. Black, board chairman of the Pacific Gas & Electric Company, stood looking from his fourteenth-floor window. Traffic was pouring from freeways and bridges into the congested streets of the city. A look of regret clouded his face, but it passed quickly.

"We are destroying what we had," he said. "Or at least some of what we had. But there is room for many, many more people out here, who all will be able to live better than they have ever lived before in their lives."

Buried deep in the prognostications of his research department is a clue to what is happening in the rural areas of Northern California. They have been growing at a somewhat faster rate than the cities of Northern California, and the predictions are that this trend will increase, in defiance of the national trend.

In the sparse commuter valleys of North Bay, among the redwoods of Humboldt, beneath the glacial cone of Shasta, in the mountain fastness of the Sierra Nevada, along the flat monotonous richness of the Great Central Valley, there is yet space. To expect that it will remain is like betting into a straight flush.

Part III

THE QUIETER WEST

11

OREGON

Green and Gangly

Indians called the big bold river *Ouragon*. There was no one around to argue about it until a United States sea captain named Robert Gray appeared in 1792 aboard his ship *Columbia*. He eased cautiously through the pounding breakers, sailed upriver to anchor, and named the river for his ship. At that time the Columbia River was part of a territory just as foreign, and considerably more hazardous, than Siberia today.

When Lewis and Clark explored the area in 1805, after their overland journey from St. Louis, they found a stretch of the Columbia that was flowing southeast, away from the Pacific. This gave them pause, but soon they realized that such perfidy is typical of this mightiest river of the West; it also flows northward in Canada on its way to the United States.

Lewis and Clark followed the Columbia to its mouth. They were on the Indians' freeway; the Columbia was a trade artery for fifty to sixty thousand Indians all over the Northwest. Their favorite

spa was Celilo Falls, where they made canoe portages and built sal-
mon-fishing stands out on the rocks over the falls. The Indian merchants of this turnpike were the Wishram tribe, who lived at Celilo.
They peddled to the Chinooks, who lived westward at the mouth of
the Columbia, to the Yakimas of the north, and to the Umatillas and
other plains Indians in eastern Oregon.

Lewis and Clark spoke enthusiastically about the Columbia,
and John Jacob Astor was a man who knew a good thing when he
heard about it. From New York, he arranged for a cadre to set up
a fur-trading post named Astoria at the mouth of the Columbia. It
was the first commercial settlement by Americans on the Pacific
Coast, and it had its troubles. Soon a British sloop brought news of
the War of 1812. Astor's man at Astoria sold out to the British
in a hurry at a good price. In a few years the Hudson's Bay Company
held a grip of iron on the Oregon Territory. Its man in Oregon was
Dr. John McLoughlin, a wise agent who dominated Oregon for
twenty years by being reasonable with his enemies. Today he is called
the King of the Columbia, and the Father of Oregon.

Though the fur trade was at its peak at this period, in 1839,
there were only one hundred and fifty-one Americans in all the Oregon country—which included the present states of Oregon, Washington, and Idaho, and parts of Montana, Wyoming, and British Columbia. There were only slightly more British citizens, and the two
countries skittishly held joint control of the territory. Tension grew.
James K. Polk was elected president of the United States on the crest
of the "Fifty-four-forty or fight!" hysteria. But for once, reason prevailed. The two nations compromised on the forty-ninth parallel, thus
fixing the northern boundary of the Western United States. The only
tip of Canadian land jutting south of that latitude is Vancouver Island.
That's been compromised, too; Victoria is its main city, and American tourists take that over each summer, to the considerable satis-
faction of the people of both countries.

Just as anyone else who comes unglued when the road is over-
crowded, the Indians were angry at the white men who were trapping
their beavers and catching their salmon and running back and forth
along their freeway. One Indian massacre followed a deadly epidemic
of measles which had decimated their tribes. The Cayuse, who had
never had measles before, quite reasonably blamed it on the white
man. Eventually the Army Cavalry rode up, and in 1859 most
Northwest Indians signed a peace treaty.

A barmaid on Applegate Creek near the Rogue River country
wrote in 1854 to her niece back East: "Em, I should like to have you
here, but a young lady is so seldom seen here that you would be in

danger of being taken by force." History does not note whether the
promise of violence brought the young lady out by return stage, but
we do have Daniel Webster's remarks, made in Congress about the
Columbia River Country: "What do we want of this vast, worthless
area, this region of savages and wild beasts, of shifting sands and
whirlpools of dust, of cactus and prairie dogs? To what use could we
ever hope to put these great deserts or these great mountain ranges,
impenetrable and covered to their base with eternal snow? Mr. President, I will never vote one cent from the public treasury to place the
Pacific Coast one inch nearer Boston than it is now."

Despite Webster, Oregon territory gave way to Oregon State
in 1859. Portland, founded before its rival, Seattle, was a healthy
town, but it also was already apathetic. Wrote Harvey Scott: "A few
persons talked about (statehood) with languid interest, and wondered
when the government of the state would be set in motion." There
was no boozing, no run on gunpowder, no dancing in the streets.

In 1877 a brave Nez Percé Indian, young Chief Joseph, made a
monumental retreat of a thousand miles before United States troops
rather than surrender the beautiful Wallowa Valley. He and his
people lost the valley, but when he died in 1904, he was buried beside Wallowa Lake in the valley for which he had fought. There is a
white man's town there now named Joseph.

Oregon's east-west railroad, the Union Pacific, arrived in the
early 1880's. Homesteading reached a peak. The wheat fields of
eastern Oregon turned green and gold.

A reform leader, William S. U'Ren, campaigned across Oregon
in the early days of the century for what came to be known as the Oregon System: the initiative, referendum, and recall.

In the midst of an unhappy revival of the Ku Klux Klan about
1930, Oregonians calmly elected a Jewish governor, Julius Meier.

Because the Bonneville Dam had been built on the Columbia
River in the middle Thirties, Oregon was ready for its boom in
World War II. To Portland shipyards and aluminum plants came
war workers from every state; Portland grew by ninety thousand
persons in three years. A war town named Vanport, at Portland's
northern edge, held forty thousand of them and ranked for a while as
Oregon's second largest city. The town disappeared on Memorial Day
in 1948 when the dikes of the flooded Columbia River gave way;
eight lives were lost.

But Portland did not disappear when the war boom burst. There
were plenty of Portlanders left to enjoy the Vicecapades of 1956–59,
which produced sound, fury and Pulitzer Prizes, but—despite the
solicitous attentions of Bobby Kennedy—led to the conviction and

sentencing of only three of the one hundred and seventeen indicted men: Big Jim Elkins, the star witness for the prosecution; one of his henchmen; and the district attorney, who was found guilty of failing to make an arrest at a party where there was gambling for charity.

There were only eight thousand Indians left in Oregon in 1960, but they had won a point. They were calling the Columbia River by the white man's name, not by their old name of *Ouragon*—but the white man was using their name for their state.

◇◇

The forests and high desert of Northern California do not cease; they become Oregon. In the quietening mood of California towns north of San Francisco, one senses that Oregon may be a different matter altogether from California. But there is nothing to suggest the totality of the contrast. The line that separates California and Nevada from Oregon is the forty-second parallel, where Spanish authority once ceased and British influence took over. In California, the adventuresome recklessness of the conquistador and the sophistication of the caballero left an imprint. The sober, bland and often prim New Englander was the first to follow the British into the Oregon Territory, and his mark is etched indelibly on the face of Oregon. Historians have made much of the fork in the Oregon Trail near the Snake River in southeast Idaho, where the wagon trains of immigrants separated. Farmers and merchants took the northern trail over the Cascades into the rich Willamette Valley of Oregon; the gold hunters headed south over the Sierra Nevada toward Sutter's Mill.

Once such a trend is set, the strong force of selective migration augments the pattern. Loggers and more farmers followed the agricultural pioneers into Oregon. For California, fortune hunting still is a powerful factor in migration; the gold is gone, but the lure of other riches sparkles like a grail—even though it may be involved in the prosaic acts of growing prunes or building houses.

Oregonians, who are alarmed by California anyhow, insist that the Oregon kind of growth is more solid. They crave stability. They take no chances. They do not enthusiastically solicit military spending or industry or migration. They are afraid that industry would destroy their rivers and streams and their air. At the same time, massive amounts of the waters of the Columbia River, flowing along the state border at the north, have been used upriver in Washington in one of the most frightening industrial processes known to man: production of plutonium in the eight reactors at the Hanford Atomic Products Operation of the Atomic Energy Commission. A continuous air monitoring program is conducted over Oregon and Washington by the General Electric Company, which operates Hanford, to guard against radiation. Water, ground, and vegetation are sampled each month for radioactivity over an area of twenty-five thousand square miles. But Oregonians have had little to say about the coming of Hanford, either before or since its function became known.

The New England heritage of Oregon is apparent in the names of city and towns: Portland, Salem, Albany. It is also evident in the church spires and trim white farm houses of the Willamette Valley. It is sensed on its college campuses; Joaquin Miller, the poet, wrote of his school days in Oregon, "I have never since found such determined students and omnivorous readers. We had all the books and none of the follies of great centers." The conservative heritage is felt most dramatically by the newcomer who has flown from a place like San Francisco into Oregon's only city, Portland. There are some sights which will look familiar, but very little that will *feel* familiar. Portland lies in the green, rolling valley of the Willamette River, near its junction with the Columbia. It has a glossy new air terminal, efficient freeways, a well-designed shopping center which ranked as the largest in the world when it was completed in 1960, two smart new hotels, a superb new Memorial Coliseum which Portlanders refer to as their Glass Palace, a new zoo, mental hospital, bridge, docks, schools, and sparkling new office buildings. Much of this construction followed a civic stirring in 1954, when voters approved a thirty-one-million-dollar bond package.

But by 1961, Portland voters had turned their backs on this orgy of reconstruction and were rejecting progressive bonding proposals and even school-district refinancing. Portland was stunned by the 1960 census. The city had expected a substantial increase; instead, the census revealed a drop of about one thousand, to 372,676. The overall metropolitan area had grown since 1950 at a rate almost exactly that of Oregon as a whole—slightly less than the national average. After a forty-percent increase in state population during the World War II boom between 1940 and 1950, this decline left Portland and all of Oregon badly shaken. There is no reason for such alarm now; the lumber business, the backbone of the Oregon economy, has been through a major readjustment, and its soft spots are being bolstered rapidly by new industry.

In 1962, Portland was like a virtuous maiden, rejected at the crest of an impetuous first love and swearing never again to proffer her favors. She will get over it. The irony is that she fancies herself the victim of the passion for growth in which she shared hesitantly and with grave misgivings. Portland embraced the idea of progress, because she had concluded it to be a necessary evil. Convinced by the census that she had not succeeded, simply because she was not bigger, Portland longed for a return to the familiar and comforting pattern of austerity.

But most of Portland's liabilities are psychological. Its business attitude has been widely negative, and its people are inclined to be insecure about the attitudes of others toward Portland. The city still seethes with adolescent wrangling: between the east and west sides of the Willamette River, which divides the city; between rural Oregon and Portland; between Oregon and California, and Oregon and Washington; and between Portland and Seattle. Portland will grow out of this, too.

Portland is smaller than Seattle, but each city has about two million people in its economic hinterland. Battle is being waged over several hundred thousand of these people because the hinterlands of the two cities overlap. The reasons for this friction are immediately apparent when one looks at a terrain map of the Northwest.

Portland and Seattle are the only two large cities of the Northwest. They are less than four hours apart by automobile, closer in travel time than Portland and some Oregon towns east of the Cascade Mountains, or Seattle and Spokane in eastern Washington. The Columbia River gorge that separates Oregon and Washington is the fastest east-west route for rail or highway in either state. Because of this, Portland can match Seattle in trucking rates even to the extreme northeast of Washington near the Canadian border, a hundred airline miles closer to Seattle than to Portland. The increasing use of barges on the Columbia favors Portland in this economic battle.

One surprising area of overlap is Alaska. By customary ocean routes taken from both cities, Portland is eighty-three miles *closer* than Seattle to Anchorage, Alaska. Seattle traditionally has had Alaskan shipping as its own plum, but Portland is gaining. The city also has a narrow lead over Seattle in coastal shipping, but both are far behind Los Angeles and San Francisco.

The rivalry between Portland and Seattle is heightened by the periodic relocation of distribution facilities from one city to the other. Several major manufacturing distributors have moved from Seattle to Portland in recent years, citing lower Oregon taxes and a more central location in relation to markets in Oregon, Washington and

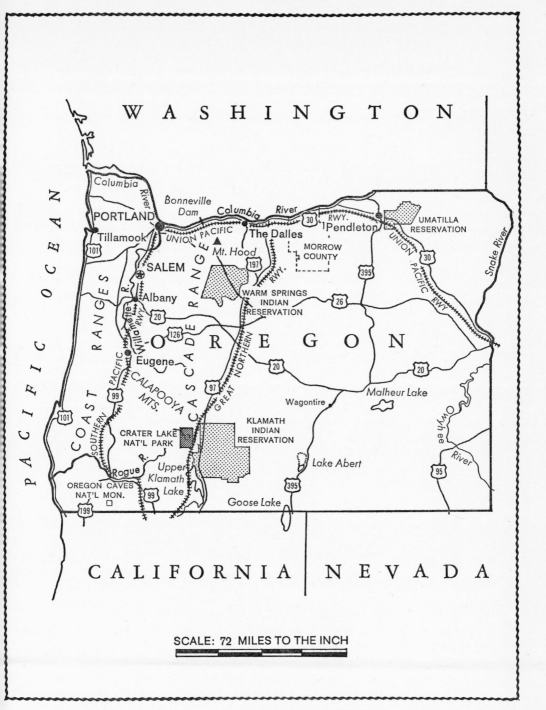

Oregon

Idaho. Regional post-office facilities have jockeyed back and forth between the two cities. They are now in Seattle. This has been a political game, not an evidence of any trend.

Portland staged an exposition during the centennial of Oregon statehood in 1959. Seattle showed small interest; but Portland wasn't able to resist a look at Seattle's World's Fair in the summer of 1962, although it didn't talk much about the Seattle extravaganza.

A happy moment in the history of Portland-Seattle relations came when the Hotel Multnomah in Portland (which has no sales tax) took a puckish five-column advertisement in Seattle newspapers. Headlines read:

> SEATTLE,
> DISBAND
> *Your tax structure is*
> UNBELIEVABLE

The text read gleefully, in part: "We don't hide a city tax in your hotel bill, and slip it to a bureaucrat. Or even a county tax. Or a state tax. Oh, there are some of you who pay twenty cents to get your car back across the Columbia River when you return to Seattle on your cigarette run, but most of the people we know row." As a "salute to freedom," the Hotel Multnomah pledged to wash and iron shirts free for Seattle visitors.

The frothy fun of the Portland hotel's advertisement subsided only slightly when it was realized that the hotel is owned by the Western Hotels chain—which has headquarters in Seattle.

Economists insist that rivalry between Portland and Seattle will proceed to a climax in which one city will assume a dominant role, taking over what Dr. William Bunge calls the "higher functions" of distribution and services. If so, the temper of the two cities at this time seems to favor Seattle, which has been united and galvanized by its World's Fair.

M. J. Frey, publisher of the Portland *Oregonian*, has been blunt in chiding Portlanders for their recurring apathy. In his first address as Portland Chamber of Commerce president in 1961, he spoke of the "stupidity" of the divisive fight between East Side and West Side (of the Willamette River) which caused a long delay in the construction of the Portland Memorial Coliseum. This fine hall eventually was built near the fifty-million dollar Lloyd Center and the new Sheraton Hotel on the East Side. Architects had recommended the West Side, at the center of downtown Portland, in an area slated for widespread urban renewal. The site finally chosen was cramped and offered inadequate parking. The fight prevented completion of the

Coliseum in time for the centennial celebration in 1959. Another symptom of Portland illness was displayed when a magnificent design for a circular arena of prestressed concrete—submitted by the architects, Skidmore, Owings & Merrill—was rejected in the face of short-sighted protests from the lumber industry, which has overriding influence in this state of forests.

Not all of Portland's schisms are involved with the Seattle rivalry or the tension between East Side and West Side. There is a lingering hostility toward Portland in rural Oregon—and this includes all of the state outside the Willamette Valley, a north-south trough of farm and timber land extending about one hundred and eighty miles southward from the Columbia River to the Calapooya Mountains, and about fifty miles east and west from the Coast Ranges to the Cascades. In this valley live two out of three Oregonians. Metropolitan Portland, part of the valley, accounts for one in two Oregonians.

East of the ten-thousand-foot-high Cascades is two-thirds of the land area of Oregon, but only eleven percent of its voters. Most of this part of the state is high desert and ponderosa pine forest; even in timber, it contrasts with western Oregon, where Douglas fir predominates. In eastern Oregon the largest town is Pendleton, a round-up center of only 14,434 people.

Eastern Oregon is the most emphatically rural sector remaining in the Pacific Coast states.

At one stretch along Highway 395, I drove for more than forty miles through high desert without sight of human or animal life. The highway winds along beside Lake Abert, a forbiddingly desolate alkali lake beneath the Abert Rim, the largest fault scarp in North America. The rim rises two thousand feet above the plateau, running for nineteen miles; its lava cap ends in a sulfurous precipice. The only movement on this desert was that of cloud shadows racing across sagebrush and greasewood. Late in the afternoon, I stopped near a one-house hamlet called Wagontire, as several cattle plodded across the highway. The slant rays of the dying sun made a carpet of the sagebrush, and the road led through it toward the horizon like a tiny macadam trail. But this seemed like an urban center; Wagontire was the first house I had come across in sixty miles. Atlases published after the 1960 census list Wagontire, but show no population figure. It appeared to be three on the day I was there: a woman who offered to pump gas for me, her husband, who sat inside their little store and talked tersely of the need for rain, and a small boy who wanted to confirm that the car I was driving was a Mercedes-Benz.

In 1962, when filings for the primary election closed in Morrow

County, more than two thousand square miles in size, it was discovered that no one—Democrat or Republican—had filed for district
attorney. Of the county's fewer than five thousand residents, only three
are lawyers, and none of them wanted the job.

The circulation of the Portland daily newspapers throughout
the vast rural areas of the state has made them stronger than those
normally found in cities of its size. They provide home delivery as
distant as four hundred miles away. Until August, 1961, when
Samuel I. Newhouse bought the Oregon *Journal*, Portland claimed
rank as the smallest city in the United States with competitive daily
newspapers. (The labor-union-backed *Reporter* continued publication
as a tabloid daily, in the wake of Portland's turbulent newspaper
labor war.)

In many Oregon towns considerably larger than Wagontire, but
almost as remote, Portland looms as a gargantua. The isolated rancher
or lumberman in Oregon still has some distrust for the city slicker.
The editor of the small-town weekly is quick to deride Portland.
An Oregon *Journal* editorial stated: "They like to use the words
'hicks' and 'sticks' as applied to themselves, with the implication that
these are a part of the city dweller's vocabulary. The fact is, we never
hear city people use them. The only time we ever see them is in the
writings of the upstaters. . . . Some of these gentlemen have such
a good thing in perpetuating the myth that Portlanders look down
upon and seek to exploit upstaters they will never give it up."

This schism, based more on prejudice than fact, is disappearing
as Oregon's fine highway system is expanded. The Dalles, for instance,
a town eighty-three miles up the Columbia River from Portland, is
forty-five minutes closer to Portland by car than it was fifteen years
ago.

Now, as it develops a program of annexation, Portland is having
trouble with its closer neighbors. Its largest annexation from 1940 to
1961 was two square miles—and this was almost half of the total for
the two decades. The city has been indifferent to annexation in an era
when other Western cities have been thriving on it—and, incidentally,
running up astronomical percentages of population expansion. When
Portland finally went out to seek some fringe areas in 1961, angry
cries arose from the suburbs. Again, the *Journal* stepped forward in
apologetic conciliation with an editorial headlined: *Portland Not Big,
Bad Wolf*. Portland has instead been, the *Journal* suggested, "a very
reluctant dragon indeed."

Toward California, Oregonians have an attitude of well-veiled
hostility. It is bred of many things, the most basic of which is a

personality clash, which is sometimes as vivid today as it was more than a century ago between the Spanish don in Oregon and the New England migrant. Another cause is the bittersweet tincture of mistrust, jealousy, and awe in which the small and quiet so often hold the big and brash. There is an element of dependence, too, which is not calculated to make Oregonians like California any better. The giant to its south is a hungry market for Oregon lumber and for its rich crops of vegetables and fruits; Californians are the predominant tourist in Oregon, and tourism is Oregon's third major source of income.

Californians enjoy visiting the moist greenness of the Northwest coast, a contrast from most Californians' environment, and they also enjoy moving to the Northwest. Oregon's principal source of migration in modern years has been California. This does not inject as schizoidal a relationship as one might think; those who leave California to live in Oregon are making a sharp change for a purpose, and they usually are aware of it. Among reasons for coming, they cite California smog and congestion, and the desire to raise their children in a smaller community. The Oregon town of Medford, in the beautiful Rogue River Valley, has become a haven for retired Southern Californians. Those who later return to California—and they are not insignificant in number—talk mostly of their depression at heavy Oregon rainfall and a sense of remoteness, and their nostalgia for the live-and-let-live freedom of California. One California executive who served a three-year tenure in Portland returned gratefully to Southern California. "The theme of the statehood centennial in 1959 was Frontiers of Tomorrow," he said. "But it was typical of the Portland attitude that most people seemed to be looking back to the frontiers of yesterday. Our biggest problem in Portland was to pull the city, dragging and screaming, into the twentieth century." The physical aspect of Portland, now teeming with new construction, does not support his attitude, but there is much beneath the surface of the city that does. A negatively oriented group called Taxsavers, Incorporated, epitomized the complacency of Portland.

Portland planners, with an eye toward California, envision vaguely a metropolitan area extending southward from Olympia, Washington, at the foot of Puget Sound, across the Columbia River to Portland and down through the Willamette Valley to Salem, the handsome capital town of Oregon, and to Eugene, the site of the University of Oregon. It is a distant dream. Eugene passed the fifty-thousand mark for the first time in the 1960 census; Salem only approached it. They are the second and third cities of Oregon in size—and their residents like it this way.

Stanley Grove, manager of the Salem Chamber of Commerce, is a former Southern Californian who prefers life in Salem. His offices are in a charming two-storied home on a tree-lined street.

"Half the members of my board of directors attended high school together here in Salem," Grove told me. "Everybody went to school around here. They are descendants of pioneers. There are a hundred farms in this area that were homesteaded and are being run today by grandchildren of the homesteaders. The kids build new houses close by the old farmhouse and stay on. They are stable and conservative.

"We have a good, quiet social and cultural life. There must be fifteen or twenty dancing clubs. In the winter, members dress formally, have cocktails and dinner, and dance until twelve or one o'clock. Each club may have three or four dances a year, and some people will belong to as many as three of them. We have a civic concert series, and Willamette University has a concert series, and there are a thousand members in the Knife and Fork Club, which brings good speakers. The Portland Symphony makes three or four trips down here a year. Of course, with the freeway now, Portland theaters are less than an hour away. We have bridge clubs here in Salem; people even put on their tuxedos and long dresses to meet for dinner and bridge. Then, of course, we have hiking and fishing and gun clubs—very big in this part of the country—and a lot of golf."

One vivid contrast between Oregon and most of the rest of the West is that status is more involved with genealogy than with one's role in the community or with economics. The tradition of the covered wagon is important; if there is one in your past, you are a member of the elite, even if you are broke. It does not seem to matter who your ancestors were at the other end of the Oregon Trail; it is important only that they came here early. The covered wagon, in this regard, is not much different from the Mayflower. In contrast, the descendant of an early settler in California may be inclined to talk about it, but he will have trouble finding anyone who will settle down and listen.

The Oregon pioneer even stands atop the Capitol, a strikingly handsome white-marbled building, which was completed in 1938 after a more traditional statehouse had been destroyed by fire. On its rounded tower is a twenty-two-foot-high bronze statue, covered with gold leaf, of a pioneer holding an axe in hand, ready to begin building a log shelter.

The Capitol is at the head of a well-planned mall of state buildings which eventually will extend for eight blocks. Four of the projected structures are completed; a seventy-five-year plan for the remainder includes an auditorium topped by an amphitheater. The

Capitol has a television studio adjacent to its press rooms in the basement; such startling progressiveness is not without precedent in Oregon, which—despite its conservatism—was the first state to employ fully the initiative, referendum, and recall. The state also led in setting high employment standards for women and children. More recently, it has ranked as one of the first states to institute effective civil-rights legislation. It was the first state to provide for popular election of United States Senators. Its migrant-labor statutes are progressive.

By incidental contrast, Oregon is also one of the few states that does not provide a governor's mansion. This has proved no handicap for its governor, forty-year-old Mark Hatfield. He is a brilliant, handsome, and progressive Republican with an impressive potential and a solid record. The Oregon budget is balanced. Its schools and services rank high. Hatfield has fought hard to reorganize the Oregon government on the cabinet system. He has also exercised a record number of vetoes as governor, and has been sustained without exception.

Hatfield was elected to the Oregon House of Representatives at the age of twenty-eight, after a campaign which stemmed from a classroom dare while he was associate professor of political science at Willamette University, whose campus is across State Street from the Capitol. For six years, during three terms in the house and senate, Hatfield arranged to teach classes at eight and nine in the morning and, during terms of the legislature, to rush across State Street in time for the ten o'clock session. When he was elected secretary of state in 1956, he resigned from the faculty. In 1958 he was elected governor, and in 1962 he won reëlection. (No Oregon governor in this century has served two full terms. The governorship has been studded with ill omens; three governors have died in office after being reëlected, and a fourth resigned. Although the term is for four years, seven governors served during the twenty-year period preceding Hatfield's election.) It is Hatfield's hope that his second term will also be interrupted—by elevation in 1964 to the Vice Presidency. As one of the brightest stars among Western Republicans, he is regarded as a suitable running mate for any of the Eastern Presidential candidates.

The personal story of its governor is somewhat typical of the character of the state. Hatfield was born in a small Oregon town, the son of a railroad blacksmith and a school teacher. His press secretary, Travis Cross, still has a 1932 Christmas program from the Salem First Baptist Church, listing him and the future governor as appearing together. Hatfield graduated from Willamette University in

Salem, went into the Navy and saw action at Iwo Jima and Okinawa before returning to Stanford University for a master's degree. (During Hatfield's stay at Stanford, Governor Dewey was defeated by Harry Truman in his bid for the presidency. Hatfield was freshmen counselor at Encina Hall; the freshmen knew their man well enough to drape his room in black after the Dewey defeat.)

Shortly afterwards, a plane crash killed the three key Republican politicians of Oregon, including Governor Earl Snell. Hatfield, within one year of his doctoral dissertation, decided to go home to Oregon and enter politics. He took a job at Willamette, and a year later became a state representative.

At the Oregon State–University of Southern California football game in 1957, Hatfield sat behind his good friend Gerald Frank, a wealthy young merchant, and Frank's pretty date, Antoinette Kuzmanich, daughter of a Yugoslavian longshoreman in Portland. She and Hatfield were engaged and married within the ensuing year. Returning from their honeymoon in Carmel, California, the bride was indoctrinated promptly into the pitfalls of Oregon politics. The wedding had taken place shortly after his victory in the primary for governor, and the Oregon press criticized the two for leaving the state on their honeymoon. The bride got a second, stronger taste of Oregon politics on the eve of Hatfield's election as governor in the following November: Democratic Senator Wayne Morse uncorked the smear that Hatfield had been awaiting since his entry into politics. Driving a car at eighteen, he had struck and killed a seven-year-old girl.

Hatfield, the blacksmith's son from the West, was considered an ideal choice for Nelson Rockefeller's running mate had Rockefeller been nominated for the Presidency at the 1960 Republican Convention. Instead, Hatfield was chosen to nominate Richard Nixon with a crisp and eloquent twenty-sentence speech which began with one of the livelier gambits of that dull political season: "The White House is not for sale—its lease is up for renewal."

Hatfield is the strongest governor Oregon has had for many years. But the state's dominant political figure has been the irascible United States Senator, Wayne Morse, who was first elected as a Republican in 1944 and more recently reëlected as a Democrat. Long dominated by Republicans, Oregon now has a Democratic plurality. Its other senator is Maurine Neuberger, the capable widow of former Senator Richard L. Neuberger, a distinguished liberal who through his extensive writings was the foremost spokesman of the Northwest until his death in 1960. Mrs. Neuberger is a breezy and casual woman who already had made a reputation as a fellow lawmaker with her husband in the Oregon legislature. In the Senate, she has dug in to carry on her husband's unfinished business: dedication of the Oregon Dunes Park, billboard regulation, Point Four youth projects, and the International Medical Year. She has become known for her fight for smog-control legislation, for a bill to convert the nation to the metric system, and for a widely publicized outcry she made in 1961 against watered-down hams.

Senator Morse's party-hopping has weakened his value to Oregon. He has complained bitterly that both the Eisenhower and Kennedy administrations have discriminated against Oregon—but much of it is his own fault. He bolted the Republican ticket in 1952 to campaign for Adlai Stevenson. In 1960, as a Democrat, he campaigned for his own candidacy against Kennedy during the presidential primary in Oregon. At about the same time that he fought the appointment of John Connally as Secretary of the Navy, he was blasting the Kennedy administration for closing Oregon's only naval installation. California has twenty naval installations and Washington eight; Oregon now has none. In 1960, almost one-fourth of federal defense expenditures went to California; Washington received more than three percent, and Oregon only about one-tenth of one percent.

The more immediate solution to Oregon's economic limbo is industrialization; and Governor Hatfield has made earnest efforts to rally Oregonians to encourage new industry. Oregon, overwhelmingly involved in the lumber industry, has risen and fallen with trends in building construction around the nation. The state has enough trees to rebuild every house in the fifty states; one-fifth of the nation's standing timber is here. Unemployment zooms during seasonal lags in logging. To offset this, an active industrial development committee has been at work, with a small budget, under the direction of Hatfield's old friend, Gerald Frank. The state has set up a hundred-thousand-acre industrial park on the Columbia River. Several large new plants involved in production of pulp and paper and electronics have been built here and elsewhere in Oregon under this impetus. In a Portland suburb, the electronics firm of Tektronix, Incorporated, has an impressive recent spiral of growth. Near Portland, but across the state line in Washington, Dow Chemical Company is constructing a large plant on the Columbia River. Oil companies are involved in coastal and inland explorations. Industrial leaders are flown to Oregon and entertained through a fund contributed by Oregon businessmen.

The Port of Portland is being developed aggressively; it is now the largest dry-cargo port on the Pacific Coast. As California farmlands give way to subdivisions, farmers of the fertile Willamette Valley have begun to step up production of vegetables and berries;

several million tons of frozen foods are packaged there now each year.

In the lumber industry, large operators are swallowing up the small lumberman on every side; reforestation and the steady conversion to tree farms require tremendous reserve capital like that of Weyerhaeuser, Georgia-Pacific and Crown Zellerbach. Today Oregon is growing more timber each year than it cuts. The lumber industry is finding ways to minimize waste with new lumber products (in the cutting, ten percent of a tree becomes sawdust). The pulp-and-paper industry has grown sharply in Oregon.

"We are not trying to experience a boom in population," Hatfield said. "We are not in the same growth status as our sister states. Probably the majority of our people are pleased that we are not. Oregon has been able to look at other states' experiences and problems and has learned to alleviate the intensity of pressures that subsequently develop here. We think we can have playgrounds and payrolls at the same time. There are Oregonians like Stewart Holbrook, the author, who see Oregon as a great wilderness area in which man hunts and fishes and roams without the restrictions of an industrial society. But this point of view is diminishing. Our economic development program more than anything in our history is drawing the state together. Portland is not looked on as just a metropolitan monster trying to dominate, but as an economic center whose wealth depends on areas outside the city. I would like to be remembered as a job builder. Only out of more jobs can come a wealthier Oregon—wealthy not only in the material sense but in terms of good living and a happier existence."

The vision of a wealthier Oregon will not be impeded by power shortages. The Northwest is loaded with hydroelectric power. In 1960, for the first time in fifteen years, the Bonneville Power Administration conceded a surplus of power. The BPA is the federal agency charged with wholesaling—both to private and public power distributors—the power generated at Bonneville Dam, forty miles east of Portland on the Columbia River, and at other federal dams. It supplies more than half of the power consumed in the Northwest. It has operated at a deficit since 1959.

The Columbia starts its mighty run in the Canadian Rockies. It courses northward, then turns south for almost five hundred miles during its descent to the United States border. It crosses east Washington and then turns westward to form the border between Washington and Oregon. It is 1,210 miles long; its peak spring flow is five-sixths that of the Mississippi River. Already harnessed in Washington by the Grand Coulee Dam and near Portland by the Bonneville, the Columbia was the center of negotiation for sixteen years between the United States and Canada before the signing in 1961 of the Columbia River Treaty.

The treaty has opened a new can of worms in the simmering feud over public versus private power. It provides for four new storage dams: three at the headwaters of the Columbia in Canada, and the long-discussed, three-hundred-and-thirty-million-dollar Libby Dam on the Kootenai River in Montana, which will back up a reservoir extending into Canada. The aim of the project is to control the Columbia's flow at its origins in Canada (and its tributary, the Kootenai, in Montana) so that power generators at ten completed or planned hydroelectric dams on the Columbia in the Northwest United States may operate at top efficiency in low-water as well as high-water stages.

Before construction could begin, the project grew snarled in politics. It was agreed that in return for building its three dams, Canada would receive payment for half of the additional power produced on the Columbia. Controversy developed in Canada over disposal of the Canadian share of Columbia River power. Neither British Columbia, the Canadian province through which the Columbia River flows, nor the Northwest can now use all of the power generated in their areas by existing facilities. There is plenty of evidence to point in both directions—that public-power fanatics are planning shrewdly for the assumed power needs of coming generations, and also that they are reveling in a sort of power gluttony.

But two developments in 1962, one in this country and one in Canada, compounded the alarm of private power interests and a large number of Westerners, who by nature are more suspicious than most Americans of federal intrusion. With consumption of Bonneville power about thirty million dollars below maximum output of its generators, the Interior Department in 1962 faced a dreary alternative. It had to find a market for more power, or raise its rates. In the gamesmanship of public power, a rate raise is a humiliating admission of failure. Instead, Bonneville's administrator, Charles F. Luce, a Kennedy appointee, began to preach the virtues of a concept which is a major step toward the utopia of public-power fanatics: a regional intertie, or interconnection, of high-voltage transmission lines which would allow BPA to market its surplus federal power in California— and in theory, permit California to return off-peak, steam-generated power to the Northwest, if the need ever arose.

There is not yet in America any real regional intertie of public power. Clearly it would be a more portentous move than intra-regional power developments like the Tennessee Valley Authority and Bonneville, which utilize the natural resources within a region for its own development. A regional federal power intertie involves grave ideologic decisions. It would be a long step in the direction of nationalization of power. Public-power philosophy calls eventually for a nationwide grid uniting all public power production, transmission, and distribution in one mighty federal monopoly with which private companies could do business only on federal terms and subject to federal control.

Public power protagonists are hoping to stampede the United States into nationalization of power by warning that Russia is overtaking us in the production of electric power; *ergo*, set our government free to make all the power it can, whether we can use it or not. American production of electric power in 1960 was two and a half times greater per capita than that of Russia. There is no chance for Russia to overtake this nation in power production for at least twenty years—no chance even then if a healthy and balanced competition continues in this country between public and private power. There is nothing to suggest that a public power monopoly would be any more effective in maintaining our power lead over Russia than would a private power monopoly.

A regional intertie such as the Interior Department has sought from Bonneville would require about a thousand miles of super-high-voltage transmission lines from the Columbia down through California, at a cost estimated as high as a third of a billion dollars. California private power interests immediately objected when this was proposed. They already had announced plans for a third, minor private power interconnection between the Northwest and California, which has some of the same characteristics. Four private power companies of California already had set up their own power pool within the state to channel off their own surpluses. Still, some California state officials estimated wildly that the state could save up to eight million dollars a year through taking excess Bonneville power. In the Northwest, the intertie generally was favored, largely because it was the alternative to a raise in power rates to BPA customers in the Northwest.

At about the same time that the intertie controversy reached the white-heat stage, the legislature of the Canadian province of British Columbia—without a dissenting vote—expropriated private power companies in British Columbia. Premier W. A. C. Bennett, the Social Credit party leader who led the coup, was quoted as saying, "Free enterprise needs a little pruning now and then." With the nationalization of power taking place upstream on the same Columbia River which is the source of the current treaty dispute, the public power argument burgeoned in the Western United States.

The West would not exist as it does today without Hoover Dam serving Southern California, Grand Coulee and Bonneville in the Northwest, and the Upper Colorado Project in the Rocky Mountain states. But this same West voted predominantly against the New Frontier in 1960. Politically, it is a conservative region. In the power fight, private companies are likely to receive resounding support from the average citizen. Most of the old prejudices against the vested power interests belong to another generation.

The nuclear era has put Americans in a state of such insensitive resignation to astronomical degrees of power that it is very hard to stir up awe over a dam, no matter how many times longer it may be than the Empire State Building lying on its side, or whether the concrete that was poured into it would bury forever the relatively few unpaved portions of America. At Bonneville, on a Sunday afternoon visit, I decided to forego my tour into the bowels of the powerhouse. Instead, I watched for an hour from atop the navigation lock, as Uncle Sam did his best to get along with two couples in a small motor cruiser who had signaled that they wanted to go through the lock and up the Columbia from Bonneville.

The cruiser was about a twenty-eight footer; the navigation lock at Bonneville is five hundred feet long and it will accommodate an eight-thousand-ton ship. The master of the lock peered downriver at the boat and began to manipulate his valves. He closed the upstream gates. Then he pumped out the lock chamber to the downstream level. Finally the downstream gates swung open.

But by now the Sunday afternoon sailors had lost power, and their little craft was pounding up against a granite quay. While the two women aboard peered anxiously, the two men fumbled with their starter and checked their gas tanks. Finally, one of them scrambled ashore for help. The gates of the lock were yawning above them, and the lock master was staring in disbelief. Twenty minutes passed. Two boats arrived upstream to pass through the lock in the opposite direction; inexorably, the gates swung closed. In his tower, the lock master shook his head, and turned his valves to flood the lock again.

The Columbia is big, broad and bold. It is the smaller rivers of Oregon that mean most to Oregonians and to thousands of out-of-state visitors who return each year as if mesmerized. The Rogue River in southern Oregon, and the McKenzie are the best known. To trout fishermen, such country is a mecca; to those who revel in rustic isolation around fast running water and green trees, it is a balm.

To understand Oregon, one must feel at home with its back rivers and its deep forests. And one must know that even the city-born Oregonian is not speaking casually when he tells you about his last fishing trip. In Portland, an old friend told me he had given up fishing. "Look," he said, still angry. "You know I was born and brought up in Oregon and fished all my life on the Rogue. Took the wife and boys up to the same spot every time, right in the woods. Hauled in some bedsprings once, and built a cupboard there in the woods where I kept canned food and bedding so I didn't have to haul it in or out. No cabins around. Didn't want any. But the last two times we've been up there, we've seen this same guy about half a mile upriver. It isn't the same, with somebody else around. We hauled the bedding and the food out this last time. I'm through. There's nowhere you can go anymore in Oregon without running into people."

Even Californians, who have plenty of beach of their own, flock to the four hundred miles of rugged Oregon beach, all but twenty-three miles of which is state-owned and available to the public. For the fisherman, the coast is the avenue to salmon and flounder; for the casual strolling tourist, the prizes are big, colorful glass floats which have broken free from Japanese fishing nets and drifted across the Pacific.

The small, quiet coastal towns like Tillamook, the cheese center, are memorialized by the natives in doggerel: "Trees, cheese, ocean breeze—and mud up to your knees."

Nothing quite so explicit has been devised to categorize Portland. For half a century it has called itself the Rose Capital of the World, and its black police cars have roses painted on their sides. But the Oregon *Journal* has noted with an editorial sigh that the title of Rose Capital of the World also has been claimed by Newark, New York; Tyler, Texas; and Columbus, Ohio.

Portland is proud of Mount Hood, which is visible from downtown on clear days. As a symbol, its centennial commission designed a montage of salmon leaping up falls, with Douglas fir trees, the Bonneville Dam, and Mount Hood in the background. But nothing has caught on and stuck as a symbol of the character of the state. Perhaps it is because Oregon is many things to its people, and not yet sure enough of itself to rely on a single one.

12

WASHINGTON

The Gentle People

Life is simpler for tourists in Washington because of two English sea captains, Cook and Vancouver. Cook sighted the coast of Washington in 1778 during a search for the Northwest Passage. In 1792 Vancouver turned inland and charted Puget Sound. There he set about implanting English names like Rainier, Whidbey, Vashon and Bellingham. A lot of other Washington names are Indian; it is harder to ask directions to Snoqualmie or Snohomish, to Kooskooskie or Klickitat.

Except for fur trappers, the Indians were almost alone until 1843 in that part of the Oregon country which is now Washington. In that year, the first of the American wagon trains moved out over the Oregon Trail from Missouri. With them, returning from a trip to Boston to plead for his Indian missions, was a missionary doctor named Marcus Whitman. The missions were saved, but four years later, Whitman, his blond wife Narcissa and fifty of their people were killed by Cayuse Indians. Around Walla Walla, his name is commemorated today by a college, a park, a museum and a centennial.

Salem became capital of the new Oregon Territory in 1849. The few settlers north of the Columbia River rebelled at the remoteness of the territorial government. In 1853 Congress approved splitting the Oregon Territory, and the name of Washington was proposed for the new territory. Stephen A. Douglas suggested Washingtonia, to avoid confusion with the national capital. Congress ignored the recommendation, but Douglas was right; there has been plenty of confusion.

Lumbering began to prosper during the California Gold Rush. At Seattle, which had been settled in 1851 by a party of twelve adults and twelve children, logs were coaxed down a hillside to the waterfront. The route of the logs became known as Skid Road. Later saloons and brothels sprang up there, and the phrase entered the language as *skid row*.

In 1860, the Puget Sound *Herald* carried its editor's plea for bachelors to devise plans of bringing "marriageable white women" to Seattle. Eastern newspapers had already grown derisive of "squaw marriages" between white men and Indian women. Asa Mercer, a young newcomer, had been made president of the University of Washington, but there was no student body. It struck Mercer that there was not likely to be one, either, unless there were some women in Washington. He made two journeys to the East to bring back brides. Only eleven dared the trip on the first try, but forty-six went on his next; one of them he claimed as his own. A few of the Mercer girls saw San Francisco first and wouldn't go on to Seattle.

The move for statehood grew frenzied in 1888 after a summary of federal rivers-and-harbors grants for the previous eighteen years showed that California, as a state, had received almost a million and a half dollars, while the Washington Territory had been given only five thousand five hundred dollars. Statehood came in 1889.

The completion of the Northern Pacific Railroad in 1883 set off a boom, though its trains were compelled at first to back forty-five miles from Tacoma to Seattle. Ten years later came Jim Hill's Great Northern. In that decade Washington had quadrupled in population.

Gold was discovered in Alaska in 1897, and Seattle was the port of embarkation for thousands on their way to the Klondike and the Yukon. John Rosene, from Chicago, was disappointed in gold, but he was struck by the inadequacy of ships in Alaska trade, and he became Seattle's first shipping baron.

In the early twentieth century apple fever spread over the Wenatchee Valley. But Swedes and Norwegians were attracted to logging, which in the first quarter of the century made Washington the largest producer of lumber in the nation, and inflicted desolation on the forests.

Henry J. Kaiser, who began his career as a paving contractor in Washington in 1914, returned to Washington in 1939 as half-owner of the Seattle-Tacoma Shipbuilding Corporation. In the early Forties another Kaiser shipyard at Vancouver, across the Columbia River from Portland, spewed baby aircraft carriers down the ways into the Columbia and out to the Pacific. At seven West Coast shipyards in World War II, Kaiser built 1,490 ships, including one-third of the United States' merchant fleet and fifty small carriers. After the war, he leased two surplus aluminum plants near Spokane and built a gypsum plant in Seattle.

William Edward Boeing took his first plane ride in a seaplane on Seattle's Lake Washington. The first plane he built, in 1916, flew seventy-five miles an hour. During World War II, his company and two others built almost thirteen thousand Boeing-designed B-17 Flying Fortresses. Today the Boeing 707 dominates the jetways of the world.

The caliber of Washington politicians had grown so hopeless in 1932 that the Seattle *Times* parodied the campaign for mayor of Seattle by backing an obviously unqualified bandleader named Victor Aloysius Meyers as a puppet candidate. The *Times* paid his filing fee and assigned a staff writer, Douglass Welch, to create and report his campaign each day on page one. Meyers lost, but he liked politics. He ran later for lieutenant governor, without the help of the *Times*, and was elected.

During the Depression, workers came from all over the nation to build Grand Coulee Dam on the Columbia River.

In the winter of 1942, scientists in secret session at the Davenport Hotel in Spokane chose the site—along the Columbia in southern Washington—of a strange factory first called Hanford Engineer Works. It was a well-kept secret—until Hiroshima and Nagasaki. Plutonium is made at Hanford, and the waters of the Columbia used to cool its awesome fires.

Dave Beck, the son of a carpet cleaner, quit high school in Seattle to drive a laundry truck. His climb appeared steady, right up to the presidency of the International Brotherhood of Teamsters. By 1962, when he went finally into federal prison, it had been eleven years since he first was indicted on a tax evasion charge, and had resigned as a regent of the University of Washington.

In the apple town of Okanogan, in the highlands of north central Washington, a Seattle bank economist, about to speak to the assembled members of the chamber of commerce at its annual banquet in 1960, reflected that it was a pleasure to find chamber-of-commerce members convening without any signs of self-importance. He remarked to the Okanogan man on his left that it was wise for a group like this not always to feel the pressure of getting big things done.

"Once in a while some of the boys get heated up," the Okanogan man replied, "but they always get over it."

At that moment, to the surprise of the Seattle economist, the inevitable after-dinner graph was exposed. It was an extraordinary chart; a heavy black line rose resolutely up and across the graph, then plummeted, in red.

The explanation was disarmingly brief. "This line in black," said the Okanogan chamber of commerce secretary, "represents what we took to be the population explosion in Okanogan County. The red line at the right represents the adjustment we had to make after the 1960 census."

The little town of Okanogan had held almost even. It had lost only twelve residents in ten years. But the population of the county as a whole had declined by twelve percent.

Okanogan has not been an exception to the Northwest pattern. Rural areas have declined, and cities have held even or grown only modestly. Like Oregon, Washington was unchanged in its population rank among the states between 1950 and 1960. Its growth was most notable in the previous decade. The probability is strong that another surge will come as the aftermath to the Seattle World's Fair of 1962. The respite from rapid growth in Washington has been used well by its citizens: in Seattle, it gave time for introspection and adjustment of goals. After passing through two trying decades of mixed emotions, Seattle has recaptured its sense of direction. It has always been a pleasant city in which to live, and its people have been loathe to risk change. Left to themselves, they would not encourage new industry or in-migration. But there has been enough foreshadowing of unemployment and depression to jog them into remembering that a city must move on, or drift backward. The Seattle World's Fair was a direct consequence of the evolving civic conscience, which might be expressed in this way: "If it weren't for the future needs of our children, we'd prefer to be left alone. But our children will need jobs if they are to stay here and enjoy this rare livability. Let's go look for new business."

The fair has filled a need far greater than its obvious economic stimulus. Complacency had begun to set in. There was no burning issue; no one in the twelve counties around Puget Sound, where 1.8 million of Washington's 2.9 million people live, seemed to find much reason to be angry. Farming, lumbering and fishing were not thriving, but Boeing was building good airplanes and missiles and running away with the jetliner market. Nobody seemed hungry. The new downtown library was one of the handsomest in the nation, and a bevy of good new restaurants had opened. As usual, Northwest writers were writing glowingly about the Northwest, and there was no more graft than usual in the Capitol at Olympia. So everyone took to his boat on weekends and long summer evenings, and headed for the snow in the winter. Sure, there was a lot of rain, but where else could you live like this?

The best boating waters of America lie east and west of Seattle, and snow-capped mountains rise proudly on both sides, but it is never very cold and never very hot. A six-thousand-dollar salary will support as many of the amenities around Seattle as nine thousand dollars in a city of the East or Midwest. There are enough tourists to keep the city lively; and as California grows more crowded, more people are escaping to the Northwest to live—and bringing money. Jim Owen's University of Washington Huskies have marched into the Rose Bowl for two years in a row; the second time, in 1961, more than thirty thousand Northwesterners followed their team south on the twelve-hundred-mile trip to Pasadena. Milton Katims, the West Coast Leonard Bernstein, leads the Seattle Symphony from its new opera house out into the villages of the forests, and conducts compositions by Washington composers. There is more than a little culture: the University of Washington is thriving, a Municipal Art Commission was formed in 1952, and a master development plan was adopted in 1957 along with a new zoning code. There is even a group called Seattle Beautiful, Inc.

But a few years ago a handful of Seattle leaders smelled trouble.

Boeing had been backed against the wall once, and the company had come out fighting with the 707 jetliner and the Minuteman missile. But Seattle remained a one-industry city: Boeing was it. Governor Albert D. Rosellini was looking for more industry. Population as concentrated as that of the Puget Sound area could never be sustained again by old Northwest reliables such as logging, fishing, and farming. While the state hunted more industry, why not stage a good fair like the 1909 Alaska-Yukon Pacific Exposition?

It was not, of course, that simple. The most stubborn resistance to a world's fair came from within Seattle, which was a surprise to

many. It was also eloquent testimony to the depth of feeling of some
in Seattle against the growth of the city. For thirty months, the progressive faction of the city which backed the fair worked under a
cloud of litigation. There was a series of restraining orders and legal
challenges, but the fair board won each case. During the fair, an
official said defensively, "This area has grown. The Puget Sound is
a magnet. Whether we bring in new people and industry on a long-
range basis, or whether we bring them in immediately through the
fair, they see what is nice about living here and they stay. I don't
think they can blame us entirely at the fair for all the people who
settle here!"

Even before the fair opened in the spring of 1962, its success
had made its mark on the city. Opposition had given way to apathy
only months before its opening. A civic inferiority complex typical of
Seattle was at work: the fair was going to be a Seattle fair, and therefore it would not be much good. But two factors worked steadily in
the fair's favor: it was conceived as a showcase for American scientific
advance, and Seattle is the closest major city to the Orient and, incidentally, to Russia. Moreover, on the final day of Congress in 1959,
Senator Warren Magnuson—a practical politician known as "Mag-
gie" around the state—had squeezed through an unprecedented nine-
million-dollar federal appropriation for the fair.

The fair president, Joseph E. Gandy, an automobile dealer in
Seattle, flew to Paris and won the sanction of the Bureau of International Expositions. He asked for, and received, a BIE commitment to
withhold its recognition from all other U. S. fairs during the decade,
thus cold-shouldering the New York Fair of 1964. BIE recognition
insured the participation of many nations in the Seattle Fair. Seattle
businessmen raised four million five hundred thousand dollars. With
the aid of a bond issue, the city of Seattle pledged ten million dollars
for fair buildings which have remained as a permanent civic center:
the opera house, theater, and exhibition hall. The state of Washington appropriated another ten million dollars for an eighteen-thousand-
seat coliseum. With its monorail and space needle and other facilities, the Seattle Fair investment soared to eighty million dollars. As
the fair site took shape, Seattleites nodded in proud approval. Trees
were planted on downtown streets, news kiosks gave a touch of
Parisian gaiety, hotels and motels were booked solid, and suddenly
Seattle residents were being courted by long-lost friends and relatives
from distant cities.

All this was just what Seattle needed. Forgotten were the
phrases of gloom and doom: chronic unemployment, lack of diversification, remoteness from manufacturing centers, provincial outlook,

downward trend in forest industries, squeeze on farmers, labor strife, high living costs.

"What Washington needs most," Governor Rosellini told me before the fair opened, "is a more optimistic attitude on the part of its people, and more realistic and factual news media. There is too much negativism, too much inclination to suppress the confidence that lies naturally in many of the people."

The success of the fair quashed most of that negativism— for a time, at least. Harold Mansfield, assistant to William Allen the president of Boeing, said, "You have the feeling that maturity is just around the corner. The fair has developed an awakening aspiration. There is new thinking in the Northwest that is struggling to make itself felt. It isn't in polite company yet, but it eventually may prove to be more vigorous and unique than that from some of the older thought centers of the nation. We have an advantage that way in the West; our approaches may appeal to more people since we are a little more like the majority than, say, New Yorkers."

But, of course, a fair is a fair, no matter how cataclysmic the impact of several million summer visitors in a city of fewer than six hundred thousand people. With the Spacearium dark and the girlie shows gone, with the Seattle Symphony instead of the Philadelphia Orchestra playing in the new Opera House, what is Seattle?

It is the newest major city in the land.

It is the most densely populated city in the West.

It runs close behind San Diego, in the other Western corner of the nation, as the fourth most populous city in the Western states, and the nineteenth in the nation. Like San Diego, it both suffers and is enhanced by its corner position. Unlike San Diego, which is enshadowed by Los Angeles, Seattle is the biggest thing in sight for seven hundred miles in any direction. It lays effective claim to the title of third largest market in the West, after Los Angeles and San Francisco.

Seattle is the center of a colonial state whose economic stability will be determined in large part by its current attempts to meet more of its requirements within its borders. Except for food, forest products, and transportation equipment, Washington produces only thirty-seven percent of the goods it requires.

Seattle is also an expectant city. "We don't move in such deep grooves here as back East," said William Allen of Boeing, a Montana native. "The younger people feel untrammeled. Opportunity is unlimited, as compared with older sections of the country. The Northwest offers so much more in pleasurable living than most parts of the country. A person getting started, with a small income, can have pleasures here and do things that he couldn't do elsewhere with the same income. Take the Boeing Company. A very large number of Boeing employees—and I don't mean executives—own boats. They go in droves. It's not unusual to be in a little cove in the San Juan Islands on a summer evening when from around the corner will come ten little boats with outboards, all traveling together. They go ashore, make camp, go water skiing, fishing—all right out in front of Seattle, having the world's best time.

"This environment can be taken advantage of, and our people still make the effort to achieve something of significance and service. There is a very real maturity here in this area. There isn't the provincialism that there once was; travel in itself is doing a great deal to eliminate that, and the jets we make here are playing their part. We certainly think in a broader sense than we used to."

Seattle is a city of people intensely interested in ideas. Walter Straley, president of Pacific Northwest Bell Company, has lived previously in San Francisco and San Diego. "Strangely enough," he said, "I find more people up this way involved with ideas. There is less talk about other people and more talk about ideas. I wouldn't call it a higher intellectual or even more cultural part of the country, but there is certainly a lot more knowledge in the Northwest about regional environment and tradition, and more involvement in it, than in Southern California." The environment does not seem to foster the intellectual complacency that exists in many California cities. The Puget Sound region has a capable group of regional writers such as Nard Jones, Stewart Holbrook, and Murray Morgan; all of them are known and read.

It is a rugged but naïve city. Douglass Welch, the Seattle humorist, recalls that once George Sessions Perry excused himself from a dinner party during a research trip to Seattle. An hour later he was back. "I took a stroll around downtown," Perry is said to have announced. "Aren't you folks just a mite short on sin?" Victor Rosellini, a leading Seattle restaurateur and first cousin of the governor, said, "The only trouble is that the town is full of Scandinavians. They do all their eating and love-making at home." Despite stringent efforts, the Sunday liquor ban was not relaxed during the Seattle Fair. Bar liquor had not been legalized in Washington until 1948.

Seattle is an overwhelmingly friendly city. There is no suspicion of strangers, no aloofness, no effort to measure up the visitor. Seattleites enjoy entertaining, and they do it buoyantly—in their homes or clubs or on their boats. On the wooded beaches of Hood Canal, beneath the wilderness of the Olympic Peninsula, it still takes only a few

Washington

minutes to dig enough clams for a giant pot of chowder, and one can enjoy eating it in the company of some of the most cosmopolitan people on earth. In towns like Aberdeen, on the rainy western slope of the Olympic Peninsula, families made wealthy by lumber live in unostentatious comfort. They are likely to be active and generous patrons of the arts, both regionally and nationally; they are discriminating travelers, and well-read.

"This region seems to be rooted," Walter Straley said. "There is a Scandinavian, wood-chopper kind of background which makes you feel that despite heavy in-migration, Washington will not explode. If you walk into a room filled with people around Seattle, you'll see the sturdiest, finest-looking bunch of people that you'll ever meet."

There is a greater sense of regionalism in the Northwest than in California. It is part of the feeling of roots, of moderation, almost of gentleness. Seattleites have the easy air of people who have been around for a while and who plan to stay. Sophistication is not an issue. The family unit is taken more seriously than in most of the other new cities of the West; there is not the same fragmentation of family life. Some of this can be credited to the heavy proportion of European immigrants in Washington, but much of it is because even in the highly urbanized area of Puget Sound, the prevalent traditions are those of the logger and the farmer, not of the industrial city dweller. Industrialization and its evils are relatively new elements in Washington.

The dominant physical fact of Seattle is water. The city is built on hills that lie between Lake Washington and Puget Sound. The Sound is part of a two-hundred mile extension of the Pacific which begins as the Strait of Juan de Fuca, along the Canadian border. As this arm of the sea turns southward, it becomes Puget Sound. Seattle lies a hundred miles inland from the ocean shore, and it is almost equidistant from the borders of Oregon and Canada. It is a seaport but, like Portland, it is far from the sea. Visitors who look from the hills of Seattle westward across the waters of Puget Sound are often not aware that the jagged mountain peaks on the western horizon are the heights of one of the densest wildernesses on the continent. The rain forests on the western slope of the Olympic Peninsula are the wettest places in the nation, with an average annual precipitation of one hundred and thirty-five inches. Here on the Olympic Peninsula, Justice William O. Douglas of the Supreme Court led Congressmen on a back-breaking hike in behalf of legislation to maintain wilderness areas. The highest peak of the Cascades, a backbone which separates the lush green of western Washington from arid eastern Washington, is Mount Rainier, the lofty white sentinel which emerges to crown the mountainous Seattle backdrop when the rain clouds disappear.

Seattleites have set out lately to dispel the city's reputation for rain. Its annual rainfall is less than that of Chicago, New York, Boston or Pittsburgh, but it does not seem that way. Outside my room during the spring of 1961, a weather sign flashed almost without variation for a week: *Rain, Cloudy; Rain, Cloudy.* For half an hour one morning it changed to an insistent *Fair, Fair*—but during that time the sign was almost obscured by a downpour.

There is enough rain to give Seattle a justified reputation for its flowers and shrubs, which subtly enhance the homey feeling of the city. Even the newer residential subdivisions have a stronger aura of permanence than those of California. The effect of abundant rainfall on landscaping is part of the reason; so is Seattle architecture, which is more apt to be traditional than ranch-style. The moderation of the Washington personality is reflected in its architecture. Even handsome new downtown Seattle office buildings tend toward marble instead of glass and steel. The leisure revolution has brought a new emphasis on western Washington real estate. There is fevered activity in subdividing remote forested tracts on river fronts and lakefronts and the waterfront of Puget Sound. Cottage sites sell for as little as two hundred and ninety-five dollars, and fishing boats can be had for two or three hundred dollars.

The islands of Puget Sound—three hundred of them, including one hundred and seventy-two habitable islands of the scenically majestic San Juan group—give this water world its character. The cruise on speedy ferries from Anacortes through the San Juan Islands to Sidney, in British Columbia, is undoubtedly just what is claimed for it: America's most beautiful water trip. The ferries weave among these wooded, hilly islands with hard turns to port and starboard, darting into hidden coves with storybook names like Friday Harbor, Lopez, and Orcas. The distant horizons range from Mount Rainier, far to the south, northward to the Golden Ears of Canada's Coast Ranges. On these islands live families who find no reason to visit the mainland more than once in several years. The sandspits and glacial fiords of the San Juans are becoming more familiar to tourists, but their wilderness character will be preserved forever by the deed restrictions of many privately owned islands. Seaplane service is the only link with the everyday world for scores of residents not served by telephone or radio communication. Their signals are known to the pilots who fly over the San Juans daily; an unfurled strip of canvas or a brightly-colored ball raised on a pole will bring a plane swooping down to a landing in a protected cove.

This same frontier regard for the individual extends to the crews of the ferries. I pulled into line at Anacortes twenty minutes before a scheduled ferry sailing through the San Juans. Cars, buses and trucks in several lanes almost obliterated the waterfront.

"Fifty-fifty chance you'll get on," the ticket seller said cheerfully.

Every car in line was taken aboard, including one station wagon from California that pulled up, tires squealing, one minute before sailing time. The deckhands squeezed it aboard by rocking a tiny sports car until they could move it sideways, leaving room for the Californians to edge aboard at a weird angle, their car almost hanging over the stern. It was so expert a display of custom packing that passengers, watching from a deck above, applauded.

Hood Canal plays an important role in the leisure life of the Puget Sound area. It is not a canal, but an eighty-mile long finger of tide-washed channel, usually two to three miles wide, running down the eastern edge of the Olympic Peninsula. On its shores summer homes are shaded by towering cedar and fir. Its waters are a placid aquatic playground. From its western shore, stub roads lead up into the Olympic wilderness, past lakes rimmed by dense forest, ending in rugged trails leading higher to plateaus and mountain meadows beside cascading streams and through forest aisles.

Nature speaks with a varied vocabulary in this Puget Sound area and its call has a compelling impact on those who live here. No other great American urban center is so inextricably interlocked with nature as Seattle. But it has been the character of its people to enjoy nature calmly, without proclaiming regional blessings in the manner of the go-getter. In a frank effort to whip up more boosterism on the eve of the fair in 1962, Pacific Northwest Bell staged a contest in Oregon and Washington: the public was invited to write "Why I'm Wild about Washington"—or Oregon. Ten thousand answers came in during the first month. The adjectives appearing most frequently were *cool, green, hospitable, uncrowded, promising,* and *growing.* The entrants wrote of their pleasure in being removed from hurricanes, tornadoes, droughts, dust storms, blizzards and the sweltering heat that they associated with regions where they had lived previously. A fierce pride in the Northwest was the predominant tone; it showed itself in entries which took the form of poems, paintings, songs and even complete orchestrations.

Washington residents are proud of the challenges of nature. As a train bound for Seattle headed into the most precipitous and winding part of its roadbed through the Cascade Mountains one night, a mischievous writer finished his dinner and casually asked his waiter to bring him a pousse-café. The waiter gazed at him silently, then took his order to the bartender at the opposite end of the diner. The writer met the bartender's sudden stare without a flicker of expression, and the performance began. The bartender and his helper knew the track well; they expected every sudden lurch and they anticipated the direction of every long, slow turn. Working together, pausing for each turn, bracing themselves and their bottles, they slowly built up layer after layer of liqueur in the tiny glass. Ten minutes later, the drink was done, each layer sharply defined; now the trick was to get it down the length of the car without a bump or swerve which would cause the layers to merge. The waiter took his time. Eyes from every table were on him as he made his way, step by step, toward the customer. Finally he set it in front of him. The drink was flawless. The moment obviously required some comment and the customer was equal to the challenge. He barked at the waiter, "You didn't bring me no spoon to stir it with!"

No region can exist on amenities, not even its love of environment. The artificial economic stimulus of the Seattle Fair is fading. As it is almost everywhere, agriculture is decreasing in economic importance in Washington; despite the vast wheat ranches of eastern Washington, fewer people are supported by agricultural income now than two decades ago. Only about half as much timber is being cut in Washington as twenty-five years ago, and employment in the basic lumber industry has declined; there has been a tremendous expansion in pulp-and-paper-manufacturing employment, but it is not quite large enough to offset the decline in lumber jobs. The big growth in Washington employment has been in the aircraft industry. Boeing has stayed strong during the inevitable shift of emphasis from conventional aircraft to space vehicles. But in terms of employment, the growth of this industry is leveling out. Fishing and mining are of minor economic importance now to Washington. During 1961 and 1962, economic indicators in Washington were at about the national average. The state remained far behind the dazzling economic development pace of California and other Western states such as Arizona and New Mexico.

What support can Washington show for the population growth which it confidently expects? Its economic future is shrouded in more popular misconceptions than that of any other Western region. They involve a fictitious land called the Inland Empire, which by tradition ties together eastern Oregon, Washington, the panhandle of Idaho and western Montana. They involve public power, which is not the great industrial lure for the Northwest which it is assumed to be. They involve Alaska, for which Seattle is ceasing to be the gateway. They involve the lumber industry, which is undergoing vast change.

But there are other more hopeful factors in the Washington pattern that will tend to support the hundreds of thousands of new residents whom many demographers believe will throng into Washington before 1970.

Spokane is Washington's second biggest city (181,608). It is in the rolling pine forests and wheat land of eastern Washington, close to the Idaho border. Because the Cascade Mountains present a natural barrier between western and eastern Washington, regions of sharp contrast, Spokane has been considered the capital of the so-called Inland Empire, generally defined as including those parts of the four states enclosed by mountains. The Inland Empire has been a favorite device of economists, who recall that Congress passed a bill in 1886 to create a state called Lincoln of the area; it was pocket-vetoed by Grover Cleveland. But fast highways, extensive new telephone installations, and the airplane have minimized the barriers that encircle the Inland Empire. Each segment has drawn closer to the other communities and interests of its own state. Spokane remains a natural market and distribution center for much of this area, but statistics charting automobile travel and volume of telephone calls among cities suggest that today Spokane's ties are strongest with Seattle, across the state. The growth pattern of Spokane has been closely related to that of Seattle; Spokane faltered between 1950 and 1960, like Seattle, when a lag in the aluminum industry depressed its aluminum plants and an Air Force base was closed.

Between Spokane and Seattle lies the Grand Coulee Dam, which spawned the aluminum industry in Washington in World War II and later made possible the establishment of the Atomic Energy Commission's plutonium plant at Hanford. Farms and towns have sprung up in the arid Columbia River Basin of central Washington as irrigation has reached out from Grand Coulee to two and a half million acres of land which in 1950 supported only limited dry farming. The Moses Lake region is so productive that its acreage was farmed in the late 1950's by speculators who lived in motels and hired mechanical crews to sow, cultivate, and harvest their crops of sugar beets, hay, potatoes, beans, or wheat. The population of this Columbia Basin Project rose from about thirty thousand in 1950 to more than seventy thousand in 1960. Its period of boom is past, but more land will be irrigated, and growth in the basin will be steady.

There is exaggerated faith in Washington that the Grand Coulee and the Bonneville public power projects on the Columbia

River provide cheap power which attracts private industry to the Northwest. In a survey for the State of Washington in 1960, Dr. William Bunge concluded that "the Pacific Northwest has lost its meager low-power-cost advantage since the Ohio Valley can add units of power, based on strip-mined coal, cheaper than hydroelectric capacity can be added in the Pacific Northwest." Industry which has been lured to the Northwest by low power costs has proven to be highly automated, providing meager local employment; also defeating Northwest prosperity is the fact that the public power bill is paid in the nation's capital, not in the Northwest. Dr. Bunge's survey showed too that abundant water has not been an important factor in locating industry in the Northwest.

Another nebulous asset to the Northwest is the legend of the Alaska boom. If you inquire around Seattle for the heralded Alaskan gateway, it becomes elusive. Steamship passengers bound for Alaska embark from Vancouver in British Columbia. Automobile traffic reaches the Alaska Highway at Dawson Creek in British Columbia after crossing the Canadian border at several points east of Seattle. The only passenger gateway from Seattle to Alaska is the Seattle-Tacoma International Airport, where four airlines provide daily service to the big new state.

The Alaskan boom was overplayed at the time of statehood in 1959. It has leveled off; much of it was based on military activity. Alaska fishing, its largest industry, is in danger of decline. Piqued by high shipping rates, Alaskans are giving vent to their resentment of Seattle shipping interests by trading more with other cities, including Portland. Historically, Alaska has been a captive market for Seattle merchants and shippers. From its beginnings, everything worn, eaten, drunk or used on the Alaskan frontier was sold by Seattle firms and handled across Seattle docks. Everything produced in Alaska, from furs to salmon to logs of Sitka spruce, flowed back into Washington, if for no other purpose than to be auctioned, labeled, sawed, or dried for further export. The Alaskan Gold Rush built Seattle as a city. But with declines in Alaskan defense spending, notably evident by 1961, there was sharp reaction in Seattle, the home base for labor unions, construction firms, and building suppliers operating in Alaska.

Alaska remains a huge, underdeveloped state in need of vast amounts of risk capital before it is to become an important economic factor in the Northwest. It is eight times larger than the state of Washington, with a total population about one-third that of Seattle. There were only three hundred and sixty-seven farms in Alaska in 1960, half of them part-time. Income from fishing is more than twenty times greater than that from farming. In 1959, the value of coal mined in Alaska surpassed that of gold. Alaskans are improving highways and airports in attempts to induce more tourism, which soared during the Seattle Fair.

An increasing amount of Alaska's supplies are shipped through Prince Rupert, British Columbia. Shipping lines to Alaska historically operate at a loss during slack winter months; cargo for some Alaskan ports is often so slight that the runs are uneconomical. But in 1962 rail-barge service was inaugurated between Seattle and Seward, the terminus of the Alaska Railroad. Fast-ship ferry transit was introduced six days weekly between Prince Rupert, Haines and Skagway, touching the Alaskan panhandle towns of Ketchikan, Wrangell, Petersburg, Sitka and Juneau. Notably, the ferry system bypasses Seattle; there is no passenger-ship connection between Seattle and Prince Rupert, and the roundabout highway trip from Seattle to connect with the Alaskan Highway means that the city is out of the main flow of overland traffic. Even by jet, Anchorage is three hours—more than fourteen hundred miles—distant from Seattle.

Today, Alaska's resentment against Seattle is perfectly natural, in the light of its eclipsing relationship of dependence. In the past there has been profiteering by Seattle shippers and suppliers, but there has been profiteering also by Alaskan retailers, who are likely to be in business there because they hope to make a faster profit, and who alibi stiff mark-ups on goods by making slurring references to the high shipping costs from Seattle. The situation has led to some lively outbursts, especially since Alaskan statehood.

In 1961, the United States Post Office announced a plan to send mail to Alaska by truck—a seventy-two hour run—instead of by ship, taking a week or more. Governor Rosellini of Washington protested in behalf of the Washington-owned Alaska Steamship Company. Senator E. L. Bartlett of Alaska wrote Rosellini a blunt letter in which he stated, "Your intervention suggests a lack of comprehension of Alaska's changed political status. Now that Alaska is a state, the governor of Washington should not seek to decide an internal matter concerning Alaska any more than should the governor of Alaska intervene in a governmental situation concerning Washington State."

Another source of tension has been the fishing of Alaskan waters by Seattle boats. About sixty Puget Sound purse-seine vessels cruise north in the summer to Alaskan salmon grounds west and southwest of Juneau, a marine wilderness of mountainous virgin forests, trout-filled streams, islands and interlaced waterways shrouded in rain and fog. A bill passed by the Alaskan legislature in 1961 was interpreted in Washington as potentially barring non-Alaskan boats from the salmon areas in years of low yield. The Washington legislature considered—but shelved—a retaliatory proposal. Formal protests were made to Alaska by Governor Rosellini and others. This touched off an exchange between Governor William A. Egan of Alaska and Rosellini.

"For decades," Egan wrote Rosellini, "Alaskans sought and fought for statehood in order to free themselves from outside controls largely centered in the State of Washington. These, at various times in our period of territoriality, have included control, or efforts to control our fisheries, our shipping, our labor organs, our industry and our political decisions. . . . Passage [of the salmon bill] resulted in a storm of protests from and unbecoming to the State of Washington and deeply resented by Alaskans."

Sometimes Seattle bristles and fights back. An editorial in the Seattle *Times* in 1960 attacked the Anchorage *Times* for its charges that Seattle interests were responsible for a discriminatory freight-rate schedule that set shipping rates between Japan and Alaska ports thirty percent higher than between Japan and other West Coast ports. Said the Seattle paper: "We take exception to the blame heaped unfairly on Seattle by the Anchorage newspaper. What does it mean by 'Seattle' anyway—the city government of Seattle, the Port of Seattle, the people of Seattle, or what? None of these had anything to do with it. There's nothing new about this. The Anchorage *Times* is accustomed to making Seattle a 'whipping boy' for Alaska's woes and problems, as if some dark and sinister plot were afoot here to hamper Alaska's growth and development. Fortunately the true facts about Seattle's enduring support for Alaskan development are well known among thoughtful residents of the new state."

Another key factor in the economic future of Washington, one equally burdened with misconception as the subject of Alaska, is the sweeping change in forest industries. These attained their peak employment in Washington in 1951. In the next decade, employment in sawmills declined thirty-one percent; in logging, twenty-seven percent; and in plywood mills, nineteen percent. Employment in the pulp-and-paper-industry increased nineteen percent.

Declining employment in the forest industries has been caused largely by automation. The result has been the virtual disappearance from the map of some small lumbering towns, and a slowdown in growth of cities like Tacoma, a dirty industrial city south of Seattle. Tacoma was almost static in population between 1950 and 1960. Its economic strength stems from forest products and military bases, and it is the headquarters of the Weyerhaeuser Company, which in terms of mills and forests is the largest timber company in the world.

It was Weyerhaeuser which introduced the concept of the tree farm about 1940. Since then, twenty thousand tree farms comprising fifty-five million acres have been assigned by private owners to perpetual production of wood. This plan represents one of the strongest hopes for the future of the Northwest. Now second-growth timber is being cut and more trees are being grown each year than are being cut; the timber industry is compensating for the haste and greed of its pioneers.

Despite the economic fallacies of its past, Washington has economic aces up its sleeves which—in the tradition of legerdemain that characterizes a great deal of the westward tilt—are likely to facilitate a massive growth in population. One of them is involved directly with the moderation and good conscience which mark the people of Washington: productivity of Washington labor ranges up to fifteen percent higher than the national average. Northwest people work hard. Labor disputes in Washington have been minimal in recent years.

The remoteness of Washington from national markets and raw materials is offset by its attraction for the footloose industries which today are locating rapidly in such "amenities" areas of the West as Puget Sound. In the years ahead, this same remoteness may become Washington's greatest asset. In terms of shipping costs, Seattle is closer to Tokyo than to Chicago. All of the Orient lying east of a north-south line down the center of India is in a zone where shipping costs from Seattle are less than those from New York City. The potential of American trade with Red China is a controversial imponderable. The gross national product of China today is close to that of Great Britain. Oriental economics may mean as much to the Western United States in years ahead as the European Common Market means today to the Eastern United States.

Washington's future will rise with the growth of California. With each million in population added by the giant to the south, Washington sheds another fragment of its remoteness from major markets. Washington also grows in economic strength as the enterprising entrepreneurs of the state take wing. The abstract factor in any civic growth formula is the quality of its people. It would be unwise to bet against old-timers like Nick Bez, who owns floating fish canneries in Washington and in Alaska, but who has given more and more of his time to his West Coast Airlines, which serves close to seventy towns and cities between Calgary, San Francisco, Salt Lake City, and Great Falls, Montana. When he showed me boarding figures for the current month, it was with an air of almost parental concern. Bellingham had boarded sixty-four passengers, whereas Olympia, the capital of Washington, had boarded only twenty-eight —less than one a day. Bez's line serves more small towns than any comparable airline in the nation. He keeps at it in good cheer and deep faith. "The people will keep coming," he said. "Some days I think I'd like to give away a dozen of these towns that we serve, but then I remind myself that this is our last frontier."

The Northwestern businessman is a traveler. Recently George Weber, the vice president of a large Northwest advertising agency, pointed to a map and showed me where his men were. One was in Honolulu, another in Guatemala and a third in Mexico City, each on business for Western Hotels. A fourth was in Chicago at the National Homebuilders Show, representing Weyerhaeuser interests. Another was in New Orleans in behalf of the Washington State Apple Commission, and the last was in New York City doing business both for the General Insurance Company of America, which has home offices in Seattle, and for the Canned Salmon Institute.

Walter Straley senses a "gulf that separates the Northwest from California, which is accustomed to migration. Seattle has grown much faster than the rest of Washington, but it's not California-type migration. I would guess that such massive migration is just now beginning. The migration that still follows the sun into the Southwest will give Oregon and Washington more people in the late 1960's than anyone is now forecasting. Two things begin to look good to you after a while in metropolitan centers of California: clear air and plenty of water. The Northwest has both."

And it has, above all, an extraordinary breed of Westerner. It is easy to explain economic indicators and population densities; it is harder to explain people. But it is the people of Washington who will make it great.

13

THE MOUNTAIN NORTH

Idaho, Montana, Wyoming

Lewis and Clark left St. Louis in mid-May of 1804, but it was a year later when they finally crossed westward into Montana. That day an inch of snow fell and covered the wild flowers of the plain, and Clark noted in his journal that this was a "verry extraodernarey climate."

Not until September thirteenth did Lewis and Clark cross over Lolo Pass into what is now Idaho. On their return from the Pacific Coast in May, 1806, they made friends of the Nez Percé Indians, setting the stage for seventy years of peace between that tribe and the white man—a peace broken by the white man's perfidy.

Until the fashion changed, about 1850, Europeans favored beaver hats for men and wraps for women. Beaver trappers ranged the Mountain North. A few years later gold seekers trod the Oregon Trail through Wyoming. By 1858, a daily stagecoach rolled over the trail, from Atchison to San Francisco. In that same year, gold was found in Montana, and later the Bozeman Trail forked off to the north from the Oregon Trail. Gold turned up in Idaho in 1862, and Idaho City began its boom. At Virginia City, Montana, in 1864, the Montana *Post* was founded as Montana's first newspaper and gold was struck at Last Chance Gulch, later to become the main street of Helena, the Montana capital. Henceforth Montana was to have more than its share of buccaneers. Even before its mining tycoons pirated fortunes from each other, there were the foragers of grass: Texas longhorn cattle, which became a big factor in the Mountain West, were driven up into Montana for the first time in 1866 on a search for grass.

The first Union Pacific train in Cheyenne arrived in 1867. Nine years later, General George Custer took his stand against the Sioux on Montana's Little Big Horn River, and the only thing certain about that day is that Custer should have stood in bed.

In the 1880's it began to be apparent that Butte was built on the richest hill on earth. A cast whose principals included Clark, Daly, and Heinze acted out the torrid corruption of Amalgamated—later called Anaconda—Copper Mining Company.

The Northern Pacific pushed across Idaho and through Montana by 1883, stimulating cattle raising and wheat growing. But Montana never has unjumbled the checkerboard of land ownership that Northern Pacific caused. To encourage building the railroad, Congress voted Northern Pacific the largest land grant in Congressional history: twenty-three thousand square miles of Montana, every alternate section in a strip eighty miles wide along its line. It was an area three times the size of New Jersey, but there were only a few who thought the land was good for anything at all.

In Wyoming, sheepherders and cattlemen began to hate each other. (Sheep eat grass clean at ground level, leaving nothing for cattle. Cattlemen claim that cattle will not go where sheep have grazed and that sheep pollute the water holes.) There was a truce in 1909 after five cattlemen went to the Wyoming penitentiary for killing two sheepmen and a herder in the Tensleep Battle.

Cattlemen hated cattlemen too. The first blacklist in the West was probably the one of alleged rustlers drawn up by cattlemen in Johnson County, Wyoming, in 1892. The cattlemen called themselves the Regulators; the settlers and ranchers of Buffalo who mobilized to meet the Regulators called themselves the Home Defenders. Fifty cattlemen and gunmen rode from Cheyenne to shoot the rustlers dead, but federal troops locked them up after two were killed.

Wyoming wasn't entirely without gentility. It was admitted to statehood in 1890 with a clause in its constitution making it the first state to grant full suffrage to women.

In January, 1899, the Montana senate set out to elect a United States senator. The two protagonists of Montana's copper war, W. A. Clark and Marcus Daly, were the stars of the show. Clark wanted to be senator; Daly meant to beat him. Talk of bribery was on every tongue. Fred Whiteside, a state senator, displayed thirty thousand dollars in currency which he announced had been given him by Clark's agents to buy his vote and that of four others. A grand jury convened, but ruled there was insufficient evidence of bribery. Eighteen days later, Clark was elected United States senator—but resigned after an investigation by the United States Senate. Then he teamed up with F. Augustus Heinze, a mining engineer, who later double-crossed his partner. Daly died; Standard Oil, which had bought Anaconda Copper, froze out Heinze; Teddy Roosevelt's trust busters froze out Standard Oil. Anaconda survived it all, and has done all right in Montana.

To the northeast, at Great Falls, in a bend of the Missouri River, Jenny Lind and Harry Lauder appeared at the Great Falls Opera House. Down by the railroad tracks in Great Falls, some solid citizens built two white, two-story houses as the town whore-houses. Later the parlors became the county home; now, even the county home has moved out.

Jim Hill, a tough hero with tough dreams, was responsible for Great Falls' existence. His Great Northern Railroad brought the homesteaders westward in a boom that started in 1910, after the Enlarged Homestead Act of 1909. All went well as long as it rained and wheat grew on the unirrigated plains just as Hill had said it would. But about the time World War I ended the rains stopped, the rush began for food and beds at the Salvation Army citadels, and the homesteaders were ruined. Between 1921 and 1925, one of every two Montana farmers lost his farm by foreclosure. Eleven thousand farms disappeared.

The Butte Union Hall, headquarters of Local No. 1 of the Union of Mine, Mill & Smelter Workers, was blown up in 1914, and martial law, no stranger to Butte, was enforced once more. On the night of August 1, 1917, masked men dragged an International Workers of the World organizer named Frank Little from his bed; they broke his leg and hanged him. In Wyoming, in 1922, Secretary of the Interior Albert B. Fall leased the Teapot Oil Reserve to Harry F. Sinclair. He shouldn't have; the oil belonged to the government. Sinclair went up for three months, and Secretary Fall received a three-year prison sentence and was fined three hundred thousand dollars.

Drought was the pervading fact of the era. In 1925, as the drought continued in Montana, a story circulated among stockgrowers about a Missouri River boatman who was stuck on a sandbar. He saw red when a rancher stepped up to the shore and took a bucket of water as the boatman struggled to free himself. "Hey, you put that back!" the boatman yelled, and the fight started.

There's been a lot of other violence in this Mountain North. Montana, which has more earthquakes than any other state, lost a mountainside, and twenty-eight persons were buried beneath it, on the night of August 17, 1959, in Madison Canyon near Yellowstone Park. Around the Mountain North, old-timers shrugged. Some think the good Lord has had His doubts about their part of the country all along.

◇◇◇

On the Snake River Plain in southern Idaho, near the Strategic Air Command base at Mountain Home, a service-station attendant tried to discourage me from taking a back road to Sun Valley. "I wouldn't ride over it in a jeep," he snorted. "Three cars came in here this week off that road and they all had been shaken apart."

With that assurance, I took the back road, heading northeast toward the Sawtooth Range. The asphalt ended, and a narrow ribbon of dirt wound off through glens of willow and alder and cottonwood and Rocky Mountain ash, past herds of sheep. Houses fell behind. In a ravine at the turn of a hairpin curve, a sheepherder's wagon stood beneath a great lodgepole pine, his stovepipe extending through the roof of the wagon. Ahead and above were mountainsides dense with fir and cedar and pine.

At a mountain crossroads called Dixie stood a two-story frame house, deserted, its windows cracked and open. A house trailer was parked nearby, and a faded wooden sign pointed down an even more tenuous lane to hamlets named Pine and Atlanta. Then the road soared through green valleys and curved through forests like a roller coaster. A blue lake shimmered in the distance. Here and there, a weathered, abandoned farmhouse, its roof collapsed, subsided into the landscape.

There were no cars but mine. I had forgotten the joy of driving a lonely back road where a man has a choice to drive on the left side of the road if it beckons, or in the middle if he is so inclined, without single lines, double lines, broken lines, passing lines, or center islands. Hawks flew up in the road ahead, and a great bald eagle soared from a cliffside nearby. The road led over Wild Horse Creek. At a sudden ninety-degree turn, I saw my trail of dust for miles behind.

An hour later another sharp turn to the left revealed a wheat field, the first on this road. The road led to the end of the field, and turned sharp right; somehow it seemed satisfying to detour around this man's field. On the horizon appeared the only sign of habitation in an hour: a cedar fence, and soon a red barn, and a brick farmhouse. Civilization, a speck on the horizon at first, was emerging again. The road was leaving sheep country and entering wheat country. The wind rippled the sea of wheat almost within arm's length of the car at both sides, bringing a strangely pleasant suggestion of vertigo. Soon a grain elevator appeared against the sky, and then a sign announced Hill City: two or three houses, a general store, and the grain elevator at the terminus of a railroad spur.

It was almost dark, but a road crew at Hill City was grading. The road was hopelessly blocked by mounds of earth. I stopped the car and got out.

"Didn't expect anybody else in tonight," the foreman said, with a broad smile. "Thought we'd work on until dark and knock off early tomorrow. Guess I'd better move some of this dirt and let you through."

A little farther on, at Corral, the progress of the graders began to be evident. Blacktop resumed, and with a sense of loss, I pulled in at the Corral store and post office. It was little more than a weather-beaten shanty, and it looked deserted, but inside, the man who served as postmaster and proprietor chatted pleasantly.

"They tell me we'll be getting some city traffic in here one of these days," he said. "They're talking about grading this road all the way over past Dixie to Mountain Home." His face was impassive, but the prospect did not seem to excite him.

This kind of West is with us still, but nowhere else in such generous supply as in the Mountain North of Idaho, Montana, and Wyoming. These states serve as a counterpoint to the theme of change in the other eight states of the West. Though they differ vastly within themselves and from each other, they are bound together by the almost aggressive reluctance of most of their people to sacrifice their affinity with the land and the past. On the timetable of the American West, the Mountain North lies decades away from the mood of urgency which grips its neighbors in the coastal states and, to an increasing degree, those to its south. The Mountain North is a balm to the harried West.

There are many reasons for this, both historically and in the present. Above all, there is the compelling fact of wilderness. I drove for days through these three states and then, enraptured by their beauty but frustrated as a reporter, I took to the air. There is immense solitude in this land, and unlike most other areas, that sense of solitude is only accentuated when the country is seen from the air. Man's mark is minute and inconsequential. Nowhere in this Mountain North does a city rise to break the mood. The biggest town of Idaho, Wyoming and Montana in 1960 was Great Falls, Montana, with 55,246 people. The three states are larger in combined area than Texas, New York, and New Jersey; yet their combined 1960 population of 1,672,024 was about one fifth that of New York City.

Nor is there any expectation that this wilderness is soon to be conquered. Population projections for the coming years are of the most modest nature, not only well below the Western rate of growth, but in general below the national average. There is a lot of pioneering yet to be done. Winters are bitterly cold, and summers can be hot; the climate will not bring the millions here. Freight rates are discriminatorily high, and state industrial development commissions— despite their protestations to the contrary—are wooing industry with considerably less enthusiasm than other Western states. While these man-made obstacles exist, industry will not overwhelm the Mountain North. There is an immense friendliness among the people of these states, but their leisureliness and remoteness are not characteristics which will act as magnets for a scientific, industrial, or educational explosion. The Mountain North is not on the main line, and the sense of hope and destiny which brings the millions to the rest of the West is not yet felt here.

In each of these respects, these three states bear some resemblance to the Deep South—with the obvious exception that crises of prejudice are almost totally absent from the Mountain North. But in their loss or slow growth of population, and in the sense that both regions are off the main path of progress, many parallels can be drawn.

The sheer geography of this wilderness has worked against its best interests. Idaho is divided in two by the barriers of the Clearwater, Salmon, and Sawtooth Mountains. Its northern panhandle and much of northwest Montana face naturally toward Spokane in eastern Oregon. Southern Idaho is in the Salt Lake City orbit. By tradition, there are three capitals of Idaho: Boise, Spokane, and Salt Lake City. Fashion-conscious Boise women may shop in Seattle, San Francisco, or even, on a lark, Los Angeles, 893 fast miles away.

Western Montana is mountainous mining and timber country

oriented toward the Pacific Coast. The eastern two-thirds of the state becomes part of the Great Plains, looking toward North Dakota and the Twin Cities. Its interests are in wheat and oil. Montana boundaries, as Ross Toole wrote in his book *Montana: an Uncommon Land*, "seem almost to have been drawn deliberately to frustrate economic unity and good sense." In *The Great Plains in Transition*, Carl Kraenzel analyzed the influence of eighty-eight federal governmental functions in Montana and found they tugged the state variously toward Spokane, Denver, Lincoln, Minneapolis, Salt Lake City, Portland, San Francisco, Kansas City, Chicago, Seattle, Omaha, Sacramento, and St. Louis; only seventeen of the agencies had headquarters within Montana itself.

Wyoming depends on Denver to the south or Billings to the north for its distribution of goods. The state has only about two hundred settlements with any habitation at all; of these, only half are populated by more than one hundred persons. Cheyenne (43,505), the capital and largest town, is in the Denver orbit.

Transportation is unbelievably complex in the Mountain North. Highways and railroads make east-west connections reasonably good, but because of mountains, north-south transportation is difficult. No railroad links northern and southern Idaho, and there was no highway until 1927. Cheyenne and Boise are trunk-line stops for major airlines on east-west routes. But feeder-airline service in other towns of these three states is a chancy thing, and weather tends to make a mockery of their slim schedules during much of the year. In many smaller towns airports have the look of the 1930's; sometimes it is difficult to tell an airfield from a pasture. In the Montana wilderness, smoke-jumpers will drop from a plane to fight a forest fire; it will take them a few minutes to arrive over the scene of the fire, they will fight it for several hours, but it may take days to walk out of the wilderness and back to a habited area.

These are the surface problems of a contemporary wilderness, but they conceal more serious crises. Wary of the future, youth has been deserting these states for greater opportunity elsewhere. The populace which remains behind tends toward stolidity and laissez faire.

Montana is freeing itself from the colonial coils of The Anaconda Company, but its sense of liberty atrophies because there is no surge of constructive motion in any other direction. Anaconda surrendered its death grip on the Montana press by selling off its seven company-owned daily newspapers in 1959 to the Lee chain. Perhaps political morality in Montana has improved since the brazen days

CANADA

WASHINGTON

OREGON

NEVADA

UTAH

IDAHO

MONTANA

WYOMING

Coeur d'Alene
Moscow
Lewiston
BOISE
Mountain Home
Sun Valley
Corral
Hill City
Twin Falls
Burley
Craters OF THE MOON NAT'L PARK
Pocatello
Idaho Falls
Rexburg
FORT HALL IND. RES.
SNAKE RIVER BASIN
Snake River
SALMON RIVER MTS.
CLEARWATER MTS.
BITTERROOT RANGE

Kalispell
Flathead Lake
FLATHEAD IND. RES.
GLACIER NATIONAL PARK
BLACKFEET IND. RES.
Missoula
HELENA
Butte
Anaconda
Bozeman
Livingston
Great Falls
Havre
FORT BELKNAP IND. RES.
FORT PECK IND. RES.
Glasgow
Fort Peck Reservoir
Missouri River
MINUTEMAN MISSILE RANGES
GREAT NORTHERN RWY.
C.M.SP. AND P. RWY.
Billings
Miles City
Yellowstone River
CROW IND. RES.
YELLOWSTONE NATIONAL PARK
GRAND TETON NAT'L PARK
Jackson
Cody
WIND RIVER IND. RES.
BIG HORN MTS.
Big Horn
Sheridan
Buffalo
C.B. AND Q. RWY.
Casper
Rock Springs
Flaming Gorge Res.
Laramie
LARAMIE MTS.
CHEYENNE
UNION PACIFIC RWY.

SCALE: 105 MILES TO THE INCH
0   105   210

Idaho–Montana–Wyoming

when Anaconda and its opponents bought legislators and judges, but the state's political leaders are so diverse today in attitude that they are not directing their state.

In the Senate, Majority Leader Mike Mansfield and Lee Metcalf are two distinguished liberal Democrats. At the capitol in Helena, a conservative Republican lawyer, the late Donald Nutter, moved in as governor in 1961, promising to revitalize the state with industry and new population. But his greatest effort was directed toward decreasing expenditures and eliminating a six-million-dollar state deficit. He confined himself to a skimpy six-hundred-dollar annual expense account. "It is going to be like pulling teeth to get industry into Montana," Governor Nutter said only weeks before his death in a plane crash in Montana in 1962. "A lot of Montanans are resentful of the idea of a lot of industries coming in here. I don't want Montana to become a congested area like Los Angeles. We have some of the best fishing and hunting and scenery in the United States, and many of our people would like to leave it that way. I'd like to see our growth gradual. The ideal situation would be to have our growth just keep pace with increasing government costs. We'd be able to do all the things we need to do in Montana and not have a lot of big industry."

Nutter's successor as governor, Tim Babcock, a conservative Republican, carries on the tradition. In the fall of 1962 he testified in Washington against a proposed dam on the Flathead River which he termed an "unsound expenditure of the taxpayers' dollars that would cost the people of this country two hundred and fifty-nine million dollars they do not need to spend." Governor Nutter and the 1961 legislature slashed educational budgets and cut back spending for welfare, state health services and custodial institutions—even though the vicious Montana prison riots are modern history. Nutter justified this policy on the grounds that industry which might be enticed to Montana would be most interested in the state's fiscal solvency. But it is more likely that the voices of Anaconda and the Montana Power Company, still loud and clear in Montana, were dominant in shaping the Montana budget. These two giants no longer have interlocking directorships, but Anaconda still is Montana Power's largest customer (fifteen to twenty percent of its total billing, down from a high of about forty percent) and their political goals are highly compatible and equally reactionary.

Why then, if these two companies' political strength in Montana is so great, do two liberal Senators represent the state? In part, because they can do Anaconda and Montana Power less damage in Washington than in Montana. And also because Montanans are individualists above all, and personality is a weightier political factor than issues.

Mansfield, a former history professor at Montana State University, believes that the first need of Montana is for a "vigorous and vocal effort to sell the state and its resources to private industry and the general public." He considers the major problems of the state to be "its erratic climate, distance from major market areas, the fact that major industry in the state is largely of an extractive nature, and the migration of its young people away from the state." As a cure, he supports expanded research in soil and water conservation to stabilize the agricultural economy; new industry to process and prepare for market materials already available within the state; full development of low-cost hydroelectric power, and the adjustment of freight rates.

Metcalf, the other Montana senator, followed Mansfield into Congress when the latter moved up from the House to the Senate in 1952. Metcalf was elected to the Senate in 1960 after establishing a liberal voting record in education, labor, conservation, and Indian affairs. A former attorney and associate justice of the Montana Supreme Court, he is a fiercely partisan public-power advocate who has pushed for construction of the giant Libby Dam in northwest Montana which would back water into Canada, and for federal dams on the Flathead River in western Montana and on the Big Horn in southern Montana.

"Federal expenditures have kept the Montana economy going," Metcalf wrote. "The Defense Department has spent hundreds of millions of dollars in Montana at the Malmstrom Air Force Base in Great Falls, the Glasgow Air Force Base, and the Minuteman complex in central Montana. Montana is thirty percent federally owned; in other Western states an even higher proportion of land is federal. Growth of the West depends much on federal investment." However, he mirrors the Mountain North attitude when he remarks that "this year's bustling missile site may again be prairie within a decade. But the community which shares in the development of wood and water is likely to be growing still at the end of this century."

Metcalf foresees industrial jobs in Montana through the development of forest wealth and timber-products manufacturing. Pulpwood potentials are barely tapped. New dams may bring new industry, like the Anaconda aluminum plant built soon after Hungry Horse Dam went into operation near Flathead Lake in northwest Montana. Webb & Knapp has scheduled the construction of a steel mill near Butte. Bureau of Reclamation projects will permit irrigation of thousands of additional Montana acres, boosting agricultural jobs. There are increasing numbers of tourists, including thousands of out-of-state hunters who pay license fees of up to one hundred dollars for a combination permit to fish and to hunt elk, deer, moose, antelope, bear, mountain sheep, goats and birds. The tourist industry is close to displacing mining as second in importance to agriculture in Montana.

Mining goes on in Butte's "richest hill on earth," but the raucous past is fading. One Butte leader told me, "Right up until the last year or two, national magazines have strained and scratched to perpetuate our wild past. It won't work. We've come of age."

Out of Butte Hill, Anaconda has taken more than three billion dollars in copper, gold, silver, zinc, and manganese. There is no evidence that Butte copper is running out, but automation and a declining market have set off another depression in the long series that Butte has known. From the point of view of the miner, this one looks permanent. Montana, long heralded for its copper, has produced in recent years only about one-fifth as much of the metal as Arizona, and less than one-half as much as Utah. Butte is perhaps the world's most famed company town; if it has come of age in any way, after the scandalous oppression of its employees for many decades, it has been in providing excellent recreational and social facilities for miners. Unfortunately the best of these are being disbanded in interests of economy.

Silver Bow County, in which Butte is located, began its present population decline in 1957. Mining methods have changed; the twenty-seven hundred miles of underground tunnels and shafts are almost deserted and the industry has shifted to automated open-pit mining. In its Berkeley pit on the edge of Butte, trucks race day and night up and down the spiral benches, to and from electric shovels which gouge the ore eight tons at a scoop. The trucks dump the ore into the cars of Anaconda's railroad, over which it is hauled twenty-five miles west to the smelter at the town of Anaconda.

On every side of the Berkeley pit are grimy shacks and slag piles. Backed against the pit is Meaderville, once a flashy town of sin, now dingy, listless, and half-shuttered. A sign reads: *If You've Never Seen Colusa Club, U. S. A., You've Never Seen Meaderville*— but the front window is smashed and Colusa Club, U. S. A., looks as though it has been long deserted; we may never see Meaderville. From its gambling halls came men, such as Milton Prell, who now work less precariously at their calling in the satin and plush of Las Vegas casinos.

I re-read sections of John Gunther's *Inside U. S. A.* as I roamed the West. Inevitably, as with any reportage no matter how expert, much of Gunther's material on the West has been dated by events of the westward migration since he toured the West in 1945, and since he revised his book in 1951. Only in the Mountain North did the general tone of Gunther's Western chapters hold true in 1962. In itself this seems eloquent testimony to the unchanging nature of the three states. In Montana, the state with the slowest rate of growth of the three during three of the four past decades, one of Gunther's plaints has had a parallel. In 1945 he reported seeing an inch-long item in the Helena newspaper announcing the abandonment of a Great Northern Railway branch line between the towns of Armington and Neihart. In Butte in 1961 there was consternation because the Interstate Commerce Commission had authorized the Great Northern to discontinue its last two daily passenger trains between Butte and Great Falls. In its heyday, during sixty years of service over this 171-mile run, the Great Northern offered Pullman and dining-car service. In later years, passenger service declined to a Diesel-powered passenger car, and the volume of traffic did not seem to justify even that. It is rare in the West today to see curtailment of services of any kind; changes are in the opposite direction.

There is sickness in any region which retrogresses, even though much of the rest of the West, by contrast, offers evidence of ills which result from too precipitous a move forward. "Change?" sighed Michael Stephen Kennedy, editor of the Western historical magazine, *Montana*, and director of the superb Montana Historical Society Museum across from the state capitol at Helena. "Historically we've been progressive in Montana, but now I'm afraid we're going backwards. We are paying the penalty of the generations which have left the state."

Yet there is a certain charm accompanying this aura of retrogression. The area with the greatest rate of growth in Montana between 1950 and 1960 was Mineral County in the far west, where the Diamond Match Company built a plant and the population zoomed from about two thousand to three thousand. In odd contrast, as if to compensate for the sparsity of population, the Montana capitol teems with legislators. A modest population increase between 1950 and 1960 led to an attempt to seat ninety-four members of the lower house—which proved at first to be a physical impossibility.

Liquor laws are amiably flexible. Bars sell whiskey by the bottle, but prices average about two dollars a fifth higher than those at the state liquor stores, which close inconsiderately at six in the evening. Gambling still is overlooked in many parts of the state. Among the few things about which Montanans seem to be disturbed is the price of gasoline, which is in the neighborhood of forty cents a gallon. The gas is refined in Montana from oil pumped in the eastern part of the state, then is piped westward four hundred miles to Spokane, where it may sell for a dime a gallon less than in Montana. Refineries say their distribution costs are greater in Montana because of the sparsity and isolation of markets, but understandably Montanans grumble.

The people of Montana run the gamut of sophistication. In Butte's newest motor hotel, a maid watched in fascination as a guest applied hair spray from an aerosol can; she had never witnessed the ritual before. At an opposite extreme, friends in Butte, when talking about their son who had just finished college in the East, avoided charges of pretension in Montana by not mentioning Harvard by name.

One of the charming patricians of the state is Robert Corette, a Montana Power Company vice president and lobbyist whose ranch near Butte is astride the Continental Divide; his house is on the Atlantic side, but rain that falls on his fields a quarter of a mile to the west finds its way into the Pacific. He showed me results of a public-opinion poll taken to learn what Montanans thought the relationship was between Anaconda and Montana Power. The results were eloquent: Montanans still appeared to regard Anaconda with considerable hostility but to think of Montana Power as fair friends; at the same time, the impression prevailed that Anaconda controlled Montana Power. Anaconda does not—Montana Power had 32,579 stockholders in 1961 and Anaconda was the first and most vigorous with protests at a recent power rate increase.

Traditional hostility between private power and the Rural Electrification Administration still is strong in the Mountain North. One battleground is a five-mile stretch of farmland between downtown Billings and the Yellowstone Country Club. The REA services many of the homes along the south side of Rimrock Road; on the other side, Montana Power lines string out to the Country Club and its adjacent subdivision. With the job of rural electrification admittedly ninety-seven percent complete, President Kennedy in 1961 outlined a new challenge for the REA: to work through its coöperatives in leading local development programs and studies which will create more jobs in rural and small town areas. In 1962, a dispute flared between REA and the private power interests which won their fight to build a portion of the transmission lines to distribute electricity generated by the Colorado River Storage Project in Colorado, Utah, New Mexico, Wyoming and Arizona. The REA charged private power with obstructionism—a typical argument in the continuous Western struggle between private enterprise and the long arm of Washington, which so often has proved the only one strong enough to effect some of the massive and costly hydroelectric and irrigation projects which have helped to build the West. At this moment the checks and balances implicit in this kind of competition seem to be working well. Neither private nor public power is winning all the fights. For instance, though the Idaho Power Company won its fight to develop Hell's Canyon on the Snake River, in Montana there are twenty-five REA coöperatives—twelve of them in the service area of Montana Power. Seven of the twelve buy their full power requirements from Montana Power; four buy power both from Montana Power and the federal government, and one is wholly a government customer. The cost of the power REA buys from Montana Power's system of thirteen hydroelectric plants is greater than that of the power bought from the federal Bonneville system, but less than that which REA pays to the Bureau of Reclamation for power from other federal hydroelectric sources in Montana. In the inviolate statistics of dollars and cents, the case for public versus private power in Montana can be considered a draw.

No one has described the cattle ranches of the northern West more vividly than the late artist and writer, Charles M. Russell, in his book *Trails Plowed Under*, which appeared after his death in 1927. The ranches he described of that day strongly resemble the prosperous ranches of today in Montana or Wyoming: "Most of the cow ranches I've seen lately was like a big farm. A bungalow with all modern improvements, a big red barn that holds white-faced bulls an' hornless milk cows. The corrals are full of fancy chickens, there's a big garage filled with all kinds of cars, and at the bunkhouse that sets back where the owner and his family can't see or hear them, are the hands. . . . The bungalow, that's got electric lights an' hot and cold water. There's a piana that you play with your feet, and a radio, a Mah Jong set, and a phonograph. The owner, if he's an old-timer, don't care for this. He'd rather camp in the bunkhouse and talk to some old bowleg about cows that wore horns . . ."

The most fascinating rancher I ever met was Vivienne Hesse, a tall, straight woman of indeterminate age who has lived all her life around Buffalo, Wyoming. Her blue eyes brim with fire in a face which shouts defiance to wind and sun and time.

"I'm ninety!" she announced when I could refrain no longer from asking the unforgivable question. I protested that I knew this could not be true, and her expression grew benign. "Well," she said, with an eloquent shrug, "there isn't anybody old enough in our county to deny it!"

Miss Hesse's brothers became Wyoming bankers. She grew up and lived until recently on the family ranch near Buffalo. "We raise cattle for respectability, and sheep to pay the bills," she explained.

Whatever her age, she thought nothing of driving alone almost four hundred miles across Wyoming to visit a friend, and then taking a raft trip down the Snake River, on which I first met her.

It was Hamilton Basso who wrote: "The notion keeps growing on me that in order to know Wyoming—to know it as a New Yorker knows New York or a Parisian knows Paris—you have to be an Indian." Wyoming is cattle and sheep and range. Wyoming is dude ranches, big-game hunting, and trout fishing, oil fields in the center of the state, and the majesties of the Grand Tetons and Yellowstone in its northwest corner. It is the Frontier Days Celebration in Cheyenne each July, an annual six-day rodeo first held in 1897. Sioux Indians stage tribal dances, there are parades and square dancing in the streets, and the best cowboys tangle with bulls, broncos and steers. But also in Cheyenne the first ICBM base in America was built.

The temper of the Mountain North is revealed again in the comment of Cheyenne's Cliff Bloomfield, a savings-and-loan firm's president: "The word 'boom' implies, sooner or later, 'bust.' We haven't had, and aren't going to have, either one here in Cheyenne." He seems right. Cheyenne has shown steady growth over the years as Wyoming's largest town, but in 1960 that meant only 43,505 people.

A payroll appropriate to rugged Wyoming is burgeoning in the mountains of southwest Wyoming. Under great secrecy, pilot plant crews from United States Steel and FMC Corporation are at work at Kemmerer on a joint venture to produce metallurgical coke from non-coking coal. As this book went to press, the unconventional technique being explored at Kemmerer seemed likely to revolutionize the production of elemental phosphorus—and to be of significance to vast Western regions with low-grade coal deposits.

Except for Alaska, there is no American state on which the passage of time and man has left so small an imprint as Wyoming. From the point of view of the Western tourist, it is a sanctum sanctorum, a natural green belt in an age of urbanization. But there are some in Wyoming who feel the state must reinforce itself with a cushion against periodic depressions in wool, livestock, and oil. One of these is Senator Gale W. McGee, one-time history instructor at Notre Dame and at the University of Chicago, who took leave from his post as professor of American history at the University of Wyoming in 1955 to serve as legislative assistant to the late Senator Joseph C. O'Mahoney. In 1958, in his first campaign, McGee defeated the incumbent Republican senator, Frank A. Barrett, who never before had lost a political race. McGee promptly made a name as one of the most thoughtful and courageous of Democratic freshman senators. "Wyoming is in desperate need of a massive and accelerated development of our vast repository of natural resources," he said. He and Wyoming's new senator, Milward Simpson, a Republican, regard uranium resources in Wyoming as a considerable aid to its future development. They also have prodded Washington and talked eloquently on behalf of Western conservation.

But its two senators are not typical of Wyoming. More characteristic are the residents of Big Horn—exactly one hundred of them in 1960—whose post office is in the corner grocery store. In 1961, when they learned that Washington was allotting funds for a new post office in Big Horn, they sent word that the government should save the money. The Post Office Department forthwith canceled its call for bids.

Such restraint in federal spending is not ordinarily associated with a state which has had Democratic leaders, but it is typical of the individualism of the West. Wyoming's sixty-four-year old former governor, Jack R. Gage, is no stock character; as secretary of state, he petitioned the legislature for a cut in his budget, received it, and ended the year with an unspent balance. He is a former postmaster and a Western writer, author of *Tensleep and No Rest*. No booster, he recently said: "Among the continental states, we happen to rank next to the bottom. In my thoughts alone, this is somewhat of a blessing." Gage became governor, like seven other Wyoming governors, by being elevated from the office of secretary of state. His announcement in 1962 that he would seek reëlection is as eloquent an example of Wyoming individualism as could be found. He scoffed at the politicians' customary bravura that he is running at the plea of thousands. Gage said: "I do not feel that I am anyone's glowing gift to Wyoming—in fact, Wyoming has done much more for me than I can hope to do in return. I do not think I have all the answers; nor have I heard all the questions. At the same time, I know that I have my teeth into this job. I know what it takes. I like it, and announce the fact that I will run because I want to very much." His modesty was not politically effective. Gage and the United States Senator whom he had appointed, John J. Hickey, were thrown out of office by the electorate in November, 1962. Wyoming voters were quarreling with the fact that Hickey, as governor, had been appointed to succeed a senator who died.

Idaho extends the Mountain North tradition of individualistic senators. Montana had its isolationist Burton K. Wheeler; Idaho had its banjo-plucking Glen H. Taylor, who ran afoul of the Henry Wallace third-party debacle in 1948 and moved on to California to become a wig manufacturer. Before Taylor, Idaho's best-known citizen was another isolationist and a famed non-partisan, William Edgar Borah, whose portrait hangs in a Capitol corridor at Boise above his words: "We may go back in sackcloth and ashes, but we will return to the faith of our fathers. America will live her own life. The independence of this republic will have its defenders."

Idaho's most prominent politician in recent years has been Senator Frank Church, a Phi Beta Kappa from Stanford University. His spellbinding keynote address at the Democratic National Convention in 1960 marked him nationally as a youngster who intended to get ahead; back home in Idaho it apparently helped to give him a reputation, even among many members of his own Democratic party, as a man considerably more radical than his constituents. The Church story is a classic tale of ambition. He won a national American Legion contest in oratory as a high school debater; his award included a scholarship at Stanford. He graduated from Stanford Law School and established a private legal practice in Boise in 1951. In 1956, by a narrow margin, he repulsed a comeback attempt by Glen Taylor in the Idaho Democratic primary for senator, then ousted the incumbent Republican by a large plurality. By 1960, he was stumping Idaho and the country for Kennedy. In 1962, he was reëlected.

Among Republicans of the Mountain North, Idaho's Governor Robert E. Smylie, also a lawyer, is the best known. He took office in 1954, served two four-year terms, and, in the fall of 1962, won a third term. (His opponent enlivened the campaign by espousing legalized gambling in Idaho.) This uncomplicated, personable man has made a contribution toward unifying the diversified people and regions of his state. If Idaho is to develop an identity and to move ahead, the miners and lumbermen of its remote mountainous northern panhandle, adjacent to the Canadian border, must find some affinity and common goals with the people of areas like the predominantly Mormon agricultural towns in the desert on the state's southeast border. It is almost five hundred miles between the north and south borders of Idaho. As late as 1919 there were only five miles of paved road in Idaho. Air transportation has not overcome the handicap of geography.

"There has been a measurable development of state pride and unity of purpose in recent years," Governor Smylie said. "It was very seldom, for example, that Idahoans ever saw their state flag. It is now fairly common. We have obliterated the mountain barrier across the state, in terms of communication between people, with the help of such basic improvements as telephone service, airline schedules, and better highways."

Smylie's favorite highway project has been the construction of a

highway following the route of Lewis and Clark across Idaho, a goal
for which he worked closely with Senator Church. There had been
no road at all on the route, though engineers still regarded it as the
easiest east-west route across the foot of the Idaho panhandle. Opened
in 1962, Idaho's Lewis and Clark Highway leads one hundred and
seventy miles through the wilderness from Hamilton, Montana, to
Lewiston, Idaho. In eight years under Smylie, with the aid of
federal funds, Idaho built or completed more roads than in any previous *twenty-year* period. School districts were consolidated and re-
organized, reducing the number from about twelve hundred and fifty
in 1947 to one hundred and ten in 1962. The state has trebled its
budgetary investment in education during Smylie's administration,
and tourist business has been promoted.

During these years, Idaho saw the growth of its first major
manufacturing industry: the processing of its huge potato crop and
the installation of starch factories. About one-third of Idaho farmers
grow potatoes; it has become the largest potato-producing state. The
largest Idaho markets are in California; to the huge metropolitan
areas of San Francisco and Los Angeles go Idaho cattle, starches, and
lumber. The West Coast population explosion is viewed by shrewd
Idahoans as a prime long-term market for their products.

One of Idaho's few tycoons is Jack Simplot, an energetic man
whose empire embraces lumbering in the California Sierras, Idaho
livestock, a sulphuric acid plant and several potato-processing
plants producing potato starch, and instant and frozen French-fried
potatoes. Simplot believes that Idaho's future is unlimited, and
that most people of the state fail to understand its potential.

Jim Brown, general manager of the respected Idaho *Daily
Statesman* at Boise, has generally supported industrial development
since his first New Year's Eve in Boise. He had come to Idaho from
Michigan and at midnight, he recalls, "I relented and bought a drink
around the city room. I kept expecting noise, like in Michigan. At
ten minutes after twelve I asked, 'Where are the whistles?' My boys
explained that there wasn't one in town. So we launched an editorial
campaign for industry. In general, it's been useless. Basically Idaho
does not yet want industrial growth."

But the Morrison-Knudsen Company, active in construction and
engineering in thirty-nine countries, has its executive offices in Boise.
And there is a baby boom at Idaho Falls, near where the Atomic
Energy Commission maintains its national reactor test station on a
desert reservation one hundred miles square. Here too is the nation's
first plutonium-fueled power reactor. The sharp rise in silver prices

in 1962 stimulated mining activity, which centers in the Coeur d'Alene
area of northern Idaho. The state leads the nation in silver production.

Although Boise is small (34,481), it is the least insular town in
the Mountain North. Its metropolitan area population is about eighty-
five thousand, and annexation is beginning. It can be considered the
capital of the only frontier except Alaska that remains in the United
States. It is intriguing to observe in Boise the first stirrings of the
wider outlook which will surely descend on this area in the decade
ahead.

Idaho may turn the corner from agricultural to industrial state
by 1975, but today there is a trout stream five minutes away from the
state capitol. Boiseans still can go duck hunting before work, fifteen
minutes away from the city, and skiing and high-lake swimming
are only an hour or two away. Now Boiseans find that these accustomed pleasures are being cited as lures in livability for industrial
newcomers.

One exciting saga of corporation growth has occurred in their
midst. Almost unnoticed by Idahoans, the Boise Cascade Corporation
has become one of the behemoths of the lumber industry. "Some of
these great old-timers," smiles R. V. Hansberger, its forty-two-year-
old president, "don't understand how this could have happened. They
aren't quite aware of how big we are; it would shock them if they
did know. We haven't concealed it, but we purposely haven't publicized what a giant we are."

Hansberger is a Minnesota native who attended the Harvard
Graduate School of Business Administration and served between
1947 and 1954 as assistant to the executive vice president of the
Container Corporation of America. Then he struck out for the West.
After three years in Portland, he went to Boise and quietly began
putting together a corporate empire in lumber. In 1956, the parent
company had three sawmills in Idaho; by 1962, it owned fifteen in the
states of Washington, Idaho, Oregon, and Colorado. It has increased
production of lumber by five times to become the second largest soft-
wood lumber producer in the country. It increased its wholesale
building-materials plants from six to fourteen, and its retail stores,
scattered throughout the Northwest from Seattle through Colorado,
from seventy-eight to one hundred and twenty-nine. Sales rose from
thirty-five million to more than one hundred and thirty million
dollars; company employees went from seventeen hundred to almost
seven thousand; its stockholders increased in number from three
hundred to about three thousand; its net earnings in 1960 were more
than three million dollars. Hansberger's major coup was a merger

which resulted in the construction of a profitable pulp-and-paper mill as part of the corporation. Today the net worth of the corporation is in excess of one hundred and twenty-five million dollars.

"Just in the past year or two," Hansberger said in 1962, "we have been getting visits here in Boise from Eastern bankers. Their personal prejudices against investment in a state like Idaho take a back seat to their realization of the opportunity and potential development of this area."

Hansberger has assembled a youthful executive staff, almost exclusively men with Eastern university backgrounds. The pattern of a young and dynamic corporate group against a complacent regional background is explosive. But Hansberger and his staff enjoy Idaho, and they are accepted graciously—with the silent understanding that the newcomers won't flaunt either their "fancy" backgrounds or unfamiliar living customs.

Boise Cascade men are active in local and state politics; employees hold public office in both parties. One is speaker of the Idaho House. Hansberger himself has served as president of the Boise Industrial Foundation and the Boise Art Association.

There seems to be no sense of sacrifice or condescension on the part of urbane Easterners who move West to this contemporary frontier. So long as opportunity can be found here, as in the case of the Boise Cascade, the Simplot and the Morrison-Knudsen organizations, the more adventurous Easterner appears to be just as intrigued with his new environment as were the moguls who came west to run the mines and build their new empires. The Easterner who wants to maintain his Eastern business pace in this Mountain North often can run far ahead of the pack—and still find time to take his boy hunting once or twice a week, or to spend long weekends with his wife boating at Payette Lakes or skiing at Bogus Basin. The handicap of isolation from Eastern or West Coast cities can be overcome easily by the jetliner. United Air Lines has claimed for Boise the distinction of the highest passenger business per capita of any city which it serves. The Boise businessman can be in Denver, San Francisco, or even Chicago and New York faster than he can reach some of the closer towns of equivalent size to Boise in Wyoming and Montana which do not yet have major airline service.

Hansberger's secretarial troubles at Boise Cascade offer an intriguing example of one aspect of the westward tilt. "It's been hard to find good secretaries around Boise for Boise Cascade executives," he told me in his office one morning. "Girls just aren't trained locally to what we consider the role of a secretary in modern business. At a time when we were trying to get some good new men from Harvard, I needed a secretary. We gave one of the deans at Harvard Business School the assignment of finding one. The idea of bringing a little girl all the way out here from the East was kind of incredible, but he turned up with a delightful girl who had grown up in Boston with all of the Boston accent, and had some adventuresome spirit in her. She had come out to the University of Colorado and been at the top in her class, then gone back for an advanced Radcliffe course, and turned out to be one of the top in her class again. She came to Boise, and turned out to be one of the best secretaries I ever had.

"Of course, we were bringing a lot of young men into the company, and the inevitable happened: she married the star salesman of our corrugated container division. She stayed on with her job, but then the other inevitable happened: she had a baby girl and decided to make a career of being a mother.

"Anyway, her reports on Idaho were so glowing that her sister and her husband came out from Boston. Two of the girls' brothers have been out, and the other day their parents came out from Boston for a visit. We introduced a little bit of Idaho to Massachusetts, and they are wonderfully compatible!"

Hansberger does not overlook a subtle asset of the frontier personality. "There's some kind of discipline that gets into an individual when he has to live pretty close to nature," he said. "This is not only a community which is nestled in nature; it's an agrarian community, and there's something that's good for a person in having to wrestle with nature for a living."

Land still is cheap in the Mountain North, and there is excess water. Agriculture will increase, and processing industries will grow faster in food, lumber, and minerals—all notable Idaho resources. Idaho will show the way, and Montana and Wyoming eventually will follow the inevitable path of urbanization and industrialization. It will not happen tomorrow, but it will come on with what will seem—to the people of the Mountain North—like a rush. One hopes that it will not change them much.

It should not change people like Steele Barnett, a former Forest Service ranger in Idaho, who was so proud of his record of no lost time that even when injured in a fire and taken to a hospital he was back fighting the fire before the day was over. It should not change his wife, a city girl who had agreed to go with him on his forest job when he was assured there would be electricity available. There was, but it was a mile from their remote mountain cabin. She went, and stayed.

It will not change Jim Brown, the newspaper manager at Boise, who made three telephone calls to the acting governor of

Idaho about a reader's backed-up sewer line during the afternoon that I sat in his office. "That poor woman was getting the runaround from every politician she called," he explained. "This is the kind of thing a newspaper is for."

Nothing seems likely to change Larry Mills, a blunt and taciturn man who served four terms in the Idaho House of Representatives, one as speaker, and who later became a Boise Cascade executive. He took off on an office holiday to fly with me through Hell's Canyon, whose five-thousand foot deep canyon channels the angry Snake River as it flows north along the western border of Idaho toward the Columbia. We flew low over the mountainous wilderness and primitive areas of central Idaho where there is no habitation as far as the eye can see. Further south, Mills pointed down to the ranch where he had grown up. Back at Boise he told how as a child his grandmother had come by boat from Ireland to San Francisco in 1863, and walked almost all the way from San Francisco to Idaho City. Mills would not flinch if he had to set out walking for San Francisco today.

Nothing, one hopes, will change the political contradictions of an insurance partnership like that of Stein-McMurray in Boise; McMurray has been state chairman of the Republican Party, and his partner Stein served in 1960 as chairman of Idaho Citizens-for-Kennedy. Or the atmosphere of tolerance in which a Japanese-American was made president of the Boise Junior Chamber of Commerce; or the happy acceptance of the handsome Basques of southern Idaho—the largest Basque colony in North America—who are sought out eagerly as husbands and wives by the Anglo-Saxon community.

One would not like to change country in which I saw a man in the upstream meadows of the Snake River walking back toward his little farmhouse, his shoulder pouch hanging heavy with trout. He strode confidently, with purpose, a man bringing home dinner to a waiting and expectant family.

No future industrialization should be allowed to mar the life of the school teacher who turned down a promotion to county superintendent of schools because it would preclude his summer work of guiding raft floats down the Snake River.

The Mountain North still belongs to God. Its population is thin, and when one does not see a human being for a good many miles, the human seems more important. Values count more than they do in places where people begin to get in each other's way—and that will not change in the Mountain North, not for a long time.

14

COLORADO

A Tug of War

Thomas Jefferson was strongly criticized when he paid Napoleon fifteen million dollars for the Louisiana territory in 1803; it wasn't worth half the price, his critics in Congress said. Eventually one tiny corner of this territory became northeast Colorado.

Far over in the southwest corner of Colorado, Indian cliff dwellers had come and gone. The ruins of their culture remained on a forested, flat-topped mountain called Mesa Verde. Zebulon Pike was sent out to map the Louisiana territory in 1806, and discovered the peak that bears his name. He didn't make it to the top, and in his journal stated the opinion that the peak could not be scaled.

The first permanent settlement in Colorado was not established until 1853, in the beautiful southern valley of San Luis. Five years later, the trails called Overland and Santa Fe were thronged by gold-hunters. This was the Pike's-Peak-or-Bust gold rush, the beginning of Central City, Fairplay, Golden, Boulder, Colorado City (now Colorado Springs), and Buckskin Joe. Horace Greeley rushed out from New York to have a look and take a census. Wide-eyed, he reported to his readers in the *Tribune:* "As yet the entire popula- tion of the valley—which cannot number less than four thousand, in- cluding five white women and seven squaws living with white men —sleep in tents or under booths of pine boughs, cooking and eating in the open air."

In the same year, 1858, the Rocky Mountain *News* made its debut and put out an extra to headline Greeley's reports on the gold rush; it has been publishing steadily ever since. It began cautiously: it was built on piles in the center of Cherry Creek so that it would be equally acceptable to the jealous gold camps of Auraria and Den- ver City, on opposite sides of the creek. Diplomacy didn't pay off; a flood washed the building away. The *News* received word of the election of Lincoln by Pony Express from St. Joseph, Missouri, six hundred and sixty miles away, in four days, as telegraph lines only reached Denver in 1863. But even then they were a sometime thing: storms, Indians, and buffalo were against them.

The railroads came between 1870 and 1890, and Denver soared in population from 4,759 to 106,713. The Rocky Mountain backbone of Colorado was a barrier to railroads; the Union Pacific took an easier grade through Wyoming, and Denverites built a rail- road north to meet it at Cheyenne. To surmount the Rockies, narrow- gauge railroads were built in profusion. The Denver and Rio Grande was the first to use narrow gauge, and the scenery from some of its roadbeds is among the most spectacular in the world.

Colorado's fight for statehood was won in 1876, a century after the Declaration of Independence, and Colorado was nicknamed the Centennial State.

Silver strikes at Aspen and Leadville brought little booms, but the silver market collapsed in 1893 and the state faced a serious de- pression. It reacted by voting in woman's suffrage, the second state to do so. By the end of the decade, Colorado's virtue was rewarded: the Cripple Creek gold strike was the biggest in its history.

In 1895, the Denver *Post*, a three-year-old failure, was bought by a one-time bus boy and curio salesman named Harry Tammen, and a lottery promoter and speculator named Frederick G. Bonfils. A sermon appeared every Sunday in the *Post*. It was typical of the Bonfils-Tammen sense of humor that at one time the sermons were written by an inmate of the state mental hospital.

Mining declined as the new century began. Colorado turned to its farms. Sugar beets prospered in the irrigated plains of eastern Colorado, and the names of the mining camps changed tone as gold and silver petered out: Last Chance, Grubstake, Hard Times.

Moxcy Tabor ran the Brown Palace Hotel in those days, and the Rockefellers ran the big Pueblo plant called Colorado Fuel & Iron Company, which made rails and barbed wire. The Boettchers and the Hugheses ran about everything else. The governor was a member of the Ku Klux Klan who served time for mail fraud.

The Community Chest plan originated in Denver in 1887. The first juvenile court was inaugurated by a Colorado county judge named Benjamin Barr Lindsey, but an eight-hour work day for underground miners was unanimously voided by the Colorado Supreme Court.

The Ute Indians had long been shunted off into a barren corner of Colorado. Since the discovery of oil and uranium there, it has been known widely as one of the Four Corners—the only junction of four states—and the Utes' royalties already are greater than the sum Thomas Jefferson paid for the Louisiana territory.

◇◇

The unyielding wilderness of the Rockies spreads southward through Colorado. This is still the primitive West, touched only spottily by the restless, striving spirit of the New West. Endowed by God and revered by man, it is too close to heaven to be marred yet by man's lemming instincts, or to be scarred by the scavengers of change at any cost. The average altitude of Colorado is sixty-eight hundred feet. Within its borders are fifty-six of the eighty-eight highest mountains of the United States; all fifty-six are higher than fourteen thousand feet.

But these Rocky Mountains serve only as the fulcrum for the westward tilt; they are not a part of it. Thus a dichotomy has developed in Colorado.

Denver is the eastern outpost of the New West. Within its five-county metropolitan area in 1960 lived half of the 1,753,947 people in Colorado. Four out of five Coloradoans live within a fifteen-mile strip along the eastern slope of the Continental Divide. It is only a moment from the center of the state's financial life on Seventeenth Street in Denver, or from the mile-high steps of the state capitol, to the sky wilderness of Colorado. In the past Denver has been a dozing giant, part Eastern, part Western in outlook. Today it is bulging like other booming Western cities, but a few miles away there is man's country still. Denver itself is a city for men who are not awed by big things, a city for men who know how to live at ease beside mountains; the precipitous Front Range of the Rockies rises omnipotently from the plains, and Denver rises with it.

The gloss of the new Colorado shows up in a handful of sleek structures built in downtown Denver since World War II, but they have not triggered any widespread awakening to civic problems in planning and urban renewal. The men responsible for most of the new buildings, the Clint Murchison group and William Zeckendorf, were outsiders who made their imprint on the city and then retreated. John Gunther wrote of the "Olympian inertness" of Denver; its inertness has been shattered once or twice since then. The old magnates are dying, and the new are clawing for position. But the new quickly grow to behave a great deal like the old. Denver once was a closely controlled and conservative city, complacent to the verge of backwardness, but it has been jolted out of that for a time, though complacency tends to close back in like quicksand.

Like San Francisco, Denver recalls a giddy, gold-lined past. Its great wealth still is in the hands of a relative few. There is a gulf between traditionalist Seventeenth Street and nearby towns like Littleton, which has felt the greatest impact of the Martin Company's Titan missile plant. The weight of power still lies with the old guard, but the weight of numbers lies with the new. If Denver follows the pattern of cities further along in the transitions brought on by the westward tilt, the weight of power will accrue to the many, the old will be swept out, and the new guard will have a moment in history to prove if it has anything better to offer.

The Great Divide in Colorado is not only a demonstrable physical entity; it is also an outlook. Colorado lies astride the Divide. The arid, dormant plains beginning on Denver's eastern edge are not part of the Western story. To the west, beyond the Great Basin and the Sierra Nevada, Colorado faces the whizzing, zooming Pacific Coast. To its north is the comparative emptiness of Wyoming, Montana, and Idaho. To the south and southwest are the stirring, sprawling cities of Albuquerque, Phoenix, and Tucson. These directional forces tug at Colorado and make it seem at times like an island, wavering toward the new and back to the old, toward the city and back to the wilderness, toward industrial urbanization and back to the plains and cattle and dry farming.

Within a few weeks late in 1961, these things happened in Colorado:

On a sub-zero winter night, a hungry, howling wolf gave chase to a Diesel truck as it wound through the snow and over Loveland Pass, crossing the Continental Divide with a Denver-made missile in tow.

In the lofty wilds of the Sangre de Cristos in southern Colorado, a range war broke out when a new landowner set out to fence off his seventy-seven-thousand-acre ranch. Spanish-Americans whose families had lived there since before the land was American protested that the land was theirs for grazing. There were charges of kidnapping, assault, and robbery. Tempers were so hot that the Colorado governor flew into the village of San Luis to plead that the matter be left in the hands of the law.

A Pueblo city councilman captured a mountain lion in a cave and gave it to the Pueblo Zoo.

At isolated Aspen, once a silver-mining town and now a cultural magnet, a long and blessed silence was broken after the Federal Communications Commission granted a construction permit for Aspen's first radio station.

At about the same time, in a dining room on the sixteenth floor of the new Denver Club Building the club manager was playing a game of musical chairs. Members had disagreed violently about selling their former Victorian clubhouse to Clint Murchison, the Texas financier, who wanted to erect an office building on the site and give the club the top three floors. That the deal was finally made was evidence of change in Denver. The club's ornate mahogany dining-room chairs, stiff-backed and uncomfortable, were reupholstered in a rust-colored fabric and moved to the new quarters, but the decorator rebelled at their continued use—and so did some of the members. Contemporary chairs, shaped more to the human form, were covered in the same fabric and substituted quietly in many parts of the dining room. Now one can tell a great deal about a Denver Club man by the chair he chooses.

The man who first took me to the Denver Club was Elwood Brooks, a country-style banker from Kansas who came to Denver in 1942 to head a sick and dying institution, the Central Bank and Trust Company. It was the smallest of Denver's banks, and it was not one of the six great banks that formed the Denver Clearing House and, with the aid of interlocking directorates, controlled Denver banking. But Brooks was a maverick; with advertising, liberal lending, and a folksy image, he shocked and horrified Denver's old guard, men like the late Claude Boettcher, whose sugar beets, cement, potash, banking, and real estate had made him one of the nation's wealthiest men. By 1960, however, any investment of one thousand dollars made in Brooks' bank stock at the time he took over had risen to a value of $13,841, plus $4,932.15 in cash dividends, an increase in value of 1,284 percent. Brooks has wooed the country banks (there is no branch banking in Colorado) and brought in big deposits from them. Now he has passed some of the old Big Six and is a major factor in Denver banking.

Seventy-two years old when I lunched with him in 1961 at the Denver Club, Brooks was white-haired but still erect, keen, and friendly. The dichotomy was evident again: though Brooks preferred the former, Victorian clubhouse to the high, sleek modern clubrooms looking out toward the peaks of the Front Range of the Rockies, he chose one of the contemporary chairs at the table where we ate.

As conservative Seventeenth Street began to grow accustomed to the brash banking methods of the newcomer from Kansas, other things were changing in Denver. Palmer Hoyt, a vigorous newspaper editor, was brought in from Portland in 1946 to revive the Denver *Post*. It was with the backing of Hoyt that Quigg Newton, a lawyer born in Denver and schooled at Yale, was elected mayor at the age of thirty-six. Mayor Ben Stapleton had bossed Denver since 1923; Hoyt and Newton broke his machine soon after World War II. Newton did not entirely live up to his billing as a reform mayor, but he was a symbol of a remarkable transition in the *Post* and of the general though erratic trend toward progressiveness in Denver. Soon men like Murchison and Zeckendorf were dropping into Denver to look around. Denver wasn't sure it liked the idea of big-city promoters, but Murchison maneuvered quietly and soon had changed Denver's skyline with the Denver Club Building and with the First National Bank Building, twenty-eight stories high. Zeckendorf built a downtown center which includes the eight-hundred-and-eighty-room Hilton Hotel and a two-thousand-two-hundred-car garage, a skating rink, and department store.

Brooks recalls Zeckendorf's travails with admiration and amusement. "Zeckendorf came in and tried to buy the old courthouse property. The old birds sat out there and chewed tobacco and told stories. Some of the property owners nearby took surveys to show that Zeckendorf's hotel and his big four-basement garage would cause their walls to slant. Zeckendorf was kept in the courts for four years before he could take title to the property. He never gave up. He bought the old Daniels & Fisher department store and brought in the May Company to merge with it and occupy space. Then he brought Hilton in for the hotel. Some of the old-timers did everything they could to beat Zeckendorf, but he wouldn't be licked."

As outsiders have in so many cities around the West, Murchison and Zeckendorf came to make money, but what they did for the face of Denver gave the people of the city poise and self-confidence. The change continues, erratically, in the hands of old and new Denverites. One of them is Cris Dobbins, once an office boy to Claude Boettcher, raised as his son, and now chairman of the board of the vast Ideal Cement Company and of the old-guard foundation which holds that firm, owner of the Brown Palace Hotel, American Crystal Sugar Company, American Potash, and big blocks of stock in Great Western Sugar, Denver U. S. National Bank, and the First National Bank. John Evans, Sr., president of the First National Bank, is a grandson of the man who built Colorado's first railroad and who was made governor of the territory by President Lincoln. The Coors family in nearby Golden does equally well in producing porcelain for scientific and electronic use, as in brewing beer. Robert Six heads Continental Airlines' home office in Denver. The Shwayder Brothers in Denver are among the world's largest makers of luggage. The Gates Rubber Company of Denver is sixth-largest in the nation.

The single greatest economic impact in the area has come from the Martin Company, which in 1957 opened a twenty-seven-million-dollar plant near Denver for production of the Titan missile. In five years the nearby town of Littleton grew from six thousand to fifteen thousand people. About twelve thousand people were employed by Martin in Denver in 1961. Martin's success in recruiting personnel insured Denver's future as an important industrial center. Martin has been able to lure the people it wants to Denver away from every city in the nation except San Francisco; the icy winters of Colorado do not seem to be a hiring liability, even in competition with balmy Southern California.

Martin chose Denver as the site for its Titan plant after examining ninety-four cities in thirty-three states. Some of the reasons are enlightening: Denver is a metropolis in a remote area, but central for an industry in which components are coming from both East and West coasts. (When I visited the Martin plant there were Titans with two color patterns. Those with black-and-white tracking marks were destined for Cape Canaveral; those painted with the military star-and-bar were to go to Vandenberg Air Force Base on the opposite coast, in California.) The mountainous terrain minimizes the thunderous noise of static missile tests. The labor market is considered good. (Engineering and technical personnel were drained promptly from the Denver area by Martin when it opened. For a time, ninety percent of such personnel were imported from outside Colorado. In most recent years, however, the number of Coloradoans has risen to forty percent in this critical field, and the proportion continues to rise.) Climate and recreation potentials are regarded favorably, and

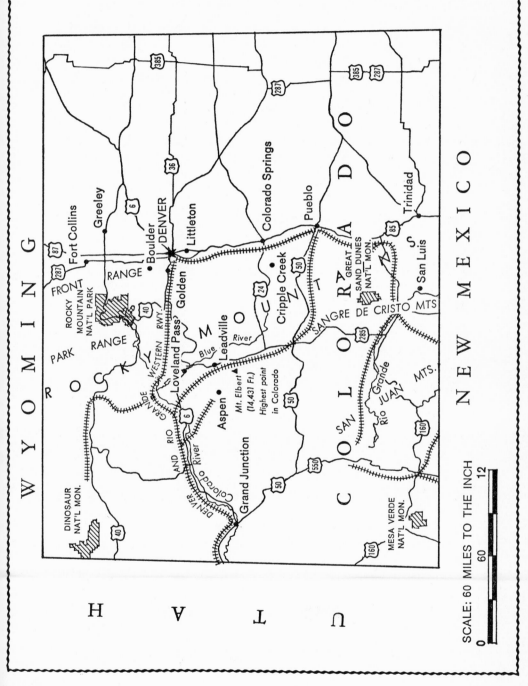

SCALE: 60 MILES TO THE INCH

0   60   12

Colorado

colleges and universities are improving rapidly. Excellent transportation facilities—rail, motor, and airline—are available. No longer is Denver a health center. It is an industrial center with a healthy climate.

Some of these same factors have applied in the selection of the Denver area for other notable additions to the scene. The Air Force Academy and the North American Air Defense Command headquarters are at Colorado Springs, sixty-seven miles south of Denver; at Boulder, twenty-seven miles northwest, the University of Colorado has been joined recently by laboratories of the National Bureau of Standards and of the new University Corporation for Atmospheric Research. Six million subscriptions to ten national magazines are processed in Boulder at an Esquire, Inc., computer center. Here too the geographic location, at the center of the western two-thirds of the nation, is the major factor.

In the living room of his snug modern home on a modest street in Boulder, Dr. Walter Orr Roberts flicked off the pro football game on television and waved goodbye to his son and daughter who were driving thirteen miles up into the Rockies, to Roosevelt National Forest, to cut down a Christmas tree under the supervision of forest rangers.

From the kitchen came the sound of dishes; his wife Janet, a Boulder city councilwoman and vice mayor, was at work. It was a Sunday afternoon in December. On a brick wall behind Dr. Roberts as he talked was a mounted photograph of distant nebulae, part of the work that had brought this Massachusetts-born solar astrophysicist to the West. He is a pioneer in learning the effect of sun spots on communications facilities.

When Dr. Roberts moved to Boulder in 1947, the University of Colorado was not strong in sciences, and the research tradition was not evident. Off campus at Boulder, there was no scientific activity. Now, there are large and vigorous research programs on campus, and the University of Colorado has assumed from Harvard the major role in the High Altitude Observatory at Boulder. About one thousand people are employed at the Boulder research laboratories of the National Bureau of Standards. In a decade, Boulder has become a substantial scientific center, and Dr. Roberts has developed the High Altitude Observatory into one of the most challenging environments for pure research in the nation. He heads the new National Center for Atmospheric Research at Boulder, formed to study the entire atmosphere, including the circulation of winds, the meandering of the jetstreams, changes of climate, the role of dust and water vapor and atmospheric chemicals like carbon dioxide, and the interaction between ocean and atmosphere. The National Science Foundation is the sponsor of the Center.

Whereas the High Altitude Observatory is interested primarily in the sun and its effect on the earth, the National Center for Atmospheric Research is studying the whole atmosphere. It was created because scientists conceded that there was a critical lag in what we know about the atmosphere—man is learning to leave it before he understands it.

Dr. Roberts is making his new center an intellectual mecca for men working in such varied scientific disciplines as chemistry, mathematics, physics, and meteorology. "We all will be working together, feeding ideas back and forth, trying to develop underlying notions of what makes things go," he told me. "We will be the principal center in the United States whose objective is development of the underlying knowledge of the atmosphere without regard to specific practical applications—basic research, in other words."

The new West is in harmony with Roberts and his laboratory. "Our scientists are happy here. It's not only the scenery and the skiing; it's the people, the open spirit, informality, that help to make it a lively place. The West has a great attraction for people. Wherever new things are being started, new ideas are bound to be promoted. New groups build up new ideals and new objectives. There is a chance for the fresh start, the something better."

While his wife busies herself with city council, Dr. Roberts pleads the virtues of long-term civic planning and conservation. "The people of the West seem to be meeting most of their challenges. But I wonder if we are doing enough to preserve our clean air, our water, and our out-of-doors? We have some very serious growing pains.

"All over the West, we must pay some very specific attention to evaluating what factors have brought people here, and making sure that we preserve these factors. We need much more vigorous effort by planning boards and redevelopment groups for adequate parks, traffic control, and water supply."

As he talked, the Roberts children came home, dejected. There had been bumper-to-bumper traffic into the national forest. Such a monstrous traffic jam had developed on icy roads that they had turned back. So, on the front range of the Rockies, Mrs. Roberts dried her hands, left the kitchen, and led her children to the supermarket to choose their Christmas tree.

Dr. Roberts grinned. "I guess that's part of what I mean," he said.

Boulder is the scientific and educational diamond in the necklace that Palmer Hoyt and his Denver *Post* call the Rocky Mountain Empire. As the *Post* sees it, the empire extends from Canada to the Gulf of Mexico, from the Missouri River to the Sierra Nevada. Under Hoyt the *Post* has become one of the better newspapers of the West. Its opposition in Denver is the Scripps-Howard tabloid, the Rocky Mountain *News*. But the *News'* barbs at the *Post* are mere slivers compared to the javelins heaved by Gene Cervi, the son of an immigrant coal miner, in his small-circulation Denver weekly, *Cervi's Journal*. A sort of Western Harry Golden, Cervi is only an harassing gadfly to the elephantine *Post*, but he has helped to maintain an expectant unrest in the Denver press world that is in the great tradition of the city. Denver claims the oldest active press club in continuous existence in the nation; among its past presidents are Damon Runyon, Gene Fowler, and Westbrook Pegler. On its walls are photographs of every President since McKinley, and with the exception of Harry Truman, each has been presented personally to the club. There have been only three club stewards in more than eighty years: a Chinese who served for forty-seven years until his death in 1927; a Jew who served until his death in 1946, and Jimmy Fillia, a Greek, who has been at it since. A club legend is that the Chinese steward staked Damon Runyon to two hundred and fifty dollars for his assault on New York City.

The relation to their city of Hoyt and his big *Post* and Cervi and his little *Journal* has all the characteristics of the classic press rivalry that is rarely seen today. Hoyt and the *Post* have done big things for Denver; Cervi has shrieked in anguish at some of them, and chided the *Post* and the *News* alike when he judges them guilty of opportunism—which is usually. Cervi has an ebullient sense of humor and the reluctant cynicism to be expected from an angry man who organized the American Newspaper Guild chapter on the *Post* and later became a minor but vocal opposition publisher. Toward Cervi, Hoyt has the aloof tolerance of the successful metropolitan publisher. A respected author and lecturer, Hoyt will ignore Cervi or, at most, express confidential disdain for his attacks on the *Post*, but a suspicion lingers that there are days when he envies Cervi his fun as self-appointed watchdog of the hi-jinks of the vested interests.

Hoyt is no ordinary newspaper publisher. He calls himself editor, and he works in his shirtsleeves behind an open door adjacent to his newsroom. He is that splendid anachronism: a highly literate publisher, and a scrapper.

"When I first came to Denver in 1946," he said, "the mother of a well-known Denver doctor met me and my wife at a cocktail party. She wanted to know where we had come from. We told her. She was quite rude and said, 'We don't want new people in Denver.'

I said, 'Well, when did you come to Denver?' She said, 'Many years ago,' and I asked, 'Well, weren't you new then?' She said, 'Well, yes,' but that she hadn't thought of that as being germane. These are the real old-timers here, but you don't find this attitude much among businessmen, because the dynamism of this new Denver has taken hold of them and they are part of it now. The friction between old and new is receding; the outsiders have been the magnetos, the catalysts, the gadflies."

Hoyt regards the old Denver as similar in insularity to Portland. "I once told the Portland Chamber of Commerce that Portland was a great city and was going to grow; that the people who were in charge twenty years ago weren't interested in growth, and that somebody else was going to come in and take over. It's been that way in Denver to a large extent: a lot of outside money and all kinds of people have come here with new ideas and an eagerness and drive that have revived the city."

In Denver, as in most inland Western cities, many of the new-comers are from the West Coast. Many of them have hurdled the inland cities in their first move from the East, South, or Midwest, and later retreated to Denver.

"This region holds much of what America really means," Hoyt said. "Here in the Rocky Mountain empire may exist America's happiest blending of old with new, of sturdy tradition with modern convenience, of outdoor vigor with atomic-age cosmopolitanism.

"One of the things we've carried on long fights for at the *Post* is the proper development of reclamation: power, water—everything. When I was in the Office of War Information in Washington in 1943, I took on those Congressmen who didn't believe in the West, who thought that development of these big dams was sheer waste. Hell, those dams have been one of the reasons we've been able to pay so damn much income tax!"

The relative aggressiveness of the *Post* has not endeared Hoyt to all of Denver. He told me, "Frankly, when I finished my first five-year contract in Denver in 1951, there was a good deal of wishful thinking that I would leave. When I first talked to the Chamber of Commerce, old Mayor Ben Stapleton, who believed in a certain kind of Denver, made a pretty good crack. When I came here, we started a campaign to change the street signs. They were incredibly bad; you couldn't read them. As I got up to talk, he said that those street signs were good enough for Hoyt to get into town by, and they'll be good enough for him to leave by, too! But we took on everything we could find that would help the city. There was a cocoon of insulation, and nobody gave a damn. I think we print more foreign news in the

Post, for example, than any afternoon paper in the country, except possibly the Philadelphia *Bulletin*. We have one of the biggest news holes [total inches of news matter] of any afternoon newspaper in the country. We try to have a liberal, informed newspaper. We supported Kennedy—yes, I'm a lifelong Republican—not so much because we wanted him as because Nixon didn't seem to know what he was going to do."

The official *Post* summary of its crusades runs the gamut. It includes Anti-Pollution of Streams, Beetles (Spruce Bark), Dirty Streets and Sidewalks, Dog Leash Law, McCarthyism, Police Burglary Scandals, Quackery, and the State Penitentiary Mess.

But across town in his little publishing shop with his four-man staff, Cervi is unimpressed—or at least appears to be unimpressed. "Carl Sandburg said, 'Why can't there be a metropolitan weekly?'" he says, sputtering and fuming characteristically. "We are. We are the only weekly newspaper in America that advertises the Rolls-Royce. We are the only weekly in America that hopes to God it is never discovered by *Time* magazine. Some day we may get around to discovering Mr. Luce—who does he think he is, going around the United States discovering people? We've got better than six thousand paid circulation, and our readership includes the people who make this community tick. I believe you've got to be constantly nagging and scolding, at the price of a burdensome unpopularity."

Cervi's antics include announcing in his own editorial column a Name the Editor Contest for a nickname that "could cause the editor of *Cervi's Journal* to 'become human.' . . . The prize is $152 ($100 plus $52 inflationary allowance) for the reason that we don't want some of our Republican friends muttering thru [sic] the halls of the Denver Club that 'the sonofabitch wants to pay off in New Deal dollars. . . .' "

Until 1962, Cervi, a former Colorado State Democratic Party chairman, printed the syndicated columns of Morrie Ryskind, whom Cervi views as a "paid battler of the right." "When that Los Angeles Times-Mirror Syndicate salesman conned us into taking Ryskind on the grounds that the paper needed 'balance,' we should have suspected the door was being opened to every manner of right-wing zealot and fanatic, the same being found in surprising abundance among some of our highly placed citizenry," Cervi wrote. "Ever since we started running [the columns], a type of reader heretofore unknown to us has come forward with flushed and angry face to take exception to our occasional editorial rebuts attached to the Ryskind columns. If this gets out of hand, we shall not hesitate to throw Ryskind out of the paper. [Later, Cervi did drop the Ryskind column.] We'll admit it. In the case of political convictions, we are not unlike the frontier judge who said, 'Bring the no-good horse thief in here for a fair trial and then take him out and hang him.' Somebody give us one good reason why we should publish material offensive to our sense of right. . . . It would be utter nonsense for us to provide a forum for those Ryskind views we consider harmful to sound public opinion."

I suggested to Cervi that he had entrapped himself with such an admission; his logic was precisely that of most publishers who scrap or edit liberal columnists. Most publishers honestly believe more in George Sokolsky than in Murray Kempton, and, like Cervi, are loathe to publish material which is offensive to their own sense of right.

Cervi, a stocky man with bushy eyebrows, simply grinned. "My father fell under the spell of Eugene Debs in the coal camps," he said. "But my mother got tired of all the funerals in the coal camps and we moved west when I was ten. She said, 'Now, I want you to amount to something!' That was the Republican in her. So I've really had all the benefit of the socialist philosophy without any of its ills, because I believe in private property. I also believe in editors being in politics. If not, why are you in business? I say openly what the others can't say. A lot of editors would like to be better men, but their economic survival is dependent on their supporting *other* big business. What is there but spirituality and politics?"

Cervi believes that Denver is now "hell bent for respectability," that "a lot of the vigor is gone out of it and we've got suburbanitis and country clubitis. That strong, vigorous, no-good show-off from the country is gone from the legislature. The ranches are larger, fewer, and corporate interests are taking over. Colorado is growing sedate politically. Me, I'm the sonofabitch who carried the hod around here forty years ago and I don't forget it."

I asked Cervi if he saw some new world within grasp of the West.

"Naww," he said. "You're romantic—like me. It won't work. It's gone too far."

But there is constant talk of that new world in the seminars of the Aspen Institute for Humanistic Studies, high in the Sawatch Range of the Rockies, a hundred and seventy-one miles west of Denver. The late Walter P. Paepcke, chairman of the Container Corporation of America, founded the Institute in 1950, after a bicentenary celebration honoring Goethe at Aspen had attracted one of the most remarkable gatherings of scholars, poets, and men of affairs ever brought together in the nation. There is a nine-month series of two-week programs designed—and priced—for the management level of American business. The moderators are men of international stature, and the participants are assigned reading that ranges from Aristotle, Plato, Samuel Johnson, and de Tocqueville to Horace Mann, Theodore Roosevelt, and Herbert Hoover.

The Aspen Music Festival and Music School thrive in the summer. In winter, there is no better nor more varied skiing than in this most beautiful mountain setting in America. At Aspen, I had dinner in the home of a family who had all but abandoned themselves to nature, and who seemed among the happiest of people. Both parents came from well-established families, one in Pennsylvania and one in Southern California; he had rebelled against the quest for fame and fortune and was working as a ticket-taker at a ski lift. When he was off duty, his family joined him, and my last glimpse of them was as they skiied off at the summit of the highest ski lift above Aspen into the dazzling, limitless blue and white of the Rockies.

Not far from Aspen, the Colorado River, a narrow but angry stream near its headwaters, cuts through thousand-foot canyon walls, gathering snow and momentum for its turbulent 1,440-mile plunge through the Southwest and into the Gulf of California. Its drainage basin covers one-thirteenth of the area of the United States and includes parts of Wyoming, Colorado, Utah, New Mexico, Nevada, Arizona and California. Without the Colorado, Los Angeles could not be a metropolis, rich desert farmland could not be tilled, scores of towns would not exist, water skiers and power boaters would not cavort in the desert, Grand Canyon would not be a canyon, and Southern California would lack the power (from Hoover Dam) which has helped to give it industrial muscle.

Entire careers have been involved with the endless legalities of the water rights of the Colorado River; in 1963, differences which had festered since 1922 between Arizona and California on this issue were being judged after the lengthiest argument ever scheduled by the United States Supreme Court. By the terms of the 1922 compact, seven and a half million acre feet of Colorado River water annually were allotted to the Upper Colorado Basin (Colorado, New Mexico, Utah, and Wyoming), and eight and a half million to Arizona, Nevada, and California—with the major share going to California. Because Colorado is a source of six major river systems, including the major tributaries of the Colorado, the state has been party to more interstate water litigation before the Supreme Court than any other state.

Even within Colorado, water is an edgy matter. Western Colorado, with thirty-seven percent of the total area of the state, has sixty-nine percent of the state's surface water yield. East of the Divide lies sixty-three percent of Colorado's area, including most of its farm-lands, but only thirty-one percent of its water. To augment metro-politan Denver's water supply, in 1960 a twenty-three-mile aqueduct was tunneled under the Rockies, bringing waters of the Blue River to Denver.

Naturally enough, water has been an obsession with such reign-ing Colorado politicians as Steve McNichols, a cold-eyed but capable Democrat who was chairman of the National Governors' Conference in 1960–61; former Senator John A. Carroll, cosponsor of the saline water conversion bill introduced by the Kennedy administration; and Senator Gordon Allott, an Air Corps veteran who has been a surpris-ingly successful Republican campaigner in a state which is conserva-tive but Democratic. Both McNichols and Carroll were displaced in 1962 by Republicans.

South of Denver on the eastern front of the Rockies lies the celebrated "Newport of the Rockies," Colorado Springs. The lux-urious Broadmoor Hotel has expanded with a new lake-front wing and a convention hall which its architects called the largest hyper-bolic paraboloid in the world. At the Air Force Academy, the seven-teen angular spires of the wing-shaped new chapel soar above the flat squareness of a complex of buildings so vast that a Congressional grant of one hundred and sixty million dollars was not enough to pay the cost; the Air Force Academy Foundation has augmented construc-tion funds by unannounced but formidable amounts. Two million visitors a year stream into this aerie; its grounds are forty-eight times the size of Monaco.

To blast a sixty-six-million-dollar tunnel into the granite base of Cheyenne Mountain, near Colorado Springs, the Army Corps of Engi-neers has brought in hundreds of coal miners plus the Utah Construc-tion Company. The tunnel will serve as the combat operations con-trol headquarters for the North American Air Defense Command. When completed in 1965, it will be large enough to accommodate buildings, automobiles and enough food and water for the NORAD staff of three hundred and fifty. It will operate its own power plant behind huge blast doors which will seal off the buildings inside in the event of nuclear attack.

Until its completion, the combat center of NORAD, which must flash the alarm before United States bombers or missiles are unleashed, operates in a four-story building of sand-colored brick. This is the nerve center which controls a network of installations that extend across the northern fringe of the free world from Alaska to England. As you approach the center, Pike's Peak is directly ahead and above. Moments later, with an Air Force major close by your side, you are trying to adjust your eyes to the darkness of a battle room. A two-story-high projection of North America, the Iconorama, dominates one wall. Some sixty squadrons of interceptor aircraft all over North America are under the Air Defense Command, standing by to roar into the air on three-minute notice to investigate unidentified aircraft detected by SAGE, the NORAD radar system.

I noticed that code letters and numbers on the Iconorama were clustered off Seattle and Los Angeles. My escort explained that these represented airborne U. S. interceptors, flying faster than sound toward two unidentified aircraft.

Beside a leather chair is a yellow telephone labeled JCS (Joint Chiefs of Staff) ALERT NET. EMERGENCY USE ONLY. The line offers instant communication with the White House, the Canadian prime minister, the Pentagon war room, SHAPE in Europe, or SAC headquarters at Omaha. At the left of the Iconorama are wall panels installed for the BMEWS (Ballistic Missile Early Warning System). The old-fashioned SAGE warns of unidentified aircraft; BMEWS warns of missiles. It is a detection system of three bases in Greenland, Alaska, and England with radar screens the size of football fields, designed to give the United States fifteen to seventeen minutes' warning of ICBM's fired from Russian territory.

Another wall panel at Colorado Springs speaks tersely but eloquently of Anglo-American coöperation in the new English BMEWS base. It reads, UK ALARM LEVEL, and it would indicate the severity of an enemy raid as monitored in the United Kingdom. Beside it is another panel labeled MINUTES TO GO. There is room for only two digits; it will never read higher than seventeen.

On the opposite wall, a stark red bulb burned. I asked the major about it. He grinned. "That means someone is in this room who is not cleared for classified information," he said. "When you came in, that light went on, and panels flashed off which cited United States readiness in terms of numbers of nuclear weapons, defensive missiles, and rockets, and interceptor aircraft." He pointed toward another panel, labeled PREDICTED IMPACTS. It is a panel which, one hopes, will never flash.

As I left, the Iconorama indicated that the aircraft off Los Angeles and Seattle had been identified. North America stood again, for the moment, unchallenged.

15

UTAH

Gold-Plated Zion

"Give us ten years of peace and we will ask no odds of the United States," roared Brigham Young in 1847 to the newly arrived Mormon colonists beside the Great Salt Lake. There were no houses, no crops—only the arid land, and that still belonged to Mexico. The Mormons had been driven by fire, mutilation, and murder from their city of Nauvoo in Illinois. Their prophet Joseph Smith had been shot dead.

Three days after the main contingent arrived in 1847, the choir assembled where Temple Square is today. By 1867, the choir sang in the great Tabernacle from which its Sunday broadcasts are heard today. Out to the arid mountain valleys, Young sent detachments of colonists including blacksmiths, carpenters, millers, and tanners. They were all farmers too, and they built forts, dug irrigation ditches, fenced lands, and erected adobe or log houses. A late frost killed the first crops, and clouds of crickets moved in to devour what was left.

But sea gulls swooped in from the lake to feed on the crickets; a statue to the sea gulls stands today in Temple Square.

Young declared the State of Deseret (it means honeybee) to include what is now Utah and Nevada, most of Arizona, part of Idaho, Wyoming, Colorado, Oregon, and New Mexico, and even a seacoast strip in Southern California. By 1868, Congress had pared down Deseret to the present boundaries of Utah and made it a territory. But its citizens' petitions for statehood were blocked by federal efforts to quell Mormon polygamy. The Mormons, who had escaped to a land they dreamed of as their own, were disputed in their claim by Paiutes and Utes, by pestilence, by judges and courts, and finally by the United States Government. With the Gold Rush, they found themselves on a main trail to Sutter's Mill. But Mormons were forbidden to join the rush. "Gold is for paving streets!" cried Young from the pulpit. "The business of a saint is to stay at home and make his fields green!"

Polygamy and slavery were termed the "twin relics of barbarism" by the Republican National Convention of 1856. Mormon relations with Washington deteriorated. President Buchanan terminated Brigham Young's service as governor of the territory and dispatched the Army of the West to Salt Lake City. It was 1857; Young's ten years of peace were up.

But the Utah War was never fought. Federal troops stayed in Utah for three years until the outbreak of the Civil War, but a pardon was negotiated and the soldiers returned to fight the Confederates. Mormons skirmished only with marauding Utes.

In 1869, the transcontinental railroad was joined at Promontory. Spurred by a new exposure to the outside world, there occurred the strongest of several church schisms—the Godbeite rebellion of 1870. It involved a plan for developing mining in Utah, which had been opposed by church leaders. The schism led to the organization of the Liberal Party, the first powerful anti-Mormon movement in Utah. For years to come its voice was the gentile Salt Lake *Tribune*. (In Utah, anything non-Mormon is known as gentile.) In opposition, the Mormons organized the People's Party. It was quite a while before the labels of Democrat and Republican meant anything in Utah politics.

By 1884, the federal government was sending deputies on night raids to break up polygamous families. They were called "polyg hunts," and the "cohabs" were jailed. A church leader was sentenced to four years in the penitentiary for polygamy. In 1890, the church surrendered; a manifesto was published renouncing polygamy. Six years later, Utah was admitted to statehood.

By 1959, it was clear that the doctrine of insularity proscribed by Brigham Young had undergone drastic change. The Mormon choir—by radio, recording, and tour—was becoming as heralded as any vocal group anywhere. Mormon missionaries were proselyting all over the world. And during that year, in an act which seemed to embrace the idiom of the secular world, three hundred members of the Mormon choir appeared on a network television show from Los Angeles to receive a Grammy award for their hit record, "The Battle Hymn of the Republic."

◇◇◇

In the minds of two million Mormons, including George Romney, a prospective candidate for president of the United States, Zion is that booming, gold-plated spiritual empire which fans out from the spires of the majestic Mormon Temple in the heart of Salt Lake City.

The temple is off limits to all but the most sacrosanct of Mormons. It is almost equally difficult to explore the power patterns of their Church of Jesus Christ of Latter-day Saints. Those patterns are poorly understood outside Mormon country, and heatedly distorted within.

The confusions which have colored American attitudes toward Mormons rise periodically—most recently in Michigan, where George Romney sought and won the governorship in 1962. An active Mormon, Romney is typical of much that is best in Mormonism; he is energetic, thrifty, scrupulously moral, and possessed by an almost fanatic zeal.

Polygamy has ceased to be an issue in Mormon country. Conformity is not yet a threat. Through faithful tithes, shrewd investments and business operations, the church has attained spectacular wealth. It is fast becoming—if it is not already—the richest church, on a per capita basis, in the world. Unquestionably it controls the greatest aggregation of capital in the states of the Rocky Mountain area. It grows grapefruit, digs coal, raises cattle, mills flour, processes sugar, and writes insurance. Estimates of its church and temple construction program in the past decade run far in excess of half a billion dollars. The percentage of tithing never was as high as in recent years.

Yet all is not well in Zion. As the historic isolation of Mormon country is broken down by jet travel, as the agrarian economy of

Utah turns industrial with the invasion of missile plants, the church fights harder to maintain its benevolent domination of Mormon lives. The civil and social institutions of Mormon country—centering in Utah but spreading into other Western states—are under siege by forces of political conservatism and the autocracy of the Mormon church, a power personified by what Bernard De Voto called the Mormon ecclesiastical oligarchy. In the main, it is a benign oligarchy. There is much to recommend the church as a force for constructive living.

From the gold-leafed statue of the Mormons' Angel Moroni atop the tallest spire of the Mormon Temple in Salt Lake City, the thriving empire of Zion looks out past the granite statue of Brigham Young at the head of Main Street. It encompasses at least seventy-one major pieces of downtown Salt Lake City commercial property and a hefty number of the city's businesses. Zion already has a foothold in New York City, where a Mormon-owned skyscraper will be completed in 1965, and now it has begun to spread its influence to the rest of the world. In 1962, Mormons had completed ten churches in Europe and had begun construction of forty-seven more. Seventy-six other buildings were in the planning stage and one hundred and twenty-nine properties had been purchased.

Snowballing church assets are responsible for a surge in its world-wide missions. There are temples in Canada, Hawaii, Switzerland, New Zealand, and England, and close to two thousand mission branches or congregations. For its size, the Mormon church proselytes more actively than any other church in the world today. Nine thousand Mormon youths, most of them nineteen to twenty-two years old, are serving their voluntary stints in all parts of the world as missionaries, supporting themselves on their own resources or on contributions from friends and family. Fewer than one-third of the church's two million members live in Utah, although of the nine hundred thousand people of Utah two-thirds are Mormon. Mormons are numerous in Idaho, Nevada, Arizona, and California. Mormon power in politics and commerce is felt throughout the West. There are Mormons scattered through all fifty states and in thirty-five other nations.

Naturally enough, however, the social temperament of Zion is sensed most strongly in Salt Lake City. At dusk on a May Saturday there, I watched boys and girls promenading along Main Street, peering leisurely in shop windows, holding hands, joking, and laughing. A sidewalk artist stood sketching a child as the mother and father looked on; they held hands too. Bicycles zooming along the sidewalks among pedestrians were ridden by adults as well as by the young.

Movie houses were uncrowded; restaurants, which serve plain, wholesome food, were quiet. The dress of the people was simple, their conversation naïve. On the faces of the young was a guilelessness unlike that of the young in the coastal cities of the West or of larger cities anywhere in America.

To Brigham Young's left, in the lobby of the church-owned Hotel Utah, the Saturday church supplement of the *Deseret News*, the church-owned daily newspaper, was being read by a score of the faithful. Upstairs in the handsome Sky Room, the cocktail menu featured non-alcoholic drinks like the Wasatch Awakener ("Strong espresso coffee—frosty with shaved ice, capped with a ball of our super-rich ice cream, $1.10"); even the Wasatch Awakener is forbidden to Mormons. Out the window past Temple Square, the River Jordan glinted in the sunset.

In one block near the center of Main Street are clustered many of the landmarks of small-town America: Kress, Grant Stores, Woolworth, Walgreen's, Penney's, National Shirt Shops, Baker's Shoes, National Dollar Stores. At the foot of Brigham Young's statue a tall new office building rises; the church is landlord to Kennecott Copper here. Across Main Street are offices of KSL, the church-owned radio and television outlets, and of the *Deseret News*.

On the hillside behind the hotel, a thirty-two-story Mormon office building is rising to supplant some of the older buildings housing the Women's Mutual Improvement League, the Sunday School Union, the Mutual Improvement Association, the Temple Bowling Alley, and the adult education center of Brigham Young University.

Higher still on the hillside is the Utah capitol. From its steps, the city stretches away into the infinity of the violent desert to the southwest, and to the narrow oasis of the Wasatch Mountain strip to the south. To the east, the city rises in tiers until it can climb no farther into the Wasatch. To the northwest is the Great Salt Lake, shrunk and drawn away from its shoreline by drought; noxious, deserted and burdened by the raw sewage of the city.

The long north-south Wasatch oasis of Utah is the central island of the Mormon empire. It has been invaded by change, but it resists as stubbornly and as secretively as any polygamist ever resisted a United States marshal. A paternal provincialism distinguishes the Mormon hierarchy, and the skyrocketing wealth of the church enables it to maintain its historic independence; it is its own welfare state. Mark Twain is said to have remarked that the only thing as thoroughly organized as the Mormon congregation was the Prussian army. Today the Mormon church has a greater hold on its members than does the Roman Catholic church, or any other in America.

Mormons tend to fall into four categories. The first are the purists, who will ask waitresses to remove coffee cups from restaurant tables. The Mormon "Word of Wisdom" bans alcohol, coffee, tea, and tobacco. More practical Mormons, the second type, like George Romney, live their religion earnestly but try to minimize its conflict with American customs. A third type is the "jack Mormon," as one United States Senator from another state described himself while he drank whiskey during an interview. The fourth, by official Mormon standards, is no longer a Mormon at all. He is the polygamist, now violating church as well as federal law. Most polygamists today live in remote areas of Utah—or in the Strip Country of northwest Arizona, isolated from the rest of Arizona by the Grand Canyon, and almost inaccessible to the stranger.

In apology for polygamy, the church points out that less than three percent of male adult Mormons practiced polygamy in its heyday, about 1880, and that when instigated originally it was not against the law. I talked to one Mormon church official in Salt Lake City whose grandfathers both were polygamous; each had five wives, about the average for polygamists. Among his maternal grandfather's wives were two pairs of sisters. But his own wife, he admitted freely, "just doesn't see how a woman could have consented to such an arrangement." I also met a Mormon farmer who was visiting Salt Lake City for the first time; what he wanted most, instead of seeing the sights of the city, was to meet his father for the first time. Like many devouts of other faiths, contemporary Mormons can become tangled in the web of their own theology; a monogamous Mormon who has been a widower one or more times is expected to live in heaven with all his wives—a dividend of paradise which would be enough to drive some men and women in the other direction.

There were two revealing glimpses of the Mormon temperament when the Western Governors' Conference convened in Salt Lake City in 1961. Governors, their wives and staffs, and newsmen were guests of Utah's Governor George Dewey Clyde at an after-dinner theatrical given by two Salt Lake City women. With pantomime, original verse, and a few props including a washboard, farm dresses and some even less sophisticated accouterments, the two women gave a fifty-minute presentation perhaps most charitably described as a naïve joshing of the humble life of the Mormon pioneer and farmer. Some of the audience enjoyed it immensely, but for most of the visitors it seemed an interminable performance. The varied reception to the program symbolized the sweeping gradations in sophistication among Western states today.

The other glimpse came at the formal state dinner on the final night of the conference, and it was more alarming. On the program between two groups of singers there was listed a "special feature." As Governor Clyde rose at the head table and began to speak of the vigilance of Utahns in protection of Americanism, men in Russian army uniforms dashed into the banquet hall, shouting in Russian, and declared themselves in control of the gathering and the hotel. The mock Russians were students of a Utah National Guard Reserve linguist school. Their appearance was climaxed with an anti-Communist declaration—in English—by the National Guard adjutant general of Utah, who had been conducting a series of anti-Communist seminars. This gentleman was followed by a double quartet from the incomparable Mormon Tabernacle Choir, predictably singing "The Battle Hymn of the Republic."

Most political issues in Utah are more provincial. In a state plagued by water shortages, it is no surprise that the governor's primary distinction is as an expert of world-wide acclaim in the highly specialized field of irrigation engineering. Governor Clyde, a Mormon and a Republican, succeeded one of Utah's best-known citizens, J. Bracken Lee, who served two terms as governor.

Lee was one of only three non-Mormon governors in Utah history. He was born in little Price, Utah, and was mayor there for six terms. He won his first election by two votes; it was contested, and he paid more in attorney's fees than the total of his salary as mayor, twenty-five dollars a month, during the two-year term. He was beaten once when he ran for Congress, and again when he campaigned for his third term as governor. In 1962, he failed to win the Republican primary for United States Senator.

"All told," he said, counting slyly on his fingers at lunch in Salt Lake City, "I guess my box score is about eight wins and seven losses." For a moment he munched meditatively on a roll and then amended the count. "No, by golly, even counting that time I got beat for justice of the peace in Price—and I never wanted a job anyhow where I handled money—I think I've lost only five. I guess it just seems like more when you lose."

Lee is open-faced and disarming, a rash and brash politician of the old school. When I first visited him in 1961, it was in the decrepit City Hall at Salt Lake City where he had got himself elected mayor. On the day we talked, he was feuding with his five commissioners, all Mormon—not on religious but on budget lines. The fight was over lawn mowers and music. The city needed twelve hundred dollars to buy lawn mowers, and the commissioners had voted as a bloc against Lee to borrow the money from the city building fund. Most city votes seemed to go five-to-one against Lee.

"At the same time we are borrowing money for lawn mowers," the mayor argued plaintively, "the commissioners have a contract with a band to play ten concerts in city parks at a cost of three thousand eight hundred and fifty dollars. It seems silly to me that we don't have money for lawnmowers, but that we do have money for free music."

Lee is the man who, as governor, decided he didn't believe in sending money overseas and withheld his federal income tax payment. (The government attached his bank account and collected.) As mayor of Salt Lake City, he has had a little more to say about taxes on the local level. He balanced the city budget for the first time in ten years—then lowered the tax rate for the first time in twenty years.

Such fiscal policies delayed such badly needed civic improvements as a sewage treatment plant, new streets, new civic and service buildings, and downtown redevelopment. The city hall dated to 1894 and the public library to 1905 when a twenty-million-dollar improvements bond was approved in 1962. There had been no debt at all—city or state. Utah believes in pay-as-you-go. Economic conservatism still is in charge.

"Everything we had was run down," conceded Mayor Lee. "But you can't throw money away and still keep up your city. We can do without luxuries."

Bracken Lee must be labeled an eccentric in tax matters. When his own Republican leaders quashed his bid for a third term as governor (because of his frontal attack on Eisenhower policies), he took to the road to plead for repeal of the income tax. Yet he is not as absurd as he may sometimes sound. He is mayor of a city with a high content of political archaism, but he cannot be dismissed as a member of the lunatic fringe.

Though not a Mormon, a fact which makes him a rarity among successful politicians in Utah, Lee married a Mormon, and all but one of their four children are members of the church. "I've always contended," he said chuckling, "that if you're not actually anti-Mormon, they won't hurt you too much."

Mormon financial growth is a spectacular, though shielded, success story. I asked Lee if through his acquaintance with church officials he could make an estimate of church wealth.

"I have no guess as to the wealth," he answered. "I do know that the net income exceeds a million dollars a day. . . . You look at their annual report and they show income of better than three hundred and sixty-five million dollars a year. And of course you consider it net because it's non-taxable, that part of it. Involved in that may be profits from stocks and properties that they own as well as tithing."

That answer, openly tape-recorded during our interview, seemed startling—if for no other reason, because Bracken Lee is a gentile politician in a Mormon state, and had aspirations for the United States Senate. His answer was to become an "incident" in Mormon annals. There have been a good many "incidents."

From the best available evidence on the vast church holdings in real estate, commerce, and securities, its investment income, combined with the faithful tithe of two million Mormons, the total might readily reach that figure. In any case, it was the only answer to any general question on Mormon finances I received over many months of inquiry. Its wealth is the most harshly-held secret of the church. Until recently, the annual public statement by the church itemized disbursements; when they soared to fifty-five million dollars, disbursements were no longer made public. The income of the church has not been announced in any public report of modern times.

Other churches withhold financial statements, and, after all, there is nothing scandalous about a prosperous church. But my prying afforded me some insight into the regrettable attitudes that still prevail among Mormon leaders toward the gentile outlander who leaves the beaten Utah path to probe.

I telephoned Mayor Lee's friend Orval Adams, a Salt Lake City banker and chairman of the Mormon church's finance committee. I repeated Mayor Lee's statement, and asked Adams if he cared to comment.

There was a long pause. "Did Brack tell you that?" Adams asked.

I repeated that he had.

"It's not our policy to discuss income," Adams said firmly.

Later I mailed a similar inquiry to Henry Dinwoodie Moyle, who ranks next to President McKay in the Mormon hierarchy and who is the financial wizard of the church. Many Mormons give him credit for its phenomenal financial growth. Moyle had been genial when I met him before the Lee incident. Now he did not answer my letter; a note signed by a secretary stated that my inquiry had been referred to the church historian. I heard no more. A subsequent inquiry by mail to another church official brought no reply. Others have found their information sources to be silent when their investigation has extended beyond the limits encouraged by the church.

One example bordering on censorship occurred when Robert Cahn wrote an article about Utah published in 1961 in the *Saturday Evening Post*. The section of the article dealing with polygamy was "edited" after advance proofs were seen by Mormon leaders. The late Walter Budge, as Utah attorney general, had talked to Cahn about the extent of polygamy in Utah. Budge, a Mormon, was standing for reëlection at about that time and was quoted in the article as being anxious to stamp out polygamy, and having "reason to believe there are still at least twenty thousand Utah men, women, and children involved in polygamy." But much of the article devoted originally to polygamy had been deleted before publication. A Mormon church official who had seen the proofs told me that Budge had been "prevailed upon" to contact the *Post* and request modification of his remarks.

"He shouldn't have talked up like that," the church aide told me, smiling, "but it was an election year."

With the Budge incident in mind, I went to a friend who is a Mormon leader in Southern California and showed him the first draft of this chapter, mentioning my inability to reëstablish communication with the Mormon hierarchy. Promptly there came a six-page letter from President Moyle. Nowhere in it did he answer any questions regarding the extent of income of the church, but he did say:

> I called Mayor Lee and asked him the source of the information which he gave you that the Church's income was in excess of One Million Dollars (sic) a day. He frankly stated he had no source, that he didn't know and that that was pure speculation upon his part. Unfortunately his speculation conveyed, unintentionally, I am sure, serious misinformation.

Even before Moyle's long letter, a brief note had come from Bracken Lee on the stationery of the mayor of Salt Lake City. It was not difficult to detect a certain aroma of crow in these lines:

> There appears to be one comment in the interview with me that is incorrect and that is where I estimated to you the net income of the L.D.S. Church as being a million dollars a day. I have no way of knowing this, nor do I know anyone who could give me this figure.

The contradiction is probably involved with accounting techniques. The reticence of the Mormon church to discuss its wealth is understandable. Most Mormons are people of modest income, but their rigid ten percent tithe is not the end of their financial obligation to the church; they give heavily of their time and remaining funds to the construction of temples and churches, and to the church welfare program. A poor Mormon farmer educated to the high standards of his church might occasionally bristle at some family sacrifice necessary to meet his tithe if the extent of church wealth were commonly known.

An inventory of Mormon business holdings would include the major Salt Lake City department store, ZCMI (Zion Co-operative Mercantile Institution, fifty-one percent owned by the church, with a three-million-six-hundred-thousand-dollar branch); a major interest in the Utah-Idaho Sugar Company (wholly owned, with assets of close to ninety million dollars); Hotel Utah (with a seventeen-story annex now under way), Hotel Utah Motor Lodge and Temple Square Hotel; the Deseret Book Company, largest book store in the West with annual sales exceeding one million five hundred thousand dollars much of which goes to underwrite the church publications program; KSL radio and television, the CBS outlets in Salt Lake City (a majority interest); Zion's Securities Corporation, a real estate management firm; ranches of vast size in Florida, Canada, and Georgia; sugar acreage in Hawaii; and real property in most areas all over the world where Mormon stakes are established. At the fall general conference of the church in 1961, President McKay announced creation of the Deseret Title Holding Corporation; previously he had speculated publicly on setting up a banking system to handle church finances, since the Zion National Bank, once church-owned, had been sold.

In Boise, Idaho, a responsible citizen said, "The Mormons aren't a church any more; they're a business." In Salt Lake City, another told me, "There is no two-way property deal in Salt Lake City. Every deal is three-way. One way or another, the church figures in every real estate transaction."

But President Moyle wrote in his letter:
We could use a much larger income than we have in carrying out our spiritual purposes. Our corporate holdings are confined almost exclusively to a few pioneer corporations of the state, the Church's interest in most of which arose out of necessity of its coöperation in the first instance. Our income from this source is relatively negligible. Over the years the value of the corporate holdings has increased, but we are not primarily a business organization.

One flare-up of feeling against this spiritual and financial monolith came in Salt Lake City after the Mormon-owned Brigham Young University bought the city-owned Forest Dale Park and golf course as a prospective junior college campus.

"The deal was made through the Chamber of Commerce crowd and the church," recalled Mayor Lee. "They had private meetings. I don't think the public found out about it for a couple of months after the sale was made."

The record is clear in this case, unlike the matter of church income, and it bears out Mayor Lee. The sale was first reported in the pages of the gentile Salt Lake City *Tribune*, and later it was contested in the courts. As this book went to press, the case was undecided, and golfers still had the run of the course.

The effect of the church is felt in every area of Utah life, and by every Utahn—Mormon or gentile. A moral barricade has retarded secular institutions in Utah. Its criminal system is archaic: why bother to improve jails and prisons, when you won't be needing them if you are a good Mormon? Years ago, it was advantageous for a prisoner to tell his jailer that he was a "LDS"—the abbreviation by which Mormons speak of themselves. Once the church ignored or disowned criminal offenders among its ranks; now a Mormon boy may be executed occasionally in Utah, but the high emphasis on moral values among Mormons and the attention to family life make crime less of a problem in Utah than in most states. Crime rate statistics are, however, contradictory. Only in the crimes of murder and non-negligent manslaughter does Utah rank low in comparison with other states. Under the prodding of Dr. Arthur Beeley, dean emeritus of the Graduate School of Social Work at the University of Utah, the Utah legislature in 1961 approved without a dissenting vote a bill creating a unique state agency charged with observing criminal justice procedures. The action was spurred by serious prison disturbances, an inadequate juvenile court system, lack of coördination among law agencies, and the use of obsolete methods of punishment.

Salt Lake City police recently began enforcement of an ignored 1907 Utah statute which prohibits smoking or possession of tobacco by anyone under twenty-one. A companion statute makes it illegal to sell, give, or provide tobacco to anyone under twenty-one. "You can drink in private, so you drink," a Mormon physician told me. "But if you smoke, you can't avoid smoking in public, so you don't smoke." Minors cited by police under these reactivated statutes were required to pay fifteen-dollar fines or to attend a two-hour lecture at which the evils of tobacco were stressed. Some citizens have protested bitterly that a religious credo of the majority was being forced upon the minority.

Yet it is reassuring to see how little bigotry there is on either side, gentile or Mormon. And the absorption of the Mormon with his church seems to be contagious; Utahns of all faiths are among the most church-going people.

His status in heaven is spelled in remarkable specifics for the

Nevada–Utah

SCALE: 94 MILES TO THE INCH
0   94   288

Mormon. An abundance of relatives enhances his standing; thus his obsession with genealogy. The massive church genealogical head-quarters across from Temple Square has copies of most of the birth and death records of many European countries. It is often thronged, especially by the elderly making ready for heaven. Some members of the church believe they have traced their ancestors back to the years before Christ. The Mormon discovering such ancestors will be bap-tized in their behalf, vicariously bringing salvation to members of his family who died before the founding of the church. Polygamy has done nothing to simplify Mormon study of genealogy. One unique by-product of this interest is found in the medical school at the University of Utah, which has done valuable research in muscular dystrophy. The disease is assumed to have hereditary causation; no better place for hereditary study could be imagined. One basis of the church's opposition to alcohol, tobacco, coffee, and tea is the preser-vation of the body; Mormons believe they live on in heaven with their earthly bodies.

The Mormon youth programs, through the Mutual Improve-ment Associations, are intensive. Two thousand teams from through-out the church participate in annual basketball and softball tourna-ments. Music and drama festivals are held each June in Salt Lake City. Biennial dance festivals draw eight to ten thousand participants in Salt Lake City. Church youths over the age of twelve meet one night of each week for prayer, talks, skits, debates, and music. Every Mormon family is expected to gather for a weekly evening service of prayer and talk, and daily family prayers are customary. There are more than five hundred seminaries near public schools where Mormon children may go for released-time religious instruc-tion; more than six thousand Mormon college students attend in-stitutes for religious education near gentile college campuses.

Two of the most publicized facets of the Mormon church are totally compatible with more ordinary creeds: its choir and its welfare system. The church holds idleness and waste to be sinful. Even mem-bers like George Romney and Ezra Benson regularly go out into fields to help with food crops, which flow into a network of provisions for the needy throughout the Mormon world. Thirty canneries are oper-ated by Mormon stakes, or parishes; one operates a soap factory. A Mormon coal mine in southern Utah is manned by church volunteers with only a few union miners as supervisors. To one hundred and fifty storehouses throughout the United States and Canada go Mormon-grown, Mormon-harvested, Mormon-canned or Mormon-packaged food, Mormon-sewn clothes, Mormon-mined fuel. The Deseret label is on tuna canned in San Diego, on peanut butter jarred in Dallas, on blue jeans sewn in Salt Lake City.

The Welfare Square storehouse in Salt Lake City alone distributes half a million dollars' worth of food and clothing in a year— much of it in trucks without identifying insignia, on orders filled out by block workers visiting the needy and authorized by stake bishops. Records are kept of every welfare order; Mormons are expected to repay the church if they are able. On a squaw dress in Welfare Square I saw the tag: "This dress was made by a new convert who has the use of only one hand. Grantsville Stake." An aged but nimble clerk, one of the many volunteers, proudly told me, "This is what the outside world doesn't realize. If the Mormon church didn't take care of its own people, the government would have to." Then he asked me to lean over, and whispered in my ear, "God bless you."

The same unquestioning spirit of giving pervades the best-known of all Mormon institutions, its Tabernacle Choir. Its broadcasts have been heard each Sunday since 1929, and its records and world concert tours have brought both critical acclaim and wide popularity outside the Mormon world. It was in 1959 that their recording of "The Battle Hymn of the Republic" made with the Philadelphia Orchestra became a record hit; nothing quite like it has happened before or since in the history of popular music. There was keen rapport between choir and orchestra—a total of almost five hundred musicians—during their recording sessions. After "Battle Hymn" was cut, there was a hushed moment while all waited for the flashing light of the engineer to know if it was "a take." When the flash came, a bassoon player lifted his instrument above him with a white handkerchief tied around it and waved it in surrender. The tension broke with a roar.

The arithmetic of the choir is incredible. It averages about three hundred and sixty-five members, all unsalaried and all residents of the Salt Lake City–Provo area. From this relatively small area has emerged one of the consistently great choirs of the world. It regularly evokes the amazement reflected by a New York newspaper critic's query after the choir sang at Carnegie Hall in 1958: "Where on earth do the Mormons find so many admirable voices?"

The Sunday broadcasts are half-hours of musical warmth and dignity which have done much to divert attention from the memory of past Mormon polygamy. Richard L. Evans, who announces the hymns and reads brief, non-sectarian devotional messages, has become the closest thing in religious broadcasting to a matinée idol; he gets an awesome amount of mail, and his books sell heavily.

The choir conductor is Richard P. Condie, a tall, urbane man who formerly taught music at the University of Utah. Before a recent Thursday night rehearsal in the Tabernacle, Condie sat in the front row of the choir loft, wearing a sport shirt and brown slacks, and identified members of the choir as they took their places: doctors, housewives, teachers, secretaries, businessmen, two beauticians, and two electrical linemen. Some were listening intently to a playback of their previous Sunday broadcast, which filled the arched ceiling of the century-old Tabernacle. Dr. Frank Asper, the choir's senior organist, rose from the five-manual organ to shake hands. A gentle, soft-spoken man with bushy, unruly gray hair, he presides over one of the most intricate and mightiest organs in America.

At seven-thirty, Condie raised a small stick and turned to face his choir: the sopranos and contraltos in tiers to his left, the tenors and basses to his right. Effortlessly, suddenly, the vast, disciplined voice of the choir soared through the Tabernacle. But Condie tapped his stick and interrupted them. He does this more frequently than most choir leaders. The sopranos usually take the brunt of his chiding; when choir members imitate Condie, it is in a whining voice to say, "Sopranos, I know you are there, but why don't you sing? I thought all of you were going to pass out!"

Choir practice is a good-humored occasion, running the gamut from prayer to riotous laughter. Here Mormon pride and camaraderie are at their best. Choir members are dedicated to their leader and to their calling, a signal honor in their church. It is evident in their concern when Condie heckles gently, "I know some people who take the music home and study it, and they're good people, too!" Or when he stops the choir in full flight and roars, "The words! The words!"

At the time that I attended rehearsal, the choir had been involved in several strenuous sessions, recording a Civil War album. But Condie would not allow them a dull Thursday night practice. "Put some interest in it," he pleaded. "I can tell you're tired because you haven't changed moods at all! But it's got to sail, to flow like springtime! We can't afford to slip!"

Less devoted and disciplined choirs would not have responded, but the Mormon Tabernacle Choir began again, and their voice was the voice of springtime.

The choir's albums have sold more than a million copies, but success in the commercial world of recording does not seem to spoil the spontaneity of the choir. Even singers who drive forty-five minutes from Provo for rehearsals and services refuse reimbursement of expenses. Male singers buy their own choir robes; only the women receive theirs without charge. Lester Hewlett, its business manager, stepped out of his profitable coffee, tea, and jam business to give his time without salary to the choir. Choir membership is considered a position of Mormon aristocracy, and a waiting list always is at hand.

Although the Mormons have a reputation for taking care of their own through their welfare system, Utah would have blown away during the Depression had it not been for federal aid; one in four Utahns was on direct relief, and the state ranked second in per capita volume of relief spending.

Like it or not, Utahns are in the grip of the Mormon church on one side and once again the federal government on another. There are elements both of salvation and of philosophical irony in their debacle. Political and church leaders are almost belligerent in their independence of Washington subsidy, but one-fourth of personal income in Utah is from the government, and the per capita annual income remains three hundred dollars below the national average.

Drought and the lure of steady wages in new Utah missile plants are responsible for the abandonment of much of Utah's scarce farmland. Between 1950 and 1960, thirteen of the twenty-nine Utah counties lost population, although the state increase was twenty-nine percent. Rural Utah has relatively little to lose. It is sparsely inhabited at best, and its hardy settlers seem to be in the process of giving it back to nature. It will probably not be until 1967 that irrigation waters of the Upper Colorado River Project will reverse the trend.

Faced with the inevitable, President McKay of the Mormon church has become a booster of Utah industrial development, even though it may mean federal dependence. Mormons are industrious workers. "When church authorities hear of their people goofing off on the job," said Gus Backman, manager of the Salt Lake City Chamber of Commerce, "they send out investigators."

Wages from the Utah missile industry in 1961 were estimated at sixty-three million dollars—a pittance in a factory city but a bonanza in Utah. About one-third of this payroll was concentrated near Brigham City, where the Thiokol Chemical Corporation is building the first-stage solid-fuel rocket for the Minuteman. The change in this city is symptomatic of the transitions of Zion. Dean Beeley believes that the influx of industrial population will reduce the proportion of Mormons in Utah by 1970 from about sixty-four percent to as little as thirty-five or forty percent. His projection is thought by some to be extreme; nevertheless, the effect of this incoming population is a factor behind the current fanatic proselyting of the Mormon church. Only by increasing its church rosters as fast as newcomers dilute the Mormon majority can the church hold its dominant position in Utah affairs.

Until 1956, Brigham City was a quiet Mormon town of six thousand people. It was rimmed with fruit orchards, but after Thiokol came, the orchards became housing tracts, and the population doubled. Among the new residents of Brigham City are a heavy proportion of gentiles. The same is true in Ogden, a railroad junction and distribution center and the second largest city in the state, where Marquardt Aircraft Company has its Bomarc missile plant. Boeing has a Minuteman assembly plant here as well, and Hill Air Force Base, with twelve thousand civilians on its payroll, is the largest employer in Utah. Some of the in-migrant flow is Mormon—sons and daughters of citizens who had left Utah in search of opportunity, but who have been encouraged to return as opportunity developed in the state. Industrial growth will be steady, but it will never approach the runaway proportions of the West Coast cities.

Utahns do not consider defense industry as industrial development; they understand that it is there because Utahns have a reputation for giving a good day's work for their wages and because of geographic proximity to missile bases. A lot of residents would prefer to see no jobs than to see jobs which disappear. President McKay said: "The Mormon Church is interested in developing the character of man, and we don't like our members to be dependent on the government. If a man is going to work eight hours at a missile plant, he should also work eight hours on the land and have eight hours for his sleep—that would keep him out of mischief! People should keep cows and chickens, have small farms and stay independent."

Until 1939, Utah had relied almost entirely on mining and agriculture. Then Remington moved into the state with a small arms and shell plant, and citizens took a fling at factory jobs because that was all there was. The federal government became aware of Utah's strategic geography; it was at the center of the eleven Western states, midway between Canada and Mexico; it had the only substantial city in a thousand-mile belt between Denver and the Pacific. In came air bases, supply and ordnance depots, and proving grounds. A two-hundred-million-dollar government steel plant was built at Geneva; at the end of the war, U. S. Steel bought it at surplus for less than fifty million dollars. Then came two dozen satellite industries dependent on steel. Iron and coal deposits of Utah are vast, but the steel industry is dominated by Eastern interests. Kennecott operates the largest open-pit copper mine in North America at Bingham, twenty-eight miles southwest of Salt Lake City; it has produced almost six billion pounds of copper since 1906. But until recently,

Kennecott left nothing behind in Utah. Its Utah Copper Division had always been operated by engineers. That is changing; both Mormon and gentile leaders of Utah reminded Kennecott officials firmly of their obligation to Utah. Kennecott has public-relations people in Utah now, and the company is increasingly active in charity and civic affairs.

From the earth in remote southeastern Utah come other treasures that help to make the state more prosperous. The rugged, red-rocked town of Moab came alive in 1952 when an unshaven prospector named Charles Steen made a one-hundred-fifty-million-dollar uranium strike at Mi Vida Mine. Until that moment, Moab was a sleepy Mormon town, a center for farms and cattle ranches, of only twelve hundred persons. Within a decade, its population had risen to six thousand, and Charles Steen had become a working millionaire. He built a nine-million-dollar uranium reduction mill and financed additional uranium exploration. At forty-one, he is held in awe by the townsfolk of Moab—less for his luck than for what he has done to provide jobs in Moab. He is one of the few men made rich by uranium.

The typical two-man teams of uranium prospectors have vanished from the Colorado Plateau, all the way from Wyoming at the north to New Mexico in the south. At Moab, ore trucks roll over the Colorado River to Steen's mill with about fifteen hundred tons a day of uranium ore taken from their pods (not veins) in surrounding mines. It takes ten men one day to extract one hundred tons of ore, which is converted into six-hundred-pound drums of yellowcake—U_3O_8 concentrate—at the Moab mill. Each drum brings about forty-eight hundred dollars from the Atomic Energy Commission. The miners earn about one hundred and seventy-five dollars a week, but living costs are high. Moab is remote, but the seventy-piece Utah Symphony from Salt Lake City has made its way there, and an annual conference on uranium brings specialists to Moab from many nations.

The marvel is that Moab has only quintupled in population. After the uranium strike of 1952 came important oil discoveries in 1956 at Paradox Basin, seventy miles south. More recently, major potash deposits have been found.

Twenty-five miles southwest of Moab, oil-company roads have made more accessible the spectacle from Dead Horse Point, more than two thousand feet above the water surface in the gorges knifed by the merging of the Green and Colorado Rivers. Here is one of the most surrealistic panoramas of America, a museum of intricate erosion patterns in shadings of red and orange: ridges, towers, buttes, fins, spires, tapestried cliffs. It has taken uranium and oil to expose to tourists the wilderness of southeast Utah. The landscape is worth seeking out. A hardy kind of tourist is discovering the rewards of southern Utah; though the visitor is neither solicited nor pampered, Mormon isolation has at last been penetrated enough so that he is at least welcome.

The Colorado and the Green Rivers surround the Mormon island on the east and south with a geographic decisiveness that neither modern communications nor tourist facilities has entirely pierced. The Green comes down out of Wyoming and Colorado to traverse the eastern length of Utah. In more than seven hundred miles of river there are only four crossings, and its gorges are deep and vertical.

The back country on either side of both rivers is arid, forbidding, inaccessible plateau and mountain desert. Almost exactly at the center of the states' boundary, the Colorado dashes down its gorges from Utah into Arizona. Here the Glen Canyon Dam is scheduled for completion in 1964. Its reservoir will be one hundred and eighty-six miles in length, and it is higher than any dam in the nation except Hoover, rising seven hundred feet above the Colorado to span the sandstone flanks of the canyon about a quarter of a mile apart. The principal unit of a Bureau of Reclamation project, the Glen Canyon will provide power and irrigation water for five states.

Some of the canyon country is eerily familiar at first glance; it has been used repeatedly as settings for films. This is the area of massive, colorful cliffs, sand dunes, and groves of desert cedar around Paria and Kanab in southern Utah. Kanab is the gateway to the north rim of the Grand Canyon; it also performs another vital function: its residents are old hands at the movie business. They provide not only food and lodging for the caravansery, but Indians, extras, horses, dogs, and children as well. There is even a Kane County Extras Organization. In 1961, the area was the scene of shooting for *The Three Sergeants*, a refilming of *Westward the Women*, which had been filmed many years before in Kanab, and other films starring John Wayne and Richard Boone. The attitude of the mayor of Kanab, Bernell Lewis, is a refreshing contrast to the growth fetish of most mayors: "There is no other country to match ours for color, for natural beauty, or for that wilderness feeling so essential to Western film entertainment."

In southwest Utah, known to Utahns as Dixie, the climate has been borrowed from Arizona and the Southern California desert. The sun grows perceptibly hotter and brighter within a few hours' drive southward from Salt Lake City, down through Mormon villages and small farms squared off by long stately lines of Lombardy poplars like English hedgerows. The streets of the towns are wide, the houses stark but solid, all centered around the ward chapels or—in Logan, Manti, and St. George—around startlingly imposing temples in which are performed the rites of the church: marriage, baptism, and the mystical six-hour endowment rite for the more dedicated teen-age youth. The main north-south highway of Utah is 91, which comes down out of Idaho through the towns of the Wasatch oasis strip, bearing in a gentle southwest arc and respectfully skirting the margin of the Great Basin—the barren bowl that fills the void between the Sierra Nevada and the Rockies.

Nephi, one of the towns which bears a Book of Mormon name, is the southern outpost of the Wasatch oasis along Highway 91; it is in towns like this that the full flavor of Utah fills the senses of the gentile outlander. "Mormon country," Wallace Stegner once wrote, "will be the sticks for a good while to come." Nephi is a good town, and its people must be good people to battle its dry fields for wheat; it is the seat of Juab County and is on the slopes of Mount Nebo. These are names of religious significance to Mormons; the town itself is named for a patriarch who, according to the Book of Mormon, came from Judea to America during the Babylonian captivity.

In Nephi, the town creek went dry in 1960 for the first time since the 1880's. The state lent the local water company money to dig wells, and thus saved a third of a million dollars' worth of crops that summer. There were vacant houses when I stopped there, and a filling station attendant told me that he expected many more residents to leave. His son had quit farming to go to work for Thiokol in the north and had taken his family with him.

In his campaign in 1962 for a third term in the United States Senate, Wallace Bennett, a wealthy Salt Lake City car dealer and former president of the National Association of Manufacturers, stressed the problems created in rural Utah by the migration to the towns and to Salt Lake City. Utahns regarded the contest between Bennett and his Democratic challenger, Representative David S. King, a liberal, as a test of liberal strength; King was soundly beaten. Both Senator Bennett and Senator Frank Moss have sought to speed up phases of the Upper Colorado River Project which will divert irrigation water into central Utah and may help to halt the exodus from the land. The central Utah project will reclaim two hundred thousand acres of desert, but in 1962 an eight-year drought had made its completion date of 1967 seem an eternity away to the central Utah farmers with whom I talked.

Yet Mormons are patient, unpretentious people, and it is rare to hear them complain. It is expected of Mormons that they work hard, play quietly, and resist the pressures of the world. To see such traits preserved in an era of spreading commercialism and conformity is remarkable. Mormons have retained more of the pioneer spirit of mutual aid, group interest, and of the nobility of work, than most other Americans. The dilution of the Mormon majority by industrial expansion will strain these traits, but the church is resisting its dilution with all of its powerful resources and organization.

If the individualism which has shaped the West is to be weakened by conformity, Zion will be among the last to surrender.

Part IV

THE
SOUTHWEST

16

NEVADA

Test Tube of Change

Julia Bulette was the first white woman to reach Virginia City in 1859 after the discovery of the Comstock Lode, the richest of all bonanzas. She came from New Orleans and was thought to be French, but in fact her name was Smith, and she had been born in Liverpool. She was a prostitute and was strangled to death seventeen years after she came West by a lover who took her furs and jewels. He was promptly hanged, and the ceremony was the occasion of one of the most riotous holidays ever celebrated in Virginia City.

By then, Nevada was a state. In 1864, Abraham Lincoln needed votes for the Thirteenth Amendment, and in order that Nevada could line up against slavery in time, its new constitution was telegraphed in full to Washington at a cost of $3,416.77.

Virginia City was the site of a hundred saloons and as many as twenty-five thousand inhabitants. From the Comstock Lode, discovered in 1857, came about three-quarters of a billion dollars' worth of silver before the lode ran out near the turn of the century.

In 1867, the six-story International Hotel in Virginia City was equipped with the first elevator west of Chicago. Piper's Opera House was one of a score of theaters and music halls which drew the finest entertainers of the day. Silver and gold made empires for John Mackay, James Fair, James Flood, and William O'Brien, as well as paying for much of the San Francisco that existed before the fire of 1906.

Down the mountainside in Carson City, named for Kit Carson, the emigrant trains refitted, the Pony Express set up a relay post, bullion was deposited with Wells Fargo, and Snowshoe Thompson began his perilous mail run over the Sierra to Hangtown, California.

But not much was happening in the vast wastelands of sand and rock and alkali dry lakes to the south. Many years earlier, the springs and meadows of Las Vegas had been a landmark on the Old Spanish Trail between Santa Fe and the California missions. In 1855, William Bringhurst arrived from Salt Lake City with thirty young men assigned by Brigham Young to "go to Las Vegas, build a fort there to protect immigrants and the United States mail from the Indians, and teach the latter how to raise corn, wheat, potatoes, squash, and melons."

The Paiutes were uncoöperative. They raided Mormon fields but planted none of their own. The Mormons mined silver but thought it was lead, and for five years they could not understand why the metal cast so poorly in bullet molds. When they left Las Vegas they were broke and discouraged—the first of a long line like them.

In Tonopah, near the center of the state, a mining boom around 1900 brought a miner named Cal Brougher, who fell in love with Tonopah's first widow, a woman named May. May was stubborn, but Brougher hopefully hauled lumber across the desert to build Tonopah's first frame house. Just as it was finished, May married another miner who lived in a tent. Brougher sold the house and got drunk. The house still stands.

In 1905, on a platform under a mesquite tree, an official of the San Pedro, Los Angeles, and Salt Lake Railroad explained a plan. In two days, a land auction brought two hundred and sixty-five thousand dollars for twelve hundred lots, and a tent city rose. The railroad became part of the Union Pacific; the tent city was Las Vegas.

The next boom in Las Vegas came in 1931 when construction began on Hoover Dam, but even that migration has been forgotten in the night-and-day cavalcade of California cars that have zoomed across the desert since the end of World War II.

On the night after hearing the Mormon Tabernacle Choir rehearsal in Salt Lake City, I sat in a Las Vegas hotel watching the most lavish of all American night-club shows and one of its nudest—a revue which derives from the Lido in Paris. The West is extreme in its contrasts.

The highway leaves Utah in the red-rocked Zion country, slashes through the northwest Strip country of Arizona, and enters Nevada near the 114th meridian, an arbitrary border which separates one of America's most conservative states from its most flamboyant.

The scenery does not change along the long straight border between Utah and Nevada. From the air, it all seems equally part of the tanned, barren Great Basin. But the temperament changes abruptly. Ely, Nevada, tempts Utahns across the border to gamble by offering bargain bus rates from Salt Lake City which stress togetherness: $5 single, $7 double. Just within Nevada, on its Idaho border, is a town of a hundred people named, by petition of its citizens, Jackpot.

In uproarious contrast to the more stolid attractions of Utah, Las Vegas, the largest city of Nevada (64,605), draws tourists with lures which rank in declining order of appeal from gambling to night-club shows, uncommonly alluring girls of varied callings, and —a poor fourth—Hoover Dam and Lake Mead, thirty-one miles to the southeast, the Western Hemisphere's highest dam and largest man-made reservoir.

Mormons are powerful in Nevada; their churches are the most prominent in the state. The state was settled by Mormons; its first town was Mormon Station, now known as Genoa. Until the population growth of Nevada after World War II diluted their voting strength, the Mormons were a fearsome specter to gambling interests. Members of the church could have swung an election on the gambling issue if it had been put to a vote—but it has not been on the ballot since it was approved in 1931 at the polls, and it is not likely to be.

The gross profit of almost three hundred casinos in Nevada was more than two hundred and sixteen million dollars in 1961. Tourist spending in Nevada—mostly because of gambling—is almost triple that. Each year about thirteen million dollars goes into the Nevada state treasury because of a sliding-scale tax which ranges from three to five-and-a-half percent of net casino profits. As a source of state income, gambling revenue is about equal to the two percent state sales tax.

Nevada has fewer than three hundred thousand residents.

Seventh state in area, it ranks forty-ninth in population; only Alaska is less densely inhabited. It is more than twice the size of New York State, but its people could be quartered in some ten-by-twenty block areas of New York City.

Sixty percent of Nevada's people have income related to gambling. Whether Mormon or not, they know that without gambling the financial structure of their state would be shaky. This makes most Nevadans expert rationalizers. Senator Howard Cannon, a Mormon and a former Las Vegas city prosecutor, says, "I have no compunction whatever in representing our state's gambling interests in Washington. I am not a gambler myself; Mormons are usually not gamblers. But I sense no conflict of interest. Gambling is legal in Nevada. It is, at this moment, my state's leading industry."

Its Mormon population gives Nevada incongruity, but this is only one facet of the state. Nevada is a tale of two cities. Three of every four Nevadans live in or just outside Las Vegas or Reno. In mood, the two cities parallel the two major California cities. Los Angeles goes to Las Vegas; San Francisco goes to Reno. There are conservative third-generation leaders in the northern cities of both states. The southern cities, now dominant by weight of numbers in the politics and economics of both states, have not had time to develop entrenched, complex power patterns. Reno people regard Las Vegans as crass, commercial, and lacking in taste—just as San Franciscans long felt about Angelenos. In Reno, which grew slowly, failure until recently to agree on such projects as a convention center was attributable to leadership paralysis. Reno people explained this away by saying that they were more deliberate, less money-mad than Las Vegans.

Las Vegas astonished even itself with its dispatch in developing in 1959 a $6.5 million aluminum-domed building for conventions, just a few blocks from the fabled hotels of the five-mile Las Vegas Strip. To the surprise of almost everyone, the new facilities graduated Las Vegas from a random tourist town to a busy convention center. From such national conventions as the Junior Chamber of Commerce, the World Congress of Flight, the American Mining Congress, and many others, it was learned that delegates seldom stay up all night in a wide-open city. Whatever they want will be available still at breakfast or at noon; there is no excuse for missing the morning session.

The number of delegates at conventions each year in Nevada is almost as great as the entire population of the state. Ten times as many tourists visit Hoover Dam and Lake Mead each year than Nevadans. Reno had its finger in the pie of the 1961 Winter

Olympics, but it is alarmed that Las Vegas has the plum of steady convention business.

One more symptom of hostility within the state is that state-wide elections are likely to split on regional lines. An eminent Supreme Court Justice, Frank McNamee, barely won reëlection in 1960 over a Reno attorney without judicial experience; McNamee has been a lifetime resident of Southern Nevada. In an editorial decrying sectional mistrust, the Las Vegas *Sun* pointed out that "in other parts of Nevada, many community leaders and public officials take pride in the assertion that they rarely come to Las Vegas and don't intend to do so. . . . A general feeling of suspicion and mistrust exists against Clark County, and particularly Las Vegas."

This hostility is the result of a dramatic shift in power to Las Vegas. In this sense, Nevada is a test tube of Western change. Its sparseness makes the tugs and bulges of growth more obvious. Clark County, eight thousand square miles in the southern wedge of the state, is the site of Las Vegas. Reno is in Washoe County, four hundred and forty-six miles to the northwest. The fifteen other counties are the cow counties. Each has one assemblyman, except Elko in the far northeast, which has two. Until reapportionment in 1961, Reno controlled the state legislature as it had done from the beginning of statehood, just after discovery of the Comstock Lode twenty miles south at Virginia City. But the 1960 census produced radical changes in Nevada. Since 1950, Clark County had grown from 48,289 to 127,016 persons, while Washoe grew only from 50,205 to 84,000. In the first six months of 1962, Clark County residents paid fifty-one percent of Nevada sales and use taxes. Clark County picked up three new state assemblymen for a total of twelve; Washoe dropped from ten to nine. Thirty years before, Clark County had sent only a single assemblyman to Carson City, but by 1961, Reno was done in.

Between Reno and Las Vegas there is very little but rock and sand, alkali-laden dry lakes, sharp buttes, and craggy mountains. The desolation of Nevada is awesome. As though in sympathetic understanding of the dreariness of travel, drivers on its fast highways are not regulated by speed limits. In such wastes, a new gypsum plant bringing two hundred in-migrants into one of the cow counties is a massive boost to the economy. In contrast, some of the cow counties lost population in recent years, even though the growth of Las Vegas made Nevada the state with the greatest growth percentage.

Nevada statistics would seem significant only in a Lilliput. But they show Nevada to be exhibiting the classic symptoms of the westward tilt. The election of Governor Grant Sawyer in 1958 was

the warning bell. Not a Nevadan—in the historic sense of the old
Nevada mining or cattle families who controlled the state almost
despotically for many years—Sawyer was born in Idaho, schooled in
Oregon, and had lived in Elko for eleven years as an attorney before
being elected governor. He was new and unknown in politics. It was
the first time a stranger had been elected to an important office in the
state, and his victory was assured by a Las Vegas majority. The new
people like him were outnumbering the old.

Sawyer is no statesman, but he has brought verve and enthusiasm into Nevada government, where they were needed badly.
When he moved into Carson City, the nation's smallest capital (5,059),
he found caves where prisoners recently had been interned in the
nearby state prison, built before Nevada came into the Union. There
was no prison chapel. Woman prisoners were confined to top-floor
rooms and never permitted out for exercise. Sawyer instituted modest
prison reforms, rebuilt the frightful state orphans' home, tripled the
staff of the boys' detention facility and instituted a parole system.
Within several years, that system progressed from an archaic institution to one with a high rate of rehabilitation.

But as might be suspected, crime rates in Nevada are appallingly
high. In 1959 it had the highest rates of robbery, burglary, and
larceny in the United States. Governor Sawyer insists the rates are
high because of youngsters from out-of-state who come to Nevada
for all-night whoopee; Nevadans, he maintains, sin no more than
most. Although data to support his premise is elusive, it is credible.
Residents of Las Vegas and Reno are seldom habitués of their resort
casinos. For most of them, as for most visitors, the glitter soon turns
to glare; the expense is too heavy to permit the habit.

But not only in crime has the inrush of people been an ordeal
for Nevada. Abundant land is not the only answer to problems of
crowding, and the race to expand facilities is constant and tense in
Las Vegas. Though there are more than twelve thousand rooms
available there for tourists, permanent housing has been periodically
in short supply. A new airport terminal serves an armada of planes
astonishing for a town so small: more than a hundred commercial
airline flights each day, and more than a million passengers each year.

School buildings all over the state were squalid. Under enlightened lobbying from men like Dr. Guild Gray, former superintendent of schools in Clark County, the 1955 legislature enacted a
two percent sales tax which made funds available for new school
construction. "There were actually cracks in our school floors," Dr.
Gray recalled, "where the kids could lose their pencils." Two maximum bond issues have been voted in Clark County and more than

twenty-five million dollars spent on new schools; despite such stringent efforts, there are still double sessions in some schools.

But Clark County has managed to institute programs which are studied by school administrators across the nation. One of them is its program for emotionally disturbed children, a weighty factor in an all-night, wide-open city like Las Vegas. Another is the integration of fourteen wildly diversified school districts into one county-wide district. Eighty-five miles northeast of this gambling capital in Virgin Valley—still in Clark County—are farm communities like Mesquite and Bunkerville, settled by Mormons and almost inaccessible until relatively recent highway construction. Equally in contrast is Boulder City, a government town beside Hoover Dam, where gambling is banned, and professional and highly skilled technical workers live. Seven in ten of the children of these families go to college after high school graduation. In the northwest corner of the county is Indian Springs, near the Atomic Energy Commission's Yucca Flats proving ground. Here, in 1961, was a three-teacher elementary school. At Searchlight, a tiny mining town, there was a one-room school. Some years ago, it was pointed out that several houses of prostitution were operating in Searchlight—one of them within four hundred yards of the school and thus in violation of a Nevada statute. It was suggested seriously that the school be moved.

If a motley array of facilities such as these, with more than thirty thousand pupils, can be administrated in a single district, one of the fondest dreams of American educators can be realized. In the opinion of the Educational Facilities Laboratory, an affiliate of the Ford Foundation, the Clark County district is functioning; the laboratory chose it from among the districts of the West as an example of consolidation and healthy growth. The conscience of a gambling city may be a factor in making it work. Dr. Gray, a Stanford graduate with school experience in three states, told me that he had never worked in a community where there was so much wholesome interest in education as in Las Vegas. "I have never seen such strong P-TA's as in Las Vegas, under good leadership—not just mothers' clubs. A large percentage of our P-TA presidents have been men, many of them power figures in the community," he said. Another factor certainly is money—most of it coming today from the tourist. Nevada has the highest per capita income of any Western state: in 1960, $2,844. Nationally, it was led that year only by Connecticut, Delaware, and the District of Columbia.

One of the more incongruous phenomena of the westward tilt in Nevada is Las Vegas' attempts to woo industry, a characteristic it shares with other Western cities. Gladwin Hill described this in the

New York *Times* as comparable to "Paris touting its Y.M.C.A., or Detroit talk shifting from cars to camellias." The Southern Nevada Industrial Foundation was launched as a joint effort of Las Vegas officialdom on the premise that industry and gambling are compatible. Its task is a classic challenge in diversionary tactics. Visitors' eyes bug out at non-industrial activity in Las Vegas, like the sign long posted in a Strip casino proclaiming 4:30 A.M. mass each Sunday—at a time of morning when the naïve are sometimes charmed by what they mistake for family sentiment: all those middle-aged men strolling hand-in-hand with their daughters toward their hotel rooms.

To divert the serious-minded from such images of Nevada, the Foundation sends teams across the nation to advertise that Nevada also has adequate power, water, and labor, cheap land—and no income tax. A favorite gambit to disarm skeptics is the argument that twenty-six states have legal gambling—four of them with higher incomes from it than Nevada. But though New York may take in ten times more revenue from race-track betting, and California six times as much, it is impossible to ignore the fact that no other state is as dependent on gambling as Nevada.

The industrial center of all Nevada is at Henderson, between Las Vegas and Hoover Dam, where the Basic Magnesium plant of World War II was sold as surplus by the federal government to Nevada. There, or nearby, are electronic and machine factories, chemical and mineral producers, and manufacturers of exotic fuels. Pleasant living conditions give promise of strong future industrial growth. The sun glows bright during eighty-three percent of the hours of potential sunshine, and with summer air conditioning, the climate is a delight to anyone accustomed to the East or Midwest. If his wife is alarmed by the distractions of Las Vegas, the industrial worker can commute to his Henderson job just as easily from Boulder City, a one-time government town whose city charter still proscribes against liquor and gambling in the hope that sloth and lust shall not corrupt, nor croupiers break in and steal.

Casino operators are not overly pleased about the little industrial boom of Southern Nevada. The industrialists' ploy, obviously, is to rid Nevada of its dependence on gambling. If they succeeded, and there were another way for Nevada to support itself, the gamblers infer, there might come a day when the state would vote out gambling. But A. E. Cahlan, general manager for many years of the Las Vegas *Review-Journal*, remembers Nevada in the days before gambling and predicts that "other states will join us in legal gambling before you see us giving it up." Senator Cannon, insisting that Nevada has more churches per capita than any other state, says, "We have a

responsible way of life within the framework of our laws. If we
continue to control gambling as we do now, there is no prospect of
opposition." Governor Sawyer, who appoints the five-man Gaming
Commission and its enforcement arm, the three-man Gaming Control
Board, is convinced that Nevadans would not vote out gambling "unless it began to control the state, instead of the state controlling
gambling."

The state is not likely to risk federal intervention—and possible strangulation of its golden goose—by hanky-panky with the
underworld. The 1961 Nevada legislature passed a civil rights bill,
something which would have been inconceivable two years before,
partly in the hope that it would head off federal probes into Nevada
gambling. The devious logic involved was that the Kennedy administration was interested in civil rights, and that if Nevada showed
Washington it was trying to go along, Washington might not punish
Nevada with a gambling probe. In the same legislative session, gamblers fought a proposal to raise the casino tax. One assemblyman
reports that a casino spokesman blurted in a closed hearing, "Look!
You leave us alone, and from now on you'll get an honest count!" The
legislature left the casino tax unchanged and state income from that
tax promptly soared all out of proportion to tourist increases.

State control over gambling increased sharply after state licensing of casinos was invoked in 1945. One major aim was to eliminate
ties between Nevada gambling and organized crime outside the state.
Federal investigators have discovered political manna for themselves
in the form of unsavory characters who own "points," as they are
called in Nevada, in casinos. Nevadans rebut by conceding that some
"point holders" were convicted of felonies many years ago, but have
had exemplary records since. Nevada law insists that "point
holders" be free of conviction only in the five years prior to their connection with a casino. The late Morris Katleman, whose son Beldon
was the owner of El Rancho Vegas, served time during 1920 and
1921 in the Nebraska State Penitentiary on a charge of aiding and
abetting grand larceny. His prison number was one which a crap-
shooter might envy: 7777. Some convicted bootleggers from the
Prohibition era have "points" in Nevada casinos; selling liquor is a
minor part of their role in Nevada and they grow almost sanctimoni-
ous in defending their names against such little ironies as bootlegging
convictions.

George Ullom, former Las Vegas city manager, has a blithe
outlook. "Some of these casino operators were law violators elsewhere
—because they were gamblers. Here, they still are gamblers, but they
join the chamber of commerce."

Understandably, such men are loath to speak up. They hire platoons of press agents for their hotels, casinos, and show rooms, all of them with *carte blanche* to buy dinner, drinks, or lodging for anyone whose credentials suggest that there is a possibility they may add to the chorus of Nevada ballyhoo. Men like Jake Freedman, once of Houston, who built the Sands Hotel, and Moe Dalitz of the Desert Inn, have gained the respect of the community, as have most operators in Reno, where gambling is less heavy and more controlled by long-time Nevadans. But the reticence of gamblers is legendary.

One exception is Wilbur Clark, whose name has been associated with the Desert Inn in Las Vegas since its opening in 1950. In 1948 he walked with me across hot bare sand and traced an outline of the mammoth hotel he planned to build. At that time few believed that Las Vegas could support a hotel of such size; a dozen more as big have come along since.

Clark is a little-schooled man with all the keenness of judgment and flair for risk that mark the good gambler. He has somewhat less than a one-fifth interest in the hotels with which he is associated, but his honest face and his obsession for meeting people have been well exploited by his partners. Though he has done as much as any man to create the image of Las Vegas as a safe place for the folksy tourist to pause and look about, little has been known about him. One afternoon recently, in the living room of his big home beside the hotel golf course, Clark cut off his telephone calls and sat back to talk. While a tape recorder hummed, I nudged his memory.

"I was born in Keyesport, a little town in southern Illinois. I was only nineteen when I decided to go West," he said. "I hadn't seen my dad since I was nine years old. We were poor. I started walking and hitching rides. In about eight or nine days I landed in San Diego. I was walking through Kansas City on the day that Herbert Hoover was nominated, in 1928.

"My first job was bussing and washing dishes at Leighton's Cafeteria in San Diego. It smelled so bad it made me sick. I worked there nine days. When I walked out, I said, 'I'll never walk in this place as long as I live.' It must have been fifteen years before I had to go in there, and it still had the same smell. It finally closed down —the smell must have killed it.

"My next job was as an elevator operator. I didn't have a high school education and I was very little. I didn't weigh over a hundred and ten pounds. It was tough getting a job. Soon I landed work as bellhop in San Diego at the Knickerbocker Hotel. In 1931, gambling came into Nevada. I quit and thumbed to Reno, figuring I'd hop bells in some big hotel.

"Well, there were just two little hotels, and of course I couldn't get a job. I run into this fellow we used to call Tomatoface Ryan, and he got me a job working for Jack Sullivan, a big tall guy with a scar on his face. Eddie Ryan took me up to him and Sullivan said, 'This kid looks like he could do anything.' He called a dealer over and said, 'Break this boy in to be a crap dealer.' That's how my gambling career started.

"Then I became a wheel dealer and a twenty-one dealer. I worked all over the country—Saratoga, New York, Palm Springs, on the gambling boats. The last time I worked for anyone was in 1937—I was always on my own from then. I started my first little bar in San Diego in 1941. It was called the Breakers Club. I sold that place and made a little profit. Then I bought another little beer place which I opened seven days before Pearl Harbor. In a year or two I had quite a few places and made a lot of money.

"Then in 1944 I came over to Las Vegas and bought the El Rancho Vegas, which had started but was a failure. I wound up with sixty percent, which I still had when I sold it in 1946. Then I came down the street across from the Last Frontier Hotel and bought this acreage where we are now sitting. It was a lot of sand and sand hills. I wasn't very sure I was going to be able to do what I planned. I went as far as I could go in building a hotel, and I ran out of money. I stopped work; I figured I never could lose something that I don't owe anybody any money on. I just set there, exactly one year to the day. I started again and got stopped again.

"Then I met these fellows who came in with me, and we made a deal and we opened up the Desert Inn on April twenty-fourth, 1950. It took me six years. Right now we have close to two thousand rooms and a payroll of roughly fifty thousand dollars a day here and at the Stardust across the street. I imagine our gross this year would show thirty million dollars on both hotels counting casinos, food, whiskey, the whole works. But I wouldn't want you to hold me to those figures exactly—we've got about a hundred and fifty auditors.

"When I first came to Las Vegas, there couldn't have been over eight or ten thousand people. Now we're like the hub of a wheel, surrounded by Los Angeles, San Francisco, Salt Lake City, Denver, Phoenix, Tucson, and San Diego. This town is on its way to being one of the biggest world centers of conventions. Me, I'm a thirty-second-degree Mason, but Cardinal Cushing and myself were on page one of the local paper. In the next paper was Cardinal Cushing *and my wife* and me on page one.

"Kennedy has stayed in my hotel. The finest people in the world come here. We've had Chief Justice Warren and Tom Clark and

Cardinal McIntire and Errol Flynn and governors and senators and, of course, all the show business people. I've had three different audiences with the Pope, two with the one that died and one with the new one. I'm half-owner of a horse that has the world's record at six furlongs. I've been living pretty good.

"One of the things in my life—I always said if I can ever get my name to be known, then I'm rich whether I got any money or not. It's very simple to get into trouble in life, especially in the business I've been involved in. I feel good about going through life without really getting into trouble.

"When I first came out West I went three days without eating, and I came close to getting into trouble. These days, three hundred and sixty five days a year, I can meet a hundred or two hundred people each day. I've met every type of person, in this country and Europe. It's a funny thing: if I'm introduced to a stranger as Mr. Clark, it means absolutely nothing. But the minute they say, 'This is Wilbur Clark,' people perk up. I figure my name is known, and that makes me rich."

The casinos of Las Vegas are showpieces of cynicism. They do not rely on the percentages of odds—which on Nevada tables is as low as 1.36 percent for the house on the back line of the crap table, and 1.41 percent on the "come" line. What brings the millions into the cash boxes of Nevada casinos is what the house calls the "playing percentage."

As Wilbur Clark puts it: "A guy will stand to lose more than he'll stand to win. It's the human factor. A man will walk up to a table with a hundred dollars in his pocket. If he wins ten or fifteen, he's happy and he quits. But he can't take it. He's got to come back and get another ten or twenty. If he loses that ten or twenty, he doesn't quit; he stands there until he loses the hundred."

The big gamblers of Las Vegas a decade ago are not around today, but the gross grows higher. The typical tourist expects to pay for his fun with losses of from fifty to five hundred dollars in the two or three days he stays, and he seldom disappoints the management. He can get an honest game and good odds; Nevada casinos do not need to cheat and rarely do. Only once have I spotted a crooked deal—and that was in favor of the customer. A visiting physician had just attended a woman who had stumbled and fallen down a flight of stairs. The house manager, who knew him slightly, was grateful and led the doctor to a twenty-one table. The doctor protested that he didn't enjoy twenty-one; the manager insisted, and introduced him to the dealer. In ten hands, the doctor won more than two hundred dollars. Then he picked up his chips and left the table. With a small smile, he said, "I think that's plenty for a house call."

Bright young businessmen are the casino bosses today, replacing the old-time gamblers who could tell by the shift of a shoulder or an eye whether a dealer or player was honest. "It's like Bobby Darin instead of Al Jolson," I was told by Eddie Fox, who in his dancing days was a member of the Chaney and Fox team. Talking in the Silver Slipper casino in Las Vegas, Fox's eyes darted regularly toward the show he directs, watching the movements of his dancers, comedians, strippers and the waitresses as they moved about between shows. It is the duty of the Las Vegas beauties to "dress the house" by mingling with patrons while off-stage; their sex life, more often than not, is their own business.

Fox has been a show producer in Las Vegas since 1951, during an era in which the last hold-outs of the entertainment world—Danny Kaye, Jack Benny, Noel Coward—succumbed to the lure of big Las Vegas salaries. ("I heard Herbert Hoover was doing a week in Vegas," said Joey Bishop. "I didn't know he had a hit record.") Fox has competed against the big-salaried hotel performers by giving his customers earthy burlesque that goes on until dawn. Nudity has been employed to pique tourist interest in a town where audiences have become overstimulated and blasé. The most flamboyant shows and the greatest names in show business must be juggled constantly to hold audiences. An integral part of entertainment once was the capacity of the audience to be amazed; in Las Vegas, audiences are amazed by nothing except a tourist who goes home with his winnings. An audience roared with laughter one night in Las Vegas when a flat-chested girl acrobat broke a shoulder strap and rushed in embarassment to the wings; the chorus girls, without a bra among them, had just left the stage. The most insidious influence of Las Vegas is its destruction of wonder: the wonder of sex, the wonder of chance, and the wonder of oneself. Everything is settled fast in Las Vegas.

Like the lava outcroppings of its desert, Nevada has become a molten overflow of the American passion for excess. It is a long way from Plymouth Rock. Some kind of a full circle was traced when the National Council of Catholic Women met in convention at Las Vegas, four thousand strong, just at the time that Las Vegas chorines were stripping to the waist and below for the first time. To many Nevadans, it was the vindication of a fond premise that Las Vegas is simply the finest town in the nation for a good time. But it was also testimony to the gradual but methodical erosion of our mores and moral standards. Nowhere else, and at no other time in our history, have the conventional temptations of man been packaged so glibly and been so widely accepted as in Las Vegas.

The efforts of investigators from Kefauver to Kennedy to show ties between Las Vegas and the criminal underworld are almost irrelevant. What does say something about the American character is that the Las Vegas package—glamorized gambling, glossy prostitution, and incomparable cynicism—has been accepted as a tourist standard. Through the shrewdest of promotion, Las Vegas has made the grade. It is not a dirty name; it is, instead, the weekend dream of most Americans. An amazing proportion of them are managing it. They are never again quite the same after Las Vegas: not because of what happens, but because it happens in the open, without sanction but without embarrassment. Las Vegas is remarkable not for what it offers, but for the fact that it is so casually received. Nothing quite so drastic, in its way, exists anywhere else in our country.

Reno casinos are relatively tame; they have neither the tension nor the high stakes. Pretty divorcées make no effort to hide the fact that they are hired as shills at the gambling tables; they openly make penciled notes of their wins and losses for the house. Entertainment is less sophisticated than in Las Vegas. There are fewer nude shows, smaller orchestras, fewer top-name entertainers, and a profusion of girl trios—a species of entertainment which would empty most Las Vegas clubs. In Las Vegas the closest thing to folksiness is The Mint, where each dealer wears an apron imprinted with the name of his native state. At Reno, the Nugget casino displays $50,000 in gold; in Las Vegas, you may peek at a million dollars in silver. Church notices are found on the dressers of Reno hotel rooms, and across the street from the Mapes Hotel and its casino one is reassured to see a Woolworth's and an ordinary bank. On the Las Vegas Strip, on the other hand, the visitor soon is starved for some contact with reality—for sidewalks or shade trees or houses. Once in Las Vegas I found myself ordering a sack of candy from a dime-store clerk. I didn't want the candy and I wasn't conscious of having set out to look for it; I made the purchase because I was so pleased to see a dime store and a candy counter.

One of the two remarkable entrepreneurs of Reno is Harold S. Smith; some credit his father and the Harold's Club he founded in 1937 for casinos gaining the stamp of acceptability from Nevadans. Harold's has a reputation for kindness to losers; traditionally, they don't go home broke. Club records show refunds to losers of more than half a million dollars in 1960, with the state casino tax deducted in advance. In such a hospitable town, it is no surprise to hear the dire prediction that Las Vegas has gone too far, and may kill gambling in Nevada. The other big name in Reno gambling is William Harrah, who opened a casino next to Harold's Club in 1946 and soon pulled ahead of the older casino in volume. Harrah, who went at his business like the former UCLA engineering student which he is (he even retained Stanford Research Institute for a survey on his customer potential) led an influx of casinos to the shores of nearby Lake Tahoe at Stateline, where California and Nevada meet.

Near Reno are the Nevada shores of Lake Tahoe, the cobalt-blue gem of the Sierras. Beside Lake Tahoe are busy new towns like Tahoe Keys and Incline Village. Sparks, once a railroad junction just east of Reno, has burgeoned with subdivisions and shopping centers and doubled its population to eighteen thousand in six years. At its little Chamber of Commerce, Mrs. Wilbur Junk shook her head and smiled when asked why. "We're trying to figure that out," she said.

At Carson City, palmistry salons and casinos have their place on the little main street along with the Nevada Supreme Court and the capitol. In the capitol I looked up Nevada marriage and divorce statistics and found that marriage is far more profitable to Nevada than divorce. The state is far ahead of any other in the rate both of marriage (two hundred and fifteen per thousand population) and divorce (thirty-four per thousand population). The easy marriage laws of Nevada have meant more to neighboring Californians than its six-week residence law for divorce; marriage, after all, appears to be more fun and even quicker.

The road up Gold Hill from Carson City is steep and winding. At its peak is Virginia City, at the site of the Comstock Lode. The town has become a real-life, boardwalk amusement park, and from the windows of the Old Comstock Saloon, the Crystal Bar, the Red Garter, the Silver King, and the Mark Twain Saloon, the symbols of Carte Blanche, Diners' Club and American Express reassure today's tourist. At the Sharon House, the walls are lined with paintings of Julia Bulette, but in the rear, installed in a place of more contemporary honor, are photographs and scoring records of the Virginia City High School basketball team, state champions for three successive years.

It is brutally plain in Virginia City, as all over Nevada, that mining is in distress. The ore is running out or has become too low-grade for profitable mining; there are easier ways to find it today. Mining towns like Pioche, north of Las Vegas near the Utah border, are becoming ghost towns. The winds of Nevada, which push searing sand ahead of them in summer or bring winter blizzards, eat away at tottering walls and abandoned smelters in remote sites seldom sought out by the tourist: Hamilton, Rhyolite, Leadville, Midas, Rabbithole—all deserted. In 1940, Nevada produced more than five million ounces of silver. By 1959, the figure had dropped to seven hundred and eighty-six thousand. Its gold output had dropped from three hundred and eighty thousand ounces to one hundred and twenty-four thousand. Nevada, famed for gold and silver, produces far less of both than Utah.

Desolate little Tonopah, where the mining boom came early in this century, has another excuse for hanging on now because of the renewed activity at the nearby nuclear test site of the Atomic Energy Commission. A few new cement-block houses appear side by side with relics of mining-camp houses built sixty years ago out of anything at hand: barrels, bottles, or square oil cans filled with dirt. But towns like Tonopah are dying too. The youth are moving away, and the only sign of growth is a new filling station or two to cater to increasing highway traffic.

Of all the mining towns, Virginia City does best today by mining the tourist. It is a sorry fix for a town which poured forth more than half a billion dollars worth of gold and silver in three decades to help build San Francisco, to finance the Mackay Cable Company, to contribute to the Union cause in the Civil War and propel Nevada to statehood, and to enrich families who still live nobly from its wealth in several parts of the world. Many Virginia City buildings have burned or been razed, but a trust fund has been set up hopefully for the restoration of those remaining. A county zoning ordinance proscribes conformity to 1870 architectural style for any new buildings erected in town by any of the five hundred residents there now— or any who might still come to stay.

It does not seem likely that many will. Like a once-hot mama, Virginia City has lost the treasure that men pursued—and yet she goes on offering to dance. Across the wasteland to the south, a new hot mama dances all night, and she is pursued. Perhaps the real trouble between Reno and Las Vegas is that Reno is forever linked with the grandiose past of Virginia City. The new girl down south shows no sign even that she remembers the fading old *grande dame* of the north.

17

NEW MEXICO

A Double Life

Western television serials would be even more awkward if the name first given to the capital of New Mexico in 1609 had stuck. It was called *La Villa Real de la Santa Fé de San Francisco de Assisi*, which translates as The Royal City of the Holy Faith of Saint Francis of Assisi. The part that stuck was Holy Faith. With that name, Santa Fe made good, and the town became the Western terminus of the Santa Fe Trail.

New Mexico was settled from the south—not, like much of the rest of the West, from the east. New Mexico, for almost three centuries before statehood, looked toward Mexico City and, in turn, toward Spain. Cast in this contrasting mold, New Mexico has never surrendered many of its differences from the surrounding West.

Spanish adventurers began filtering into New Mexico with the rumors of 1539 that the Seven Cities of Cíbola teemed with treasure. All that Francisco Vásquez Coronado found were Indian villages, and all they teemed with when Coronado arrived were Indians. The Spaniard didn't learn; he pursued another bum tip in 1541 after a Cicuye Indian called the Turk told him of vast treasures to the east. Coronado marched into west Texas and into Kansas without finding treasures; he never thought to drill for oil.

Coronado and his army left in disgust. Two Franciscan friars stayed behind; they meant to be missionaries, but both were murdered within a year. Coronado's report on the territory to the Spanish viceroy was not precisely glowing, and the Indians were left alone for forty years, until three more Franciscans bravely marched up from Mexico. They too were killed. All this was an irresistible challenge to the Spanish, and so in 1590–91 a colonizing expedition led by Gaspar Castaño de Sosa moved up the Pecos River with one hundred and seventy persons. For his troubles, Castaño was returned in chains to Mexico City by his own people, who ruled that he had made an unauthorized entry into this formidable new land.

Castaño's chains did not frighten two Spaniards named Humaña and Bonilla, and so they made an unauthorized entry three years later. This one had a different plot: Humaña murdered Bonilla, and Indians killed Humaña.

The hero of the piece is Don Juan de Oñate, who spent his own mining fortune in colonizing New Mexico in 1958–99. He went broke. For his troubles, he was fined and banished by the Spaniards on grounds he had mistreated the Indians, the friars, and his own viceroy.

In 1609, Don Pedro de Peralta, who knew where he stood with the viceroy, founded Santa Fe and became governor of the colony. In 1610, across the plaza from where a Harvey Hotel now stands, he built El Palacio Real, which remained a seat of government under five varying flags until 1910; in 1960, it appeared on a 1¼-cent stamp as the oldest public building in the United States. Santa Fe was settled before Boston or New York, but to the delight of those who lived there, it didn't catch on in the same way.

The Spaniards gave up the hope of treasure in New Mexico; its colonization became largely an exercise in missionary zeal. In 1640, forty Pueblo Indians who refused to be converted were hanged. In 1680, the Indians revolted; the Spaniards fought their way out of a trap at Santa Fe and retreated southward to El Paso. The Pueblos promptly annulled their Christian marriages, tore down the churches, and were especially solicitous of baptized Indians: they washed them with soapweed in the Santa Fe River to cleanse them of their stain.

This period of religious freedom for the Indian existed only until 1695, when De Vargas led a Spanish army which recaptured New Mexico. The Franciscan missions were restored. (Ten of the original thirteen can be seen within a few hours' drive of Santa Fe and Albuquerque). One of them was the largest in the Southwest, the Acoma Mission on a sandstone plateau rising three hundred and fifty-seven feet above the plains; every grain of sand and drop of water that went into it was carried up the precipitous cliffs during a forty-year construction marathon.

Albuquerque was founded in 1706, and named for the contemporary viceroy of New Spain. By 1790, the total population in New Mexico, including Indians, was only 30,953. Two years later, Pedro Vial blazed the Santa Fe Trail from Santa Fe to Independence, Missouri. In 1800, the Santa Rita copper mine near Silver City, the first important mine of the region, was discovered. The land went from Spain to Mexico in 1821. But the influence of the south, after three centuries, was diminishing. Soon settlers' wagons were crossing the plains from the East.

Santa Fe was occupied peacefully by American forces in 1846. For decades, New Mexico fought for statehood, but it was impeded by Indian massacres, floods, small cattle wars, disputes over borders, and a whimsical laxity on the part of its officialdom. This reached a nadir in the reputed sale of the Santa Fe Spanish Archives as wastepaper by a territorial governor in 1870.

But statehood came finally in 1912, when the population of New Mexico had risen past one-third of a million, and New Mexico was on the threshold of its discovery as a place of tourist joys and of balm to the tubercular. And a pair of New Mexican individualists known as Billy the Kid and Geronimo went on to their rewards, although not in time to save television.

◇◇◇

The United States Supreme Court concluded one of its lengthiest cases in 1960 by ruling on a border dispute which had existed between Colorado and New Mexico since 1919. Yet four decades of confusion over an indefinite border has been a relatively minor aspect of the identification problem endured by New Mexico.

The New Yorker once published a map of the United States as it is envisaged by New Yorkers. New Mexico just wasn't on it. New Mexicans in the East, trying to telephone home, contend with long-distance operators who want to route their calls through Mexico City. Other Americans compliment them on their good English.

They are not even safe from confusion by other Westerners; a New Mexico governor recently received a letter from a California gunsmith who wrote that he had made weapons for kings and emperors, and would be honored to make a pair of pistols for the President of New Mexico. The New Mexico tourist division receives inquiries about drinking water, passports, currency exchange, and language barriers.

Yet New Mexico observed its fiftieth anniversary of statehood in 1962. It is the home of about one million Americans who are uniquely and simultaneously involved both with past and future.

Santa Fe is the oldest capital in the United States. Its Governors' Palace was built in 1610, ten years before the Mayflower set out from England. From within its adobe walls have ruled five governments: Spanish, Pueblo Indian, Mexican, Confederate, and United States.

But today the era of atom and missile has been superimposed indelibly on the state. The impact of a nuclear economy on any state is great; in New Mexico, a sparsely settled state, it has been so overwhelming that New Mexicans have grown schizoid on the subject. Their attitude is: "It is another world from New Mexico; if it is to exist here, let it. But it is not part of our life." At Los Alamos, a white-collar employee may happen to be the corn priest for an Indian pueblo. He is granted four days off the job to preside over the corn dance; friends from among the scientists at the nuclear laboratory turn up to watch the dance. Indian women from the San Ildefonso Pueblo are baby-sitters for the children of Los Alamos scientists. Physicist and native alike are apt to rush off together at any hour on a field trip to Indian pueblos, through Navajo country, into Mexico, or to an abandoned mining town. The cultural interchange is intriguing, but it is on a human basis, not a philosophical one. Oliver La Farge, the writer, who lives in Santa Fe, compares the nuclear establishments of the state to the old International Zone of Shanghai: "They aren't a part of New Mexico even though they give a lot of employment to New Mexicans. They will never become part of the state."

Besides employment, these same nuclear establishments have brought a host of literate and cultured families into New Mexico. Whether Los Alamos and White Sands become part of the state or not (and it is likely they will, in every way), the people who have come to New Mexico because of Los Alamos and White Sands are certainly already a part of New Mexico. Inevitably they are gripped by the humor, charm, beauty and traditions of the people and the country of the Rio Grande Valley—the central strip of the state running north from Albuquerque past Santa Fe to Taos.

The average distance between the Jémez Mountains along the

west to the Sangre de Cristo range of the Rocky Mountains, at the east of this valley, is about forty miles. It is about a hundred and sixty miles from Albuquerque to the high mountain-pass country that begins north of Taos. It is virtually impossible to remain immune to the magnetism of this valley and its diverse people. The Rio Grande itself is not much to see; there is very little in it. Its waters are drawn off in irrigation ditches for most of its length, with the result that the river is at wading depth most of the year. Eight inches of rainfall annually is all that is expected along much of its course through New Mexico. But so far its underground storage appears endless. No one has characterized the Rio Grande better than Will Rogers, who was shocked when Clyde Tingley, a former New Mexico governor, told him of a plan to use its water for a bathing beach at Albuquerque.

"You can't do it, Clyde," Will said. "Why, you ought to be out there right now, irrigatin' that river to keep it from blowin' away!"

All of the Rio Grande Valley in New Mexico is high and dry, and it becomes scenically more inviting as one moves northward. That such a valley as this, filled at every turn with history, wearing the enduring marks of Indian, Spanish and Anglo (the New Mexican term for non-Spanish) cultures all at once, should be living a double life with the atom and the missile is one of the great incongruities of the West. This valley has the openness, the ruggedness and the restless individuality that characterize most of the West, but it also has a third dimension, a depth in time. Just as all the geologic layers stand exposed in the walls of Grand Canyon, here in this magnificently picturesque valley all the anthropological layers are exposed. The tiny Pueblo of Sandia has been occupied for more than thirty thousand years; the Spanish explorer Coronado made it his headquarters in 1540–41. Archeologists trace other pueblos as far back as 500 A.D. Eighteen distinct Indian pueblos of New Mexico, looking like toy towns, are inhabited today.

The finger of time has moved through this valley, leaving traces of the ancient Indian, abundant evidence of later Indian cultures, the colonial Spanish and modern Spanish-American culture, and remnants of the American frontier era. Filling-station civilization has not yet threatened to bury any of them. Instead, recent years have brought artists, writers and scientists who have fallen under the spell of this third dimension. The sense of timelessness overwhelms; it is so obviously bigger than the invasion of any single wave of culture that it is a cohesive force. This is not a country which lures the type of in-migrant eager to superimpose Eastern or Midwest patterns as in the sunshine of Arizona or Southern California. The New Mexico in-migrant does not think for a moment that he will change the land; there is too much evidence all around him that others have tried for thousands of years, without effect. But people have been coming to New Mexico at a great rate. Albuquerque more than doubled in population between 1950 and 1960, moving from 96,815 to 198,856 people. It is the only city of the state; next come Roswell, Las Cruces, and Santa Fe, all with under forty thousand people. New Mexico had fewer than seven hundred thousand people in 1950; by 1962, it stood at about one million. There is very little to explain growth here except the power of the atom—and the charm of the land.

From the desert of White Sands and Alamogordo at the south, to the uranium fields of Jackpile and Grants in the west, to Albuquerque's Sandia base, to the mountains of Los Alamos at the north, the atom and missile have been the catalyst of New Mexico growth. Los Alamos is a company town of thirteen thousand people on a wooded plateau in the Jémez Mountains. It is the prime laboratory of nuclear-weapon research and, more recently, of peaceful nuclear research. At White Sands, sixty miles from Trinity, where the first atomic bomb was detonated in 1945, rocket and missile testing goes on at a proving ground. Of United States uranium reserves, sixty-five percent are in New Mexico—a fact not known when the atomic history of New Mexico began.

But the location of the vast Sandia base at Albuquerque is directly related to the prior installations. From here, the Atomic Energy Commission's operations office oversees the research and development, the testing, manufacture, and storage of United States atomic weapons everywhere. Sandia is the meeting place of manufacturers, of the AEC, and of the users—the military. The laboratory has about seven thousand employees, the largest payroll in New Mexico. Los Alamos develops the nuclear explosive parts; Sandia does the design engineering, development work, and prototype production. In the missile field, this base works on the entire warhead except the nuclear component; the latter is designed in Los Alamos but not physically produced there.

There are immense atomic support agencies in Albuquerque. One of them is Kirtland Air Force Base, administrated under the Air Research and Development Command to match weapons to aircraft or missiles. It is the Air Force special weapons' center. Also at Kirtland is a naval aviation facility with the same mission. At Sandia and Kirtland are gathered an impressive proportion of the military's scientific brainpower; it has been estimated that one-third of all Air Force Ph.D's are at Albuquerque. High-altitude medical research is also centered at the distinguished civilian Lovelace Clinic in Albuquerque, where American astronauts received training. One of several storage sites in the nation for nuclear material is located in the mountains east of Albuquerque.

The schizophrenic aspects of this nuclear invasion are inescapable. Traditions of the past and the miracles of tomorrow are not blended; they merely exist side by side. An AEC executive told me: "When my wife and I meet Albuquerque people, I always become aware that very few people know what the AEC is doing here— or even that we're here." From the earliest days of super-secrecy at Los Alamos, New Mexicans were trained to look the other way. Their lack of awareness of the monster in their midst is understandable and, so far as the AEC is concerned, entirely satisfactory. The history of New Mexico has been one of integrating the newcomer. Natives (Spanish-Americans), Anglos (those of non-Spanish heritage), and Indians are more ready to accept the individuals of this new world than they are its implications.

The use of the terms *native* and *Anglo* is unique in New Mexico. The Spaniards, who arrived before the Anglos, earned their title as natives. In the mountains of northern New Mexico and in Santa Fe there still are as many natives as Anglos. They are distinctly Spanish, not Mexican, in appearance and manner and tradition.

In all of New Mexico except the eastern plains country adjacent to Texas and considerably influenced by its social attitudes, there is vastly more respect for the Spanish-American culture than in other parts of the West. But *tejanos* (originally the Spanish word for Texan, but now corrupted to mean any prejudiced person) are increasing. Opposition to the Texas influence led to passage of anti-discrimination laws recently in Albuquerque. The Spanish culture is not considered to be merely a part of the romantic history of the region, as in Southern California, but it is a part of contemporary New Mexico life.

New Mexico is so bilingual that until recently ballots were printed in both English and Spanish. Political tickets often are balanced between native and Anglo. Natives like the late Senator Dennis Chavez blend the Latin temperament with politics. What is regarded elsewhere as political corruption still exists as a kind of sport in this state. Where there are prominent families like Montoya, Espinosa, Apodaca, Valdez, Armijo, Aragon, Chavez, and Archuleta, the native vote controls part of northern New Mexico. Traditionally votes are delivered at the direction of the *patron*, the landowner.

There has been a great deal of cash on the line in past New Mexico politics. Will Harrison, the astute New Mexico political columnist, tells of the night when the Associated Press, in a burst of good intentions, set up special election wires in an attempt to smoke out results from native precincts in the mountainous north.

"How many votes you got up there?" inquired an AP reporter as the night wore on.

Back came a native voice: "How many you need?"

New Mexico politics still are crude. The thievery of some past governors has been an open joke. Periodically the voters send back Edwin Mechem, a competent Republican attorney and former FBI agent, for an interval of relatively sound administration. Mechem is one governor who does not sweep state offices entirely clean of opposition party employees during his tenure. He concluded his fourth term in 1962; no other New Mexico governor has served a third term. Senator Clinton Anderson, one of the most literate of senators, has been a considerable asset to New Mexico; even his mortal enemy Lewis Strauss, the former chairman of the Atomic Energy Commission, whose appointment to the Department of Commerce Anderson almost single-handedly defeated in the Senate, has spoken of him with respect.

When Dennis Chavez defeated Patrick J. Hurley in a Senate race in 1952 by what was announced as a margin of about five thousand votes, Hurley contested the election. Before the fun was over, a United States Senate committee had probed and condemned New Mexico election procedures. Registration books had turned up in unexpected crannies, some with torn, burned, and water-smeared pages, and ballots had been burned. One ballot box, its keys locked inside, was opened in front of a bevy of witnesses; inside, observers found only the keys and a *ristra*, the string of red chili peppers used so widely in New Mexico both as food and decoration.

The principal lobbying forces in the Capitol at Santa Fe are conservative in practice but Democratic by affiliation, an anomaly found frequently in the West. A lot of the lobbying is for jobs. For years, a convenient formula around the capitol allotted patronage in the form of janitorial and clerical jobs to the natives, with a smattering of better jobs going to the native elite. But native patronage has declined in the onrush of Anglo in-migration.

One of the newcomers of another era, who came to Santa Fe in 1932 with a mild case of tuberculosis and was soon cured, is one of the most admired figures of the Los Alamos scientific family. Dorothy McKibbin, a gentle and gracious woman, was one of the first employees of Los Alamos. Today, as in 1943, her office is not at Los Alamos but in the back of an inconspicuous arcade near the historic Plaza of Santa Fe.

"Maybe the reason they haven't fired me," she says, with a disarming smile, "is because I remember so many things they didn't have time to write down."

At the start of World War II, Mrs. McKibbin was working in a native-and-Indian trading post that soon went out of business. Suddenly she was offered a secretarial job.

"I was given twenty-four hours to decide," she recalled. "I couldn't find out one darn thing about the job. I decided to take it. I met a man representing himself as a Mr. Bradley; he was Dr. Oppenheimer. I was made secretary to the housing manager and told to ask no questions. It was March, 1943. In May, the rest of the offices around the patio moved on to The Hill (Los Alamos); Army engineers had finished their building. I was left here in Santa Fe with an assistant. There were sixty or seventy people a day coming in the office, and usually more than a hundred calls. The sign on the patio outside identified us as U. S. Engineers. Everything was so secret that all our office notes were destroyed at five P.M. We were kind of on the front line, exposed to enemy agents, and everyone was suspicious. G-2 was active. The security story of Los Alamos is almost as intriguing as getting the bomb made. Intelligence agents were always worried about somebody up on The Hill. They were in the bus station, on trains, in drugstores, everywhere around Albuquerque and Santa Fe."

Mrs. McKibbin recalls that Klaus Fuchs, the Russian spy who worked at Los Alamos and admitted passing on atomic secrets to Soviet agents in New York, Los Alamos, and London, baby-sat "for the wives on The Hill during camping trips, and went on camping trips with other families."

There is less of a problem these days for G-2. Russian scientists have visited Los Alamos, and subdividers have moved in. Scientists are free for the first time to escape bleak governmental rental housing and to build the houses of their wives' dreams. Cape Cod saltboxes stand beside California ranch houses, Territorial adobe next to Georgian, all facing across the valley toward the imperturbable Sangre de Cristo mountains. Bingo is played each Friday night at the American Legion Hall. There is a Little League, horseback riding, a rodeo and county fair in summer, Veterans of Foreign Wars, Elks, Kiwanis, and Lions. Good signals come in over three television channels at Los Alamos. Despite a steady construction program which has boosted the investment in Los Alamos past the two-hundred-and-seventy-five-million-dollar figure, Los Alamos wears a placid, unexciting demeanor.

It is more pleasant for scientists "now that everything seems to have been declassified," in the words of Dr. Thomas Milton Putnam, Jr., a soft-spoken, thirty-nine-year-old researcher who is at work on fundamental plasma physics. "We can write notes, which wasn't possible before. We have visitors and free communications; we can publish. In the period before the Geneva conference in 1958, everything was born classified."

Putnam has been at Los Alamos for ten years, six of them in Project Sherwood, which is working toward controlled thermonuclear reaction. He came to Los Alamos from Berkeley, where his father was a professor of mathematics at the University of California. At Los Alamos, operated by the University of California, Putnam likes the "academic atmosphere," and his family is able to ski and fish. Schools are good, although there is a rapid turnover in teachers; Los Alamos has a disproportionate number of bachelors, and a pretty school teacher can be as certain of marriage in Los Alamos as was the Harvey Girl who headed west in the last century.

Night lights burning in the Los Alamos laboratories have been a symbol of the continuing enthusiasm there, even during the period of the nuclear test ban. Enthusiasm shows in the animation of technical conversation around cafeteria tables, and in the easy humor and interchanges among research people. In the basement of a laboratory used by Project Sherwood scientists are two thousand tall capacitors, used to store electric charges; this collection of capacitors is referred to as Sherwood Forest. Los Alamos' most exclusive club is made up of twenty present and former Los Alamos employees, now scattered over the globe, who were exposed to "greater than safe" doses of plutonium radiation. Each two years they submit urine specimens. So far, all is well, but the status of their red blood cells is of consuming interest to Dr. Thomas L. Shipman and his laboratory, which is concerned with radiation effects on the human being. Affectionately, he calls his club of twenty the IPPU; *Pu* is the chemical symbol for plutonium.

Dr. Norris E. Bradbury, who succeeded Oppenheimer as director of the Los Alamos laboratory, has on his desk a magazine cartoon showing a shipboard mutiny; the caption reads: "You made your mistake when you put things to a vote." The cartoon is misleading; Bradbury is an ingratiating and politic administrator very much interested in the image of Los Alamos, in housing for his families, and in finding new ways of keeping his men's wives happy.

"I have a profound interest in the morale of people in this community," he explained. "If the wives aren't happy, their husbands can find a job anywhere else within five minutes—and will. The responsibility for the community here is in the hands of the Atomic Energy

Commission, but the *way* people live here becomes of great interest both to me and to the AEC."

Despite dissatisfaction with housing conditions—now being alleviated by private construction—the turnover in the Los Alamos scientific population has been low. Dr. Bradbury attributes it not merely to dedication, but to the unique facilities which Los Alamos offers research people which are unavailable elsewhere in the nation. One problem he has faced in recruitment is the mistaken motion that this part of New Mexico is desert country like Alamogordo, far to the south.

The same homing instinct applies in remote Los Alamos as it does throughout the West. "We've discovered many people who were here during World War II when things were pretty tough, then moved on, and now just can't wait to get back here to retire. They couldn't wait to leave the place, but as they look back over the years, they sense that this was the life."

"If Los Alamos should ever become a ghost town," observed Frank C. Di Luzio of the Atomic Energy Commission, "it would be one of the prettiest and best built ghost towns in the history of civilization—but I don't think it's going to happen."

All told, one-sixth of the AEC's total expenditures are in New Mexico. In related nuclear facilities, three hundred and seventy-six million dollars had been invested in Los Alamos and Albuquerque by 1960. In the latter alone, the AEC and its related contractual and military agencies employed about twenty-four thousand people directly in 1960; if this number is multiplied by a factor of 1.5 to arrive at the number of people in business and services supported by such a force, a massive majority of the Albuquerque work force is accounted for. Albuquerque officials claim that their dependence on the military and the atom has dropped below a fifty-percent-employment factor, but their attitude is optimistic. Albuquerque is an atom city.

It is also a gangling shoestring city with its pueblo-style homes sunny and serene outside the gates of Sandia. The setting here is for those who like their scenery tough and hard. Harsh, bony mountains and tawny mesas flank Albuquerque on east and west, and five extinct volcanic cones loom to the northwest. Albuquerque itself is almost a mile high, a fact which in decades past brought tuberculars thronging to its sanitariums. Tuberculosis was controlled, and the economy shifted from "lungers" to the atom. The city's fears now are that government installations may close or cut back. There does not seem to be much chance of it; this is the heart of the United States's nuclear-weapons research and development. Light industry has been coming into Albuquerque lately, but it is restricted by the sparseness of the population in its market area. Albuquerque seeks closer ties with Phoenix and Tucson to its west and with El Paso, in the panhandle of Texas, to its south; four-city conferences have been held annually for the past three years to seek ways to advance tourist business, airline service, industrial development, and to attempt to influence Congressional legislation.

In no comparable city of the West does one hear as much general criticism of the city's newspapers. Though there is token opposition between the Scripps Howard afternoon paper and the independently owned morning *Journal*, both are accused widely of negativism. But one newspaper shrine is here: a modest house at 900 Girard Southeast, the home of Ernie Pyle and now a memorial library. "We like it," Pyle once wrote, "because our front yard stretches as far as you can see, and because old Mt. Taylor, sixty-five miles away, is like a framed picture in our front window. We have seen sunrises so violently beautiful they were almost frightening, and I'm only sorry I can't capture the sunsets and the thunderstorms and the first snows on the Sandias, and take them east and flaunt them in people's faces." If Pyle were alive today, he would be seeking another home farther out—his mesa is covered with houses that block the view.

There is plenty of room left in New Mexico, however. From the gas-rich Four Corners country at the northwest corner of the state, to the even richer oil fields of the southeast, around Hobbs, and the cattle ranches of the south and east, New Mexico still has space. One of Pyle's eulogies of the Rio Grande Valley was quoted in a national land-promotion scheme in 1961 to sell "one full acre of sunny enchantment in booming New Mexico" in the south-central desert of New Mexico, at $199 an acre.

Socorro, seventy miles south of Albuquerque, still calls itself the Free State of Socorro in New Mexico; it is part of an old Spanish land grant and maintains that it never has technically become part of the United States.

On the Mexican border, west of El Paso, the village of Columbus is making a modest comeback. There were three thousand people here before bandits claiming to be part of Pancho Villa's forces raided and burned Columbus in 1916; the town's population dwindled quickly to three hundred, where it stood early in 1960 when Columbus made a bid for elderly residents living on fixed incomes of two hundred to three hundred dollars a month. There is a Pancho Villa Saloon, a Pancho Villa Museum and a Pancho Villa State Park at Columbus, but history does not note whether Villa led the raid— or even knew of it.

Growth at Alamogordo is more realistic. Before the Manhattan Project was set up sixty miles away at Trinity in World War II, Alamogordo had a population of about four thousand. By 1950, it had grown to 6,783, but by 1960 it had 21,622 residents, a boom caused by Air Force research and development programs at Holloman Air Force Base.

The New Mexico town which has resisted growth most doggedly is the center of the state's charm. Santa Fe lies sixty-two miles north of Albuquerque in the valley of the Rio Grande. Northward, the valley floor climbs, and so does the rainfall. The mountains grow greener and more appealing. Santa Fe, with 34,175 people in 1960, is almost seven thousand feet high. It has survived two decades since the establishment of the nearby Los Alamos laboratory without any population bulges beyond the national average. Santa Fe may be the most cosmopolitan town in the nation. Here live the writers Oliver La Farge, Witter Bynner, Ruth Alexander, and Winfield Scott. Part of the literary crowd is Paul Horgan, who lives at Roswell, and Frank Waters of Taos. There are bookish traditions; Peggy Pond Church, Edna St. Vincent Millay and Willa Cather wrote here. For a time, D. H. Lawrence was up the valley at Taos. The Santa Fe architect John Gaw Meem is widely known. Designer Alexander Girard is based here, and Theodore Van Soelen and Randall Davey, both Santa Fe residents, have national reputations as painters. Peter Hurd is on a ranch not far away. The late John Sloan led a school of Santa Fe painters, and narrow, unpaved Canyon Road remains the site of artists' studios where the paintings are no better or worse and the conversation at showings no more or less pretentions than in Greenwich Village or in North Beach or any other mecca for artists.

Santa Fe's museums are the finest in the Southwest. Its opera, in one of the most appealing outdoor amphitheaters ever built, lures men of the caliber of Stravinsky, who has been associated with the company since it was founded in 1957 under the prodding of John Crosby, a young New York-born conductor who came to New Mexico as a student in 1940.

Although local bankers note with asperity that the funds of some of the wealthier Santa Fe residents remain in Cleveland, Chicago, and New York, considerable wealth from the Midwest and East has come to Santa Fe. It is largely the character of its inmigrants that has held Santa Fe against the onrush of modernity which might have destroyed the charm of its heritage. Its high adobe walls conceal delightful gardens in the tradition of Spain and Mexico. Its streets are narrow and winding, half of them still unpaved; when I was last there, no street went straight through town in any direction.

Although there is a central plaza, and this is a town of fewer than forty thousand, the stranger is likely to get lost. But no one objects, not even the stranger. When he was mayor, Leo Murphy once joked to his city council, "Where you made your mistake was when you let cars in." A previous mayor met the plea of a Canyon Road resident for street repairs with the sturdy rejoinder, "It's just plumb wore out. There's nothing we can do about it." Despite a great burst of anti-paving sentiment, a Santa Fe street named El Camino del Monte Sol was paved in 1956; the curb, however, was realigned after a sculptor with a pickaxe had hacked out the section in front of his house often enough to make his point.

In Santa Fe civic affairs, there is little agreement; as expected in a town of individualists, everyone has his pet project. City council sessions are broadcast, primarily for the reassurance of a potent lobby of citizens who resist change. Mayor Murphy tried for four years before pushing through a city sales tax to produce revenue increase to up police protection in Santa Fe when vandalism by juvenile gangs became a pressing problem. When I was in Santa Fe four of the eight city councilmen were natives; the police magistrate was named Rumaldo E. Chavez. But it is among the natives of Santa Fe that startling poverty exists, though, in the Latin tradition, the city does not worry much about such matters. At Christmas, some among the rich, like the poor, hang red chili peppers on their doors, and light candles in paper sacks of sand; these are *farolitos*, and long lines of them on plazas and in front yards and patios bear mute testimony to the bond between native and Anglo.

Those who come to Santa Fe are drawn in part by the racial and cultural diversity of the community. Without being patronizing, the newcomers try to stress the native and Indian heritage of the area. Half a century ago, in a burst of enthusiasm for modernity, the pueblo buildings of Santa Fe were being submerged by clapboard and shingle. It was the leadership of a corps of artists and writers recently arrived in Santa Fe that produced a calculated return to traditional pueblo architecture. Its houses are distinguished by their adobe construction, rounded corners, and flat roofs over stripped logs called *vigas*. Floors are usually brick or tile. The somewhat more stately Territorial style is equally distinctive. Of this school, the State Capitol at Santa Fe, with its simplicity of line, is one of the most beautiful capitols in America.

There is no unlikelier place in the West for a subdivider to settle than Santa Fe. But one who has succeeded, in a restrained fashion, is Allen Stamm; he has built about thirteen hundred homes at Santa Fe since World War II, and has been personally responsible

Arizona–New Mexico

for accommodating a goodly share of its population growth. At first
Stamm was urged to leave Santa Fe alone. Cautiously he polled
service clubs and civic groups about their hopes for the Santa Fe
future and came up with the answer that if growth was inevitable,
at least it should be planned and controlled. He agreed to keep his
tracts away from older sections of the town, and to build to the south
and west. Even there, he has politely adhered to pueblo and Territorial styles, tossing in a few of what he calls "bastard California"
ranch style. Some Santa Feans seemed unhappy about a shopping
center that Stamm was planning in 1962, but their attention has
been largely diverted to the more distressing challenge of plans for a
crosstown freeway as part of the interstate highway system.

Growth can be a majestic thing, but one can grow only sad at
the prospect of the changes which inevitably will be forced on Santa
Fe. There is no town in the West which more immediately whets the
inquiring mind, soothes the jaded eye, or solaces the downhearted.

One man whose love for Santa Fe is obvious and overwhelming
is James Webb Young. In the advertising world, he already is a
legend. As senior vice president of J. Walter Thompson Company
in New York in 1928, Young awoke one morning and realized he no
longer felt the same pangs about whether his client sold more cereal
than its competitor. Today he commutes between Santa Fe and New
York as senior consultant to the firm he left soon after that fateful
morning. Although he is regarded as a senior statesman of the advertising industry, his heart is with his twenty-thousand-bushel apple
orchard in the Jémez Mountains near Santa Fe. When he took the
land over, it was a bleak, abandoned homestead. Applying the
Madison Avenue techniques he helped to formulate, he has become
one of the few successful entrepreneurs of Santa Fe. He markets his
Winesaps as Sparkling Burgundy Apples, and his Golden Delicious
as Champagne Apples. When hail threatened to wipe out his entire
crop one year, he capitalized on catastrophe by advertising that unless
apples had the telltale marks caused by hail, they weren't genuine
Champagnes or Sparkling Burgundies. It worked; he sold his entire crop.

A large, shaggy man with youthful and intense eyes, Young
is of indeterminate age. He speaks deliberately and with great
warmth, wasting no words or gestures. "I came here because I liked
the looks of the place, the people, and the climate. But having spent
all my life working, I couldn't let myself overlook an opportunity
when I thought I saw one. That's how I got into the apple business.
Very probably," he told me, "the first apples in the United States
were grown here in New Mexico by the Spanish padres."

Young was living in Santa Fe when he developed a television workshop for the Ford Foundation, started "Omnibus," and hired Robert Saudek to run it. He usually goes to Europe each year for J. Walter Thompson; he is a member of the Business Council, a trustee of the Committee for Economic Development, the author of several books, and he is now completing an autobiography called, *How to Make a Failure of Retirement.*

Young refused to leave Santa Fe in 1952 despite the entreaties of Paul Hoffman, who wanted him close to Ford Foundation head-quarters, then in Pasadena. "Finally I told Paul, 'I just don't want to leave Santa Fe for the Southern California area. I think it's made up of Iowa farmers who are trying to be South Sea islanders, and they aren't going to make it.'" Young admits that this conversation took place a decade ago. "There's been a lot of pioneering in California since then, in science and industry, and it would seem that adventurous people may be moving into California. But I'm getting old, and I think for myself I'll stay with what James J. Hill said when he first was asked to build a railroad to Los Angeles. He wasn't interested. He said that a man on whom snow never falls isn't worth a damn." As he spoke, he looked outside his window in Santa Fe, and smiled. Snow was falling.

The meeting place in Santa Fe is La Fonda, the most in-gratiating hotel in the Fred Harvey chain. It is a great tiered mound of adobe on San Francisco Street, between the Plaza, which is lined by historic buildings, and the Cathedral of Saint Francis, an impressive successor to a series of churches built on the site since 1622. At dinner one night in La Fonda, as huge snowflakes swirled outside, I sat in front of a big crackling fire and was served distinguished Spanish food by Effie Jenks, a silver-haired Harvey Girl. She had been working the counter in the Alvarado Hotel in Albuquerque, we computed, before I was born. She agreed to let me drive her home so that she could show me pictures of her gold mine at Bland, a ghost town southwest of Santa Fe.

If one can believe the legends of the early West, Harvey Girls married into fame and fortune. Effie said it wasn't so—but she has a gold mine all her own. She was not one of the Harvey Girls hired in Chicago or Kansas City and exported to the West by the Santa Fe; she made it West on her own. After four years of college in Nebraska, Effie said goodbye to her parents at their ranch in South Dakota, and went West to seek her fortune. At Albuquerque, in 1923, she ran out of money and became a Harvey Girl. It took Effie thirteen years to pick a husband, and he was no titled lord or silver baron. Thomas Harry Jenks was a pioneer and a miner, but a picture of his great-

great-grandfather, Sir Rowland Hill, an inventor of the postage stamp, is on many stamps of many lands.

Effie gave up being a Harvey Girl when she married. She had banked her tips through those years and had lived simply. When she married, she set her savings aside for an opportunity which seemed important enough to represent the long hours, tired feet, and loneliness of those thirteen years. It came sooner than she expected. Her husband died in 1941, and after Pearl Harbor Effie donned the Harvey uniform again and waited on the service men who shuttled east and west through Albuquerque. But just before his death she and her husband had been in Bland, and her heart stayed there. Effie began buying up Bland.

Most of the New Mexico mining towns had their heyday in the late nineteenth century. Gold and silver were mined in modest quantity, but then the veins ran out. Today, New Mexico has more uranium reserves than any other state; only a few gold mines still are worked. The mine at Bland was one that closed at the start of World War II and never reopened. In 1893, its population was as high as three thousand and a Denver newspaper had called the town "a new Cripple Creek." Into a sixty-foot-wide canyon at Bland were crowded a hotel, two banks, a newspaper, twenty-one saloons, an opera house and a stock brokerage office. Walls of the canyon were blasted out to make room for a stamp mill and a boarding house. Today fourteen or fifteen buildings still stand, but the only one occupied is the home of an Indian couple from the nearby Cochiti pueblo who serve as Effie's watchmen. Bland has not been vandalized by the curious and by the tourist like many ghost towns. It is inaccessible through most of the winter months, but Effie makes her way there by jeep in almost any weather when she has time off from her tables at La Fonda.

By 1962 Effie owned almost all of Bland. She had sunk her savings into it, and only a few scattered lots were not hers. Her voice quavered as she told me her plan. "It is such beautiful country, and it is the most strategically located ghost town in the state. It seems to me it isn't just for one person, but for the whole world. I hope to form a nonprofit corporation to build a resort at Bland, and allow many different charities to share in the income. I'm not sure just how soon I can do this. I'm waiting for the price of gold to go up—there is quite a little gold left in the mine, and it will help finance the project. But it must be done well or not at all. We mustn't have Bland taken over by hamburger stands and neon."

While she waits, Effie stays busy at what she knows best. She is not only mayor and mistress of Bland; she is still a Harvey Girl.

18

ARIZONA

It Leapfrogged History

One of the good guys of the mission era in the Southwest was an Italian-born Jesuit priest, Eusebio Francisco Kino. He rode like a cowboy and marched like a camel. He was a scholar, and the maps he drew of Arizona were superb. He taught the peaceful Pimas and Papagos, the Indians among whom he worked, new ways to grow crops; he brought them cattle and horses, and he defended them successfully against oppression both by military and secular rulers. It is probably no coincidence that to this day the Pimas and Papagos are among the most Christianized of Southwest Indians. They also are among the poorest.

The Navajos believe their gods sent them the oil and gas and uranium that are beginning to alleviate their poverty. Father Kino's Indians have received no underground riches from their God; they are lucky when they can get jobs picking cotton at seventy-five cents an hour. But sometimes a little money does rub off when tourists come to see the missions that Father Kino laid out, including San Xavier es south of Tucson, the most admired mission in

ather Kino died. In 1776, a year of action on the
Coast, the mud-walled presidio of Tucson was established. The city languished until the traffic of the Gold Rush to
California. Even then not much happened; air conditioning hadn't
been invented, and Tucson was just a place to get through.

A report to Congress about Arizona in 1858 got right to the
point. "The region is altogether valueless. After entering it there is
nothing to do but leave." Even as late as 1932, former United States
Attorney General Harry M. Daugherty was expressing the sentiment
of most of the nation when he derided Arizona as one of the "little
Western boroughs."

A tribe of Indians now known as Hohokams was living on the
site of modern Phoenix and Scottsdale at the time of Christ. They
channeled the waters of the Salt and Gila rivers—mere creeks by
Eastern American standards—into irrigation ditches. They also left
tiny holes in the east and west walls of a tribal building which even
the white man couldn't comprehend for years; then someone discovered that the sun shone through these holes about eight minutes
after sunrise each March 7 and October 7. The holes had been the
Hohokams' planting calendar.

But the Hohokams had disappeared forever by 1500, and no
white man settled in the area of Phoenix until after the Civil War.
Among the first of an endless and exuberant line of Arizona entrepreneurs were Jack Swilling, a Confederate officer who cleaned out
and reinstated the Hohokams' canal system, and Darrell Duppa, an
English remittance man with a feeling for whiskey and the classics,
who turned spellbinder and announced that a new civilization surely
would rise here, phoenix-like, from the ashes of the old. That it did.

On December 29, 1863, in a desolate spot of northeast Arizona
known as Navajo Springs, the territory of Arizona was established
hastily so that the first governor could be paid. John N. Goodwin
was sent from Washington to establish the government, and he had
to take his oath of office on Arizona soil before New Year's Day.
Since he was running late, he swore himself in the moment he was
safely inside the territory. The capital was subsequently moved to
Fort Whipple, to Prescott, to Tucson, back to Prescott, and finally
in 1889 to Phoenix.

Tucson was so angry about losing the capital that the legislature
gave it a university. Gamblers and madames chipped in to help start
the campus. Phoenix was given the state mental hospital, which was
expected to provide more jobs than the university.

At the turn of the century, mining was the biggest thing in Arizona. Wyatt Earp had taken matters in hand briefly at Tombstone, and the mine and railroad owners had done the same in the legislature with more lasting effect.

Soon, merchants came to Arizona. In 1872, Albert Steinfeld, seventeen years old, took a train westward from Denver to San Francisco, then a boat to San Diego, and a stage eastward to Tucson. He went to work for his uncle in a trading post established four years earlier by Aaron and Louis Zeckendorf. Thus started one Arizona empire in the south. In the north, five Babbitt brothers came from Cincinnati in 1886, and four stayed. Three of the brothers married three Verkamp sisters from their home town. Thus began an empire in northern Arizona.

In 1860, Michael and Joe Goldwater had come from California and opened a trading post on the Colorado River. Michael bought out Joe and moved to Prescott. His sons, Baron and Morris, opened a store in Phoenix. Baron's sons, Barry and Bob, took over the operation of the stores, except that Barry got into politics and wasn't around much, and in 1962 the stores were sold.

After twenty years of political shenanigans in Washington and Arizona, statehood came in 1912. The sheriff at Phoenix, a Democrat named Carl Hayden, was elected Congressman. He served until 1927, when he became United States Senator. In 1962, at eighty-four he was dean of the Senate. As chairman of the Senate Appropriations Committee, he was listened to respectfully when he spoke more flatteringly about the value of Arizona than others in Congress had spoken a century earlier.

◇◇◇

Urban Arizona is an improbable veneer of green oases on ocher desert. Clustered around the two major oases, Phoenix and Tucson, are almost a million of the state's 1,302,161 people. Their vitality and optimism have produced a kind of civic indomitability that may yet lead to one of the remarkable chapters of American history.

Arizonans are obvious victors over their awesome environment, a formidable desert state larger than Illinois and Wisconsin combined. At this moment they are the most eager people in the West. They will try anything once, and so far they have seemed able to make anything work.

Until the admission of Alaska and Hawaii to statehood, Arizona was the baby state; the fiftieth anniversary of statehood was celebrated in 1962. It still has the verve and adventuresomeness of pioneer America. Arizona has succeeded in leapfrogging history; the virility of the pioneer has been harnessed here to build dams, office buildings, and shopping centers, missiles and electronic gadgetry, golf courses and resorts, and above all, homes.

These Arizonans of the Sixties snake over the raw mountains by jeep to stake out new towns, or speed by Cadillac or plane between Phoenix and Tucson, between cotton or cattle ranch and city, between damsite or mine and town; these are transposed Americans from the pioneer era, men to match the mountains. They make war not with Indian, but, in the fashion of the era, with banker, broker, and land speculator, with the searing sun and a plummeting water table—yet they make war with the same deadly zest as did the gunfighter.

Around Phoenix especially, in the Salt River Valley, sheltered by mountains with names like Superstition, Squaw Tit, and Camelback, there is an intensity in the air that affects even the stranger. The static electricity of the desert dryness imparts sparks to many handshakes, and one comes to sense even this as a symbol.

With the mass production of air conditioning units in about 1952, Arizona was on its way. (Today, even police cars in Phoenix are air-conditioned.) Between 1950 and 1960, Phoenix jumped from fifty-first to twenty-ninth city in population, going from 106,818 to 439,170. Tucson, always about half the size of Phoenix through this decade, grew even more sharply, from 45,454 to 212,892. Both were increases of more than three hundred percent.

Since much of this population rise was the result of annexation, a more accurate picture comes from metropolitan area statistics. By this measure, Phoenix and Tucson ranked second and third in the nation (after San Jose, California) in rate of growth. Phoenix grew by 96.5 percent, and Tucson by 85.6 percent.

Throughout this decade, every kind of observer has plodded industriously from the Grand Canyon to the Mexican border, inquiring as to how it all has happened. The growth is not, as almost everyone ends up assuming, simply because of the climate; it is far more complex than that.

Phoenix is now somewhat in a golden era like San Francisco of the late nineteenth century. The mood is here; the word is out; this is the place. The city is going somewhere, and it is attracting more than an average share of people who want to go somewhere with it.

Incredibly, although such rapid growth does not tend to be stable, neither Phoenix nor Tucson is in serious trouble. They are not going to dry up and disappear like the Hohokam Indians who dug the first canals in this Valley of the Sun. Water is the obvious and overriding requirement. Besides using the Hohokam's canals, the white man also knew how to coax water out of the federal government; Roosevelt Dam, eighty miles east of Phoenix on the Salt River, was built under the first reclamation act passed by Congress in 1902. Whereas all of the Tucson water supply comes from ground-water reserves, dams on the Salt, the Gila, and the Verde rivers serve the agricultural oasis around Phoenix, and four thousand wells augment the supply.

Except in its east-central mountains, Arizona has an arid look, but wells are delivering four million acre-feet of water from beneath the searing sand each year. Abuse of pumping, mainly by cotton growers, has lowered water levels alarmingly in certain areas, and some farmers and conservationists foresee eventual depletion of underground reserves.

Arizona has fought tenaciously against California for a larger share of the Colorado River, which forms the two states' border. It looks speculatively southward to the Gulf of California, sixty miles below the Arizona-Mexico border, for eventual saline conversion. Mayor Sam Mardian of Phoenix stoutly maintains that enough water is in sight to provide for the two million residents that his planners forecast for Phoenix in the year 2000. An anomaly is helping him: agricultural irrigation requires three times as much water as residential use of the same acreage, and so when subdivisions tear into the fertile citrus groves and farmland around Phoenix, the supremely important factor of water supply becomes no more critical.

With his supply of water and his air conditioners to help him tame the desert and the heat, and jetliners to minimize his remoteness, the contemporary Arizonan has set a fast pace. He has come here not because of the traditions of the state, but to make his own traditions. He has so dazzled the native Arizonan with his strivings that the native has fallen in behind him and both are running pell-mell toward what they presume to be the promised life. The Arizonan lives well: casually, with less self-consciousness and monotony of environment than some of his coastal Southern California neighbors. An otherwise dispassionate treatise on Arizona life, *Arizona, Its People and Resources*, published by the University of Arizona Press, observes: "Arizona is the place that the newly rich Texan comes to learn to live well without ostentation." New millionaires and new factories breed like forced hothouse flowers. Behind them are more candidates, on the heels of the initial successes. So far there seems plenty of room, even though 85.22 percent of Arizona land is owned by the federal or state government. Thus the major landlord of the state becomes a native Mormon son, Stewart Udall, the Arizona Congressman whom President Kennedy appointed Secretary of Interior.

The newcomer to Arizona is seldom prepared for the variety of scenic majesties that await him in Udall's home preserve. The state is not all desert; an unbroken ponderosa pine forest extends through central Arizona into New Mexico. The image of the American West in the minds of most of the world is an image of Arizona. A predominant number of Western movies have been made in Arizona, from Sonoita near the Mexican border in the south (where *Oklahoma!* was filmed) to the red canyons of Oak Creek and Sedona, and on to Monument Valley in the mountainous north. The rangeland of "Gunsmoke" 's Dodge City is neither in Kansas nor in California, but near Sonoita. Movies set in Texas often include scenes which abound in the upraised arms of the giant saguaro cactus; the saguaro abounds in no state but Arizona, in an east-west belt seventy-five miles wide.

Josef Muench, who was working as a gardener in Santa Barbara when his first Arizona photograph was bought and printed by *Arizona Highways* in 1939, has traveled scenic Arizona as much as any man alive; he has been into remote Monument Valley with his cameras more than one hundred and twenty times. Of Arizona, he says, "It is because in Arizona the arresting framework, the very skeleton of the earth, is exposed, that the scenery is so compelling and meaningful. Its 'bone structure' is superb. Seldom does one find here the soft landscape, so covered by the 'flesh' of monotonously green vegetation as to weary the eye. Variety is built into Arizona's boundaries. Mountains poke up to 12,670 feet above sea level in the north. The high tableland, cut by profound canyons, that is Arizona's share of the fascinating Colorado Plateau, drops to a vast desert land only a few feet above sea level near Yuma. A feeling of great breadth and expanse about the land comes not alone from sheer size, but because there is always a rise from which you can view the surrounding area, something new around the next corner, surprises in the folds of the mountains and right at your feet."

At the beginning of World War II, Arizona had twice as many cattle as people. Six military bases were set up during the war in the Phoenix area alone, and as many more in other parts of the state. Several have remained active and important, but despite the military, Arizona was a land of cotton, cattle, and copper until the last decade.

Then came industrialization. It has overshadowed the three C's, even though Arizona remains the first copper-producing state, and, because of long-staple cotton, leads all states in average net farm income ($9,343 in 1959). Half of the state's industry is in the Phoenix area, and a large share of the remainder is in Tucson.

Sudden industrialization brought Arizona a substantial middle class for the first time. This social change has been a catalyst, not a soporific. More than half of the new Arizonans settle in Maricopa County (Phoenix) and another fifteen percent in Pima County (Tucson). Their average age is higher than that of migrants to other parts of the West: the largest bracket is in the forty-to-forty-nine age group. But that is changing; Arizona claims the nation's highest birth rate. Most notable, more than fifty percent of the heads of families of Arizona newcomers are professional, skilled, and managerial workers. In a study made by the Arizona Development Board, the motivations most frequently cited for moving to Arizona were health, climate, transfer, and opportunity. The factor of opportunity is coupled often with each of the others; it is the subtlest but strongest.

The largest number of new Arizonans are coming from California. Texas and Illinois are next, followed by New Mexico, Michigan, Ohio, and New York. The dominant role of California is due to a backwash of migration: the new Arizonan may have gone from Illinois or New York to California first, then pulled back to Arizona. Usually it is because he was not prepared for California's congestion. About twelve hundred families a month were moving into Arizona in 1962.

In Phoenix and Tucson, reliable estimates of home ownership run as high as eighty percent; yet almost all of these homeowners have come recently from somewhere else. They tend to align themselves with the political and social power patterns of their new home in the hope of regaining the status they may have held in their former communities. They are far from detached and disinterested in community affairs, as one might expect newcomers to be; and they act with surprising unity to give their city what it needs. In Phoenix, the newcomers clearly are in charge. In Tucson, they are gaining but not in command; the balance of power is clouded by a large segment of retired people who do not seem to care much and who are indeed in Tucson primarily for the climate. "The new crowd will win out by force of numbers," one eager young Tucson leader explained, "but by then we'll be the old crowd."

The unanimity of direction in Phoenix today is unique among Western cities. This sense of purpose was in the air before the industrial invasion gained momentum. One man who helped it to grow was Ray Wilson, a brusque, witty, old-school city manager who came to Phoenix from Kansas City in 1950, the same year that a new city councilman named Barry Goldwater took office. At that time Phoenix was plagued by prostitution, open gambling, inadequate city services and a vacuum of planning. It had averaged one new city manager every thirteen months since 1914.

Just before his retirement in 1961, Wilson said, "I came in and told the city council that if prostitution and gambling were legal, I knew how to run them and I would, because I had learned how in Sicily in military government. The council decided they weren't legal, and so I ran 'em out."

While Wilson chased out vice, fifty troubled citizens met, formed a charter-government committee and chose a slate of city officials, scrupulously avoiding declared candidates and opportunists. It has happened that way every two years since, and the slate always has won. It does not hew to party lines.

Phoenix went on a rampage of annexation in Wilson's eleven years as manager, increasing its area from 16.4 to 187.4 square miles. More important, the city government gained prestige. Good men became eager to go into civic affairs. When discussing the new climate, Wilson said, "This is a young city and state. We need the vigor of young people to run our affairs. There's nobody old around here but me. Phoenix has changed. When the electronics people and the brains started coming here, the native sons began staying and developing. We used to think we had to have a native son on the city council. Now they're so outnumbered nobody gives a damn. Youth and drive will push this state ahead."

Money helps too, and the willingness to spend it where it is needed. In 1957, Phoenix voters passed a seventy-million-dollar series of bond issues to launch badly needed civic improvements. In 1961, eleven more bond issues totaling one hundred and three million dollars were approved, for new water and sewerage facilities, an expanded airport, streets, parks, playgrounds, libraries, and municipal offices. The tax rate, stable for more than a decade, went unchanged because of the rapidly broadening tax base. The success of the 1961 bond election is traceable in part to a straightforward approach typical of Arizona: a citizens' committee mailed letters to every organization in town asking what Phoenix needed, and what the best way to get it was. The Phoenix Growth Committee, a group of seven hundred and forty-two people, was formed after each group had submitted the names of five interested persons. They were split into study groups and subcommittees, and specialists were assigned to the units. A newsman recalls, "It was something to see all of those people going at it. It was go, go, go!"

The most important member of the cast in this civic renaissance was Walter Bimson, chairman of the board of the powerful Valley National Bank, which itself has been a major factor in the surge of Arizona's economic development. Colorado-born, Bimson came from Chicago's Harris Trust and Savings Bank in 1933 when Valley Bank accounts were in serious decline. Bimson and his brother Carl promptly set about making loans with what competitors regarded as abandon. They opened branches and developed the concept of the bank as a financial department store. In 1962, it had seventy-eight branches in Arizona and averaged a depositor in every Arizona family. It is the largest bank of the West, outside of the coastal states. Walter Bimson sends his bankers out to ring doorbells and even to explain banking to Indians. He gives social teas and luncheons in his branches; his promotion schemes are infinite. To Arizona, his name is as meaningful as that of the late A. P. Giannini in California.

Bimson expects Phoenix to double its population in the current decade. "This is a conservative state politically, but not in its economic approach," he told me. Some of his current interests are the adjustment of freight rates (Detroit to Los Angeles and back by rail is cheaper than one way Detroit to Phoenix), and the development of trade and banking with the west coast of Mexico (Nogales, Arizona, is second to Brownsville, Texas, as the busiest United States portal to Mexico, and farm products are being shipped in increasing quantities from Mexico through Nogales to the West Coast).

It is an over-simplification to say that Bimson's kind of civic leadership has resulted in a businessman's government of Phoenix, for in Phoenix almost everyone seems intent on making money, and a businessman's government is representative of the majority. Union labor is weak in Arizona; it has fewer than fifty thousand members, primarily in mining and building trades. There is very little organized political strength among the minorities, though one-fifth of the state's population is made up of Mexicans, Spanish-Americans, Negroes, and Indians. Phoenicians at all economic levels take pride in their city's reputation for making millionaires. A busboy at the Westward Ho Hotel told me with a gleam in his eye that Del Webb had worked there as a carpenter. (Now Webb has finished a seventeen-story office building in Phoenix as headquarters for his corporation, which is buying and building all over the nation: redeveloping downtown Santa Monica at a cost of sixty million dollars, participating in missile silo construction in Montana and Kansas on a ninety-three-million-dollar contract, and building retirement communities in

Florida, Arizona, and California, and hotel and office buildings in many parts of the West.) A bank teller at the Guaranty Bank recalled that David Murdock, the young man who built the bank building and serves on its board, had gone broke trying to build houses in 1948 when he was newly arrived in Phoenix. Phoenix wealth is too new to be onerous even to the poor. Established tycoons who have settled around Phoenix, such as P. K. Wrigley and Fowler McCormick, flatter the native by their choice of Phoenix for their homes.

In such an atmosphere, relatively free of jealousy and prejudice, it is not surprising to see citizens pulling together toward a common goal of bettering their lives. What Arizona lacks in social consciousness is compensated for just now by abundance. Phoenix is in its golden era because everyone is a pioneer. But some year soon, unless it can resist the American pattern, power factions will begin to divide the city; banking interests or business combines and labor unions will carve out niches of control for more selfish gain; and spontaneity, initiative, and enterprise will begin to fade. There is hope, however, that Phoenix will resist the trend. What must be called the masses of Phoenix are an exceptionally enlightened urban population, acutely aware of the pitfalls which await them. It is for this reason and cities like Phoenix that there is some cause to hope the new West can profit from the miseries of past generations and older cities, and that it will hold tight to its economic and political independence.

This dream is shared by men like Dr. Daniel E. Noble, executive vice president of Motorola, Inc., who oversees three electronics factories in Phoenix. Their payroll of five thousand employees is the largest in Phoenix. Noble's industrial complex also includes two laboratories and two factories in the Chicago area and units at Riverside and Culver City in California, but Phoenix is his home office. Noble set up the first Motorola plant, a small research and development group, in Phoenix in 1948. He remembered Arizona well from 1918, when as a weak-eyed Connecticut schoolboy, he had been advised by his family doctor to get away from studies and build himself up physically. Noble spent a year hunting coyotes and mountain lions in Arizona.

Phoenix watched the first Motorola invasion with concern, fearing it would destroy the resort atmosphere of the city. Noble, whose own office is crowded with Indian artifacts, installed Mayan Indian symbols about the parapet of the first Motorola building for decorative detail, and built a derivation of a Mayan doorway for that first Motorola plant; with a setback and extensive lawn, the factory looked like an institution, not a mill, and Phoenix was happy. Noble's people were happy with Phoenix, too, and engineers and research men were easy to hire.

"The city has an ability to attract people of exceptional scientific training and capability, people of an intellectual level who expect exceptional surroundings," Noble said. "Sure, the climate is important, but Phoenix is a growing city with a freshness about it. There is a clean and active local government. People are here by choice, and they are eager to see others join them. We are moving forward aggressively; we are not following. The intellectually capable individual does not wish to live in a community where the attractions stop with the availability of limitless sunshine. There is a conscious reaching toward a higher level of maturity. There is personal identification all the way from city and state governmental problems into community projects, educational programs, and the recreational life of the city.

"This element of personal identification may fade with increasing population, but it will probably hold on longer in Phoenix than in most other cities because here politics is not 'the other fellow's business'; the whole community welfare is everybody's business. Phoenix represents a rather special group of people. The forces which cause them to select this city as the place to live are probably substantially different from those which identify the population in Philadelphia or Chicago. There is a unique effort of a population to seek out their specific requirements. The people are here because they choose to be here, and not because of serendipity or any other chance-ruled influences."

From wherever one enters Phoenix, the sleek blue Guaranty Bank Building looms highest—which is the way David H. Murdock intended it to be. Twenty stories high, it has been the tallest building between El Paso and Los Angeles, a distance of seven hundred and ninety miles. At thirty-seven, Murdock, its builder, has made his name as a disciple of the reverse theory that if you can't join them, beat them. At last count, he had built twenty-one other handsome office buildings in Phoenix, and he has done more than any other man to give Phoenix the face of a city. Through their sole proprietorship, he estimated in 1962, he and his wife own twenty-five million dollars' worth of Phoenix real estate. His detractors assume that most of this sum is offset by trust deeds and that he is one of the new breed living on depreciation. But senior bankers praise Murdock as a sound businessman and an unselfish civic leader.

Two factors make Murdock's financial growth significant. First, he is active and respected in community affairs, a rare thing for a young man who has been busy making money. Secondly, Murdock associates his success directly with the temper of the West. After one year of high school at Findlay, Ohio, he went to work at a service station. From there he went to Detroit as a riveter. After service in World War II, he bought a small Detroit restaurant, but when he married a schoolteacher named Lillie La Marca in October, 1946, he decided he could do better. He sold the restaurant, they pooled their savings, bought a house trailer and set out for the West. Eventually they stopped in Phoenix for a look, and stayed. By 1959, Murdock was an Arizona nominee for one of the nation's outstanding young men. In Phoenix, he was like a yoyo; he had helped to lead a development trend from downtown Phoenix out to North Central Avenue, the site of his bank building and a shopping center dominated by Goldwater's, which had moved out of downtown. Then, paradoxically, Murdock took on the chairmanship of a central business-district committee and invested his profits in an effort to revitalize the downtown area.

During my meeting with him we sat in his spacious offices high in the Guaranty Bank Building. Both Murdock and his wife are interested in modern art; behind him was a wall-long mural of Phoenix by a local artist, and Lillie La Marca Murdock, the Michigan schoolteacher, had just been elected president of the Phoenix Art Museum League.

Murdock is forceful, volatile, and direct. "Back in Detroit," he said, "I kept thinking, 'I need to get out where the air is clear and clean, and relax and think—where they are looking for people who can handle something.' I don't know what I might have done in the East or Midwest, but I'm sure I wouldn't have reached the point that I have here. People say to me, 'Why did you pick Arizona, of all places?' They just think of it as desert. I say this is a place where a man—if he has any ability—can prove himself. You don't have the staid methods they operate under in the East. So then people say, 'I should have gone West myself, when I was your age. I thought about it, but I had my family, and my wife didn't want to leave her friends, and I didn't know if I could find a job.' In other words, they wanted somebody to pick them up and say to them, 'Bring everything you have, in toto, and set down here, in toto, and you can go right on, you can fit in the same niche!' The ones that feel that way are still back there!"

Murdock's voice rose as he spoke. He was pacing in front of a long picture window that faced across northern Phoenix and onto the mountains that hide the ghost mining town of Jerome, and farther to the north, the Grand Canyon.

"When we came here in a house trailer, we looked at the country, the way people talked and acted. I wasn't looking for any guarantee but a place where I could create the security that I crave. People call it hunger. It's not hunger; it's simply that when you're young you love challenge more. This is the sort of thing that brings the bulk of people West. They have the courage to set out on their own. The Southwest will become rich and strong and powerful. Anywhere you have this kind of pioneering, the area grows and develops.

"I wanted a bank to move into my new building," Murdock said, "but I couldn't find one that wanted to move this far out from the downtown area. So we started one of our own. One night at a cocktail party, five of us pledged a hundred thousand dollars apiece. Before the party was over, we'd raised nine hundred thousand. The capital went to two million seven hundred and fifty thousand dollars by the time the bank opened. The six million six hundred thousand dollars in opening day deposits set a national record. In ten months we passed twenty-one million five hundred thousand in deposits.

"My company will have to expand outside of Phoenix. I've traveled all over the country looking at cities with the thought of future development. Eventually we'll be a national firm." In Phoenix, Murdock is only one in a crowd of young men who have come West with nothing but their wits and their love of challenge. Lavergne C. (Jake) Jacobson, forty-nine, came to Phoenix in 1938, penniless. His first job was at twenty-five dollars a week, as timekeeper for Del Webb, then a novice contractor. Now he is vice president and general manager of Webb projects all across America, and his net worth is about fifteen million dollars. He said recently, "Younger men like myself around Arizona just happened to be in the right place at the right time. Also, most of us didn't have much education, and that made us think and work about three times harder than anybody else."

Lee Ackerman, a polished Harvard graduate who ran unsuccessfully for governor of Arizona at the age of thirty-nine, has become a millionaire in Arizona land speculation. John Hall, thirty-seven, left a Missouri farm with lung trouble, and hit it big in Phoenix home building. John Long, born on a farm near Phoenix, is a native who has not overlooked the opportunities of his home city. He has built and sold more than seventeen thousand houses in Phoenix, including the community of Maryvale, where live fifty thousand people who have come from all over the nation to work in Phoenix's new light industry.

Jim Paul, born in Georgia, moved from Los Angeles in 1945 because smog was complicating his daughter's asthma. He had seen Arizona as a salesman for the Diamond Match Company. He began his own business by buying several hundred decrepit Los Angeles street cars at auction for three hundred dollars each. By selling the bells to hot-rodders and the trucks to mine owners, he eventually turned a large profit. When Paul first came to Phoenix in 1945, he bought thirty lots and was warned he'd bit off too heavy a chunk. His thirty houses sold promptly, and in 1949 he built the first Scottsdale subdivision. With Del Webb, he has built one of the Southwest's finest resorts, Scottsdale's splendorous Mountain Shadows, which has scores of luxury homes and two golf courses. Now he is breeding quarter horses and cattle and buying ranches. He grows fervent when he talks of the West; a millionaire several times over, he has the barely restrained vivacity of an Ivy League cheerleader.

"This country pumps new life and energy and thinking into a man!" Paul said. "You don't have to think like pappy did! A man pours into it everything he can because of the challenge on every side. Back East, there's nothing left to make the blood circulate; hell, it's all been done before your time by your great-grandfather. For the big and small alike, out West there is release from the staid, old ordinary ways of life and thinking. Even a dull man finds release. The same thing is true today as in the Gold Rush, except in a more civilized way. You can catch 'em faster than you can string 'em! It would take us just one year to get a town built for the Ford Motor Company if it decided to move out here, and you can count on it that more and more plants will. There are a lot of subtle values out here that people are just beginning to recognize. The absence of snobbery, for instance—we accept people pretty much on their own merits."

At the end of World War II, Scottsdale was only a crossroads filling station. Now there are about fifteen thousand people there, and almost everything seems make-believe except the sunshine, the sand, and the money. Scottsdale has a controlled Western look. It has been created in the image of what the Eastern visitor (called an E.V. by residents) expects of a Western town. Old Western architecture is required by ordinance, though no one agrees on just what it is. Woolworth's has a boardwalk and false front; Fifth Avenue, two blocks long, teems with sixty brand-new Old West shops. Scottsdale calls itself "the West's most Western town." It is far from that, but it has become a playground enjoyed not only by Easterners but by Westerners and even local Phoenicians, who squeeze into such restaurants as Lulu Belle's and the Red Garter right beside the visitor, and seem to be equally fascinated by this artificial reconstruction of a legendary West which never existed.

Frank Lloyd Wright built his Taliesin West fifteen miles from Scottsdale, and died there. Elizabeth Arden built her health resort, Maine Chance, a few miles from town. Among transcontinental commuters who keep homes nearby are Ernest Breech of Ford, Boone Gross, president of the Gillette Safety Razor Company, Senator William Benton, Vernon B. Stouffer of the restaurant chain, the Henry Luces, Mrs. Vincent Astor, the E. A. Cudahys, and Raymond Rubicam, cofounder of Young and Rubicam, the advertising agency. Some came first as guests of the Arizona Biltmore Hotel, eight miles west of Scottsdale, which was opened in 1929, the antecedent of an ever more dazzling line of resort spectaculars.

The intransigence of the surrounding desert helps to offset the eerie quality of impermanence that pervades Scottsdale and other resort towns of more recent vintage. But at Scottsdale the desert has been unmistakably man-fangled. One can sip German beer in a spot which calls itself "the West's most Western beer garden," or enjoy "Kosher cooking the Western way," or browse among luxury goods in the Many Goats Trading Post. Susan Hesse, a San Francisco newspaperwoman, recalls that her father, a Wyoming cattle rancher, once checked into the Camelback Inn at Scottsdale wearing the tight-cut Western suit and boots he had worn all his life. A social hostess, familiar only with the Scottsdale pseudo-West, sweetly suggested that since he had come out West, he should get some Western clothes. He checked out, never to return to Scottsdale. A line I overheard in a Scottsdale hotel lobby occasionally returns to haunt me: "Baby, you've got the tan to meet a lot of people."

At Mountain Shadows on a bright, warm Thanksgiving morning, I asked a life guard beside the pool if the weather was about usual for late November. "Beats me," he said. "I just got out here from Cincinnati myself."

Asked if she was a year-round resident, a waitress shrugged and said, "Who knows?"

"You're new here, then?"

"Sure, I'm from the Bronx. I says to myself one day, riding the subway, I don't have to take this all my life, and I get on a train for California. Any place to get away from the rat race. I turn up in Los Angeles, and two months of *that* rat race is plenty, so here I am. Who knows?"

Don Dedera, the brilliant columnist for the Arizona *Republic* of Phoenix, told me that a friend of his had been sipping coffee in the sunshine outside her Scottsdale shop earlier that week when a tourist had walked up and asked to take her picture. He'd been looking for a real native Arizona cowgirl like her, he said. Could he take her picture? She decided not to tell him that she had come recently from Chicago. He asked her how Arizona people say goodbye. She told him the first thing that occurred to her: "Many happy trails!" He was delighted and walked off murmuring over and over again to himself, "Many happy trails!"

For all its sham and showmanship, Scottsdale has a share of thoughtful citizens. Lewis Ruskin, a retired drug chain owner from Chicago who lives in the resort town, launched the Phoenix Art Museum with a million-and-a-half dollar opening day gift of twenty-four masterpieces. Along with Banker Walter Bimson he is active in the multimillion-dollar Fine Arts Center designed by Frank Lloyd Wright for nearby Arizona State University. Clarence Budington Kelland, who came to Scottsdale first in 1936 to do research for a novel, stayed to spend his winters there and has served sixteen years as Republican national committeeman from Arizona. Lloyd Kiva, born of a Cherokee Indian mother, is an ingenious artist and designer and the man who built and rents all the shops along Scottsdale's Fifth Avenue.

Writing in the *Saturday Evening Post* about Scottsdale, Peter Wyden observed that "rootlessness and boredom are more common than in most communities." The Reverend Herbert Landes, who started the Valley Presbyterian Church in the town, told Wyden that "people come here for a new life; the moral traditions aren't built up. They press their new freedom and get themselves fouled up."

This danger is inherent in any newly established community and with any sudden shifting of people. Phoenix and Tucson, which for their size have had more population influx than any other American cities, have made startlingly few calculated efforts to cope with the dangers of rootlessness. But a superficial effort to assist newcomers was launched as a promotion by the First National Bank of Arizona in its drive to overtake the Valley National Bank. The plan was conceived by Henry Haupt, who became senior consultant of the Batten, Barton, Durstine and Osborn advertising agency after his retirement to Scottsdale in 1958.

"We moved out from Chicago," he recalls, "my wife, two children and a golden retriever. I met my real estate agent in Phoenix and she was going to drive her car and lead us to our house. I lost her in traffic. That was at three P.M. It took until seven fifteen to find this house—and it was a deputy sheriff who finally found it. Two weeks after we moved in, the post office telephoned and said they had a registered letter for me, and would I please tell them how to get to this address."

Haupt's home is behind the famed Camelback Inn, but maps

around Phoenix haven't been keeping pace with the birth of new streets and subdivisions. So when Haupt became a director of the First National Bank, he speculated that thousands of other Arizona newcomers shared similar problems. He designed a newcomers' service to be offered through each of the bank's seventy branches throughout Arizona. Billboards and general advertising invited the newcomer to the banks. Trained personnel at special desks dispensed up-to-date street and highway atlases and booklets on local affairs and living conditions. As many as a thousand newcomers use the service each month at the Phoenix main office. They ask about entertainment, school districts, housing, golf courses, postal zoning, restaurants, baseball schedules, utility rates, Blue Star Mothers meetings, bus service, churches, taxes, and diaper services. Often they deposit money; one newcomers' representative was asked to step inside the bank vault with a New York woman and help unsew her cache of currency from her corset.

Some of the older newcomers are headed for towns like Del Webb's Sun City near Phoenix, the best known of several retirement towns built within the past decade in Arizona. Sun City is a town without schools; its residents must be fifty years or more in age. Here, segregation is in force—but it refers to age, not race. The population of Sun City was more than five thousand in 1962; most residents lived in two-bedroom apartments or homes for which they were paying between eighty-five hundred and twelve thousand dollars on thirty-year FHA loans. Square dances are held on Wednesdays, round dances on Saturdays. At the community center are facilities for those interested in ceramics, photography, oil painting, and sewing. Hymns sound out over chimes and organ by loudspeaker. Putting greens and the golf course are busy, and the residents ride to their shopping center in electric golf carts. Sun City seems bland and harmless, but its residents start life there with the anticipation of passengers on an ocean cruise. Perhaps Sun City will wear well, yet segregation by age, even though voluntary, seems almost as distasteful as segregation by any other standard. Sun City suggests a slow-motion movie: after the novelty wears off, it can grow maddening.

Arizonans are aggressively experimental in their attitudes toward senior citizens. Since 1957, the Tucson On Call Employment Reserve (TOCER) has made notable gains in a community plan to employ older persons of established abilities who have been discouraged in attempts to seek work because of their age. TOCER is a community effort, and its office is manned by volunteers. Financed by contributions from business, clubs, and individuals, in its first three full years of operation, TOCER registered 2,750 individuals, principally between forty-five and sixty-five years of age, and made seven hundred and fourteen job placements.

Young or old, these newcomers who make up the preponderance of Arizona population today are an aggressive group who know what they want and are doing something about it. This trait is part of the reason for the state's reputation for political conservatism. Senator Barry Goldwater is far from the most vigorous champion of conservatism in Arizona history, though he is certainly its most eloquent. The late James S. Douglas, an Arizona copper magnate and father of the former United States ambassador to the Court of St. James's, became so outraged over New Deal policies that he gave up his United States citizenship and became a Canadian citizen. Such forceful protest is not uncommon in Arizona, which was a semi-feudal state until the population growth after World War II. In the mid-twenties, one Arizonan was sentenced to two hundred days in jail for saying, "To hell with Coolidge!" Arizona called up its National Guard in the 1930's in an attempt to halt construction of Hoover Dam, on the contention that it would divert Arizona water to California. Governor Sidney P. Osborn, who served four terms and died in 1948, was the only governor of the forty-eight states who never attended a governors' conference; he did not intend to gallivant around at taxpayers' expense for a lot of foolish prattle. There is a substantial Mormon population in Arizona, and it has contributed to the state's conservatism and self-dependence.

Several months before the John Birch Society exploded on the nation in 1961, a young Phoenix banker, his eyes afire, was telling me in hushed tones of weekly meetings he attended where guerrilla warfare was practiced, on the conviction that even Arizonans would be forced to defend themselves against other Communist-dominated Arizonans on some dark day ahead. In later visits to Phoenix, I found this kind of hysteria transferred to current Supreme Court hearings on the California-Arizona water dispute or to the industrialization of the Navajo.

Goldwater's political success within his home state is due in part to his personal magnetism and the long reputation of integrity that he and his family have established. But though the conservative influence of Goldwater and Eugene C. Pulliam, publisher of two Phoenix newspapers, is felt throughout the state, it is a debatable question to what extent that influence is cause or result of Arizona's political laissez faire.

The political history of Arizona has been relatively tranquil. Its people have less interest in politics than those of its neighbors to east and west, New Mexico and California. Party lines mean little. His-

torically the state is Democratic; once six-to-one Democratic by registration, it still is more than two-to-one Democratic. But opposition
candidates have been dramatically successful since 1950; Governor
Paul Fannin, a Republican, was reëlected in 1960 by the largest
plurality in the state's history. Conservatives cross party lines with
abandon in either direction; in-migrant Republicans often register
as Democrats so that their primary votes will not be wasted.

Arizonans like Goldwater, Governor Fannin, and Congressman
John Rhodes have made a fetish of Arizona's independence from
government subsidies, but this is more talk than fact. In fiscal 1960,
close to half of Arizona's expenditures at the state level were in federal
moneys for highways, welfare, schools, and other items. Despite this,
in 1962, for three successive sessions, the legislature had failed to
provide matching funds to qualify the state to receive federal funds
under the National Defense Education Act. With seventy-two percent
of its land held either directly or in trust by the federal government,
Arizona would risk economic catastrophe if it were to practice what
some of its political leaders preach. The state is fortunate that its
eighty-four-year-old senior senator, Carl Hayden, a Democrat, is
chairman of the Senate Appropriations Committee.

Arizona is also one of the staunchest bastions of the right-to-
work legislation so abhorred by organized labor. Such legislation has
been supported strongly even in urban and mining centers where the
modest union strength of Arizona is greatest. One political phenomenon in Arizona is that conservative strength is greatest in the cities,
whereas in older areas of the nation these are the liberal strongholds.
The newly arrived white-collar worker in Phoenix or Tucson is well
paid but he may have taken a lesser job or a cut in salary in exchange
for Arizona sunshine. He is also an individualist. These factors tend
to move him away from the sphere of the prototype liberal. (The far-
right Chicago *Tribune*, which is a long way from home, is prominent
on Arizona newsstands. A more liberal daily, the Arizona *Journal*,
began publication in Phoenix in 1961 in what was to be a hard uphill
fight for survival.)

In the Arizona legislature, the words Republican and Democrat are seldom heard; they simply are not working terms. Instead,
legislators refer to the majority, which is assumed to be responsive to
banks, mines, utilities, railroads, and industrial farmers; and to the
minority, which supposedly represents union labor, Indians, Spanish-
Americans, unskilled workers, and small business. In Arizona, the
closest parallel to the so-called factory vote of Eastern cities is the
vote of Spanish-Americans, Indians, and unskilled workers—most of
whom are in the rural areas. The technician at Motorola is more

likely to vote for the candidate whose intelligence and honesty he respects; politically, as morally, he senses a freedom from the party-line restrictions of the ward or precinct he left behind.

The situation is similar at Tucson, where Hughes Aircraft Company's Falcon air-to-air missile plant, for several years the largest employer in Arizona, has brought together a highly skilled team of electronics and missile specialists. Layoffs in 1961 did not result in any exodus from Tucson; rather than leave the city, an electronics technician might turn up as clerk or salesman or service-station attendant, waiting out the production lag. The political predictability of such individualists is almost nil. And Democrat Party leaders in Arizona remember uncomfortably how the Navajo Indian nation voted overwhelmingly for Eisenhower after he promised them that they would be consulted on Indian Bureau appointments.

Among American cities, only Tucson has a higher percentage of possible sunshine than Phoenix, and only Yuma has higher summer temperatures. Both communities are sharing in the Arizona avalanche.

Tucson is slower than Phoenix. Its old Spanish traditions and its longer history are apparent in its pace, architecture, and outlook. Less than twenty-five years ago, many Tucson stores closed for three months during the summer heat, and in the Mexican tradition all business halted for daily siestas. Tucson is close to nature. The brilliant sun pervades everything. The Santa Catalina Mountains to the north, rising to 9,185 feet, are a backdrop for one side of the city. At Tucson's southern edge, the Sonora Desert plunges into seeming infinity across the Mexican border. Although Tucson has sprawled and subdivided and suburbanized, it still has not made much of an incision in the rolling, cactus-dotted desert. Ten minutes away from the Pioneer Hotel at the center of the city, one can find areas where nothing in sight bears the mark of human hand.

Despite its more leisurely pace and relative entrenchment, Tucson is feeling the impact of the young newcomer. Its Sunshine Climate Club is a brisk tourist promotion agency. In an unfortunate outburst of conformity, El Camino Real has been renamed Main Street. Dude ranches dot the desert slopes around Tucson. For half a century it was the tourist who underwrote Tucson's existence. Except for the visitors, Tucson was only a fork on the Southern Pacific and the site of the University of Arizona. But today the Tucson industrial payroll, in excess of sixty million dollars a year, is more important than anything else. A Titan missile installation consisting of eighteen sites in four counties has its headquarters at the Davis-

Monthan Air Force Base at Tucson. The new ten-million-dollar satellite telescope at Kitt Peak National Observatory, forty-five miles from Tucson, was built by the National Science Foundation with the aid of the Papago Indians, on whose reservation this "perfect astronomical peak" is located. (In return, the Papagos wrung only one promise from astronomers—to leave their pottery and other relics on the mountain peak, where they were put as sacrifices to Indian gods.)

Stretching through the desert westward of Tucson is the Army's Fort Huachuca electronic environmental test range operated by Pan American; its purposes are to explore the techniques of electronic warfare, including the jamming of enemy missile-guidance systems, and to test high-speed drone aircraft which can spy on the enemy with cameras. (The earlier role of Fort Huachuca, founded in 1877, was to confine Apache Indians to their reservation.) Twelve miles south of Tucson, beside the highway to Nogales on the Mexican border, is the Hughes missile plant. Still farther south is the Tubac Country Club, a luxury real estate development of which Bing Crosby has been chairman of the board. Large new open-pit mines have begun operation on century-old workings south of Tucson; to the north, the San Manuel mine is a large copper producer. Arizona produces five times more copper than Montana, and two-and-a-half times more than Utah. There are no siestas in Tucson any more.

Tucson bears some remarkable similarities to Albuquerque. Both were founded by the Spaniards at the base of picturesque mountains; after World War I, veterans' hospitals were built at both; both are transcontinental railroad points; both are the seats of state universities and have Air Force bases of similar size. Their population growth has been parallel.

The traditional but irrational tension between Tucson and Phoenix has been declining, as such differences usually do when cities recognize the desirability of working together on such matters as highway, air transport and tourist development. For a brief period during the Civil War, Tucson in the south of Arizona was the headquarters of Confederate troops; it is not surprising that a tradition of hostility lingered. There was jealousy in Phoenix over the growth in size and academic importance of the University of Arizona, which went to Tucson in a cynical early trade with Phoenix. (Tucsonans insist that Phoenix chose the mental hospital instead of the university because they thought it would provide more jobs, but actually Phoenix received a normal college at the same time.) But the pain for Phoenix was eased soon after World War II when voters changed the name of Arizona State College at Tempe, near Phoenix, to Arizona State University. Enrollment at Arizona State in 1962 was almost as great as the twelve to thirteen thousand on the Tucson campus. In 1962, partisans of the Phoenix university were blocking appropriations for establishment of a recommended medical school at the Tucson university, and petitioning for one at the Phoenix university. Yet most of the old tensions are confined now to athletic rivalry. The annual football game between the two schools finds desert highways as alive with traffic—there are even bicycle races en route—as in any other state on the weekend of the Big Game. There are no private colleges or universities in Arizona to share in the higher educational burden or to divert loyalties; thus Arizonans' interest in their two major state institutions is more intense than that in many states.

As the two universities became more nearly equivalent in size and importance, leaders in Phoenix and Tucson made peace overtures which would enable the two cities to pull together. In 1958, a planeload of Phoenix leaders flew to Tucson for an intercity breakfast meeting of service clubs, but fewer than a dozen Tucson men attended. In 1959, Lawson V. Smith, a Tucson native who was living in Phoenix as vice president and general manager of The Mountain States Telephone & Telegraph Company, stepped in to mediate. More successful intercity conferences developed. Phoenix and Tucson have stuck together in recent four-city conferences with El Paso and Albuquerque. The traditional combatants of the intercity war are dying from old age.

In Tucson, several families have had a strong economic grip on the city in business affairs and land holdings. The resistance of the old guard to change has been greater than in Phoenix. They have clung to the vision of the old pueblo that was Tucson, but now they are almost extinct. The average Tucsonan is proud of his city's growth. Two older families who have meant much to Arizona are represented today in Tucson by Lewis Douglas and Harold Steinfeld. Steinfeld's father Albert came to Tucson in 1872 to work in his uncle's trading post. At his death in 1935 he owned more parcels of land—three thousand lots in the city of Tucson alone—than any other man in Arizona history. His son Harold still owns the four corners of Stone and Pennington in the center of Tucson and long has operated Steinfeld's department store at one of the corners. Recently he built another department store on an adjacent corner and leased it to his top competitor. (*"Would Macy Build For Gimbel's?"* read the headline in the *Wall Street Journal.*) Steinfeld is the epitome of the entrenched conservative who is equal to the challenge of any newcomer. Yet he concedes that the development of contemporary Tucson has been "due to newcomers, or speculators, or those coming here to retire who end up back in business. Most of the old-timers have been too close to the forest; the parade has passed them by. These new landmarks are not monuments to the old families but to aggressive new citizens who have moved into the area." Yet Steinfeld is equally damning in his comments about promoters who recently have been buying arid Arizona cattle ranches, dividing them into sixty-foot lots and taking New York City office space or national advertisements to sell a piece of Arizona for a few dollars down. Of Barry Goldwater, Steinfeld says happily, "He's the kind of fellow you expect to see in Arizona."

Douglas, the former ambassador to Britain, is a relative newcomer to Tucson and only a seasonal resident, but he has lifetime ties in Arizona. Tourists still gawk at the empty, crumbling mansion his father built in Jerome, now an almost deserted ghost town, hoping to keep his son at home and interested in operating the Jerome mining properties. The town of Douglas in the southeast corner of Arizona was named for his grandfather, Dr. James Douglas, a minister and physician who was sent into Arizona in 1880 by Phelps Dodge, then a small Eastern firm, to seek copper-mine property. Although as a youth he would not linger in Jerome, Douglas has never been away long from Arizona even in the years of his diplomatic service. In recent years he has occupied a second-floor office in his Southern Arizona Bank, looking out over Stone Avenue toward A Mountain, a Tucson landmark. Douglas' walls are dotted with reminders of another era and another world: signed portraits of Cordell Hull and Pershing, and a browning, fading photograph of Clemenceau. He senses in Arizona "a considerable amount of pioneering spirit and expectation of the future among those who are coming into the state to take risks in development of its future, and only incidentally to enjoy it." Douglas himself came under fire from some old-line Tucsonans in 1960 because he sold his bank to Firstamerica Corporation, the nation's largest bank-holding company. He has been more active since then in New York City financial circles. He feels that there is "a certain belligerence in Western society. We don't like too much power out here, either among trade-union leaders or industrial leaders." But in this respect he sees the West as a national bellwether, not an exception. "In the West today, we can spot a trend more clearly than in larger communities, where people tend to become identified by groups and labels."

Yuma lies in the southwest corner of Arizona, beside the Colorado River and in the kind of terrain which fits any tenderfoot's image of how desert should look. This is low, hot, sea-level desert, about sixty air miles north of where the mighty Colorado, after passing into Mexico, empties into the Gulf of California. In irrigated groves on three sides of Yuma thrive citrus, pecan, and date. Cotton and grains bask in the searing sunshine. Summer temperatures of 120° are common, yet there were about twenty-seven thousand people in Yuma in 1962, among them earnest civic leaders who are looking forward to a day when Yuma, the hottest city in America, will become a seaport—on the Gulf of California. Even now, north of Yuma along the California-Arizona border, dams have made the Colorado River into a string of lakes rich in fish and plied by speed-boats and water skiiers.

At Yuma, the Colorado River helps to complicate one of the more intricate snarls of Western liquor laws. Winterhaven, a raucous little California town just across the river from Yuma, offers two hours of extra drinking for Yumans after their own bars close at one A.M. California bars close at two A.M., but at Yuma, the Colorado River is the zone line between Pacific and Mountain time. The capriciousness of the Colorado has kept a boundary commission of Arizona and California experts busy for almost a decade in settling the two hundred and forty-four miles of common border along the river. The river occasionally changes its course, thus forming new islands, and their jurisdiction has been in dispute.

It is more difficult to comprehend the reasons for the explosive population growth in Yuma and other Arizona towns than to understand the allure of Phoenix and Tucson. Yet unquestionably small-town Arizona life has a slow, easy charm and a remoteness from most of the complexities of contemporary life. Perhaps one need look no further than this for an explanation; if there are more people under the spell of the herd instinct in America than ever before, there surely are more people also who are eager to avoid the mob.

In Flagstaff to the north, John Babbitt, a member of a family which has dominated northern Arizona for almost a century, told me, "I don't know where they've come from, and I don't know what they're doing!" He is not upset by the precipitous recent growth of little Flagstaff, but, like many natives, he is puzzled. His reaction is typical of rural, old-line Arizonans. Flagstaff jumped from seventy-seven hundred people to almost twenty thousand between 1950 and 1961. The center of the Arizona lumber industry, Flagstaff sits placidly at the foot of the wooded San Francisco Peaks, which tower more than twelve thousand feet. To their north is the Grand Canyon. Flagstaff is a trading center for an area sixty miles southward and two hundred miles northward, including large sheep and cattle ranches. The Glen Canyon Dam construction has made a boom town out of Flagstaff; though the damsite is one hundred and thirty five miles north, Flagstaff is its railhead. The Navajo reservation begins just a few miles east, and two observatories (including the Lowell, where the planet Pluto was discovered) operate in the high, clean atmosphere near the town. The tourist is lured by the wild and varied grandeur of the scenery, by skiing, and by highways—Flagstaff is the junction point of a north-south highway with the transcontinental Route 66.

It would be difficult to say whether the Babbitt family or the Santa Fe railway is more deeply a part of the northern Arizona tradition. They came at about the same time. The Babbitts are the largest resident ranchers of northern Arizona; they carry about five thousand cows on a half-million acres of grazing land. They own general stores—called trading posts in deference to the traditions of the Old West and Indian country that they serve. Babbitt land is being subdivided for the newcomers, and Babbitt lumber is going into houses which are being stocked with furnishings and food from Babbitt stores and with cars which come from Babbitt agencies. In the upstairs offices of the Babbitt department store at Flagstaff, John Babbitt said, "Flagstaff has always been solid and conservative. Credit hasn't been anything to worry about. That's changed some; the new people may not be quite so substantial. But most of our welfare problems are people on their way through on Highway sixty-six."

Some of the most vivid scenery in the West is around Sedona, south of Flagstaff. On a spur of one of its red rock buttresses, Marguerite Brunswig Staude built the cross-shaped Chapel of the Holy Cross; it is one of those unexpected marriages of man-made and God-made beauty that one expects to find on the back roads of France. In one postwar decade Sedona grew from a one-store and post-office town and a location for motion-picture crews into a tourist mecca and retreat for artists and wealthy Easterners. On a summer weekend, it is not uncommon to find two or three thousand visitors jammed into the Oak Creek Canyon area around Sedona. Real estate values have risen five to ten times since World War II. Growth like this has driven many of its postwar settlers out. Typical of them is Ed Ellinger, a Wall Street investment analyst who bought a ranch near Sedona after World War II and began to raise horses. But his photographs and enthusiastic articles on Sedona helped to bring on the invasion, and he has moved since into the Mother Lode country of California's Sierra Nevada.

Six or seven miles north of Tucson, in the rugged foothills of the Santa Catalina Mountains, are a primitive adobe chapel and adobe house built with Indian help by an artist named Ted De Grazia. Of the nearly five thousand Westerners to whom I have talked, none stands more stubbornly and effectively than he for the simplicity of the primitive West. When I visited him, we sat on square wooden stools beside his hand-built adobe fireplace. The only water on the place was rain water that he and his wife had hoarded in rain barrels. There was no gas or electricity. De Grazia often goes to bed at dark, and is up by three A.M. to sketch by candlelight and begin painting at dawn. He does not need to live so simply; his paintings sell for a thousand dollars and more, and he is a prolific artist. A De Grazia painting of Indian children in a ceremonial dance was chosen for a UNICEF Christmas card in 1960, placing him in the celebrated company of Chagall and Tamayo.

De Grazia owns a home and studio he seldom uses in Tucson. He bought his remote homesite and built his refuge from the onrush of civilization because he and the growing West are incompatible. "I'm afraid of making money," he said. "If I made money, I'd be thinking about money all the time and I wouldn't want to paint. What money I have now, I bury. They tell me that's wrong. I tell them the hell it is. Money's no good for anybody. It makes bums out of them. I think everybody should start from scratch."

De Grazia, bearded and laconic, started from scratch. He was born in an Arizona mining camp in 1909. His father was a miner, his grandfather an Italian immigrant. "Everybody in my family figured I'd be a miner," he said. "But I was always out of step. I was painting since I can remember. When I was a kid, there weren't any psychiatrists around. Nobody paid any attention to oddball kids." He accumulated three degrees during an intermittent thirteen-year career at the University of Arizona, but his paintings did not sell. Unable to get help as an artist, he withdrew his last hundred dollars from the bank and told the banker, "I'm going to give myself a fellowship." He used the money to go to Mexico City. His paintings, vivid in color, gentle and soft, show marks of Orozco and Rivera, both of whom he studied under in Mexico. His subjects are Indians and angels and children, and sometimes the three are indistinguishably one. He paints what he feels to be the West.

As he stood looking at the cross of saguaro cactus ribs over his little mud chapel, its clay bell tolling in the wind above an open-air shrine and the tempera drawings on the walls, he said, "This is what Arizona means. The strength of a country is reflected in its art. America has no Picasso or Rivera. There is a lack of vigor and direction in our art. Now is the time for Americans to begin looking at America, and for artists to begin painting our strength, despite what some frustrated critics in patent leather shoes have to say."

When I visited his primitive little sanctuary, De Grazia was resigned to looking for another place to move, deeper into what he regards as the real West and farther from subdivisions and freeways. Bulldozers were about to invade his land; red survey flags were marching up behind the saguaro outside his chapel. "I gave permission for a new road over my property because you can't hold back progress, not even way out here," he said. "I thought I might as well make it easy for the politicians. I fought so much all my life I don't want to fight any more."

It is the vogue among writers to insist that exploding urban centers like Phoenix and Tucson are not the real Arizona, just as De Grazia would deny that they are the real West. Certainly they are not the *old* Arizona of the range, the marshal, and the badman. But the new West is indelibly flavored by the old, and in the old lies some of the keys to the hopes of the new. It is deplorable that thousands of the newcomers are neither particularly versed nor interested in the gaudy, gutty, proud, and grim traditions of the Arizona past. However, in Arizona now there is a revival of emphasis on its past. In 1962 the fiftieth anniversary of statehood focused attention on its history, and it is likely that this interest will be nurtured in the future; the nadir of indifference is past. Under the editorship of Dr. John Alexander Carroll, the Pulitzer Prize winner, *The Arizona Historical Quarterly* has had a renaissance; and Arizona's several splendid historical museums, which in the past have been the focus of more attention by non-Arizonans, are now being discovered by its residents.

The Arizona of the past, in truth, is not past; and that is one reason Arizonans do not turn about so often to look for it. The Old West still lies a mile or two off any road. One need not go to literature or to museums in Arizona to look for history; it is so recent that physical evidence remains almost anywhere away from the cities. Ghost mining towns are in such profusion, and many of them are so recent that experts clash over cataloguing them as ghost or live, and visitors have an uneasy feeling that they are staring at a still-warm corpse. One such town is Jerome, one of the greatest of the copper camps. Its population has declined from about fifteen thousand to less than two hundred, and most of those remaining cater to the tourist. Its buildings, many of them once elegant, are more or less intact, and the visitor who goes prowling may find himself a trespasser in someone's bedroom.

Nothing has changed the Arizona past in the Strip Country, the narrow northwestern triangle of Arizona bounded by the Colorado River's deep gorges and the Grand Canyon on the southeast and by Nevada and Utah to the west and north. Man remains so dwarfed and isolated by its sheer barren peaks and bottomless gorges that polygamists, excommunicated by the Mormon church, live there and defy authorities to come in after them. On meandering little roads tiny hamlets with names like Short Creek, Cane Beds, Mount Trumbull, and Wolf Hole are all that the most intrepid tourist can find.

The Old West shows through, uncomfortably and unpleasantly, in bleak towns like Eloy, halfway between Phoenix and Tucson. The town's beginnings are so vague that even the origin of its name has evaded scholars. Industrial cotton farming employing migrant laborers made contemporary get-rich-quick legends at the same time that Eloy became a haven for gamblers and prostitutes preying on the migrant worker, just as they had preyed on the Arizona miner seventy years before. As recently as 1949, an old-fashioned gun battle at Eloy resulted in the death of three persons. An angry mass meeting came next, but this one led not to hanging but to incorporation and policing. By 1960, Eloy was ready for a community workshop at which local leaders sat down with experts to plan its future, but in the 1950's it was not much different from the Tombstone of the 1890's. In *Arizona Review*, Robert C. Stone suggested that seventy years from now Eloy might be memorialized on television as the last stronghold of Western freedom and individualism. Even today, an aura of lawlessness surrounds the stranger merely driving through; there is potential violence in the stares and catcalls and gestures of a Saturday afternoon sidewalk crowd, in the harried faces of the police, in the ramshackle housing at the fringes of town where the migrant has dug in.

Eloy is one of several examples that suggest the migrant worker is in a sorrier plight in Arizona than in California. Arizona labor statutes and enforcement are not yet as advanced as its neighbor's. With cotton harvesting equipment being used more and more, the Arizona migrant is looking for urban jobs or settling in substandard housing on the fringes of agricultural towns. Some migrants are Indian, notably Papagos, for whom the substandard wages (commonly seventy-five cents an hour) represent a sharp increase in living standards. The number of Anglo-Saxon white migrants—the traditional "Okie" from Arkansas, Oklahoma, and Texas—is declining sharply as they head for the cities. The Negro migrant is increasing. But about half of the Arizona farm migrant force now is composed of Mexican nationals. In many ways, the Mexican is the most fortunate of American migrants; his living conditions are regulated by international agreement under which United States labor authorities recruit and supervise the use of Mexican nationals on United States farms. Further, a seventy-five cent hourly wage, returned faithfully to relatives in Mexico, represents a far greater buying power in the Mexican economy than in the United States.

Except for the occasional violence, the real Old West of Arizona is not in Eloy. Along the precipitous Mogollon Rim that stretches across much of north-central Arizona, forests are little changed from those which greeted Spanish explorers four centuries ago. Farther north, all through the Hopi and Navajo country, the visitor will find himself, if not in another world, at least in another era. In southeast Arizona there are cow towns which are still almost untouched by boom fever. At Willcox, eighty-one miles southeast of Tucson, in an area averaging less than three persons per square mile, the dress and language and habits of cowboy and rancher have changed remarkably little in the four generations since the town was settled. There is still the cattle auction each week at the barn on the outskirts of town, still the limitless rangeland of Sulphur Springs Valley, and now the annual festival which honors Rex Allen, star of TV's "Frontier Doctor," who was born and grew up on a ranch near Willcox and has come to occupy a rare role as both real and legendary cowboy. The dominant feeling of cattle towns like Willcox is resistance to rapid change, a reverence for the range and an abhorrence for any deviation from tradition.

This indomitability of the cattleman is obvious too in the several large cattle ranches left in Arizona. The mightiest of them is the Greene Cattle Company's ORO Ranch, operated by the family of the late Colonel William Greene, an early Arizona speculator and cattle baron who made his first big stake in the Greene-Cananea mines at Cananea, across the Mexican border in Sonora. The ranch house, whose telephones still are wireless, is reached by traveling from Prescott over fifty miles of dirt road. The ORO covers about two hundred and thirty-five thousand acres, stretching as far as thirty-three miles across high plateau and grazing ten thousand head of cattle. A day spent in riding over such vastness as the ORO's grazing land tends to make even an Arizonan feel small and to reëmphasize the credo by which editor Raymond Carlson has built *Arizona Highways* into the nation's most respected and most widely sold state magazine. Distinguished for its scenic photography and for a steadfast concentration on the less temporal of Arizona's attributes, *Arizona Highways* is constantly besieged by those hoping to publish articles of personal or commercial interest. Carlson turns such self-seekers away with the gentle reply, "Arizona is bigger than anybody who comes into it."

Epilogue

THE WEST:
AMERICA
TOMORROW?

THE WEST

America Tomorrow?

Late on a midwinter night in Manhattan, a policeman escaping the cold sat beside me in an all-night coffee shop, asking wistfully about California. He knew that salaries and climate were better in much of the West than in New York, but when I asked if he planned to give California a try, it turned out the conversation was academic.

"Who, me? No, all my family and my wife's family is within ten miles of here. I been in New York City all my life. I'm not going any-where."

In the West, similar idle conversation is founded on questions like, "Where did you come from?" or "How long have you been out here?" Standing in a bank teller's line at San Diego, I learned that the woman in front of me had moved three years earlier from Pennsyl-vania.

"How do you like San Diego?" I asked.

"It would be all right," she said, "if they ever finish with it."

There is a noteworthy contrast in the attitudes which lie behind such casual talk; the confirmed Easterner and the new Westerner often are persons of vastly different flexibility and outlook.

In much of the East there is intense interest in background and tradition; in the West, this is supplanted by absorption in the present and the future. Meeting someone for the first time, a skillful Eastern conversationalist will discover the pattern of his past: the occupation of his father, his college and social status. In the West, the opening gambits of conversation are one's region of origin, the year of migration, the neighborhood of residence, occupation, and attitudes toward school and civic affairs. The Westerner's past is apt to be more distant than that of the Easterner—not only in geography but in mind. He is busy making his future. In large part, this emphasis on present and future is because the westward migration is a youthful one. The sons and daughters of the millions of young adults who settled in the West immediately after World War II are in their teens, and they hold an important key to the future significance of the West.

"In another few years we will see what the second generation of the new Westerner is like," Walter Straley of Pacific Northwest Bell told me. "I don't think he will have that kind of provincialism typically expressed in letters back to the Midwest about how wonderful it is out West, a sort of pride in climate and flora that discourages momentarily my faith in the Western dream. Somewhere along the way, these youngsters, like their parents in their shiny new houses and cars, are going to give up their original idea of seeking comfort, and start getting interested—if they aren't already—in problems which at first will center around school and fire protection and water problems, until you have more people genuinely concerned about civic and community affairs than in almost any Eastern city you can name."

The California gubernatorial campaign of 1962 had an intriguing undertone as a testing ground of the extent of Westerners' interest in their own emergence. Of course, its outcome cannot be accepted as conclusive evidence, since issues of personality and party are dominant in politics.

In this campaign, Richard Nixon, the former Vice President, challenged the incumbent California governor, Pat Brown, a Democrat. It was primarily as a gesture of assistance to Nixon that Governor Nelson Rockefeller of New York disputed Governor Brown of California during the summer of 1962 over Brown's bullish claims of California's ascendancy over the state of New York. The flames of dispute between the governors were fanned by the New York *Times*, which itself had a special interest: its launching, in the fall of 1962, of a Western edition.

It does not make much difference at what moment in time the state of California surpasses the state of New York to become the most populous in the nation. Yet Brown had made much of this point as evidence that the state he governed was sound and prosperous. In a television speech, he spoke with enthusiasm of plans for a statewide celebration on that day when, his California population experts predicted, California would pass New York. Brown put the date in 1962, New York's Rockefeller put it in 1963, and Nixon—no doubt sincere but also in need of a campaign issue—took the position that numerical supremacy was not the point. In his reaction, Nixon, a native Californian who lost all sense of regionalism during his years in the Vice-Presidency, was typical of the Westerner who, having lived and worked in the East, is acutely aware of both the new power and old shortcomings of the West. Whether politically expedient or not, Nixon's attitude toward California's growth was more incisive than that of his opponent Brown.

In an interview during the 1962 campaign, Nixon told me: "California is the first state in many respects: soon, in number of people; already in farm products, in number of registered vehicles, in opportunity for higher public education, and in many other things. But California has hardly scratched the surface of its potential influence and impact on the nation. As California becomes the first state in other areas, it will refresh the nation; California has an individualistic, progressive population. There are people in the West who are very creative intellectually, but who are not making the contribution they should to the intellectual life of the state or of the nation because there are too many temptations in the West; life is too good. Californians must recognize that they are now first in many areas, and they have to be worthy of that responsibility. They are competing not only with fellow Californians, but with the nation."

Such criticism, while valid, was an unorthodox approach for a political underdog seeking California votes. "I wonder if they'll understand it," Nixon admitted quietly. "That's the point. They may resent it; I don't know. But this is the most exciting region in the world. It has an incredible potential. The real future of California is on the college and university campuses. Whoever is governor of this state must challenge its creative people."

It would seem a political miracle if a candidate won an election while chiding the electorate for a degree of intellectual laziness and for being loathe to assume their obligations of leadership. That Nixon took this approach at all was significant; he believed Californians might be ready to face facts. Like others, he has sensed a desire in the mind and spirit of the West to catch up with the growth of the Western body. Any leader in the West today must understand this hunger; more often than in the rest of the nation, the people in the West are moving ahead of their leaders.

In the westward tilt, as in all selective migrations, there is tur-
moil, considerable energy, and neurotic drive. But even from a neurotic push can come significant advance. The Westerner is anxious
to profit from the mistakes of older cultures and other regions.

The title of super-American, which John Bainbridge bestowed
on the contemporary Texan, would be more appropriately carried by
the Westerner, and particularly the Californian. He has come from
all the states of the nation only to be bound by new ties of regionalism
—and yet the regionalism of the West is less a matter of geographic
unity than of compatible mores and goals. The startling mobility of
the Westerner is an accelerated example of a national trend; so are
his excesses in leisure pursuit, his burgeoning income, his enthusiasm
as a consumer, his social casualness, his restless dabbling in intellectual frontiersmanship. Walter Doty, a former *Sunset* editor,
says: "I don't think of the West as a *place*, but as a *push*. It's always
pushing me. I think it pushes a lot of people."

Gradually, the nation has begun to look westward for new
trends; whatever it is, "the California way" has assumed increasing
stature. Dr. John Wendell Dodds of Stanford told me, "There's
something intangible in the appeal of the West. Today's migration
westward has the highest overall intelligence of any wave yet. Easterners visiting the West sense a kind of fermentation."

But with fermentation comes the hazard of collapse. "In the process of enjoying the West," said Dodds, "we can destroy a lot of what
we came here for. Westerners must be alerted to the immediacy of
their loss—not through ignorance of facts, but apathy." Men like
Dodds and his Stanford colleague Wallace Stegner are sensitive
about the slowness of Western progress in conservation and urban
planning. This is partly because self-criticism has until recently been
a still small voice in the West, and partly because the Western image
has been changing so rapidly that it cannot function as a rallying
point for the oncoming millions.

"The more we tend to industrialize," warned Dodds, "the more
we tend to become a duplicate of other places in the country."

There is ugliness in the West, but it has not been around so
long, nor is its shabbiness so apparent as in other areas. "The West
isn't paradise, but it's relatively much better than many parts of the
country," Stegner told me. "The atmosphere is less class-conscious,
less caste-conscious. But will this tolerance last? Perhaps, like the
scenery and open country, it will be destroyed by the people who
come to enjoy it.

"If only the image of Western virtue can be presented as an
effort to avoid mistaken progress-at-any-cost, then in-migration may

result in a good community instead of a merely growing one. It's the last opportunity we have in America. It means not merely educating the public, but bucking all kinds of lobbies. It may call for a mass movement. I don't feel like an evangelist, but somebody has got to be, or else there must be a great association of spontaneous grass-roots movements in many Western communities."

A New Yorker who moved West not for future but to escape city crowding and explore the wild life and natural beauty of the region is Joseph Wood Krutch, the author and naturalist. His home is just north of Tucson, under the towering Santa Catalina Mountains.

"If the pell-mell rush into the West is not accompanied by some controlling impulse, by some novelty of purpose," he told me, "then actually all you will have is simply another East on the West Coast. Some sense of value and ultimate purpose must be developed. The future of the West can't be realized simply by importing into the West those ideals and standards of the civilization from which the in-migrants have run away. The West did, and still does, offer a wonderful opportunity for starting a new life—a new *kind* of life—a civilization that is different from the old one. The real questions are, 'Is that opportunity going to be muffed? Will the possibility be realized?' Won't it be interesting to see the answers?"

It will be interesting, and crucial for the nation. The answers are becoming evident more rapidly than most Westerners imagine. Change is everywhere in the West, and those who resist it are falling behind. Those seeking to suggest the changes of the West have often confined themselves to such startling but superficial statistics as the geometric rise of population and of manufacturing and distribution outlets, or such figures as California's three hundred thousand pleasure boats, Los Angeles' one thousand new swimming pools each month, or the five million tourists who visit Southern California each year.

But now a more balanced portrait of Western growth can be seen. It is a landscape remarkably free of overt racial or religious prejudice or of unassuaged poverty. More nearly than any other region, the West offers freedom from prejudice and freedom from want. It also seems to offer freedom from boredom, and for the time being at least, freedom from economic or social decline. It offers more time for leisure—and more for work.

In this new picture of Western growth, West Coast editions of the New York *Times*, the *Wall Street Journal* and the *Christian Science Monitor* augment evidence of economic growth as do the new Budweiser brewery in Los Angeles, the Ford plant at San Jose, the three Motorola divisions in Phoenix, and a thousand others. The region has artists like Seattle's Callahan, Arizona's Georgia O'Keeffe and Ted De Grazia and such members of the California School as Diebenkorn and Park; photographers like Yosemite's Ansel Adams and Santa Barbara's Josef Muench; authors as diverse as Irving Stone and Joseph Wood Krutch; distinguished architects, musicians and clergy. In education and in cultural affairs, the West is bounding ahead. Its future in science and industry offers the most exciting promise any region could seek. But the growth of the West would be stunted by any considerable degree of disarmament; more diversification of industry is one of its most urgent needs.

The other most vital requirement is for state and metropolitan area planning to control rural and urban growth. The cities of the West must soon agree on plans for rapid-transit systems, or the automobile will choke them. The more arid regions of the Southwest are pumping their water from greater and greater distances. There is enough water in the West to sustain its present rate of growth for several more decades, but statesmanship is needed to effect its distribution, and the cost will grow ever greater until that day when nuclear-powered distillation and distribution of sea water become the most economic solution. That day will be a millennium for the arid West.

One giant step forward for the West would be the adoption by the federal government of a *capital* budget, to distinguish the type of repayable investments which characterize much federal spending in the West. Those federal investments which return revenue to the national treasury should be distinguished from federal spending for such current operations as national defense, interest payments, and government administration. Hoover Dam, for instance, after only twenty-seven years, has produced more revenue than its cost of construction. Long-term public investments necessary to complete the exploitation of Western resources and to accommodate the oncoming millions could be financed from a fund of which future beneficiaries would pay a just share.

After forty thousand miles crisscrossing the West by train, plane, car, boat, and foot, the region has become a personal affair for me. I love the West. I love its hard-bitten scenic majesty, its eagerness, its friendliness, its unconquerable faith in itself. I excuse its urban ugliness even while deploring it; it is too much to have hoped that its cities could have been born beautiful under the pressures of the westward tilt—but like other Westerners, I think its cities can, and must, begin to grow more beautiful. I cling to a typically Western optimism that something good for America will result from the energies and dreams of the millions involved in this greatest migration of history.

These final pages are written in an apartment in the high cliffs of Manhattan, twentieth-century refinements of those multi-storied apartment houses built into Western cliffs almost ten centuries ago by the Pueblo Indians. Less than five hours distant from Manhattan by air is that epicenter of the changing West, Los Angeles, whose lateral sprawl has been checked and which has now begun to soar skyward into cliffs like other older cities. No region nor any people monopolizes change, either physical or spiritual; nor is change to be equated with progress. America grew through its ability to absorb and digest the divergent strengths of diverse peoples. At the brink of maturity, the nation faces that moment of truth when its strength must come from within itself. The greatness of New York has lain in its capacity to serve as a crucible in which the talents and energies of all America have been distilled and liberated; the westward tilt provides the setting for another crucible from which can flow the strengths of America tomorrow.

In its beginning, the United States drew primarily on the cultures of the European. In the same way, the new West is a distillation of the older regional cultures of America. Whatever America is, the West will be more so. The urge to wester continues; now it wells up on the Pacific Coast, and poises for the leap westward to Asia. So far, the postwar resurgence of Japan has been the major bellwether of an era, long and confidently predicted, in which the American West will open the new door of commerce and cultural exchange with the Orient. Much of the hard fact of such an era lies locked in the explosive question of whether the United States will do business with Red China. So far, that issue is more likely to stir argument in Washington than in any city on the Pacific Coast; Westerners today are so absorbed in the growth of their own region that only a few are yet searching for the still newer horizon.

To the extent that the West is defensive or boastful, it demonstrates its unreadiness to wield its weight in the national purpose. To the extent that the East is ill-informed or chauvinistic about the surge of the West, it is guilty of a stultifying provincialism. There is abundant evidence of such faults today, on both sides of the land.

The Westerner who has left the West for New York is a less prevalent specimen than the Easterner who has gone West, but he has a perspective of the strengths of both East and West that usually gives him superior insight. Almost invariably, he has come to New York because of specialized activity or talent which cannot yet find full flower in the West. He is apt to be particularly sensitive to the spottiness of cultural and intellectual maturity in the West, the receding but still sturdy wave of Western sybaritism, and to a feeling that the West is not yet in the mainstream of the flow of information and ideas. Usually he admits such matters only to other Westerners; in conversation with his new neighbors of the East, he levels his fire on Eastern ignorance of the vast strides that the West is making in each of these matters. In general, the Easterner underrates the West, and the Westerner overrates it. Yet the West has moved ahead significantly, notably in the past two decades. By conventional tests of population, productivity, power resources, and creativity, the West merits recognition of its economic and cultural equality with older regions of America.

More factors act today to hold the West together than to divide it. As Westerners become more aware of this solidarity of interests, they will demonstrate their effectiveness in coping with the historic Western problems of exploitation of power and natural resources, water supply, and discriminatory freight rates.

The coalescence of Western outlook has been induced above all by migration. In his book, *Character of Races*, Ellsworth Huntington develops the relationship between migration and natural selection. He documents the thesis that migrants exhibit superior courage, resourcefulness, and initiative, and that after the stresses attendant to their migration have subsided, they contribute more than the average person toward human progress. Dr. Maurice D. Van Arsdol, Jr., a University of Southern California sociologist, goes one step beyond. "In a sense," he says, "migration is a sign of adjustment."

Throughout history, the people who move have been stronger individualists than those who stay. From the established places to the more recently settled regions have flowed originality, independence, and energy. If the move is indiscriminate or tempestuous, it is likely to fall short of its aim. If it is motivated primarily by escape, rather than by search, it is less productive. If external, material goals lead to the move, it is less hopeful to mankind than if the search is for satisfactions of the inner life: freedom, creativity, and love.

By these standards, the westward tilt receives a better than passing grade. It is a more orderly migration than most; it does not pour through floodgates because of persecution or famine. With the new Westerner, search for the new is predominant over escape from the old. He seeks material prosperity, but he strives too, within the limits of his own understanding, toward achieving his inner goals.

Acknowledgments

This book would not likely have been written except for the impetus of friendly collusion between James Michener and Bennett Cerf. To them, now that the work is done, I can sincerely express thanks.

Because of the extensive traveling involved, unusual patience was required from my daughter Jill and from those who rely on me for daily newspaper writing, notably James S. Copley, William Shea, Alex De-Bakcsy, E. Robert Anderson, Eugene F. Williams and Rembert James. To each of these go deep thanks.

The book grew with the encouragement and guidance of other good friends: Helen and Ted Geisel, Stanley Gewirtz, John Hoving, Dr. Fred Hollander, John T. Holt, Alfred Ja Coby, Robert Letts Jones, Fred Kinne, Herbert G. Klein, Stuart N. Lake, Thomas G. Lanphier, Jr., Frank Mc-Culloch, Dr. Stanley A. Moore, Scott Newhall, Ned Root, Larry Sisk, C. R. Smith, Donald B. Smith, the late Rex Smith, and Dr. Leo Smollar.

Guideposts along the way were provided by the previous studies and generous assistance of several scholars, particularly Otis Pease, Earl Pomeroy and Wallace Stegner.

At Random House, Joe Fox and Mrs. Nan Talese were of vast help in organization of material. Almost impregnable hideaways for work were provided in La Jolla by Jacquelin and Gerald Jerome, and in New York by Doris and Willis Player. Thanks are also due to my extraordinary secretary, Mrs. Robert McIver, who never lost her flashing smile. Both she and Gayle Williams devoted many hours to proofreading.

No attempt is made in the list which follows to include all of those with whom the writer has talked or corresponded; among those names missing are helpful persons in government, chambers of commerce, the business world and labor unions, and many newspapermen, clerks, law-enforcement officers, waiters, and strangers. Those named have been of great aid, but any errors or misinterpretations in the book are the fault only of the writer.

Portions of the book appeared in *Esquire, Town and Country, The Saturday Review*, in the San Diego *Evening Tribune*, the San Diego *Union*, and in other newspapers served by the Copley News Service, and appear here through their permission.

Acknowledgment is made to *The Saturday Review* for permission to reprint in Chapter One an excerpt from an article by Wallace Stegner; to *Harper's* magazine for references in the Prologue to an article by Walter Prescott Webb; and to the New York *Times* for a quotation by Bill Becker appearing in Chapter Seven.

ALASKA   *Juneau:* Henry Roloff, Commissioner, Department of Economic Development and Planning.

ARIZONA   Governor Paul Fannin, Senator Barry Goldwater, Senator Carl Hayden. *Flagstaff:* John Babbitt, treasurer, Babbitt Brothers Trading Co. *Grand Canyon:* John S. McLaughlin, superintendent, Grand Canyon National Park; Herschel Stiffler, Harvey Hotels. *Phoenix:* Lee Ackerman, president, Western Equities, Inc.; Walter R. Bimson, chairman of the board, Valley National Bank; State Senator Neilson Brown; Raymond Carlson, editor, *Arizona Highways;* Walter R. Cluer, racetrack president; Ed Cudahy, cattle rancher; Robert L. Davis, advertising director, First National Bank of Arizona; Don Dedera, columnist, *Arizona Republic;* Charles A. Esser, assistant city manager; Edward M. Hall, street-improvement administrator; Henry Haupt, retired advertising executive; Mrs. Eleanor Headlee, assistant cashier, First National Bank of Arizona; Bill Kellogg, district sales manager, Western Airlines; Mayor Samuel Mardian, Jr.; O. L. McDaniel, former chairman, Arizona Racing Commission; David H. Murdock, developer; J. Edward Murray, managing editor, *Arizona Republic;* Dr. Daniel E. Noble, executive vice president and director, Motorola, Inc.; Eugene C. Pulliam, publisher, *Arizona Republic* and *Phoenix Gazette;* Lawson V. Smith, vice president and general manager, The Mountain States Telephone & Telegraph Co.; Del Webb, developer; Ray W. Wilson, former city manager. *Scottsdale:* Charles Briley, restaurateur; Jack A. Harris, rancher; Ann Lee, theatrical producer; James P. Paul, developer. *Sedona:* Gerald C. Crary, real estate broker. *Tucson:* Dr. John Carroll, University of Arizona Press; George W. Chambers, executive adviser, Tucson Newspapers, Inc.; Ted De Grazia, artist; Lewis W. Douglas, chairman of the board, Southern Arizona Bank & Trust Co.; Frank E. Drachman, advertising director, Tucson Newspapers, Inc.; Joseph Wood Krutch, author; Mrs. Pat Martin, hotel manager; William R. Mathews, editor and publisher, *The Arizona Daily Star;* John W. Murphey, contractor and rancher; Dr. Desmond Powell, University of Arizona; Harold Steinfeld, hotel owner and merchant; Lewis Wayne Walker, associate director, Arizona-Sonora Desert Museum. *Window Rock:* Paul Jones, Navajo tribal chairman.

CALIFORNIA   Governor Pat Brown, Senator Clair Engle, Senator Thomas H. Kuchel, Richard M. Nixon. *Fresno:* Hugh M. Burns, State Senator, Senate President, pro tem. *Los Angeles Area:* Arthur Adams, photographer; Carter Barber, Title Insurance & Trust Co.; Mrs. Vivian Barclay, public relations executive; Bill Becker, western correspondent, New York *Times;* Marshall Berges, bureau chief, Time-Life, Inc.; Ernest Beyl, vice president, Communications Counselors, Inc.; Milton Breivogel, director of planning, Los Angeles County Regional Planning Commission; Norman

Chandler, chairman of the board and president, The Times-Mirror Co.; Chip Cleary, public relations counsel; Bryant Cushing, assistant to the president, Hunt Foods and Industries, Inc.; Dr. Lee A. DuBridge, president, California Institute of Technology; Dr. Philip Durham, University of California at Los Angeles; Phillip Frandson, University Extension, University of California at Los Angeles; Harry A. Gillis, Jr., industrial economist, Pasadena office, Stanford Research Institute; Dr. Walter Goldschmidt, University of California at Los Angeles; James A. Guthrie, editor and president, the San Bernardino *Sun;* Brownlee Haydon, senior editor, The RAND Corp.; Gladwin Hill, head of Los Angeles bureau, New York *Times;* William Hipple, public relations director, western area, American Airlines; Aldous Huxley, author; Dr. Abbott Kaplan, associate dean, University Extension, University of California at Los Angeles; Phil Kerby, editor, *Frontier* magazine; Stanley E. Kramer, film producer; Jack H. Mann, vice president, Western Division, ABC Radio Network; Samuel Marx, film producer; Harold C. McClellan, chairman of the board, Old Colony Paint & Chemical Co.; Frank McCulloch, day managing editor, Los Angeles *Times;* Dr. Edward C. McDonagh, University of Southern California; Leslie Raddatz, publicist; Dr. Georges Sabagh, University of Southern California; Casey Shawhan, director, press and publicity, National Broadcasting Co., Inc., Pacific division; Gene Sherman, columnist and commentator, Los Angeles *Times* and KABC; Dr. Maurice D. Van Arsdol, Jr., University of Southern California; Matt Weinstock, columnist, Los Angeles *Times;* Rose Mary Wood, executive secretary to Richard M. Nixon. *Menlo Park:* Walter Doty, editorial consultant, retired, *Sunset* magazine; Laurence William Lane, Sr., president, Lane Publishing Co.; Laurence William Lane, Jr., publisher, *Sunset* magazine; Melvin B. Lane, president, Lane Book Co.; Proctor Mellquist, editor, *Sunset* magazine; Thomas W. Ohliger, marketing manager, *Sunset* magazine. *Merced:* C. Ray Robinson, attorney. *Palm Springs:* Frank Bogert, Mayor; Phil Neary, representative, Dean Witter & Co.; J. M. F. Taylor, publisher and editor, *Palm Springs Life* magazine. *Sacramento:* Samuel E. Wood, executive director, *California Tomorrow;* Carl Zachrisson, commissioner, Economic Development Agency, State of California. *San Diego Area:* Edward T. Austin, public relations manager, Rohr Corp.; Anderson Borthwick, president, First National Trust & Savings Bank; Tom Colby, owner-operator, Lazy H Club; Thomas G. Cross, certified public accountant; Dr. Frederic de Hoffmann, president, General Atomic division, General Dynamics Corp.; J. R. Dempsey, president, General Dynamics–Astronautics; Glenn A. Dowdy, executive vice president, Associated General Contractors; Remo M. Downs, financial consultant; William Elser, president, Elser Elevator Co.; Dr. Edward D. Goldberg, University of California at San Diego; Dr. Orrin E. Klapp, San Diego State College; L. M. Klauber, consultant, San Diego Gas & Electric Co.; Bernard and Jordan Lansky, cartoonists; Jerry MacMullen, director, Junipero Serra Museum; Max Miller, author; Charles T. Newton, director of communications, General Dynamics–Astronautics; James Reading, director of public relations, San Diego Transit System;

Dr. Roger Revelle, formerly science adviser to the Secretary of the Interior; Dr. Charles R. Schroeder, director, San Diego Zoological Garden; Dr. Harold C. Urey, University of California at San Diego. *San Francisco Bay Area:* Ansel Adams, photographer and writer; Dr. Mortimer J. Adler, director, Institute for Philosophical Research; Robert C. Albrook, manager, public information, University of California; Allen A. Arthur, publicist; Mrs. Norma J. Aston, night-club owner; Albert A. Axelrod, judge of the Municipal Court; Joan Bell, head librarian, San Francisco *Chronicle;* Melvin Belli, attorney; Victor J. Bergeron, restaurateur; James B. Black, chairman of the board, Pacific Gas & Electric Co.; The Rev. Ralph Bonacker, Episcopal minister; Professor Eugene Burdick, University of California at Berkeley; Herb Caen, columnist, San Francisco *Chronicle;* Herbert Cerwin, public relations executive, George Christopher, Mayor of San Francisco; Lowell Clucas, public relations director, Crown Zellerbach Corp.; Lawrence E. Davies, head of San Francisco bureau, New York *Times;* Stan Delaplane, columnist, San Francisco *Chronicle;* Jack Foizee, military and marine reporter, San Francisco *Chronicle;* Harold Gilliam, author; Robert V. Golden, Sierra Club; Howard Gossage, advertising executive; Robert R. Gros, vice president, Pacific Gas & Electric Co.; T. George Harris, senior editor, *Look;* George Killion, president, American President Lines; Louis R. Lurie, president, The Lurie Co.; Jimmy Lyons, general manager, Monterey Jazz Festival; David Stone Martin, artist; Elton K. McQuery, director, western office, Council of State Governments; Abe Mellinkoff, city editor, San Francisco *Chronicle;* Luther Nichols, West Coast editor, Doubleday & Co.; John Wesley Noble, writer; Terrence O'Flaherty, columnist, San Francisco *Chronicle;* Rodger I. Mendes, manager of market research, Pacific Gas & Electric Co.; Mae Miller, librarian, Commonwealth Club of California; Scott Newhall, executive editor, San Francisco *Chronicle;* Polly Noyes, travel editor, San Francisco *Chronicle;* The Rt. Rev. James A. Pike, Bishop of the Episcopal Diocese of California; Kenneth R. Rearwin, vice president, Merrill Lynch, Pierce, Fenner & Smith, Inc.; Joaquin F. Reis, vice president, Kaiser Industries Corp.; Denis A. Rooksby, publisher, Hesperian House; Joe Rosenthal, staff photographer, San Francisco *Chronicle;* Jim Russell, western representative, Random House; Grover Sales, Jr., publicist; Conrad Speidel, manager, information services, Crown Zellerbach Corp.; Ted Spencer, architect; Marsha Owens, restaurateur; Benjamin H. Swig, chairman of the board, Fairmont Hotel Co.; Roy W. Taylor, public relations director, Wine Institute; Warren Titus, president, P & O-Orient Lines; Alex Troffey, coördinator of public relations, Kaiser Industries Corp.; Joe Weiner, advertising executive; Daniel Wilkes, assistant to the director, Lawrence Radiation Laboratory, University of California at Berkeley; Professor William W. Wurster, University of California at Berkeley; J. D. Zellerbach, chairman of the board, Crown Zellerbach Corp. *San Jose:* Kenneth S. Conn, executive editor, San Jose *Mercury and News;* W. G. Peyton, editorial page editor, San Jose *Mercury. Santa Barbara:* Dr. Samuel B. Gould, former chancellor, University of California at Santa Barbara. *Stanford:* Bruce Bliven, former editor of the *New Republic;* Preston S. Cutler, assistant director, Center for Advanced Study in the Behavioral Sciences. Stanford University: Peter C. Allen, Dr. John Wendell Dodds, Stirling L. Huntley, Jeff Littleboy, Professor Chilton R. Bush, Dr. Otis A. Pease, Dr. Wallace Stegner. Stanford Research Institute: David C. Fulton, Dr. Charles L. Hamman, Neil Houston, Beverly J. Taylor. *Stockton:* Dr. Robert Burns, president, University of the Pacific. *Twentynine Palms:* John W. Hilton, artist. *Vandenberg Air Force Base:* Lt. Col. Oliver Filley, Emile Genest, Maj. Robert W. Roy.

COLORADO   Ex-Governor Steve McNichols, Senator Gordon Allott, Ex-Sen. John A. Carroll. *Boulder:* Miss Pat Kelley, publicity director, University of Colorado; Quigg Newton, president, University of Colorado; Dr. Walter Orr Roberts, director, National Center for Atmospheric Research; Edwin L. Wolff, assistant to the director, National Center for Atmospheric Research. *Colorado Springs:* Lt. Col. Mark Azzolina, assistant director of information, Headquarters, North American Air Defense Command; Col. Barney Oldfield, USAF, former chief of information, Headquarters, North American Air Defense Command; Charles O'Toole, general manager, Broadmoor Hotel. *Denver:* Barron B. Beshoar, correspondent, Time-Life, Inc.; Elwood M. Brooks, chairman of the board, Central Bank & Trust Co.; E. Ray Campbell, president, the Denver *Post;* Gene Cervi, editor and publisher, *Cervi's Rocky Mountain Journal;* Dr. Robert Joy Glaser, dean, School of Medicine, University of Colorado; Don P. Herron, director, information services, The Martin Co.; Palmer Hoyt, editor and publisher, the Denver *Post;* Alexis McKinney, assistant to the publisher, the Denver *Post;* Joseph Sperte, restaurateur.

IDAHO   Governor Robert E. Smylie, Senator Frank Church. *Boise:* Gwenith H. Barnett, National Committeewoman, Republican National Committee; Steele Barnett, product development manager, Boise Cascade Corp.; James L. Brown, publisher, the *Idaho Statesman;* J. Lynn Driscoll, chairman of the board, First Security Bank of Idaho; Robert V. Hansberger, president, Boise Cascade Corp.; Dave Johnson, chief pilot, Boise Cascade Corp.; W. L. Mills, vice president, Boise Cascade Corp.; Porter Ward, press secretary to Senator Frank Church. *Sun Valley:* Winston McCrea, general manager, Sun Valley Operations.

MONTANA   The late Donald G. Nutter, Senator Mike Mansfield, Senator Lee Metcalf. *Butte:* Robert D. Corette, attorney; George W. O'Connor, vice president, Montana Power Co.; Colin W. Raff, vice president, Montana Power Co. *Helena:* Thomas J. Collins, director, Montana State Planning Board; Al Gaskill, managing editor, the *Independent Record;* Michael S. Kennedy, director, Historical Society of Montana; Edward W. Nelson, budget director, State of Montana.

NEVADA   Governor Grant Sawyer, Senator Alan Bible, Senator Howard W. Cannon. *Las Vegas:* Wilbur Clark, Wilbur Clark's Desert Inn; James Deitch, manager, Las Vegas News Bureau and Convention Center; R. Guild Gray, vice president, First Western Savings & Loan Association; H. M. Greenspun, publisher and editor, Las Vagas *Sun;*

Eugene Murphy, advertising and publicity director, Wilbur Clark's Desert Inn; Jack Pepper, advertising executive; Andrew V. Ruckman, managing director, Southern Nevada Industrial Foundation, Inc.; Henry G. Vermillion, director of information, Nevada Operations Office, U. S. Atomic Energy Commission; *Reno:* Walter H. Ramage, manager, Mapes Hotel.

NEW MEXICO Senator Edwin L. Mechem, Senator Clinton P. Anderson, the late Sen. Dennis Chavez. *Albuquerque:* Dick Elliott, public information officer, Atomic Energy Commission; W. Randolph Lovelace, M. D., director, Lovelace Foundation for Medical Education and Research. *Gallup:* W. Wade Head, area director, Bureau of Indian Affairs. *Los Alamos:* Los Alamos Scientific Laboratory: Dr. Norris Bradbury, director; Dr. Thomas Milton Putnam, Jr.; Dr. Thomas L. Shipman; John V. Young. *Santa Fe:* Will Harrison, public affairs columnist; Philip Higgins, journalist; Ed James, president, United Perlite Corp.; Effie Jenks, waitress, La Fonda Hotel; Oliver La Farge, author; Frank M. Magee, Jr., office manager, Santa Fe Opera; Mrs. Dorothy S. McKibbin, manager, Santa Fe Office, Los Alamos Scientific Laboratory; Leo Murphy, former mayor of Santa Fe; Allen Stamm, developer; William H. Vernon, president, Santa Fe National Bank; James Webb Young, rancher and director and senior consultant, J. Walter Thompson Co.

OREGON Governor Mark O. Hatfield, Senator Wayne Morse, Senator Maurine B. Neuberger. *Eugene:* Dr. Earl Pomeroy, University of Oregon. *Portland:* M. J. Frey, president and publisher, *The Oregonian;* Samuel H. Mallicoat, director, Oregon Department of Planning and Development; Ford Montgomery, general manager, Hilton Hotel; Arden X. Pangborn, editor, *Oregon Journal;* Edward D. Smith, Jr., public relations manager, Pacific Northwest Bell Telephone Co. *Salem:* Travis Cross, assistant to the Governor; Gerald Frank, vice president, Meier & Frank Co.; Oliver Williamson, Labor executive.

UTAH Governor George D. Clyde, Senator Wallace F. Bennett, Senator Frank E. Moss. *Kanab:* Whitney Parry, resort-lodge owner. *Provo:* Dr. Ernest Wilkinson, president, Brigham Young University. *Salt Lake City:* Orval Adams, chairman of board, Zion National Banks; Dr. Arthur L. Beeley, dean and professor emeritus, University of Utah; Dr. Wallace Sands Brooke, surgeon; Theodore L. Cannon, information service, Church of Jesus Christ of Latter-day Saints; Richard P. Condie, director, Mormon Tabernacle Choir; Edwin E. Dowell, director of public relations, Western Mining Divisions, Kennecott Copper Corp.; Hays Gorey, news editor, the Salt Lake *Tribune*, and correspondent, Time-Life, Inc.; Lester F. Hewlett, chairman of the board, Hewlett Brothers Co.; James E. Hogle, managing partner, J. A. Hogle & Co.; Miss Mary R. Jack, secretary, Mormon Tabernacle Choir; Mayor J. Bracken Lee; Lorry Rytting, information service, Church of Jesus Christ of Latter-day Saints; Thomas Taylor, president, Prudential Savings & Loan Association.

WASHINGTON Governor Albert D. Rosellini, Senator Henry M. Jackson, Senator Warren G. Magnuson. *Aberdeen:* Werner A. Rupp, publisher, Aberdeen *Daily World. Longview:* J. M. McClelland, Jr., editor and publisher, Longview *Daily News*. *Seattle:* Morris J. Alhadeff, vice president and general manager, Longacres Race Track; William Allen, president, Boeing Co.; Miner H. Baker, vice president and economist, Seattle First National Bank; Nick Bez, president, West Coast Airlines; Robert J. Block, president, Columbia-Cascade Corp.; Betty Bowen, Seattle Art Museum; Harry H. Cahill, general manager, the Seattle *Times;* Sidney Copeland, vice president, Cole and Weber Inc.; Ewen C. Dingwall, vice president and general manager, Seattle World's Fair; Sylvia Froula, director of publicity and promotion, Western Hotels; M. L. Graham, concessionaire, Seattle-Tacoma Airport; Milton Katims, conductor, Seattle Symphony Orchestra; Henry MacLeod, managing editor, the Seattle *Times;* Harold Mansfield, special assistant to the president, Boeing Co.; Ralph Bushnell Potts, attorney; Victor Rosellini, restaurateur; Dr. Calvin F. Schmid, University of Washington; Robert Schulman, director of special features, KING-TV and Crown Stations; Walter W. Straley, president, Pacific Northwest Bell Telephone Co.; Anne B. Swensson, magazine coördinator, Seattle World's Fair; Emmett Watson, columnist, Seattle *Post Intelligencer;* George H. Weber, advertising executive; Douglass Welch, columnist, Seattle *Post Intelligencer.*

WYOMING   Ex-Gov. Jack R. Gage, Ex-Sen. Joseph Hickey, Senator Gale W. McGee. *Buffalo:* Vivienne S. Hesse, rancher. *Cody:* Carl Putz, resort owner. *Grand Teton National Park:* Grand Teton Lodge Co.: Richard L. Erb, Raymond C. Lillie. *Yellowstone National Park:* John Quintard Nichols, director, Yellowstone Park Co.

Bibliography

American Panorama: West of the Mississippi. A *Holiday* Magazine Book. New York: Doubleday & Co., 1960.

ANDERSON, JAMES. *Idaho Looks Ahead: A Study of Industrial Employment and Population Growth in the Gem State.* Boise: State of Idaho, Department of Commerce and Development, 1960.

Arizona and the West. Tucson: University of Arizona.

Arizona Highways. Phoenix.

Arizona: The Grand Canyon State. New York: Hastings House, revised edition, 1956. Compiled by workers of the Writers' Program of the Work Projects Administration.

ASHTON, WENDELL. *Voice in the West.* New York: Duell, Sloan & Pearce, 1950.

ATHEARN, ROBERT G. *High Country Empire: The High Plains and Rockies.* New York: McGraw-Hill, 1960.

BARTLETT, I. S. *History of Wyoming.* Chicago: S. J. Clarke, 1918.

BEST, KATHARINE and HILLYER, KATHARINE. *Las Vegas: Playtown, U. S. A.* New York: David McKay Co., 1955.

The Book of Mormon.

BRIER, HOWARD M. *Sawdust Empire: The Pacific Northwest.* New York: Alfred A. Knopf, 1958.

BROOKS, JAMES E. (editor). *Oregon Almanac and Book of Facts, 1961–62.* Portland: Binfords & Mort, 1961.

BROWER, DAVID. (editor). *Wilderness: America's Living Heritage.* San Francisco: Sierra Club, 1961.

BUSCH, NIVEN. *California Street.* New York: Simon and Schuster, 1959.

———. *The San Franciscans.* New York: Simon and Schuster, 1962.

CAEN, HERB. *New Guide to San Francisco and the Bay Area.* New York: Doubleday & Co., 1958.

California: A Guide to the Golden State. New York: Hastings House, revised edition, 1954. Compiled and written by the Federal Writers' Project of the Works Progress Administration.

California Highways and Public Works. Official Journal of the Division of Highways, State of California. Sacramento.

California Information and Almanac, 1960.

California: Magazine of the Pacific. Published by the California State Chamber of Commerce.

CAMP, WILLIAM MARTIN. *San Francisco: Port of Gold.* New York: Doubleday & Co., 1947.

CARR, HARRY. *The West Is Still Wild.* Boston: Houghton Mifflin Co., 1932.

CAUGHEY, JOHN WALTON. *California.* New York: Prentice-Hall, second edition, 1953.

———. *Gold is the Cornerstone.* Berkeley: University of California Press, 1949.

———. "The Spanish Southwest" in *Regionalism in America,* edited by Merrill Jensen. Madison: University of Wisconsin Press, 1952.

———. "Toward an Understanding of the West." *Utah Historical Quarterly* XXVII (January 1959), 8–24.

Cervi's Journal. Denver.

"Change Comes to Zion's Empire," *Business Week,* November 23, 1957, pp. 108–16.

CHRISTOPHERSON, EDMUND. *This Here Is Montana.* Missoula: Montana Book, 1961.

CHURCH, PEGGY POND. *The House at Otowi Bridge: The Story of Edith Warner and Los Alamos.* Albuquerque: University of New Mexico Press, 1960.

CLELAND, ROBERT GLASS, edited by Glenn S. Dumke. *From Wilderness to Empire: A History of California.* New York: Alfred A. Knopf, 1959.

Colorado 1959–1961. Year Book of the State of Colorado.

Colorado, A Guide to the Highest State. New York: Hastings House, 1941. Compiled by workers of the Writers' Program of the Work Projects Administration.

The Commonwealth. Publication of the Commonwealth Club of California, San Francisco.

Contact. San Francisco.

COOK, S. F. *The Aboriginal Population of Alameda and Contra Costa Counties.* Berkeley: University of California Press, 1957.

———. *The Aboriginal Population of the North Coast of California.* Berkeley: University of California Press, 1956.

———. *The Aboriginal Population of the San Joaquin Valley, California.* Berkeley: University of California Press, 1955.

———. *Colonial Expeditions to the Interior of California Central Valley, 1800–1820.* Berkeley: University of California Press, 1960.

CORNWALL, J. SPENCER. *A Century of Singing: The Salt Lake Mormon Tabernacle Choir.* Salt Lake City: Deseret Book Co., 1958.

CROSS, JACK L., SHAW, ELIZABETH H. and SCHEIFELE, KATHLEEN (editors). *Arizona: Its People and Resources.* Tucson: The University of Arizona Press, 1960.

DEDERA, DON. *A Mile in His Moccasins*. Phoenix: McGrew Printing & Lithographing Co., 1960.

DE VOTO, BERNARD. *Across the Wide Missouri*. Boston: Houghton Mifflin Co., 1947.

———. *The Course of Empire*. Boston: Houghton Mifflin Co., 1952.

——— (editor). *The Journals of Lewis and Clark*. Boston: Houghton Mifflin Co., 1953.

———. *The Year of Decision*. Boston: Houghton Mifflin Co., 1961.

DODGE, NATT N. and ZIM, HERBERT S. *The American Southwest: A Guide to the Wide Open Spaces*. New York: Golden Press, 1955.

DONNELLY, THOMAS C. *The Government of New Mexico*. Albuquerque: University of New Mexico Press, revised edition, 1953.

DURHAM, G. HOMER. "The Democratic Crisis and Mormon Thought." *Ethics*, LII (October 1941), 110–15.

ERICKSON, URSULA SPIER and PEARSALL, ROBERT (editors). *The Californians: Writings of Their Past and Present*. San Francisco: Hesperian House, 1961.

ERWIN, MARIE H. *Wyoming Historical Blue Book*. Denver: Bradford-Robinson Printing Co., 1946.

EVANS, RICHARD L. *From Within These Walls*. New York: Harper & Brothers, 1959.

FERGUSSON, ERNA. *Our Southwest*. New York: Alfred A. Knopf, 1952.

FISHER, VARDIS. *Children of God: An American Epic*. New York: Vanguard Press, 1939.

FOWLER, GENE. *Timber Line*. New York: Doubleday & Co., 1933.

Frontier Magazine. Los Angeles.

FURNISS, NORMAN F. *The Mormon Conflict, 1850–1859*. New Haven: Yale University Press, 1960.

GILLIAM, HAROLD. *The Face of San Francisco: A Fond Portrait of America's Most Beautiful City*. New York: Doubleday & Co., 1960.

GLASSCOCK, CARL B. *The War of the Copper Kings*. New York: Grosset & Dunlap, 1935.

Gold Rush Country: Guide to California's Mother Lode and Northern Mines. By the editors of Sunset Books and *Sunset Magazine*. Menlo Park: Lane Publishing Co., 1957.

GUNTHER, JOHN. *Inside U. S. A.* New York: Harper & Bros., Rev., 1951

HANNUM, ALBERTA. *Spin a Silver Dollar: The Story of a Desert Trading Post*. New York: Viking Press, 1956.

HEPBURN, ANDREW. *Complete Guide to Northern California*. Boston: Houghton Mifflin Co., 1959.

———. *Complete Guide to Southern California*. Boston: Houghton Mifflin Co., 1959.

HERLING, JOHN. "The Mormons and Modern Utah." *New Leader*, May 2, 1960.

HINCKLEY, GORDON B. *What of the Mormons?* Salt Lake City: Church of Jesus Christ of Latter-day Saints, revised edition, 1954.

HOLBROOK, STEWART H. *Far Corner: A Personal View of the Pacific Northwest.* New York: Macmillan, 1952.

——— (editor). *Promised Land: A Collection of Northwest Writing.* New York: Whittlesey House, 1945.

HOLLON, W. EUGENE. *The Southwest: Old and New.* New York: Alfred A. Knopf, 1961.

HOPKINS, ERNEST J. *Financing the Frontier: A Fifty-Year History of the Valley National Bank.* Phoenix: Arizona Printers, Inc., 1950.

HOUGH, DONALD. *The Cocktail Hour in Jackson Hole.* New York: W. W. Norton & Co., 1956.

HOWARD, JOSEPH K. *Montana: High, Wide and Handsome.* New Haven: Yale University Press, revised edition, 1959.

HUNTER, MILTON R. *Utah in Her Western Setting.* Salt Lake City: Deseret News Press, 1957.

———. *The Utah Story.* Salt Lake City: printed by the author, 1960.

HUNTINGTON, ELLSWORTH. *Character of Races.* New York: John Wiley & Sons, 1945.

———. *Mainsprings of Civilization.* New York: Mentor Press, 1959.

HUTCHISON, CLAUDE B. (editor). *California Agriculture.* Berkeley and Los Angeles: University of California Press, 1946.

Idaho: A Guide in Word and Picture. New York: Oxford University Press, 1950. Prepared by the Federal Writers' Projects of the Works Progress Administration.

JACOBSON, DAN. *No Further West: California Visited.* New York: Macmillan, 1960.

JOHANSEN, DOROTHY O. and GATES, CHARLES M. *Empire of the Columbia: A History of the Pacific Northwest.* New York: Harper & Brothers, 1957.

JONAS, FRANK H. "The Mormon Church and J. Bracken Lee." *Proceedings*, Utah Academy of Sciences, Arts and Letters, XXXVI (1959–60), 145–69.

——— (editor). *Western Politics.* Salt Lake City: University of Utah Press, 1961.

JONES, HELEN L. and WILCOX, ROBERT F. *Metropolitan Los Angeles: Its Governments.* Los Angeles: The Haynes Foundation, 1949.

JONES, NARD. *Evergreen Land: A Portrait of the State of Washington.* New York: Dodd, Mead & Co., 1947.

KRUTCH, JOSEPH WOOD. *The Desert Year.* New York: William Sloane Associates, 1952.

KRUTCH, JOSEPH WOOD. *Grand Canyon Today and All Its Yesterdays.* New York: William Sloane Associates, 1958.
———. *The Voice of the Desert: A Naturalist's Interpretation.* New York: William Sloane Associates, 1955.

LA FARGE, OLIVER. *Laughing Boy.* Boston: Houghton Mifflin Co., 1929.
———. *Sante Fe: The Autobiography of a Southwestern Town.* Norman: University of Oklahoma Press, 1959.
LARSON, GUSTIVE O. *Outline History of Utah and the Mormons.* Salt Lake City: Deseret Book Company, 1958.
LAVENDER, DAVID SIEVERT. *Land of Giants: The Drive to the Northwest 1750–1950.* New York: Doubleday & Co., 1958.
———. *One Man's West.* New York: Doubleday, Doran & Co., 1943.
LINDSAY, CYNTHIA. *The Natives Are Restless.* Philadelphia: J. B. Lippincott Co., 1960.
Los Angeles, a Guide to the City and Its Environs. New York: Hastings House, revised edition, 1951. Compiled by workers of the Writers' Program of the Work Projects Administration.
Los Angeles Magazine.
LYONS, PETER. "Wild, Wild West." *American Heritage*, XI (August 1960), 32–48.

MANSFIELD, HAROLD. *Vision: A Saga of the Sky.* New York: Duell, Sloan and Pearce, 1956.
McCULLOCH, FRANK. "Will the West Take Over?" *The Saturday Evening Post*, July 8, 1961.
McGROARTY, JOHN S. *California: Its History and Romance.* Los Angeles: Grafton Publishing Co., 1911.
McWILLIAM, CAREY. *California: The Great Exception.* New York: A. A. Wyn, 1949.
———. *Factories in the Field.* Boston: Little, Brown & Co., 1939.
———. *Southern California Country: An Island on the Land.* New York: Duell, Sloan & Pearce, 1946.
"The Meaning of Wilderness to Science." *Proceedings, Sixth Biennial Wilderness Conference.* San Francisco: Sierra Club, 1960.
The Montana Almanac. Missoula: Montana State University Press, 1960.
Montana: The Magazine of Western History. Helena.
MORGAN, MURRAY. *The Last Wilderness.* New York: Viking Press, 1955.
———. *Skid Road: An Informal Portrait of Seattle.* New York: Viking Press, revised edition, 1960.
MUENCH, JOYCE R. (editor). *West Coast Portrait.* New York: Hastings House, 1946.
MUMFORD, LEWIS. *The Culture of Cities.* New York: Harcourt, Brace and Company, 1938.

The Navajo Yearbook, Fiscal Year 1951–1961.

NEIDER, CHARLES (editor). *The Great West.* New York: Bonanza Books, 1958.

New Mexico, A Guide to the Colorful State. New York: Hastings House, revised edition, 1953. Compiled by workers of the Writers' Program of the Work Projects Administration.

New Mexico Historical Review. Albuquerque.

Northern California. By the editors of Sunset Books and *Sunset Magazine.* Menlo Park: Lane Publishing Co., 1959.

O'BRIEN, ROBERT. *This Is San Francisco.* New York: Whittlesey House, 1948.

OGDEN, DANIEL M., JR., and BONE, HUGH A. *Washington Politics.* New York: New York University Press, 1960.

Oregon Blue Book, 1961–62. Compiled and published by Howell Appling, Jr., Secretary of State, 1960.

Oregon: End of the Trail. Portland: Binfords & Mort, revised edition, 1951. Compiled by workers of the Writers' Program of the Work Projects Administration.

Point West Magazine. Phoenix.

POMEROY, EARL. *In Search of the Golden West: The Tourist in Western America.* New York: Alfred A. Knopf, 1957.

———. "Old Lamps for New: The Cultural Lag in Pacific Coast Historiography." Paper delivered at meeting of Pacific Coast Branch American Historical Association, Whittier, California, Dec. 28, 1958.

POTTS, RALPH BUSHNELL. *Seattle Heritage.* Seattle: Superior Publishing Co., 1955.

POURADE, RICHARD F. *The Explorers.* San Diego: The Union-Tribune Publishing Co., 1960.

———. *Time of the Bells.* San Diego: The Union-Tribune Publishing Co., 1961.

POWELL, JOHN WESLEY. *The Exploration of the Colorado River.* Chicago: University of Chicago Press, 1957.

PRIEST, IVY BAKER. *Green Grows Ivy.* New York: McGraw-Hill Co., 1958.

REED, HENRY HOPE, JR. *The Golden City.* New York: Doubleday & Co., 1959.

RIGNEY, FRANCIS J. and SMITH, L. DOUGLAS. *The Real Bohemia. A Sociological and Psychological Study of the "Beats."* New York: Basic Books, 1961.

RUSSELL, CHARLES M. *Trails Plowed Under.* New York: Doubleday & Co., 1927.

San Diego Magazine. San Diego.

San Francisco: The Bay and Its Cities. New York: Hastings House, revised edition, 1947. Compiled by workers of the Writers' Program of the Work Projects Administration.

San Francisco Review. San Francisco.

SCHMID, CALVIN F. *Social Trends in Seattle.* Seattle: University of Washington Press, 1944.

SHADEGG, STEPHEN C. *The Phoenix Story: An Adventure in Reclamation.* Phoenix: Salt River Project, 1958.

Sierra Club Bulletins. San Francisco.

SMYTHE, WILLIAM E. *History of San Diego.* San Diego: The History Co., 1908.

Statistical Abstract of the United States, 1961, 1962. U. S. Department of Commerce.

STEGNER, WALLACE EARLE. *Beyond the Hundredth Meridian.* New York: Houghton Mifflin Co., 1954.

———. *Mormon Country.* New York: Duell, Sloan and Pearce, 1942.

———. "The West Coast: A Region with a View." *Saturday Review.* Vol. XLII, No. 18, May 2, 1959, pp. 15–17, 41.

STONE, IRVING. *Men to Match My Mountains: The Story of the Opening of the Far West 1840–1900.* New York: Doubleday & Co., 1956.

Sunset Magazine. Menlo Park.

This Is California. Menlo Park: Lane Publishing Co., second edition, 1958.

THOMAS, LATELY. *A Debonair Scoundrel: An Episode in the Moral History of San Francisco.* New York: Holt, Rinehart and Winston, 1962.

TILLOTSON, M. R. *Grand Canyon Country.* Stanford: Stanford University Press, 1935.

TOOLE, K. ROSS. *History of Montana.* New York: Lewis, 1957.

———. *Montana: An Uncommon Land.* Norman: University of Oklahoma Press, 1959.

Utah: A Guide to the State. New York: Hastings House, 1941. Compiled by workers of the Writers' Program of the Work Projects Administration.

Utah Historical Quarterly. Salt Lake City.

WALKER, FRANKLIN. *A Literary History of Southern California.* Berkeley and Los Angeles: University of California Press, 1950.

———. *San Francisco's Literary Frontier.* New York: Alfred A. Knopf, 1939.

Washington, A Guide to the Evergreen State. Portland: Binfords & Mort, revised edition, 1950. Compiled by workers of the Writers' Program of the Work Projects Administration.

WATERS, FRANK. *The Colorado.* New York: Rinehart & Co., 1946.

WEBB, WALTER PRESCOTT. "The American West, Perpetual Mirage." *Harper's Magazine,* Vol. 214, No. 1248, pp. 25–31.

———. *The Great Plains*. Boston: Ginn and Co., 1931.

WEINSTOCK, MATT. *Muscatel at Noon*. New York: William Morrow & Co., 1951.

———. *My L. A.* New York: A. A. Wyn, 1947.

Western Humanities Review. Salt Lake City.

Western Political Quarterly. Salt Lake City.

Westways. Los Angeles.

WILENTZ, ELIAS (editor). *The Beat Scene*. New York: Corinth Books, 1960.

WILLIAMS, J. D. *The Defeat of Home Rule in Salt Lake City*. New Brunswick, N. J.: The Eagleton Institute, Rutgers University, 1960.

WINTHER, OSCAR OSBURN. *The Great Northwest: A History*. New York: Alfred A. Knopf, 1948.

WOOD, SAMUEL E. and HELLER, ALFRED E. *California Going, Going . . . : Our State's Struggle to Remain Beautiful and Productive*. Sacramento: California Tomorrow, 1962.

Wyoming, A Guide to Its History, Highways and People. New York: Oxford University Press, 1941. Compiled by workers of the Writers' Program of the Works Projects Administration.

Index

 ABOUT THE AUTHOR

The son of a Southern Baptist minister, Neil Morgan became a part of the westward tilt in 1944 when he was stationed in San Diego as a Navy ensign. Born in North Carolina in 1924, Mr. Morgan graduated from Wake Forest College where he became a member of Phi Beta Kappa and served as editor of the college magazine, as well as working for the Raleigh *News and Observer*.

After leaving the Navy in 1946, Mr. Morgan became a San Diego newsman. His daily column in that city's *Evening Tribune* has won both the Ernie Pyle and Bill Corum Memorial Awards. In the last few years he has roved the West and has become one of the outstanding authorities on the current westward migration. In research for *Westward Tilt* and for his Assignment West column, which now appears in about forty newspapers, Mr. Morgan has traveled more than thirty thousand miles in the eleven Western states and recorded hundreds of hours of interviews.

Mr. Morgan lives in a house on the Pacific cliffside in La Jolla with his fourteen-year-old daughter Jill. He has written three books about San Diego, and his articles have appeared in such magazines as *Esquire, Saturday Review* and *Town and Country*.